PART 3
The Writer as Researcher

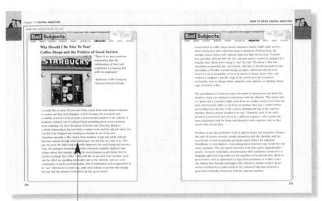

Dynamic readings that model writing for different purposes

New detailed writing assignments

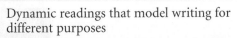

Why Do You Need This New Edition?

Nine Great Reasons to Buy This New Edition of *Backpack Writing*!

Learning to write well is the most important skill you will learn in college, no matter what your major. The new edition of *Backpack Writing* not only helps you to achieve success in college but also in your professional and public lives.

1. In Part 2, you'll find **half of the readings are new,** including selections that focus on engaging, current topics such as how children learn to lie, what to do about a dropout boyfriend who keeps dropping in, and the merits of growing some of your own food.

2. You'll find throughout the book more **examples that show you what writers actually do,** and not just long discussions about what they do.

3. In Chapters 7 through 13, the newly designed **"process maps" let you see at a glance what is expected of you** for each of the major writing assignments in the book. These process maps give you an overview of the whole writing process and help you to stay oriented as you discover ideas, write drafts, and revise your own papers.

4. In Chapters 11, 12, and 13, you'll find many **examples of provocative, engaging arguments** composed by both professionals and students, including evaluation arguments, position arguments, and proposal arguments that show you how writers take action about issues they care about.

5. In "Staying on Track" boxes throughout the book, you'll find **more examples of strategies that help you address common writing problems,** including both "off track" and "on track" examples that help to illustrate these problems for you.

6. In Chapters 7 through 13, new **"Explore Current Issues" assignments** ask you to examine a current topic—such as why wikiHow is popular, whether modest charitable donations make a difference, and whether video games can be smart—and then show you how to develop ideas for writing about the topic by responding to key questions.

7. Every reading in Part 2 includes new **"Finding Ideas for Writing" questions** that help you build on the ideas raised in what you have read and apply them in your own writing.

8. You'll find new coverage of **how to use library databases** effectively and **how to evaluate Web sources** in Chapter 15.

9. The **most recent MLA documentation guidelines** are included in Chapter 17 with visual examples from real sources as well as color-coded sample entries to help you organize the key elements of a citation.

BACKPACK WRITING

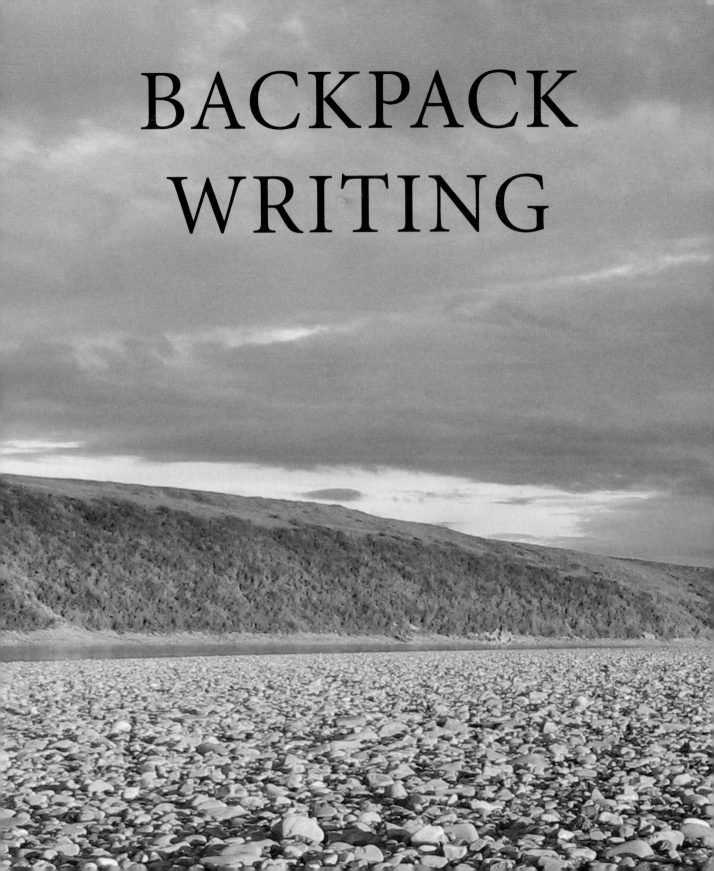

BACKPACK WRITING

SECOND EDITION

LESTER FAIGLEY
University of Texas at Austin

Longman

New York   Boston   San Francisco
London   Toronto   Sydney   Tokyo   Singapore   Madrid
Mexico City   Munich   Paris   Cape Town   Hong Kong   Montreal

Dorling Kindersley Education
Text design and page layout by Stuart Jackman
DTP: David McDonald
Cover design by Stuart Jackman

Executive Editor: Lynn M. Huddon
Senior Development Editor: Katharine Glynn
Senior Supplements Editor: Donna Campion
Senior Marketing Manager: Sandra McGuire
Production Manager: Bob Ginsberg
Project Coordination and Electronic Page Makeup: Dorling Kindersley/Pre-Press PMG
Cover Design Manager: Wendy Ann Fredericks
Cover Photo: © Lester Faigley
Visual Researcher: Rona Tuccillo
Senior Manufacturing Buyer: Dennis J. Para
Printer and Binder: Quad/Graphics-Taunton
Cover Printer: Coral Graphic Services, Inc.

For permission to use copyrighted material, grateful acknowledgment is made to the copyright holders on p. 442, which is hereby made part of this copyright page.

Library of Congress Cataloging-in-Publication Data

Faigley, Lester, date
  Backpack writing / Lester Faigley. — 2nd ed.
     p. cm.
  Includes bibliographical references and index.
  ISBN 978-0-205-74349-0
  1. English language—Rhetoric.   2. English language--Grammar.   3. Academic writing.   4. Critical thinking.   I. Title.
  PE1408.F22 2009
  808'.042—dc22

2009019864

Longman
is an imprint of

PEARSON

www.pearsonhighered.com

345678910—QGT—12 11

ISBN-13: 978-0-205-74349-0
ISBN-10:   0-205-74349-8

PART 1
The Writer as Explorer

PART 2
The Writer as Guide

Write to Reflect

Write to Inform

Write to Analyze

Write Arguments

PART 3
The Writer as Researcher

Preface

Backpack Writing starts from the often overlooked fact that writing courses make students better writers not just for other college courses, but for writing situations throughout their lives. Perhaps more than anything else I have learned about writing in my decades of teaching and practicing writing is that all meaningful acts of writing involve complex negotiations of particular subject matters, audiences, purposes, and genres. Students who learn how to adapt these processes of negotiating for particular contexts go on to achieve success in their educational, professional, and public lives.

I am pleased and grateful for the enthusiastic response of many instructors and students to the first edition. *Backpack Writing* began with the question: How do students learn best? I continue to ask that question in the second edition. These principles underlie the second edition.

Students learn best when a guide to writing is student oriented	It should start from the student's point of view, not the teacher's.
Students learn best when a guide to writing is easy to use	No matter where you open the book, the content on a particular page and the place of that content in the overall organization should be evident.
Students learn best when a guide to writing shows what readers and writers actually do	Students learn best from examples of what readers and writers do, not by reading discussions of what they do.
Students learn best when they can see examples of what works and what doesn't work	Seeing effective and ineffective examples side-by-side demonstrates strategies to employ and pitfalls to avoid.
Students learn faster and remember longer when a book is well designed	Textbooks don't have to be dull.

The second edition also maintains that the broad goals for a first-year college writing course are those identified in the Outcomes Statement from the Council of Writing Program Administrators.

1. Rhetorical knowledge	Students should respond to different situations and the needs of different audiences, understand how genres shape reading and writing, and write in several genres.
2. Critical thinking, reading, and writing	Students should find, evaluate, analyze, and synthesize sources and integrate their ideas with those of others.
3. Processes	Students should develop flexible strategies for generating, revising, editing, and proofreading, and should understand how to collaborate effectively with others.
4. Knowledge of conventions	Students should learn the common formats for different kinds of texts, practice appropriate documentation, and control surface features of grammar, mechanics, and spelling.

What's new in this edition of *Backpack Writing*

New process maps and other visual guides

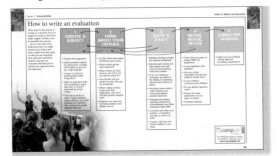

Redesigned two-page process maps lay out the process for different kinds of writing in Part 2. The process maps give students an overview of the sometimes messy process of writing and help them to stay oriented as they come up with ideas, draft, and revise.

More attention to argument

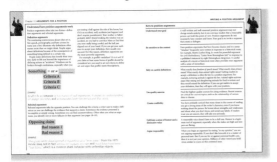

Three chapters treat in detail evaluation, position, and proposal arguments. New visual models demonstrate how each kind of argument works.

Explore Current Issues

Explore Current Issues, a new full-page writing assignment in Part 2 chapters encourages students to find ideas and write about current issues. In Chapters 7 through 13 you'll find this feature on topics such as reality television, fast-food marketing to children, smart video games, and the responsibility of government for disaster victims.

New engaging readings

In response to advice from teachers and students, half of the readings in the second edition are new. There are more longer readings and more essays of the kind written in college in this edition, including Chip Walter's investigation as to why humans kiss, Stephanie Coontz's exploration of the future of marriage, and Michael Pollan's proposal for how we can eat healthier and consume fewer resources.

Updated instruction on research

New material has been added on how to use library databases effectively and to sort the wheat from the chaff with Web sources in Chapter 15.

More ideas for writing

Every reading in Part 2 includes "Finding Ideas for Writing," new additional writing assignments specific to each reading. These assignments suggest how students might build from ideas in the readings in their own writing.

More on building from sources

New material in Chapter 6 shows how writing engages in a conversation with what has been written before on a subject and how to build on the ideas of others.

New MLA documentation guidelines

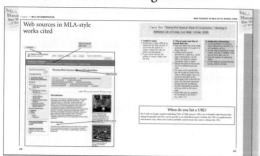

The most recent MLA documentation guidelines are included in Chapter 17. Color-coded sample entries help students to recognize and organize the key elements of different kinds of citations.

Resources for teachers and students

Instructor's Resource Manual

The *Instructor's Resource Manual*, prepared by Susan Schorn of the University of Texas at Austin, offers detailed chapter-by-chapter suggestions to help both new and experienced instructors. For every chapter in the student text, this manual includes chapter goals and chapter challenges, suggestions for different ways to use the assignments and boxed tips in the chapter, additional activities and resources, and more. It also features an overall discussion of teaching a writing class, including discussion of the Writing Program Administrators Outcomes for first-year composition. Finally, the manual offers suggested syllabi and ideas for teaching students with different learning styles.

MyCompLab

The new MyCompLab integrates the market-leading instruction, multimedia tutorials, and exercises for writing, grammar, and research that users have come to identify with the program with a new online composing space and new assessment tools. The result is a revolutionary application that offers a seamless and flexible teaching and learning environment built specifically for writers. Created after years of extensive research and in partnership with composition faculty and students across the country, the new MyCompLab provides help for writers in the context of their writing, with instructor and peer commenting functionality, proven tutorials and exercises for writing, grammar and research, an e-portfolio, an assignment-builder, a bibliography tool, tutoring services, and a gradebook and course management organization created specifically for writing classes. Visit www.mycomplab.com for more information.

About the cover

In July 2007, seven friends and I traveled in a float plane to the headwaters of the Nigu River in northern Alaska. The Nigu originates on the north slope of the Brooks Range, which stretches east to west across northern Alaska and separates rivers that flow north to the Arctic Ocean from those that flow south and west to the Pacific. The circle of stones in the foreground is the prehistoric remains of a lookout used by the ancestors of modern Iñupiaq people to observe caribou migrating through the valley.

The Nigu River flows through the National Petroleum Reserve in Alaska (NPR-A), created in 1923 but remaining a wilderness and one of the least visited areas of the United States. The NPR-A has the largest caribou herd in Alaska with over 500,000 animals along with the highest concentration of grizzly bears in the state, the nesting grounds of several rare migratory birds, and significant archaeological sites of native peoples. The NPR-A also sits on top of major resources of oil and coal. The future of northern Alaska will be determined through policies shaped by written arguments. The ability to write well can give you a voice in the future of our planet.

Acknowledgments

I am quite fortunate to work with the same team of co-creators in London, New York, New Jersey, Massachusetts, Maine, and Texas that contributed to the success of the first edition. Executive editor Lynn Huddon and I have collaborated on sixteen previous books and editions, and I much appreciate the vision she has brought to each project along with her talents as an editor and manager. She has well earned her reputation as one of the best in her profession. My development editor, Katharine Glynn, has also brought a wealth of knowledge to the book. Even more appreciated is the calmness she inspires in the often stressful process of publishing a book. Joseph Opiela, editorial director, and Mary Ellen Curley, director of development for English, have also been close to the project and have made many insightful suggestions.

Others at Longman who contributed their wisdom and experience include Roth Wilkofsky, president; Tim Stookesberry, vice president of marketing; Megan Galvin-Fak, executive marketing manager; Sandra McGuire, senior marketing manager; Laura Coaty, market research director; Donna Campion, senior supplements editor; Wendy Ann Fredericks, cover design manager; Rona Tuccillo, visual researcher; Bob Ginsberg, production manager; and Rebecca Gilpin, assistant editor. At Pre-Press, two other excellent people whom I have enjoyed working with in the past guided the book into print: Lindsay Bethoney, production manager, and proofreader Elsa van Bergen.

The experience of working across the Atlantic with Stuart Jackman, design director of DK Education in London, again has been a great pleasure. Stuart continues to teach me a great deal about using effective design for learning. I thank Oona Curley for contributing three of her excellent photographs.

I also thank collaborators in Austin, especially Susan "George" Schorn, who assisted in assembling the work of student writers and who wrote the instructor's manual. Victoria Davis helped me find readings and develop the headnotes and questions that accompany them. I cannot say enough about how much I have learned over the years from colleagues and students at the University of Texas, a few of whom are represented by their writing here.

I have benefited enormously from the advice of colleagues across the country who contributed many splendid ideas in reviews. I am especially grateful to these colleagues: Shana Bartram, *Fresno City College;* Bennis Blue, *Virginia State University;* Michael G. Boyd, *Illinois Central College;* Jennifer Brezina, *College of the Canyons;* Michael Dubson, *Bunker Hill Community College;* Jo Gibson, *Cleveland State University;* Richard Iadonisi, *Grand Valley State University;* Bradley Joseph Lint, *Indiana University of Pennsylvania;* Maureen Murphy, *Dakota State University;* Michael Pennell, *University of Rhode Island;* Eric G. Waggoner, *West Virginia Wesleyan College;* and Sara Webb-Sunderhaus, *Indiana University-Purdue University, Fort Wayne.*

Finally, without my wife Linda's deep reserves of patience in putting up with a husband who becomes distracted and grumpy when he is writing, the book would never have been written.

 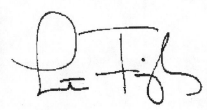

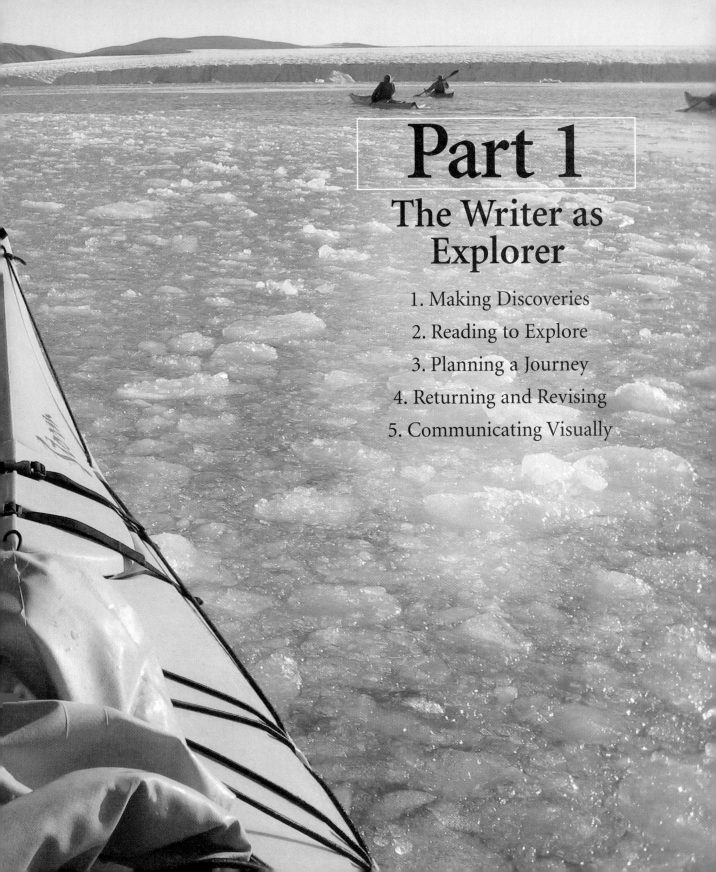

Part 1

The Writer as Explorer

1 Making Discoveries

Go outside. Don't plan where to go. Walk slowly. Look up. Look down.
No matter how familiar you are with the place, you'll see something that
you have never seen before.

Look with new eyes

Walk long enough so you forget about what is most pressing at the moment. Look for secrets that no one else sees. The dance of light in the canopy of a tree. A second-story cornice on a building. The clarity of reflections in dark puddles. The faint outline of a chalk drawing on the sidewalk. The date stamped on a fire hydrant. The dark blue of a distant slope dotted with blue-green trees.

Take in the sounds. What can you hear besides human-made noises? Even in the middle of a city you may hear birds claiming territories. Listen to the sounds wind makes. Take in the smells. Close your eyes and focus. You can distinguish different smells. Feel the leaves on different plants. Touch the trunks of trees. The world is full of distinct textures.

A city's pride can be expressed on its water meter covers. A water meter cover is also a historical document of American industry. Over the decades the manufacturers of water meters moved from New England to the Midwest, and more recently to India and Taiwan.

An aging door reveals the secrets of its construction and the rates of deterioration of its materials.

Find a territory

Writers begin by exploring. When they start writing, exploration doesn't stop. Once they start, writers find things they could not have imagined. Where writers end up is often far away from where they thought they were going.

Most writing in college concerns exploration because academic disciplines seek to create new knowledge and to rethink what is known. Colleges and universities bring together people who ask interesting questions: How does recent archaeological evidence change our understanding of Homer's *Iliad* and *Odyssey*? Why does eyesight deteriorate with age? How do volcanoes affect the world climate? How do chameleons regenerate lost body parts? How do Rousseau's ideas about nature continue to shape notions about wilderness? How do electric eels generate voltage and not get shocked in the process? How can a poll of a thousand people represent 295 million Americans with only a 3 percent margin of error?

Writers in colleges and universities respond to these questions and many others. They challenge old answers and contribute new answers. Readers of college writing expect to learn something when they read—new knowledge, a fresh interpretation, another point of view that they had not considered.

At first glance the expectations of college writing seem impossible. How can you as an undergraduate student expect to contribute new knowledge? But just as there is a great deal that maps do not show, you can find many uncertainties, controversies, and unresolved problems in any field of study. You just have to ask the right questions.

Local questions are often more interesting than broad, general questions. For example, should historic neighborhoods be preserved, or should they give way to urban renewal and gentrification, as has happened to Chinatown in Washington, DC?

Ask interesting questions

Good questions can take you to places that will interest you and your readers alike.

- Focus on an area you don't know and want to know more about.

- Find out where experts disagree. What exactly is the source of the disagreement? Why do they come to different conclusions using the same evidence?

- Analyze explanations of current trends and events. What possible causes might be left out?

- Examine proposals to solve problems. Does the solution fix the problem? Will people support the solution if it costs them effort or money?

- Compare what people claim and the reality. Often people (especially politicians) represent things and their role in making them as much better than they actually are.

Use strategies for finding a topic

Sometimes your instructor will assign a topic, but more often you will have to come up with your own topic. Look first at material from your course. You might find a topic to explore in the readings or from class discussion.

Start with what interests you. It's hard to write about topics that you care little about. If your assignment gives you a range of options, make more than one list.

PERSONAL
1. History of Anime in Japan
2. Cave exploration and conservation
3. Learning to windsurf

CAMPUS
1. Pros and cons of computer fees
2. Excessive litter on campus
3. Fellowships for study-abroad programs

COMMUNITY
1. Safe bicycle commuting
2. Bilingual education programs
3. Better public transportation

NATION/WORLD
1. Advertising aimed at preschool children
2. Censorship of the Internet
3. Genetically altered crops

Write Now

Mapping your campus

Your campus likely has an information desk for students and visitors. Information centers typically will have several brochures with maps. Visit the information desk and collect everything that includes a map. Then compare the maps. Make a checklist for what the maps show and don't show (building names, streets, shuttle bus routes, bicycle routes, parking, landmarks, hotels, and more).

Create a map for new students on your campus that contains insider knowledge that would not appear on the maps your school produces. For example, where can you find the best burger on or close to campus? The best cup of coffee or cookies? A quiet place to study? A great place to meet friends? Make a list of places that need to be included on your map. Then draw the map.

Use guides

Writers can take advantage of guides developed by libraries. Your library's online subject catalog often divides big subjects into smaller and more manageable ones. For example, if you type "nanotechnology" into the subject search window in your online catalog, you likely will get results similar to those below.

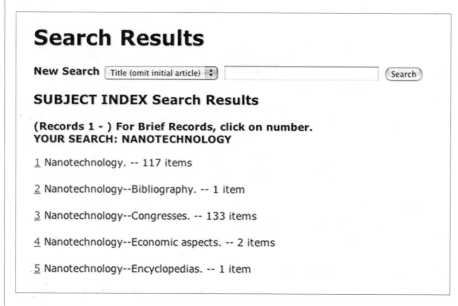

A subject search for "nanotechnology" in a library's online catalog generates a list of subtopics that may point to a manageable, specific topic.

Online subject directories including Yahoo's Search Directory provide lists of links on particular subjects.

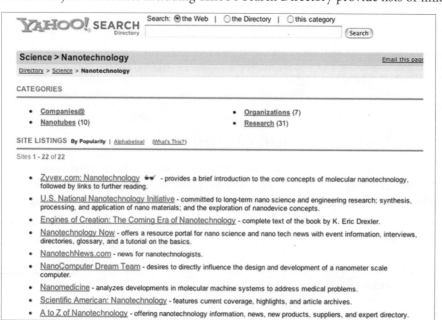

Yahoo's subject directory provides links to online sources for "nanotechnology."

[Reproduced with permission of Yahoo! Inc. Copyright © 2008 by Yahoo! Inc. YAHOO! and the YAHOO! logo are trademarks of Yahoo! Inc.]

Write Now

Make an idea map

Start with the general subject you plan to write about. State it in a few words. Draw a box around it.

Obesity in children

Next think about what can be said about this topic. At this point you don't want specifics but general categories.

problem

background

causes

Childhood obesity

possible solutions

solutions that haven't worked

The third stage is to generate topics about each category.

70% of obese children become obese adults

fast food more available

Americans consume 3800 calories a day, about twice what they need

percentage of obese children quadrupled from 1975 to 2000

problem

causes

obese children have serious health problems

Childhood obesity

children see many food ads on children's TV programs

The process continues until the topics become specific.

When you finish the map, look at how it might be translated into writing. Probably you don't want to include everything that is in the map. Get a colored marker and put a line around those parts you intend to write about.

2 Reading to Explore

Along with learning to write well, learning to think critically is the most important skill you will gain in college.

Become a critical reader

Critical thinking begins with critical reading. For most of what you read, one time through is enough. When you start asking questions about what you are reading, you are engaging in critical reading. Critical reading is a four-part process. First, begin by asking where a piece of writing came from and why it was written. Second, read the text carefully to find the author's central claim or thesis and the major points. Third, decide if you can trust the author. Fourth, read the text again to understand how it works.

1. Where did it come from?
- Who wrote this material?
- Where did it first appear? In a book, newspaper, magazine, or online?
- What else has been written about the topic or issue?
- What do you expect after reading the title?

2. What does it say?
- What is the topic or issue?
- What is the writer's thesis or central idea?
- What reasons or evidence does the writer offer?
- Who are the intended readers? What does the writer assume the readers know and believe?

3. Can you trust the writer?
- Does the writer have the necessary knowledge and experience to write on this subject?
- Do you detect a bias in the writer's position?
- Are the facts relevant to the writer's claims?
- Can you trust the writer's facts? Where did the facts come from?
- Does the writer acknowledge opposing views and unfavorable evidence? Does the writer deal fairly with opposing views?

4. How does it work?
- How is the piece of writing organized? How are the major points arranged?
- How does the writer conclude? Does the conclusion follow from the evidence the writer offers? What impression does the writer take away?
- How would you characterize the style? Describe the language that the writer uses.
- How does the writer represent herself or himself?

Write Now

Analyze information for students on your campus

No doubt your school mailed you a great deal of information when you were admitted. Schools continue to distribute information to students when they get to campus. You can find informative brochures and flyers at your school's student services building and in the health center.

Pick one of the brochures or flyers to analyze. Remember that you are the intended audience.

Write a one-page evaluation about why the brochure or flyer is effective or ineffective for an audience of college students. If it is ineffective, what changes need to be made to make it effective? If it works, what does it do well?

Look with a critical eye

Critical viewing, like critical reading, requires thinking about where the image or visual came from. Begin by asking the following.

- What kind of an image or visual is it?

- Who created this image (movie, advertisement, television program, and so on)?

The Pharaoh Menkaure (Mycerinus) and his queen, Giza, Old Kingdom, 2548–2530 BCE. One of the finest statues from ancient Egypt depicts a royal couple. Compare the statue to formal portraits of couples today. Why does the queen have one arm around his waist and the other touching the king's arm? Do you think it depicts how they looked in real life? Or how they might have wanted to look in the afterlife? How do you think people in ancient Egypt might have viewed this statue?

The following questions are primarily for still images. For animations, movies, and television, you also have to ask questions about how the story is being told.

- What attracts your eye first? If there is an attention-grabbing element, how does it connect with the rest of the image?

- What impression of the subject does the image create?

- How does the image appeal to the values of the audience? (For example, politicians love to be photographed with children.)

- How does the image relate to what surrounds it?

- Was it intended to serve purposes besides art and entertainment?

- What is it about? What is portrayed in the image?

- Where did it first appear? Where do you usually find images like this one?

- When did it appear?

Arthur Rothstein made this photograph of black clouds of dust rising over the Texas Panhandle in March 1936. Look closely at the photo. What attracts your eye first? Snapshots usually put the horizon line in the center. Why did Rothstein put the horizon at the bottom? What impression does this photo convey to you?

Working Together

Analyze political cartoons

Political cartoons make comments on politics in drawings combined with words. Bring a political cartoon to class. You can find many political cartoons on the Web in addition to ones in newspapers and magazines.

Answer these questions.

1. What is the point of the cartoon?

2. What do you need to know to understand the cartoon? Political cartoons usually make reference to current events, television shows, and popular culture.

3. Political cartoons often exaggerate physical attributes. Is anything exaggerated?

4. Political cartoons are often ironic—pointing to the difference between the way things really are and what they are expected to be. Is the cartoon ironic?

5. Why is the cartoon funny or not funny?

Organize in groups of three or four students. Exchange your cartoons and answer the same questions for your classmates' cartoons.

When all finish, compare your answers for each cartoon. Where there is disagreement, stop to discuss why you came up with different answers.

Read actively

If you own what you are reading (or are able to make yourself a photocopy of borrowed materials), read with a pencil in hand. Pens and highlighters don't erase, and often you don't remember why you highlighted a particular sentence.

Annotate what you read
Using annotating strategies will make your effort more rewarding.

Mark major points and key concepts	Sometimes major points are indicated by headings, but often you will need to locate them.
Connect passages	Notice how ideas connect to each other. Draw lines and arrows. If an idea connects to something a few pages before, write a note in the margin with the page number.
Ask questions	Note anything that puzzles you, including words to look up.

Annotate difficult readings
Much of what you read in college will deal with unfamiliar concepts, which are often defined by other concepts. Annotating a difficult reading will help you understand the relationship of concepts, and the annotations will be valuable in remembering key points when you come back to the reading later. In this passage from John Heskett's *Toothpicks and Logos, Design in Everyday Life*, the author defines function in terms of two other concepts.

A more inclusive definition of function is needed, which can be opened up by breaking the concept of function into a twofold division: the key concepts of utility and significance.

definition of function – utlity and significance

Utility can be defined as the quality of appropriateness in use. This means it is concerned with how things work, of the degree to which designs serve practical purposes and provide affordances or capabilities. A simple example is a professional kitchen knife used to prepare food: its primary utility value is as a cutting tool. In order for it to work effectively, the blade needs to possess material qualities enabling a sharp edge to be maintained and for it to remain stable in use.

definition of utlity

example – kitchen knife

affordances? odd word – author is British

Significance as a concept in design, explains how forms assume meaning in the ways they are used, or the roles and meaning assigned them, often becoming powerful symbols or icons in patterns of habit and ritual. In contrast to the emphasis on efficiency, significance has more to do with expression and meaning.

definition of significance

other examples:
computer keyboard,
pencil,
traffic light

examples of
designs for
significance

It is possible to find designs of many kinds defined solely in terms of utility or significance. Many examples of the former are products related to the performance of professional services, tools with highly specific purposes, such as a hand saw or a lathe, or medical equipment, such as an ultrasound machine. Where information has to perform a highly specific task, as in a railway timetable, the layout and type forms should be clean, simple, and directed wholly to imparting essential facts. A primary condition of utilitarian design is that it must effectively execute or support certain tasks. In contrast, a piece of jewelry, a porcelain figurine, or a frame for a family photograph has no such specific purpose—instead their purpose can be described in terms of contemplative pleasure or adornment.

examples of
designs for
utility

Map what you read

Drawing a map of a text can help you to identify key points and understand the relationships of concepts.

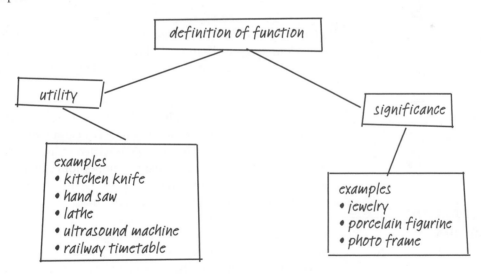

Make notes

Write down your thoughts as you read. Often you will find that something you read reminds you of something else. Jot that down. It might give you ideas for writing. Think about which ideas impress you as you read. And think about what else you might read if you want to write about this subject.

Recognize fallacies

Reasoning depends less on proving a claim than it does on finding evidence for that claim that readers will accept as valid. The kinds of faulty reasoning called logical fallacies reflect a failure to provide sufficient evidence for a claim that is being made.

Fallacies of logic

Begging the question	*Politicians are inherently dishonest because no honest person would run for public office.* The fallacy of begging the question occurs when the claim is restated and passed off as evidence.
Either-or	*Either we eliminate the regulation of businesses or else profits will suffer.* The either-or fallacy suggests that there are only two choices in a complex situation. Rarely, if ever, is this the case. (In this example, the writer ignores the fact that Enron was unregulated and went bankrupt.)
False analogies	*Japan quit fighting in 1945 when we dropped nuclear bombs on them. We should use nuclear weapons against other countries.* Analogies always depend on the degree of resemblance of one situation to another. In this case, the analogy fails to recognize that circumstances today are very different from those in 1945; many countries now possess nuclear weapons, and we know their use could harm the entire world.
Hasty generalization	*We have been in a drought for three years; that's a sure sign of climate change.* A hasty generalization is a broad claim made on the basis of a few occurrences. Climate cycles occur regularly over spans of a few years; climate trends must be observed over centuries.
Non sequitur	*A university that can raise a billion dollars from alumni should not have to raise tuition.* A *non sequitur* (which is a Latin term meaning "it does not follow") ties together two unrelated ideas. In this case, the argument fails to recognize that the money for capital campaigns is often donated for special purposes such as athletic facilities and is not part of a university's general revenue.
Oversimplification	*No one would run stop signs if we had a mandatory death penalty for doing it.* This claim may be true, but the argument would be unacceptable to most citizens. More complex, if less definitive, solutions are called for.
Post hoc fallacy	*The stock market goes down when the AFC wins the Super Bowl in even years.* The *post hoc* fallacy (from the Latin *post hoc ergo hoc,*

which means "after this, therefore this") assumes that things that follow in time have a causal relationship.

Rationalization	*I could have finished my paper on time if my printer was working.* People frequently come up with excuses and weak explanations for their own and others' behavior that often avoid actual causes.
Slippery slope	*We shouldn't grant citizenship to illegal immigrants now living in the United States because no one will want to obey our laws.* The slippery slope fallacy maintains that one thing inevitably will cause something else to happen.

Fallacies of emotion and language

Bandwagon appeals	*It doesn't matter if I copy a paper off the Web because everyone else does.* This argument suggests that everyone is doing it, so why shouldn't you? But on close examination, it may be that everyone really isn't doing it—and in any case, it may not be the right thing to do.
Name calling	Name calling is frequent in politics and among competing groups (*radical, tax-and-spend liberal, racist, fascist, right-wing ideologue*). Unless these terms are carefully defined, they are meaningless.
Polarization	*Feminists are all man-haters.* Polarization, like name-calling, exaggerates positions and groups by representing them as extreme and divisive.
Straw man	*Environmentalists won't be satisfied until not a single human being is allowed to enter a national park.* A straw man argument is a diversionary tactic that sets up another's position in a way that can be easily rejected. In fact, only a small percentage of environmentalists would make an argument even close to this one.

Write Now

Analyze opinion writing

Examine writing that expresses opinions: blogs, discussion boards, editorials, advocacy Web sites, the letters to the editor on the editorial pages of your campus or local newspaper. Read with a pencil in hand, and mark where you think there may be fallacies.

Select the example that has the clearest fallacy. Explain in a paragraph the cause of the fallacy.

Respond as a reader

Engage in a dialogue with what you read. Talk back to the author. If you are having trouble understanding a difficult section, read it aloud and listen to the author's voice. Hearing something read will sometimes help you to imagine being in a conversation with the author.

Make notes

As you read, write down your thoughts. Something you read may remind you of something else. Jot that down.

- Imagine that the author is with you. What points does the writer make that you would respond to in person?

- What questions would you have of the author? These indicate what you might need to look up.

- What ideas do you find that you might develop or interpret differently?

Write summaries

When you summarize, you state the major ideas of an entire source or part of a source in your own words. Most summaries are much shorter than the original because they include just the main points, not most of the examples and supporting material.

The keys to writing a good summary are identifying the main points and then putting those points into your own words. If you use words from the source, you have to put those words in quotation marks.

John Heskett argues that the concept of function in design should be understood in terms of "utility" and "significance." He defines utility as the degree a design accomplishes its purpose, such as how well a knife cuts. Significance is defined as the degree to which an object is designed to give pleasure or create meaning. A piece of art is an example of something designed exclusively for significance.

Build on what you read

Keeping a reading journal is a good practice for a writer. You'll have a record of your thinking as you read that you can return to later. Record your first impressions, note any ideas you find stimulating or useful, explore relationships, and write down questions. Often you can connect different ideas from different readings. A reading journal is a great place to test ideas that you can later develop for a writing assignment.

Heskett says, "It is possible to find designs of many kinds defined solely in terms of utility and significance." I'll grant the distinction, but his examples suggest that most things have elements of both.

He uses tools as objects designed strictly for utility, but look at a tool catalog and you'll see lots of bright colors and handsome cases. He uses a photograph frame as an example of significance. True enough that frames are often decorative, but a frame also has to fit the picture. The frame should use non-glare glass to reduce reflected light. A frame has to do more than just look good.

But a bigger point is that anything can have significance for a particular person. I have my grandfather's hammer. It is nearly worthless because the handle is so old and worn that it would snap if you swung it hard against a nail. I took the hammer to work one day to hang a picture, and it shortly disappeared. I searched and couldn't find it. I forgot about it, but then I noticed it in a storeroom months later and recovered it.

Write Now

Respond to what you read

Select a reading in one of the chapters in Part 2 that interests you. Write a one-paragraph summary of either the entire reading or of a part that contains a stimulating idea.

Write a second paragraph that develops one or more of the ideas in the reading. Think of some way of expanding or extending one of the author's ideas, either by relating it to your own experience or to something else you have read.

3 Planning a Journey

In some buildings, you feel comfortable and at ease right away. But in others you always feel disoriented. The problem is the layout or plan of the building.

A disorienting building lacks central spaces and signs. Directions are missing at intersections. All the hallways look alike.

Strong central spaces, like the Piazza Navona in Rome, organize neighborhoods and attract people.

Determine your direction

Poorly organized writing is like a poorly designed building. It takes too much effort to get to where you want to go. Effective writing keeps readers oriented. Writing that succeeds is organized around a central idea, much as successful buildings and even thriving neighborhoods are.

Identify your center

Often the challenge in writing is finding the center that connects your sentences and paragraphs. Probably you have had the experience of driving around looking for a store or a house without having the address. Unless you were lucky, it was probably frustrating. Knowing your center is like having an address. It makes the journey far easier.

Having a big topic like privacy is like knowing only the general area of where something is located.

BROAD TOPIC:
privacy and surveillance

SPECIFIC TOPIC:
Which public spaces should be under constant surveillance with micro-devices invisible to the human eye?

Think about where you are headed

Writing is a dynamic activity that goes back and forth between your mind and the page. Nevertheless, it helps to have an overall strategy that enables your thinking to evolve into writing that communicates with your readers.

Read your assignment again. Often the assignment will tell you which direction to go.

Reflect
You will need to think about an idea or concept in terms of your own history and life experience (see Chapter 7).

Inform
You will need to report information or explain a concept or idea (see Chapter 8).

Analyze
You will need to interpret a text or a set of data to find connections and reach conclusions (see Chapter 9).

Analyze causes
You will need to identify probable causes of a trend or phenomenon and give evidence for your analysis (see Chapter 10).

Evaluate
You will need to determine whether something is good or bad based on criteria that you identify (see Chapter 11).

Argue
You will need to take a position on an issue or propose a course of action (see Chapters 12 and 13).

Write a thesis

Central ideas in writing are often expressed in a thesis statement. Just as many urban neighborhoods grow up around strong central spaces, most writing you will do in college and later in your career will have an explicit thesis, usually stated near the beginning. The thesis announces your topic and indicates what points you want to make about that topic.

Write a working thesis

Your thesis should follow the direction your assignment calls for. These examples show how the broad subject of databases and privacy can be approached from different directions, depending on your purpose.

Describe

THESIS: My Amazon.com account has a list of every book I have purchased from them dating back ten years, plus Amazon records every item I browse but don't buy. No wonder Amazon's recommendations of what I might like are so uncannily accurate!

Analyze

THESIS: Understanding how the concept of privacy is legally defined is critical for strengthening privacy laws.

Inform

THESIS: Imagine a government that compels its citizens to reveal vast amounts of personal data, including your physical description, your phone number, your political party, your parents' and spouse's names, where you work, where you live, what property you own, what it is worth, and every legal transaction in your life, and then making that data available to anyone on the Web—which is exactly what federal, state, and local governments are doing today in the United States.

Argue

THESIS: Unlike the government, companies have almost no restrictions on what information they collect or what they do with that information. Laws should be passed that make companies responsible for the misuse of personal information and allow people to have greater participation in how that information is used.

Evaluate

THESIS: Using personal consumer data to refuse service or offer inferior service to customers who likely will not spend much money is an example of the misuse of personal information.

Reflect

THESIS: I had never thought about the consequences of data profiling until I read about Netflix's policy of "throttling" frequent users, which explained why deliveries of movies I had requested from Netflix grew slower and slower.

Analyze causes

THESIS: Many laws to protect privacy are on the books, but these laws are ineffective for the digital era because they were written to protect people from government spying and intrusion rather than from the collection and selling of personal information by companies.

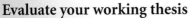

Evaluate your working thesis

Ask yourself these questions about your working thesis.

1. Is it specific?
2. Is it manageable in terms of the assigned length and the amount of time you have?
3. Is it interesting to your intended readers?

Example 1

THESIS: Steroids are a problem in Major League Baseball.

- **Specific?** The thesis is too broad. What exactly is the problem? Is the problem the same now as it was a few years ago?
- **Manageable?** Because the thesis is not limited, it cannot be discussed adequately.
- **Interesting?** The topic is potentially interesting, but many people are aware that baseball players used steroids. How can you lead readers to think about the topic in a new way?

Example 1 revised

THESIS: Home run records from 1993 through 2004 should be placed in a special category because of the high use of steroids in Major League Baseball before testing began in 2004.

Example 2

THESIS: "Nanotechnology" refers to any technology that deals with particles measured in units of a nanometer, which is one billionth (10^{-9}) of a meter.

- **Specific?** The thesis is specific, but it is too narrow. It offers only a definition of nanotechnology.
- **Manageable?** The thesis states a fact.
- **Interesting?** Nanotechnology could be interesting if some of its potential effects are included.

Example 2 revised

THESIS: Nanotechnology may soon change concepts of social identity by making it possible for individuals to alter their physical appearances either through cosmetic surgery performed by nanorobots or changes in genetic sequences on chromosomes.

Write Now

Write a bold thesis

Too much of what we read says what we've all heard before. Instead of serving up what readers likely know, try challenging readers. For example, in *Everything Bad Is Good for You*, Steven Johnson argues that video games are not a total waste of time but teach children valuable problem-solving skills.

Think of something that many people accept as common sense or general wisdom—that junk food is bad for you, reality television is garbage, or graffiti is vandalism—and argue the opposite. Or that something thought of as boring might be really interesting: bird watching, classical Indian music, or ancient Greek drama. Write a thesis that stands that common wisdom on its head.

Then write a paragraph about how you might argue for your controversial thesis. What evidence might you supply?

Plan your route

Experienced travelers have multiple strategies for getting to their destinations. Sometimes they have the route planned in advance and follow it exactly. In other cases, they know they have to be flexible, just as when you find traffic stopped and you take an alternate route. Experienced writers work in much the same way, using different strategies for different writing tasks.

Determine a plan

Get out your notes and all the information you have collected. You may find it helpful to write major points on sticky notes so you can move them around. If your topic is the effects of nanotechnology on the body, you might produce an organization plan similar to this one.

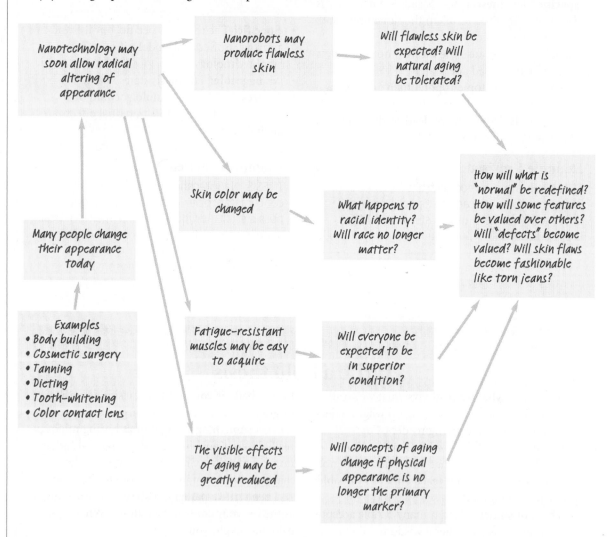

Make a writing plan

Writing plans often take the form of outlines, either formal outlines or working outlines.

A formal outline typically begins with the thesis statement, which anchors the entire outline.

A working outline is a sketch of how you will arrange the major sections.

THESIS: Nanotechnology may soon allow radical altering of the human body, which will have major social consequences.

I. Altering the appearance of the body has become common.
   A. Cosmetic surgery is now routine.
   B. Body building is popular.
   C. Most people are aware of diet and many attempt to control their weight.
   D. Tanning, changing eye color, and tooth-whitening are frequent.

II. Nanotechnology may soon radically accelerate these trends.
   A. Nanorobots may produce flawless skin.
   B. Skin color may be changed.
   C. Wrinkles and other signs of aging may be eliminated or reduced.
   D. Muscle tissue may be enhanced.

Effects of nanotechnology on the body

SECTION 1: Begin with how people change the appearance of their bodies today.

SECTION 2: Discuss how nanotechnology will accelerate these trends, giving people the potential for perfect skin, changing their skin color, and reducing aging.

SECTION 3: Move to the questions these technologies raise, such as how aging will be perceived and how race will be understood.

SECTION 4: Raise the issue of how "normal" will be defined if people can choose how they look.

SECTION 5: Expand the idea of "normal" to who will control what is desirable and how social hierarchies might be changed or reinforced.

SECTION 6: End by connecting body issues to larger issues such as who gets to live for how long.

Write Now

Make a plan

First, write a working thesis. Ask the questions on page 21.
- Is the thesis specific?
- Is it manageable?
- Is it interesting?

Revise your thesis if necessary.

Then use two of the three methods—a visual organization plan, a formal outline, or a working outline—to develop a plan for writing a paper based on the thesis. When you finish, compare the plans. Which will be easier to use for writing your paper?

4 Returning and Revising

In order to revise effectively, you must "re-see," which, after all, is
what revision means.

Evaluate your draft

Use these questions to evaluate your draft. Note any places where you might make improvements.

Does your paper or project meet the assignment?

- Look again at your assignment and especially at the key words such as *analyze, define, evaluate,* and *propose.* Does your paper or project do what the assignment asks for? If not, how can you change it?
- Look again at the assignment for specific guidelines including length, format, and amount of research. Does your work meet these guidelines? If not, how can you change it?

Do you have a clear focus?

- Underline your thesis. Think how you might make your thesis more precise.
- Underline the main idea of each paragraph. Check how each paragraph connects to your thesis. Think about how you can strengthen the connections.

Are your main points adequately developed?

- Put brackets around the reasons and evidence that support your main points.
- Can you find places to add more examples and details that would help to explain your main points?

Is your organization effective?

- Make a quick outline of your draft if you have not done so already.
- Mark the places where you find abrupt shifts or gaps.
- Think about how you might rearrange sections or paragraphs to make your draft more effective.

Do you consider your potential readers' knowledge and points of view?

- Where do you give background if your readers are unfamiliar with your subject?
- Where do you acknowledge any opposing views your readers might have?

Do you represent yourself effectively?

- To the extent you can, forget for a moment that you wrote what you are reading. What impression do you have of you, the writer?
- Does the writer have an appropriate tone?
- Is the writer visually effective? Is the type easy to read? Does the writer use headings and illustrations where they are helpful?

When you finish, make a list of your goals in the revision. You may have to scrap the draft and start over, but you will have a better sense of your subject and your goals.

Learn strategies for rewriting

Now it's time to go through your draft in detail. You should work on the goals you identify in your review. Also, look for other opportunities using this checklist.

1. Keep your audience in mind.	Reread each of your paragraphs' opening sentences and ask yourself whether they are engaging enough to keep your readers interested.
2. Sharpen your focus wherever possible.	You may have started out with a large topic but most of what you wrote concerns only one aspect. You may need to revise your thesis and supporting paragraphs.
3. Check if key terms are adequately defined.	What are your key terms? Are they defined precisely enough to be meaningful?
4. Develop where necessary.	Key points and claims may need more explanation and supporting evidence. Look for opportunities to add support without becoming redundant.
5. Check links between paragraphs.	Look for any places where you make abrupt shifts and make the transitions better. Check if you signal the relationship from one paragraph to the next.
6. Consider your title.	Many writers don't think much about titles, but they are very important. A good title makes the reader want to see what you have to say. Be as specific as you can in your title, and if possible, suggest your stance.
7. Consider your introduction.	In the introduction you want to get off to a fast start and convince your reader to keep reading. Cut to the chase.
8. Consider your conclusion.	Restating your thesis usually isn't the best way to finish; conclusions that offer only summary bore readers. The worst endings say something like "in my paper I've said this." Effective conclusions are interesting and provocative, leaving readers with something to think about.
9. Improve the visual aspects of your text.	Does the font you selected look attractive using your printer? Would headings and subheadings help to identify key sections? If you include statistical data, would charts be effective? Would illustrations help to establish key points?

Respond to others

Your instructor may ask you to respond to the drafts of your classmates. Responding to other people's writing requires the same careful attention you give to your own draft. To write a helpful response, you should go through the draft more than once.

First reading:
Read at your normal rate the first time through without stopping. When you finish you should have a clear sense of what the writer is trying to accomplish.

- Main idea: Write a sentence that summarizes what you think is the writer's main idea in the draft.
- Purpose: Write a sentence that summarizes what you think the writer was trying to accomplish in the draft.

Second reading:
In your second reading, you should be most concerned with the content, organization, and completeness of the draft. Make notes as you read.

- Introduction: Does the writer's first paragraph effectively introduce the topic and engage your interest?
- Thesis: Where exactly is the writer's thesis? Note in the margin where you think the thesis is located.
- Focus: Does the writer maintain focus on the thesis? Note any places where the writer seems to wander off to another topic.
- Organization: Are the sections and paragraphs ordered effectively? Do any paragraphs seem to be out of place? Do you note any abrupt shifts? Can you suggest a better order for the paragraphs?
- Completeness: Are there sections and paragraphs that lack key information or adequate development? Where do you want to know more?
- Sources: If the draft uses outside sources, are they cited accurately? If there are quotations, are they used correctly and worked into the fabric of the draft?

Third reading:
In your third reading, turn your attention to matters of audience, style, and tone.

- Audience: Who is the writer's intended audience? What does the writer assume the audience knows and believes?
- Style: Is the writer's style engaging? How would you describe the writer's voice?
- Tone: Is the tone appropriate for the writer's purpose and audience? Is the tone consistent throughout the draft? Are there places where another word or phrase might work better?

When you have finished the third reading, write a short paragraph on each bulleted item above, referring to specific paragraphs in the draft by number. Then end by answering these two questions:

1. **What does the writer do especially well in the draft?**
2. **What one or two things would most improve the draft in a revision?**

Pay attention to details last

When you finish revising, you are ready for one final careful reading, keeping the goals of improving your style and eliminating errors in mind.

Edit for particular goals

1. Check the connections between sentences.

Notice how your sentences are connected. If you need to signal the relationship from one sentence to the next, use a transition word or phrase.

2. Check your sentences.

If you notice that a sentence doesn't sound right, think about how you might rephrase it. Often you will pick up problems by reading aloud. If a sentence seems too long, then you might break it into two or more sentences. If you notice a string of short sentences that sound choppy, then you might combine them.

3. Eliminate wordiness.

Writers tend to introduce wordiness in drafts. Look for long expressions that can easily be shortened ("at this point in time" –> "now") and for unnecessary repetition. Remove unnecessary words like *very, really,* and *totally.* See how many words you can take out without losing the meaning.

4. Use active verbs.

Anytime you can use a verb besides a form of *be* (*is, are, was, were*) or a verb ending in *–ing,* take advantage of the opportunity to make your style more lively. Sentences that begin with "There is (are)" and "It is" often have better alternatives.

Proofread carefully

In your final pass through your text, eliminate as many errors as you can. To become an effective proofreader, you have to learn to slow down. Some writers find that moving from word to word with a pencil slows them down enough to find errors. Others read backwards to force concentration on each word.

1. Know what your spelling checker can and can't do.

Spelling checkers are the greatest invention since peanut butter. They turn up many typos and misspellings that are hard to catch. But spelling checkers do not catch wrong words (e.g., "to much" should be "too much"), where you leave off endings ("three dog"), and other similar errors.

2. Check for grammar and punctuation.

Nothing hurts your credibility more than leaving many errors in what you write. Many job application letters get tossed in the reject pile because an applicant made a single, glaring error. Readers probably shouldn't make such harsh judgments when they find errors, but in real life they do.

Write Now

Write a helpful response

Read the following first draft and use the guidelines on page 27 to write a response that will help the writer to revise the paper. Resist the urge to edit sentences and correct mechanical errors. The assignment asked the student to analyze an ad.

Analysis of an Ad

In our modern world of today, Americans see thousands of advertisements every year, we buy many products because of ads. One of the products advertised a lot is milk. I chose an Andy Roddick ad for this assignment because he is my very favorite tennis player. There was another totally awesome milk ad with Stone Cold Steve Austin, but I couldn't find it.

I found the picture of Andy in Seventeen magazine. I don't read Seventeen any more, but my younger sister does, and I needed to find an ad. Andy looks totally cool in this photo. He was on the court with his tennis racquet. His milk mustache is visible to the eye.

I suppose the milk people wanted him because he is popular and good looking. The milk ads all have celebrities and sports stars. I read that the milk people were worried that younger people aren't drinking milk and they wanted young stars to pitch milk and praise it's benefits. I guess its working because the ad campaign has been around as long as I can remember. I've even heard copycats use slogans like "Got cookies?" "Got fish?" "Got fish?" "Got sports?" and even "Got Jesus?"

The Roddick ad probably works because Roddick is good looking. As I said before, the milk people like good looking stars. He has kind of a sexy pose too. He looks like a movie star.

In conclusion, the Andy Roddick ad is a good ad because young people like Andy Roddick. If they see Andy Roddick drinking milk, they want to drink milk to.

5 Communicating Visually

The principles of good design, like those of good writing, begin with your audience and what you are trying to accomplish.

Communicate with visuals and words

The word *writing* makes us think of words, yet in our daily experience reading newspapers, magazines, advertisements, posters, and signs, we find words combined with images and graphics. Similarly, the dominant visual medium of our time, television, uses words extensively; think of the words you see on commercials when you have the sound off and the running text across the bottom of the screen on news, sports, and financial programs. Understanding the relationships of words and visuals will make you a better writer.

What do visuals do best?

We've become accustomed to deciding whether we'll need to wear a sweater outside tomorrow by looking at the colors on a weather map. But even then, we depend on words to tell us whether the forecast is for today or tomorrow, and what each color signifies. Visuals work well when they

- Deliver spatial information, especially through maps, floor plans, and other graphic representations of space
- Represent statistical relationships
- Produce a strong immediate impact, even shock value
- Emphasize a point made in words

What do words do best?

Words can do many things that images cannot. Written words work best when they

- Communicate abstract ideas
- Report information
- Persuade using elaborated reasoning
- Communicate online using minimal bandwidth

What can words and visuals do together?

Combining words and visuals allow writers to present very complex ideas: how the quick thinking of Union generals to rush soldiers to high ground at the battle of Gettysburg led to a decisive victory; how atomic structure influences ionic bonding; how the warming of oceans in the Arctic and Antarctic affects weather worldwide.

Know when to use images and graphics

Personal computers, digital cameras, scanners, printers, and the Web have made it easy to include images and graphics in what we write. But these technologies don't tell us when or how to use images and graphics.

Think about what an image or graphic communicates

- Think about your readers' expectations for the medium you are using. Most essays don't use images. Most Web sites and brochures do use images.

- Think about the purpose for an image or graphic. Does it illustrate a concept? highlight an important point? show something that is hard to explain in words alone? If you don't know the purpose, you may not need the image.

- Think about the placement of an image or graphic in your text. It should be as close as possible to a relevant point in your text.

- Think about the focus of an image. Will readers see the part that matters? If not, you may need to crop the image.

- Provide informative captions for the images and graphics you use and refer to them in your text.

Format images for the medium you are using

Images that you want to print need to be of higher quality than those intended for the Web or the screen. Pay attention to the settings on your camera or scanner.

Digital cameras frequently make images with 72 dpi (dots per inch), which is the maximum you can display on the screen. Most printers use a resolution from 300 to 600 dpi. Use the high-quality setting on your camera for images you intend to print.

Scanners typically offer a range of resolution from 72 to 1600 dpi. The higher the number, the finer the image, but the file size becomes larger. Images on the Web or a screen display at 72 dpi, so higher resolutions do not improve the quality but do make the image slow to load.

Create tables, charts, and graphs

Software makes it easy to create tables, charts, and graphs, which are often effective in conveying statistical information at a glance. Select the type of visual that best suits your purpose.

Table 25.1 — Population Change for the Ten Largest U.S. Cities, 1990 to 2000				
	Population		Change, 1990 to 2000	
City and State	April 1, 2000	April 1, 1990	Number	Percentage
New York, NY	8,008,278	7,322,564	685,714	9.4
Los Angeles, CA	3,694,820	3,485,398	209,422	6.0
Chicago, IL	2,896,016	2,783,726	112,290	4.0
Houston, TX	1,953,631	1,630,553	323,078	19.8
Philadelphia, PA	1,517,550	1,585,577	-68,027	-4.3
Phoenix, AZ	1,321,045	983,403	337,642	34.3
San Diego, CA	1,223,400	1,110,549	112,851	10.2
Dallas, TX	1,188,580	1,006,877	181,703	18.0
San Antonio, TX	1,144,646	935,933	208,713	22.3
Detroit, MI	951,270	1,027,974	-76,704	-7.5
Source: U.S. Census Bureau, Census 2000; 1990 Census, Population and Housing Unit Counts, United States (1990 CPH-2-1).				

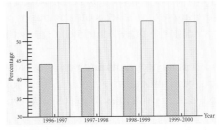

Tables

A table is used to display numerical data and similar types of information. It usually includes several items as well as variables for each item.

Bar Graphs

A bar graph compares the values of two or more items.

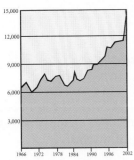

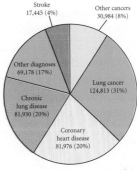

Line Graphs

A line graph shows change over time.

Pie Charts

A pie chart shows the parts making up a whole.

Working Together

Communicate with images and graphics

In a group of three or four students

Look at your textbooks for your other courses. Find one example where an image or graphic helps you to understand the material. Write briefly what exactly the image or graphic does that words alone could not. Find a second example where you think an image or graphic could be added. Write why an image or graphic would help.

Bring your examples to class and compare them with other group members. When do words work best? When is it more appropriate to communicate information through graphics and other visual media?

Understand typography

Just as people communicate with body language, texts have a look and feel created by the layout, typefaces, type size, color, density, and other elements.

Typography is the designer's term for letters and symbols that make up the print on the page. You are already using important aspects of typography when you use capital letters, italics, boldface, or different sizes of type to signal a new sentence, identify the title of a book, or distinguish a heading from the body text.

Word processing programs and personal computers now enable you to use dozens of different typefaces (fonts), bold and italic versions of these fonts, and a range of font sizes. Fortunately, you can rely on some simple design principles to make good typographic choices for your documents.

Choosing a font

A font family consists of the font in different sizes as well as in its boldface and italic forms. Although computers now make hundreds of font styles and sizes available to writers, you should avoid confusing readers with too many typographical features. Limit the fonts in a document to one or two font families. A common practice is to choose one font family for all titles and headings and another for the body text.

A Font Family

Arial Narrow

Arial Narrow Italic

Arial Regular

Arial Italic

Arial Bold

Arial Bold Italic

Arial Black

The font family Arial, shown above in 14 point, is composed of style variations on the Arial design that include a variety of weights.

Serif and sans serif typefaces

Typefaces are normally divided into two groups—serif and sans serif. Serif typefaces include horizontal lines—or serifs—added to the major strokes of a letter or character such as a number. Sans serif typefaces, by contrast, do not have serifs. Notice the difference opposite.

The typical use and stylistic impact of the typefaces vary considerably. Serif typefaces are more traditional, conservative, and formal in appearance. By contrast, sans serif typefaces offer a more contemporary, progressive, and informal look. Serif is often used for longer pieces of writing, such as novels and textbooks. It is also the best bet for college papers.

The difference between serif and sans serif fonts

The horizontal lines make serif easier to read because they guide the eye from left to right across the page.

This **SERIF** font is called Garamond

This **SANS SERIF** font is called Helvetica

Think about font style

Not all fonts are suitable for extended pieces of writing. Sentences and paragraphs printed in fonts that imitate calligraphy or handwriting are difficult to read in long stretches. For most academic and business writing, you will probably want to choose a traditional font, such as Times Roman, that is easy to read and does not call attention to itself. This book is set in 10.5 point Minion.

Choosing the best font for the job

This piece of text is in a caligraphic font and may be right for some special situations, but there is no doubt that every single reader will be aware of the struggle to decipher it.

This font is **28 point Palace Script**

This piece of text is in a handwriting font, and although easier to read than the above is still very difficult in large amounts.

This font is **17 point Feltpen**

This is about as normal a font as you can find. It is called Times Roman, for the simple reason that it was designed for use in the *London Times* newspaper, and so had to be as readable as possible.

This font is **14 point Times Roman**

This font is also very readable and is very common as it is the default font on most computer software. It does, however, require much more space than other faces.

This font is **14 point Courier**

Think about font size

It's easy to change the size of a font when you write on a computer. For most types of writing in college, a 12-point font is the standard size for the main (body) text, with headings in a larger font.

Type sizes

8 point

12 point

18 point

36 point

48 point

Height can make a difference

To ensure that what you write can be read easily, you need to choose an appropriate size. Fonts differ by height, called the x-height, as well as point size. Fonts of the same point size can look different because of height. Effective size depends on the appearance of a font, not merely its point size.

To ensure that what you write can be read easily, you need to choose an appropriate size. Fonts differ by height, called the x-height, as well as point size. Fonts of the same point size can look different because of height. Effective size depends on the appearance of a font, not merely its point size.

Both texts are set the same "size" (12 point) but they appear different because of the x-heights. Bembo, left, looks much smaller and takes much less space than Glypha, right.

Type sizes for computer monitors

For Web pages, you should consider using a larger font to compensate for the added difficulty of reading from a computer monitor. For overhead transparencies and computer-projected displays, you should use an even larger size (such as 32 point) to ensure that the text can be read from a distance.

Pixilation on the computer screen breaks up the font; thus the 12-point type in this example is too small.

You should consider enlarging to 18-point type as in this example.

Or even 32 point if using an overhead projector or a computer-projected display.

Checklist for evaluating document design

1. Audience

Who is the intended audience? Will the design be appealing to them? How does the design serve their needs?

2. Genre

What is the genre? Does the design meet the requirements of the genre? For example, a brochure should fit in your pocket.

3. Organization

Is the organization clear to readers? If headings are used, are they in the right places? If headings are used for more than one level, are these levels indicated consistently?

4. Readability

Is the typeface attractive and readable? Are the margins sufficient? Is any contrasting text, such as boldface, italics, or all caps, brief enough to be legible? If color is used, does it direct emphasis to the right places?

5. Layout

Can the basic layout be made more effective? Is there adequate white space around headings, images, and graphics?

Write Now

Design a menu

Collect menus from a few restaurants, either in print or on the Web. Study the design of each menu.

Design a menu of your own. First, you have to decide what kind of food you will serve: burgers, Italian, Thai, seafood, and so on. Second, think about the clientele you want to attract: college students, families, office lunch crowd, or another demographic. Third, list a few food items for your menu. Fourth, name your restaurant and give it a theme.

Make a sketch of your menu. Decide what graphics, clip art, and backgrounds you want to use. Then create your menu using word processing software.

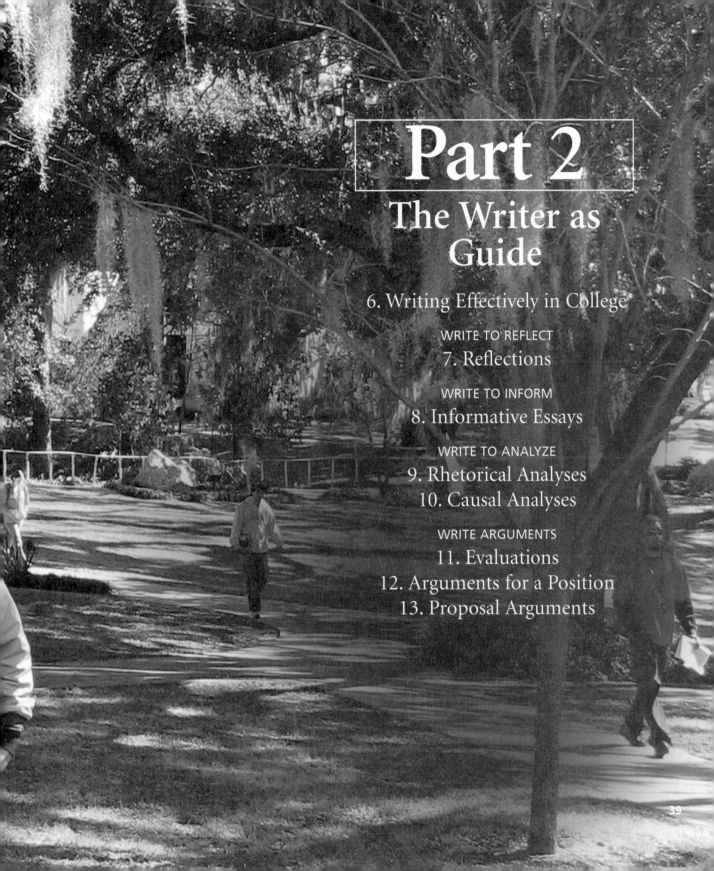

Part 2

The Writer as Guide

6 Writing Effectively in College

Writers today do many different kinds of writing for multiple purposes.

Understand the demands of writing in college

Writing in college changes from course to course depending on the requirements of the course's discipline. What is expected in a philosophy course differs from what is expected in a biology course.

Nevertheless, there are some common expectations about writing in college that extend across disciplines.

Writing in college . . .	Writers are expected to . . .
States explicit claims	Make a claim that isn't obvious. The claim is often called a thesis statement.
Develops an argument	Support their claims with facts, evidence, reasons, and testimony from experts.
Analyzes with insight	Analyze in depth what they read and view.
Investigates complexity	Explore the complexity of a subject, challenging their readers by asking "Have you thought about this?" or "What if you discard the usual way of thinking about a subject and take the opposite point of view?"
Organizes with a hierarchical structure	Make the major parts evident to readers and indicate which parts are subordinate to others.
Signals with transitions	Indicate logical relationships clearly so readers can follow a pathway without getting lost.
Documents sources carefully	Provide the sources of information so readers can consult the same sources the writer used.

Aim	Focus	Example genres
Writing to reflect	**Reflections:** Narrating personal experience and personal insights for a public audience (Chapter 7)	Journals, personal letters, blogs, memoirs, essays
Writing to inform	**Informative essays:** Communicating information clearly (Chapter 8)	Newspaper and magazine articles, academic articles, reports, profiles, essays
Writing to analyze	**Rhetorical analyses:** Analyzing what makes a text successful and why the author made particular choices (Chapter 9)	Rhetorical analysis, literary analysis, visual analysis, essays
	Causal analyses: Exploring why an event, phenomenon, or trend happened (Chapter 10)	History, accident analysis, financial analysis, essays
Writing arguments	**Evaluations:** Assessing whether something is good or bad according to particular criteria (Chapter 11)	Reviews, essays, performance evaluations, product evaluations
	Arguments for a position: Convincing others through reasoned argument to accept or reject a position (Chapter 12)	Speeches, letters to the editor, op-ed columns, editorials, essays
	Proposal arguments: Convincing others through reasoned argument to take action (Chapter 13)	Speeches, business proposals, grant proposals, essays, advocacy Web sites

Use your aim as a guide

In many cases, if you know your aim in advance, you have a good start toward how to structure your paper or project.

For example, you might want to evaluate a Shetland Sheepdog (sheltie) as a breed. For an evaluation, you know that your thesis will take the form of _____ is a good/bad, better/best/worst _____ according to these criteria: _____, _____, _____. With this guide, you come up with the following: *The sheltie is one of the best breeds because shelties are highly intelligent, extremely loyal, responsive, and easy to train.*

Chapters 7 through 13 show you how to use your aim to guide the development of your paper or project.

Working Together

Use aims to create thesis statements

In a group of three or four students

Come up with a list of subjects that your group has some interest in and knows something about. They could be big subjects like global warming or more limited subjects like your school's shuttle bus system.

As a group, brainstorm thesis statements for at least three aims. For example, on the subject of eating disorders, you might come up with something like the following.

Writing to reflect

My younger sister overcame her bulimia disorder during her last two years of high school when successes in school and in music improved her self-esteem.

Writing to inform

Anorexia nervosa is diagnosed when patients weigh 15% under the normal body weight for their height and is characterized by starvation, excessive exercise, and sometimes forced vomiting.

Writing to analyze

The causes of eating disorders are not a failure of will but are medical illnesses that take on a life of their own.

Writing arguments

Less money and effort should be spent to find drugs to treat eating disorders, and more effort should go toward teaching adolescents to deal with negative thoughts about their bodies and to develop a positive body image.

Think about your genre

Be aware of genre

Genre is a term for a kind of writing or form of communication. When you walk into your video store, you find movies classified by genre: action, animation, comedy, documentary, drama, family, horror, sci-fi, and so on. The music industry classifies music by genre: alternative, blues, classical, country, electronic, folk, gospel, jazz, rap, reggae, rock, world, and so on.

Most of the time we recognize genre in writing immediately—junk mail, a letter of application, a novel, a lease for an apartment, an informative brochure. We know a great deal more than just the form. We know, for example, that junk mail is trying to sell something, and we know to be suspicious of any offers of free products. Likewise, we know that the person writing a letter of application wants to get a job or enter a selective program.

Be aware of how genre influences style

The genre you select has a strong influence on the style you use. Compare the first paragraphs of a research report, a news article, and a blog on beach erosion.

Research report

Coastal management as a distinct practice emerged just a few decades ago, when ideas and information were exchanged through mostly conventional means. Scientists and coastal planners gave talks and presented posters at conferences and workshops, as they still do. Field trips and tours organized as part of these events highlighted problems and success stories. Agency experts prepared and distributed reports and guidelines. Academics researched problems and systematically evaluated methods to address them, reporting their results in new periodicals like the *Coastal Zone Management Journal.* Face-to-face meetings, telephone conversations, the U.S. Postal Service, and later the fax machine played key roles in the development of ideas and movement of information to address coastal problems. Working with these communication tools, professionals and concerned citizens alike drew from their personal experience, new state and federal legislative mandates, and a palpable sense of urgency to create a new practice called coastal zone management. At the time, the demand was great for scientific data and information about coastal resources and use, for tools to interpret this information, and for strategies and processes to apply it for problem solving. And the information flowed freely, albeit by slower and less sophisticated means than today.

Innovation by Design: Improving Learning Networks in Coastal Management. Washington, D.C., The Heinz Center, 2004. Print.

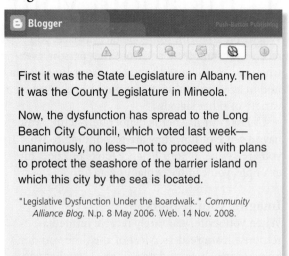

News article

When scientists consider the possible effects of global warming, there is a lot they don't know. But they can say one thing for sure: sea levels will rise.

Dean, Cornelia. "New Victim of Global Warming: The Beaches." *New York Times.* New York Times. 20 June 2006. Web. 6 Oct. 2008.

Blog

Blogger   Push-Button Publishing

First it was the State Legislature in Albany. Then it was the County Legislature in Mineola.

Now, the dysfunction has spread to the Long Beach City Council, which voted last week—unanimously, no less—not to proceed with plans to protect the seashore of the barrier island on which this city by the sea is located.

"Legislative Dysfunction Under the Boardwalk." *Community Alliance Blog.* N.p. 8 May 2006. Web. 14 Nov. 2008.

Even though each writer is writing about the same subject, notice what is different.

Sentence length	• The report has much longer sentences than the newspaper article or the blog.
Paragraph length	• The report has long paragraphs compared to the short paragraphs of the newspaper article and the blog.
Word choice	• The report uses much more formal language than the blog. The newspaper language is neutral.
Relationship with the reader	• The report and newspaper writers are distant and objective. The blog writer is passionately involved with the issue.

Write Now

Compare styles across genres

Find a newspaper article on a current social, economic, political, or scientific issue. Then find a scholarly article on the same subject using scholar.google.com/ or one of the databases on your library's Web site. Next, search blogs for the same subject using blogsearch.google.com.

Compare the styles of the scholarly article, the newspaper article, and the blog using the following criteria: overall length, paragraph length, sentence length, word choice, relationship with the reader, and use of graphics and images. Write a summary of your analysis.

Think about your audience

When you talk with someone face-to-face, you receive constant feedback from that person, even when you're doing all the talking. Your listener may nod in agreement, frown, act bored, and give you a variety of other signals.

Unless your listener is deliberately acting, you have a sense of how they are responding to what you are saying. If your listener looks puzzled, for example, you can try explaining again.

Imagine your readers

When you write, you rarely receive immediate response from readers. Most of the time you don't know exactly how readers will react to what you write. You have to think consciously about your readers and anticipate how they might respond.

Write for college readers

Readers of college writing expect more than what they can find out from a Google search or an online encyclopedia. Facts are easy to obtain from databases and print sources. Readers want to know how these facts are connected.

Good college writing involves an element of surprise. If readers can predict exactly where a writer is going, even if they fully agree, they will either skim to the end or stop reading. Readers expect you to tell them something that they don't know already.

Working Together

Analyze advertisements

Magazines sell advertising by targeting specific readers. Bring to class a magazine that you read regularly or one that you find interesting. Organize in groups of three or four students and exchange magazines with each other. Look at the articles and the advertising in the magazine.

Analyze your classmate's magazine for these criteria.

1. What is the target age group?
2. What percentages of men and women are likely to read the magazine?
3. What income level is targeted?
4. Is a particular ethnicity being targeted?
5. What else is being assumed about the audience? For magazines that cover a specific subject or activity (for example, backpacking, beauty, snowboarding, parenting, fitness, cats, and so on), what other products and services do you find being advertised?

Share your analysis with other members of your group. Ask the person who brought the magazine you analyzed if he or she agrees with your description of the target audience.

Staying on Track

Know what college readers expect

Readers expect to be challenged.
Simple answers that can be easily looked up are not adequate.

OFF TRACK
The United States entered World War II when the Japanese attacked Pearl Harbor on December 7, 1941. *(This fact is well known and not informative for college readers.)*

ON TRACK
The war with Japan actually began on July 25, 1941, when President Franklin Roosevelt froze Japanese assets and declared an oil embargo, leaving the Japanese with the choices of abandoning the war with China or neutralizing the United States Navy in order to secure oil resources in Indonesia.

Readers expect claims to be backed up with reasons and evidence.
Simple explanations without support are not adequate.

OFF TRACK
New York City is an exciting place to live, but I wouldn't want to move there because of the crime. *(Is crime really that much higher in New York City?)*

ON TRACK
Many people don't know that New York City is the safest large city in the United States according to FBI crime statistics. It even ranks in the top 20 safest cities among the 210 cities with populations over 100,000.

Readers expect complex answers for complex problems.
Simple solutions for complex problems are not adequate.

OFF TRACK
We need posters urging students not to litter so much on campus. *(Are posters alone likely to solve the problem?)*

ON TRACK
Most of the litter on our campus is paper, bottles, and cans—all recyclable—yet there are almost no recycle containers on campus. Putting recycle containers in high-litter locations along with a "don't litter" campaign could go a long way toward making our campus cleaner.

Readers expect writers to be engaged.
Readers expect writers to be curious and genuinely concerned about their subjects.

OFF TRACK
Older people have to deal with too much bureaucracy to obtain health care. *(The statement rings true but doesn't motivate readers.)*

ON TRACK
After spending a day with my 78-year-old aunt sorting through stacks of booklets and forms and waiting on a help line that never answered, I became convinced that the Medicare prescription drug program is an aging American's worst nightmare.

Think about your credibility

Some writers begin with credibility because of who they are. If you wonder what foods compose a balanced meal for your dog, you probably would listen carefully to the advice of a veterinarian. Most writers, however, have to convince their readers to keep reading by demonstrating knowledge of their subject and concern with their readers' needs.

Think about how you want your readers to see you

To get your readers to take you seriously, you must convince them that they can trust you. You need to get them to see you as

Concerned

Readers want you to be committed to what you are writing about. They also expect you to be concerned with them as readers. After all, if you don't care about them, why should they read what you write?

Well informed

Many people ramble on about any subject without knowing anything about it. If they are family members, you have to suffer their opinions, but it is not enjoyable. College writing requires that you do your homework on a subject.

Fair

Many writers look at only one side of an issue. Readers respect objectivity and an unbiased approach.

Ethical

Many writers use only the facts that support their positions and often distort facts and sources. Critical readers often notice what is being left out. Don't try to conceal what doesn't support your position.

Staying on Track

Build your credibility

Know what's at stake
What you are writing about should matter to your readers. If its importance is not evident, it's your job to explain why your readers should consider it important.

OFF TRACK
We should be concerned about two-thirds of Central and South America's 110 brightly colored harlequin frog species becoming extinct in the last twenty years. *(The loss of any species is unfortunate, but the writer gives us no other reason for concern.)*

ON TRACK
The rapid decline of amphibians worldwide due to global warming may be the advance warning of the loss of cold-weather species such as polar bears, penguins, and reindeer.

Staying on Track

Have your readers in mind

If you are writing about a specialized subject that your readers don't know much about, take the time to explain key concepts.

OFF TRACK

Reduction in the value of a debt security, especially a bond, results from a rise in interest rates. Conversely, a decline in interest rates results in an increase in the value of a debt security, especially bonds. *(The basic idea is here, but it is not expressed clearly, especially if the reader is not familiar with investing.)*

ON TRACK

Bond prices move inversely to interest rates. When interest rates go up, bond prices go down, and when interest rates go down, bond prices go up.

Think about alternative solutions and points of view

Readers appreciate a writer's ability to see a subject from multiple perspectives.

OFF TRACK

We will reduce greenhouse gas and global warming only if we greatly increase wind-generated electricity. *(Wind power is an alternative energy source, but it is expensive and many people don't want windmills in scenic areas. The writer also doesn't mention using energy more efficiently.)*

ON TRACK

If the world is serious about limiting carbon emissions to reduce global warming, then along with increasing efficient energy use, all non-carbon-emitting energy sources must be considered, including nuclear power. Nuclear power now produces about 20% of U.S. electricity with no emissions—the equivalent of taking 58 million passenger cars off the road.

Write well

Nothing impresses readers more than graceful, fluent writing that is clear, direct, and forceful. Even if readers don't agree with you in the end, they still will appreciate your writing ability.

OFF TRACK

Nobody can live today without taking some risks, even very rich people. After all, we don't know what we're breathing in the air. A lot of food has chemicals and hormones in it. There's a big hole in the ozone, so more people will get skin cancer. And a lot of people have sexually transmitted diseases these days. *(The impact of the point is lost with unfocused writing.)*

ON TRACK

We live in a world of risks beyond our control to the extent that it is difficult to think of anything that is risk free down to the most basic human acts—sex in an era of AIDS, eating in an era of genetically altered food, walking outside in an ozone-depleted atmosphere, drinking water and breathing air laden with chemicals whose effects we do not understand.

Think about how to build on the work of others

All writing builds on the work of others. After all, we write in a language countless people have used before us, giving over time each word its individual meaning. Because ideas are expressed in language, each idea is in some sense recycled. Nevertheless, every time we write, we have the potential to build on existing ideas to create new meanings.

Read to find a question

If you have general interest in a topic, often reading about that topic can help you to find a question to investigate. For example, you may have traveled to Utah, Colorado, New Mexico, or Arizona and visited one of the ruins such as Mesa Verde built by ancient Pueblo peoples and abandoned in the thirteenth century.

Archaeologists know from tree-ring evidence that the area experienced extreme drought, but the reasons for the Pueblo peoples' departure remain controversial. Reading might lead you to a specific question.

> The discovery of twenty-four dismembered human skeletons from an ancient Pueblo site in Colorado dating around 1270–1300 AD suggests that warfare along with drought might have been a cause of abandonment of communities (LeBlanc 174).

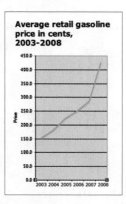

Read to find diverse points of view

Readers of college writing on controversial issues expect writers to find and represent fairly different viewpoints on those issues. People often disagree on issues that at first glance might not seem controversial. For example, the conversion of wind energy into electricity is clean, renewable, and reduces carbon emissions by displacing fossil-fuel-generated electricity. Yet wind energy is controversial for a number of reasons. Some environmental groups oppose wind turbines because of danger to birds. If you advocate building more wind turbines, you need to take into account how significant is the potential threat birds.

Although wind turbines do kill some birds, a article published in prestigious journal *Nature* in 2007 reports that the average yearly bird mortality rate per turbine is .03 or one bird killed for every 33 turbines (Marris and Fairless 126).

Read to find evidence

Readers of college writing expect any claims made by a writer to be supported with evidence. Furthermore, readers expect to be able to check the sources of facts, statistics, and other information; thus, readers expect that all sources will be carefully and accurately cited. For example, you might want to argue that the rapid rise of the price of gasoline during 2007–2008 was a major cause of a tumbling economy, but you will need statistics to argue just how big a bite out of consumer spending could be attributed to increased fuel costs.

Average retail gasoline price in cents, 2003-2008

During 2007 the rise in gasoline prices caused a 55% decline in consumer savings and less spending on cars and furniture (Weller).

Integrate sources into your writing

What you don't want to do with sources

- Let your sources speak for you.
- Fail to introduce a source.
- Fail to indicate the significance of a source for your writing.
- Fail to cite where a source came from.

What you want to do with sources

- Limit the use of long quotations.
- Check that each paraphrase and quotation of a source supports a point you make rather than make the point for you.
- Check that each paraphrase and quotation is introduced and attributed.
- Check that each quotation is accurate and properly formatted.
- Check that you cite the source of each fact that isn't well known and each quotation.

You can find more about integrating the work of others into your writing in Chapter 16.

7 Reflections

A successful reflection challenges readers to find out something about themselves.

CHAPTER CONTENTS

Writing reflections

When we reflect, we consider an idea or experience in order to come to a greater understanding of its significance. Unless we are writing in a private diary or journal, we use reflective writing to share our experience and its significance with others. Reflecting is also a way of understanding ourselves. By connecting memories of the past to our knowledge in the present, we learn about who we were and who we have become.

Reflective essays can address deeply emotional issues like family relationships, personal failings, and dramatic crises. But reflection does not always involve personal topics. In some cases, being too personal or confessional can limit a writer's ability to connect to his or her audience.

The goal of reflection should not be simply to vent pent-up emotions or to expose secrets (although when done well, these techniques can be effective). Instead, it should allow the audience to share with the writer a discovery of significance. A reflection on an important event in the history of a family should do more than focus on the writer's feelings; it should explore how each family member changed as a result.

Components of reflections

What people, places, and events stand out in my memory?	**Find a reflective topic.** Listing is one way to identify possible topics for reflective writing. You might list people, events, or places that have been significant in your life, then look back over your list and check the items that seem especially vivid to you.
Will my readers be interested?	**Consider your readers.** How interesting will this topic be to your readers? Will they want to share in your experience?
What is my purpose?	**Identify a purpose.** A clear purpose makes the reflection coherent. Your purpose is not to teach a lesson about life but rather to convey the significance of the experience—why it is important or memorable and why it is worth writing and reading about.
What key details communicate the significance of my reflection?	**Provide concrete details.** Concrete details stimulate readers' imagination and make your reflection come alive. Use factual details such as dates to provide background information. Augment visual details with your other senses: smells, sounds, tastes, and feelings. **Use dialogue when possible.** Convey interaction between people with their words.
How do I organize my reflection?	**Think about your organization.** Telling what happened in a chronological order is the simplest organization for writers to use, but it is not the only one possible. Conceptual order explores different points and links them together. For example, you might reflect on a photograph, examining details one by one and discussing how they related to your family's past.

What is the most engaging way to begin?

Start fast. The beginning of a reflection must show the writer's involvement and gain the reader's interest.

Finish strong. Effective conclusions invite readers to reflect further. Ending with a question or an issue to think about is usually better than trying to sum up with a moral lesson.

Keys to reflections

Snapshots freeze important moments in people's lives.

Tell a good story. Readers have to be interested in your story to understand the significance. Often reflections gain and keep readers' interest by presenting a conflict or a difficult decision that must be resolved.

Let the details convey the significance. Select details carefully to communicate meaning. Identify people by more than how they look. Think about mannerisms, gestures, and habits to suggest their character.

Be honest. Telling the truth about your thoughts and actions can build a strong rapport with your audience, but beware of becoming sentimental. Too much emotion may turn readers off.

Focus on the little things in life. A reflection need not reveal earth-shattering secrets or teach crucial life lessons. It may be as simple as describing something that makes you happy. Remember that small moments of significance can be just as rewarding for readers as great events.

For a reflection on an image or object, let the reflection grow out of the details. Your close reading of details and your explanation of the significance of the experience is critical.

Working Together

Reflecting on photographs

In a group of three or four students

- Look at a selection of photographs from newspapers, magazines, or a photo Web log such as Flickr.
- Have each person work with two or three photos, making a list of the people each image reminds you of, the things the image makes you think about, and the places you associate with the image. Write a brief narrative for each image.
- Share your memories and narratives with the group. Which ones strike you as the most engaging and interesting? How would you develop or change the narratives of other students?

An effective reflection

Effective reflective writing can only come after honest examination of memories, perceptions, and meanings.

Some Lines for a Younger Brother . . .
Sue Kunitomi Embrey

Sue Kunitomi Embrey was born in Los Angeles and lived there until she and her family were forced to move to the Manzanar War Relocation Camp on May 9, 1942, where she stayed until the end of World War II. She has become a spokeswoman for the thousands of Japanese Americans who were incarcerated during the anti-Japanese hysteria of that time. In this essay, she recalls the life and death of her youngest brother Tets, who spent three years of his childhood in Manzanar.

Some Lines for a Younger Brother . . .

I still remember the day he was born. It was early April and Papa came into the kitchen with a smile on his face. He said we had a baby brother. In the months to follow, we were busy carrying and cuddling the brother who was many years younger than the rest of us. When he cried from hunger and Mama was busy, one of us would run into the bedroom and rock the bed or pick him up and quiet him.

We were a family of five sons and three daughters. Money was scarce. My father ran a moving and transfer business in L'il Tokyo, the Japanese community in the shadow of City Hall in Los Angeles, but people had little money to pay him. He came home with boxes of books bartered for his services, and we spent many hours curled up in a corner reading some popular fiction story.

Tets, as we called him, was eight years old when Papa was killed in an automobile accident a week before Christmas. Tets cried because he could not give his dad the present he had made at school. The bullies would beat him up now that he had no father, he said.

Pearl Harbor was attacked by the Japanese when Tets was in elementary school. Rumors of sabotage couldn't be separated from the facts. Soon there was a

Embrey begins with her earliest memory of her brother, making it clear that he will be the focus of her reflection.

Outside events are fitted into the family's personal chronology. Embrey shows vividly the impact of the decision to intern Japanese Americans.

clamor on the West Coast for wholesale evacuation of all Japanese into inland camps. The democratic process was lost in hysteria. The grocery store which we had purchased only a year before was sold at a loss. All the furniture we couldn't sell, the plants my mother had tenderly cared for, our small personal treasures went to a neighborhood junk dealer. Tears came when we saw the truck being loaded.

On the first Sunday in May, 1942, Manzanar Relocation Center became our war-time home. Before breakfast, we walked around the dry, dusty land, to get acquainted with the landscape. The sun sparkled against the Sierra Nevada mountains to the west. The brown Inyo hills were high-rising barriers, more formidable than the barbed wire which was soon to enclose us. As we wondered how the pioneers had crossed over the Sierras, someone asked, "How long do we have to stay here?" and someone quoted from the military instructions, "For the duration of the war, and six months thereafter." Six months are forever, and forever is a long, long time.

Some order became evident within a few months after the fear, confusion and shock of transplantation from the big city to the arid land of Manzanar. Catholic nuns, who had joined the evacuees, found empty barracks and started a school. The War Relocation Authority recruited teachers from the "outside." Many of them were Quakers with a real desire to serve their fellow man.

When I asked Tets what he was studying, he shrugged his shoulders. There were no chairs, no desks, no supplies, he said. "What's the use of studying American history when we're behind barbed wires?" he asked. I tried to tell him that it would matter some day, but I was not sure any more. "Someday," I said, "the government would realize it had made a mistake and would try to correct it." His eyes were narrow against the noon sun, his whole body positioned badly to the right as he looked at me and said, "You 'da kind'? I lose fight." The colloquial speech was everywhere among the second generation. "Da kind" categorically placed me among those who argued for and defended American democracy. The second expression was used

Details about the relocation camp reinforce the sense of isolation and hopelessness it evokes.

Embrey uses dialogue to recount a significant conversation she had with her brother, one that she has remembered for many years.

constantly, but it meant different things to different people.

"Try walking out that gate," he added. "See if they don't shoot you in the back." With that, he walked away.

The rest of us managed to get out of confinement—to Chicago, to Madison, Wisconsin. Three brothers entered the United States Army. Tets was left with his aging mother and he was to spend almost three years behind barbed wires.

By 1948 when the family was partially reunited and settled in Los Angeles, Tets was in high school, or we thought he was. One day a school counselor came to the door. He reported that Tets had not been in school for several weeks and that he had been missing school sporadically for several months. He saw the shock on our faces. We had been too busy working to be suspicious.

"I'm looking for a job," Tets said, when confronted.

"But you can't find a job without a high school diploma," I protested.

"So I found out," he answered. "Learning to say 'isn't' instead of 'ain't' doesn't get you a job. They want us to have experience to land a job, but how can we get experience if we can't get a job?"

I asked him what he was going to do.

"I'm going to join the Army," was his reply.

Day in and day out, this was his argument. "I'm going to join the Army when I'm eighteen. You won't have me around to bother you and I'll be doing some traveling. I'm tired of holding up the buildings in L'il Tokyo. There's nothing to do and no place to go where I can be with my friends."

He was sure that wars were over for a while and there would be no danger. He signed up one day and was gone the next. He came home on furlough, husky and tanned, a lot taller and more confident than when he had left. He had been in training camp in Louisiana and had seen much of the country. Before he left, he broke the news to us that he had signed up for another three years so he wouldn't have to serve in the reserves. He was transferred to the West Coast and we saw him often when he hitch-hiked home on

Again, Embrey uses dialogue to show viewers a turning point in her brother's life. As in the internment camp, this argument centers on whether he should go to school, but it is clear there are deeper issues at play for Embrey and for Tets.

weekends. One day he phoned collect from San Jose. He was being shipped out to Japan and it would probably be a year before he would be back.

His hitch was almost over when the Korean War broke out. Soon after his 22nd birthday, he wrote that he hoped to be home for Christmas. He explained that he had not been sleeping well lately since some veterans had been brought into his barracks. They had nightmares and they screamed in the night. The stories of war they told could not be shut out of his mind. There was a rumor going around that his company might be going over to replace the first groups. He hoped his timetable for discharge would not change. He was worried and that was why he had not written.

Tets came home before Christmas. He came home in a flag-draped coffin, with one of his buddies as a military escort. The funeral at the Koyasan Buddhist Church was impressive. There was a change of guards every few minutes. Their soft-spoken order mixed with the solemn chants. The curling incense smoke made hazy halos of the young faces who came mourning a dead friend.

Embrey uses vivid detail to re-create her dead brother's funeral.

On December 27, 1969, I joined several hundred young people who made a day-long pilgrimage to the Manzanar cemetery. While I helped clean out the sagebrush and manzanilla, pulled tumbleweeds out of my boots, I was interrupted many times to recall facts and figures for the NBC and CBS television crews who were there to record the event.

Mt. Williamson's peak crested somewhere in the grey clouds that drew menacingly closer as the hours passed. Soon there was no sun. No seven-mile shadow lay across Owens Valley.

Dedication services ended that freezing, windswept and emotional day. I looked beyond the crowd and the monument. Out of the painful memories my mind dusted out of the past, I saw again the blurred impressions of the barbed-wire fence, the sentry towers and the tar-papered barracks. For a moment I saw again the 12-year-old boy with his head cocked, his shoulders sagging, his eyes fighting to keep open in the sun, while the long and lonely desert stretched out behind him.

Embrey ends with an almost wistful recollection of her brother.

Explore Current Issues

Can a memory make an argument?

In her memoir, *The Hypocrisy of Disco: A Memoir*, Clane Hayward describes her childhood living in and out of communes in Northern California in the 1970s with her mother H'lane, her brother Haud, and her little sister Ki. In one chapter, Clane tells about her and her brother's sporadic schooling:

At some point H'lane sent me and Haud to school. She did this in an offhand way, now and then in different places, in the middle of the school year or at the end, she didn't care. Schools are zoos run by the government to keep kids in cages, she said. Schools teach kids how to live in cages. Do you want to learn how to be straight, she would ask, with the I Ching laying open on the floor next to her, while she counted yarrow sticks in her lap. The skirts spread wide around her, incense burning, Ki chewing on one of the sticks and watching with her wide serious eyes. If being straight means wearing clothes that match and eating hot lunch, then yes, I want to be straight, I thought but didn't say.

Write about it

1. What does Hayward's description tell the reader about her mother H'lane? How do the details convey this information?

2. What does this passage tell you about Hayward? What does it tell you about her life at this time and her feelings about it? What does it tell you about her possible feelings about it now, as an adult looking back?

3. Hayward's book is a memoir, an account of her life during a specific period of time. Can a more general argument be made from her unique experiences? If so, what might that argument be?

How to read reflections

Make notes as you read, either in the margins or on paper or a computer file. Circle any words or references that you don't know and look them up.

What is it?	• What kind of a text is it? A memoir? a letter? a diary? an essay? a short story? a photographic essay? What are your expectations for this kind of text? • What media are used? (Web sites, for example, often combine images, words, and sounds.)
Where did it come from?	• Who wrote the reflection? • What do you know about the writer's background that might have influenced the reflection?
Who is the intended audience?	• What clues do you find about whom the writer had in mind as the readers? • What does the writer assume that the readers already know about the subject? • What new knowledge is the writer providing?
What is the significance of the reflection?	• Does the writer give precise, objective, concrete details? • Does the writer comment on the reflections? • What did you learn or come to understand differently by reading the reflection?
How is the reflection organized?	• Chronologically? In order of perceived importance? Or some other way?
How is it composed?	• How does the writer represent herself or himself? • How would you characterize the style? • How effective is the design? Is it easy to read? • If there are any photographs or other graphics, what information do they contribute?

My Dropout Boyfriend Kept Dropping In

(ESSAY)

Lee Conell

Lee Conell was in her junior year at the State University of New York at New Paltz when she wrote "My Dropout Boyfriend Kept Dropping In." She entered the essay in the Modern Love essay contest sponsored by the *New York Times* and was one of the five finalists out of the 1200 essays submitted. Conell's essay was published in the *New York Times* on June 1, 2008.

Return to these questions after you have finished reading.

Analyzing and Connecting

1. How does Conell describe Terry? What details does she use? How does her description of Terry affect the reflection as a whole?

2. In her reflection, Conell describes photographs she and Terry took during a visit to the Cloisters. Why did Conell choose to describe these photos? What do the photos tell about Terry? About the author? About their relationship?

3. The specter of real homelessness enters Conell's reflection a few times—for example, when she mentions how the economy can cause people to veer from their expected paths and when she mentions the campus "sleep out." How does Conell use these moments? How do they affect the reader's perception of Terry's experiment?

4. Conell admits that Terry's failure makes her feel "superior" about her own "safe choices." But she concludes by saying that this feeling "was hardly something to celebrate, and the dreamer in me knew it." What does she mean? Do you think it is an effective way to conclude the reflection? Why or why not?

Finding Ideas for Writing

Do you know someone like Terry? Or, are you the "Terry" of your family or group of friends? Choose a moment, similar to Conell's description of the visit to the Cloisters, and write a short reflection telling how this moment describes this person and your relationship to him or her. Or, if you are the adventurer, focus on how this moment represents the perceptions people have of you and your choices and your reaction to these perceptions.

In April of my freshman year, my boyfriend, Terry, decided he wanted to be homeless. Among the decisions I expected a college-age boyfriend to make (changing cellphone plans, or maybe going vegan), homelessness was not one of them.

Still, I took the situation calmly. I had known Terry since high school and had watched him pass through various phases: Goth, punk, anarchist, Marxist and Zen. When he explained that he was giving up his room to live on the farms and in the woods surrounding our Hudson Valley college town, I did not make a scene. I told myself this, too, would pass and politely asked him why he did not want to live in a house.

"I want to try to exist as free from material stuff as possible," he said.

I squinted at him. "But I like your apartment. It's in a great location."

Terry looked straight into my eyes. "This is just something I have to do for myself."

I didn't say anything. It's hard to argue with that personal power stuff.

Over dinner that evening, I told a girl who lived in my dorm about Terry's plan. "I'm really worried about it," I said.

A matter-of-fact business major from Brooklyn, she blurted, "He's crazy!" She plunged her fork into a pile of rice, and then offered a thinly veiled criticism of me: "I would never put up with that."

"He's not so crazy," I told her. "He's going to be saving a lot of money. And I can understand wanting to feel close to nature."

"No," she said. "He's definitely crazy."

My roommate was equally nonplused. Where would he keep his stuff or brush his teeth? Could a city kid like him really transition into the life of an ascetic?

I had no answers. How would I explain his decision to others? Shouldn't I have seen this coming? Several months earlier, Terry had given me the book *Into the Wild* for Valentine's Day (because nothing says "I love you" like the story of a young man starving to death in the Alaskan wilderness). That should have been a clue.

Luckily, Terry wouldn't have to worry about starvation in his own foray: he had a girlfriend with a college meal plan. I pictured myself sneaking cookies out of the dining hall and heading into the woods. People would think I was harboring an escaped convict.

An *Oprah*-esque voice in my head said: It doesn't matter what people think as long as he feels fulfilled. But another voice in my head, the one that avoided self-help books and talk shows, was less convinced. That voice told me times had changed, and we weren't in high school anymore.

CONELL: MY DROPOUT BOYFRIEND KEPT DROPPING IN

Back then, before we started dating, Terry's acts of rebellion had impressed and attracted me. Just standing next to him, a boy who wore eyeliner and a safety pin through his eyebrow, was an easy and efficient way for me to act out. But I hadn't been Terry's friend only for rebellion's sake. At heart, I understood and agreed with many of his ideas. I just expressed my agreement quietly.

His Zen phase, for example, occurred at the same time as mine, in sophomore year of high school. But while I meditated alone in my bedroom, Terry would meditate publicly: in our high school hallway, on the subway and even, as a photograph I have demonstrates, under a fountain at the Cloisters in New York City (his lined eyelids shut serenely, legs crossed in lotus, bemused museum visitors stopping to stare).

In another photograph from the same day, I also sit under that fountain, but my eyes are wide open and I'm smiling sheepishly, aware of how I stick out, a teenager crouched on the ground, surrounded by medieval art.

We were attending separate colleges when Terry and I started dating in our freshman year, but after several months Terry, unhappy with school, dropped out.

This I defended to friends who gaped at the news by telling them that he was acting against the system, against the overplanned life of studying, choosing our majors, plotting out our meek life goals. What Terry was doing, I told them, was courageous, and I supported his decision even as I spent my nights in the library working wholly within the system to plot out my very own meek life goals.

When he rented a room in my college town and took a job as a taxi dispatcher, I was glad to have him nearby. Still, with the outdoors experiment beginning, I wasn't sure how his roof-free life would mesh with my own. I had thought the enormous buildup to college — APs, SATs, and other nefarious acronyms — was supposed to pave the way to middle-class normalcy, which didn't involve having to deal with decisions like Terry's.

Sure, you might get involved in the occasional good-natured protest, but over all once you attended college, you were on the straight-and-narrow path. Or at least, if the economy didn't sink, you were on the non-homeless path.

If Terry began to spend his free time lost in the woods finding himself, meditating next to a squirrel, in a state of perpetual nirvana, where would that leave me? Laboring away under fluorescent lighting? Of course, that was what I had chosen, just as I had chosen to smile for the camera under the fountain at the Cloisters while Terry sought the meaning of life in the same spot.

It was growing dark. I had an essay to start, a test coming up. Then there would be laundry to do, followed by several halfhearted attempts at matching socks and cleaning my side of the room. I took a deep breath and looked out my window. As I watched the light change, I thought of Terry underneath that sky.

Then I realized that I was jealous.

What sort of lessons would I learn if I fell asleep each night under the stars? What would happen if I left school and followed Terry's footsteps? I knew I wouldn't do it, being overly fond of my books, my room's four walls and the Internet. Still, I couldn't stop one image from transposing itself onto my textbooks: me, lying by a brook at night, listening to its babbling, knowing I was going down my own wide-open path.

But once the experiment was under way, I realized that even when you are fully committed to treading that unbeaten path, it's not so easy to lose yourself in the woods, particularly if you're from Queens and scared of the dark. On one of his first nights outdoors, around midnight, Terry called me at my dorm. In a small voice he asked, "Can I come over?"

He had been trying to sleep in an apple orchard. As darkness enveloped him, the apple trees began to look less like trees and more like zombies with skeleton hands. Terry was frightened by the scuttling sounds in the bushes, and just as frightened when the sounds stopped.

"It's really dark," he said in a hollow, frightened voice. "I'm worried the farmer might find me and shoot me."

So I told him to come by. And I made the same offer again and again over the following weeks, when around midnight my phone would ring, and Terry would ask me for shelter. He would say it was too cold for him to sleep outdoors, or that he thought he heard rabid dogs, or that the night seemed particularly dark.

Although he did manage to spend a bunch of full nights out there somewhere, he only became edgier as the experiment continued. Whenever I saw him early in the day, if he wasn't cranky from sleep deprivation, he would be twitchy with anxiety, watching the sky for the looming dark, for a sign that the time of terror approached. Conversation centered on where his sleeping spot for the night would be, and how cold Weather.Com said it would become.

I couldn't help but entertain the ways I would have done things differently if I were in his shoes, taking advantage of the peace in a way he seemed unable to do: sitting serenely in the wilderness, studying the movements of

the stars, composing poetry about humanity's unbalanced relationship with the natural world and communing with the Disney-eyed wildlife around me. I would certainly not be scared of the dark and a few barking dogs.

Deep down, though, I knew I would be just as scared, or even more scared. And so I felt a little triumphant every time Terry's experiment went south, which happened often enough.

One night, bedded down by a river, he fell asleep with pepper spray in his grasp. Later he brushed his face with the back of his hand and immediately his eyes began to burn. Pepper spray had gotten onto his skin. Eyes smarting and sleep impossible, he walked out of the wooded area and into town, where he spent a few hours sleeping at a coin laundry before being awakened by the police. They threatened to arrest him, but let him go because they were impressed he had a legitimate day job.

That dispatcher job would prove handy during Terry's time outdoors, as it provided him with a bathroom for tooth brushing and face washing, two activities that became difficult in the wilderness. Dorms were useful for showering. The grungier Terry looked, the easier it was for him to pass as a college student, so it wasn't difficult for him to sneak into campus bathrooms.

Still, amid the run-in with the police, sleep deprivation and treks to showers, the ideology behind his experiment began to melt away. This became clear to me after I told him that the hunger and homelessness group on campus was doing a "sleep out." Students would spend one night sleeping outside a campus building to raise awareness about homelessness.

"Oh!" Terry exclaimed happily. "Maybe I'll do it with them. It'd be less scary if I could sleep near other people."

Not long after, he began spending most nights on the foldout couch outside my dorm room. In June he rented a room, at which point the experiment was declared over.

"Terry's living indoors now!" I bragged to friends.

Terry and I are still seeing each other, and he continues to live under a roof.

But my happiness at the experiment's failure had a darker side. In truth I had enjoyed watching his forays into the wilderness fail night after night because each retreat made me feel better, even superior, about my own safe choices: roof, college, stability. And Terry's final surrender only drove home the point.

This was hardly something to celebrate, and the dreamer in me knew it.

Mother Tongue

(ESSAY)

Amy Tan

Amy Tan is a world-renowned writer for her novels that concern the bonds between Chinese American mothers and daughters. She has introduced a rich world of Chinese myth and history to a global audience, but her themes of love and forgiveness are universal. Tan began writing fiction along with playing the piano to curb her workaholic tendencies, but with the publication of *The Joy Luck Club* in 1989, her talent as a writer became widely celebrated. She reflects on her career in this essay.

Return to these questions after you have finished reading.

Analyzing and Connecting

1. How did Tan's attitude toward her mother's language change over the years? Use evidence from the text to support your statements.

2. Tan writes about value judgments based on language. How does Tan account for these judgments?

3. Why was Tan's awareness of different Englishes important to her development as a writer?

4. Near the end, Tan says an insight she had as a beginning writer was to imagine a reader. Why was imagining a reader so important?

Finding Ideas for Writing

Tan says, "recently I was made aware of all of the different Englishes I do use." What different Englishes, or other languages, do you use? List each and explain the different contexts and relationships in which you use them.

MOTHER TONGUE

I am not a scholar of English or literature. I cannot give you much more than personal opinions on the English language and its variations in this country or others. I am a writer. And by that definition, I am someone who has always loved language. I am fascinated by language in daily life. I spend a great deal of my time thinking about the power of language—the way it can evoke an emotion, a visual image, a complex idea, or a simple truth. Language is the tool of my trade. And I use them all—all the Englishes I grew up with.

Recently, I was made keenly aware of the different Englishes I do use. I was giving a talk to a large group of people, the same talk I had already given to half a dozen other groups. The nature of the talk was about my writing, my life, and my book, *The Joy Luck Club*. The talk was going along well enough, until I remembered one major difference that made the whole talk sound wrong. My mother was in the room. And it was perhaps the first time she had heard me give a lengthy speech, using the kind of English I have never used with her. I was saying things like, "The intersection of memory upon imagination" and "There is an aspect of my fiction that relates to thus-and-thus"—a speech filled with carefully wrought grammatical phrases, burdened, it suddenly seemed to me, with nominalized forms, past perfect tenses, conditional phrases, all the forms of standard English that I had learned in school and through books, the forms of English I did not use at home with my mother.

Just last week, I was walking down the street with my mother, and I again found myself conscious of the English I was using, the English I do use with her. We were talking about the price of new and used furniture and I heard myself saying this: "Not waste money that way." My husband was with us as well, and he didn't notice any switch in my English. And then I realized why. It's because over the twenty years we've been together I've often used that same kind of English with him, and sometimes he even uses it with me. It has become our language of intimacy, a different sort of English that relates to family talk, the language I grew up with.

So you'll have some idea of what this family talk I heard sounds like, I'll quote what my mother said during a recent conversation which I videotaped and then transcribed. During this conversation, my mother was talking about a political gangster in Shanghai who had the same last name as her family's, Du, and how the gangster in his early years wanted to be adopted by her family, which was rich by comparison. Later, the gangster became more powerful, far richer than my mother's family, and one day showed up at my mother's wedding to pay his respects. Here's what she said in part:

Du-Yusong having business like fruit stand. Like off the street kind. He is Du like Du Zong—but not Tsung-ming Island people. The local people call putong, the river east side, he belong to that side local people. That man want to ask DuZong father take him in like become own family. Du Zong father wasn't look down on him, but didn't take seriously, until that man big like become a mafia. Now important person, very hard to inviting him. Chinese way, came only to show respect, don't stay for dinner. Respect for making big celebration, he shows up. Mean gives lots of respect. Chinese custom. Chinese social life that way. If too important won't have to stay too long. He come to my wedding. I didn't see, I heard it. I gone to boy's side, they have YMCA dinner. Chinese age I was nineteen.

You should know that my mother's expressive command of English belies how much she actually understands. She reads the *Forbes* report, listens to *Wall Street Week*, converses daily with her stockbroker, reads all of Shirley MacLaine's books with ease—all kinds of things I can't begin to understand. Yet some of my friends tell me they understand 50 percent of what my mother says. Some say they understand 80 to 90 percent. Some say they understand none of it, as if she were speaking pure Chinese. But to me, my mother's English is perfectly clear, perfectly natural. It's my mother tongue. Her language, as I hear it, is vivid, direct, full of observation and imagery. That was the language that helped shape the way I saw things, expressed things, made sense of the world.

Lately, I've been giving more thought to the kind of English my mother speaks. Like others, I have described it to people as "broken" or "fractured" English. But I wince when I say that. It has always bothered me that I can think of no way to describe it other than "broken," as if it were damaged and needed to be fixed, as if it lacked a certain wholeness and soundness. I've heard other terms used, "limited English," for example. But they seem just as bad, as if everything is limited, including people's perceptions of the limited English speaker.

I know this for a fact, because when I was growing up, my mother's "limited" English limited my perception of her. I was ashamed of her English. I believed that her English reflected the quality of what she had to say. That is, because she expressed them imperfectly her thoughts were imperfect. And I had plenty of empirical evidence to support me: the fact that people in department stores, at banks, and at restaurants did not take her seriously, did not give her good service, pretended not to understand her, or even acted as if they did not hear her.

My mother had long realized the limitations of her English as well. When I was fifteen, she used to have me call people on the phone to pretend I was she. In this guise, I was forced to ask for information or even to complain and yell at people who had been rude to her. One time it was a call to her stockbroker in New York. She had cashed out her small portfolio and it just so happened we were going to go to New York the next week, our very first trip outside California. I had to get on the phone and say in an adolescent voice that was not very convincing, "This is Mrs. Tan."

And my mother was standing in the back whispering loudly, "Why he don't send me check, already two weeks late. So mad he lie to me, losing me money."

And then I said in perfect English, "Yes, I'm getting rather concerned. You had agreed to send the check two weeks ago, but it hasn't arrived."

Then she began to talk more loudly. "What he want, I come to New York tell him front of his boss, you cheating me?" And I was trying to calm her down, make her be quiet, while telling the stockbroker, "I can't tolerate any more excuses. If I don't receive the check immediately, I am going to have to speak to your manager when I'm in New York next week." And sure enough, the following week there we were in front of this astonished stockbroker, and I was sitting there red-faced and quiet, and my mother, the real Mrs. Tan, was shouting at his boss in her impeccable broken English.

We used a similar routine just five days ago, for a situation that was far less humorous. My mother had gone to the hospital for an appointment, to find out about a benign brain tumor a CAT scan had revealed a month ago. She said she had spoken very good English, her best English, no mistakes. Still, she said, the hospital did not apologize when they said they had lost the CAT scan and she had come for nothing. She said they did not seem to have any sympathy when she told them she was anxious to know the exact diagnosis, since her husband and son had both died of brain tumors. She said they would not give her any more information until the next time and she would have to make another appointment for that. So she said she would not leave until the doctor called her daughter. She wouldn't budge. And when the doctor finally called her daughter, me, who spoke in perfect English—lo and behold—we had assurances the CAT scan would be found, promises that a conference call on Monday would be held, and apologies for any suffering my mother had gone through for a most regrettable mistake.

I think my mother's English almost had an effect on limiting my possibilities in life as well. Sociologists and linguists probably will tell you that a person's developing language skills are more influenced by peers. But I do think that the language spoken in the family, especially in immigrant families which are more insular, plays a large role in shaping the language of the child. And I believe that it affected my results on achievement tests, IQ tests, and the SAT. While my English skills were never judged as poor, compared to math, English could not be considered my strong suit. In grade school I did moderately well, getting perhaps B's, sometimes B-pluses, in English and scoring perhaps in the sixtieth or seventieth percentile on achievement tests. But those scores were not good enough to override the opinion that my true abilities lay in math and science, because in those areas I achieved A's and scored in the ninetieth percentile or higher.

This was understandable. Math is precise; there is only one correct answer. Whereas, for me at least, the answers on English tests were always a

judgment call, a matter of opinion and personal experience. Those tests were constructed around items like fill-in-the-blank sentence completion, such as, "Even though Tom was _____ , Mary thought he was _____." And the correct answer always seemed to be the most bland combinations of thoughts, for example, "Even though Tom was shy, Mary thought he was charming," with the grammatical structure "even though" limiting the correct answer to some sort of semantic opposites, so you wouldn't get answers like, "Even though Tom was foolish, Mary thought he was ridiculous." Well, according to my mother, there were very few limitations as to what Tom could have been and what Mary might have thought of him. So I never did well on tests like that.

The same was true with word analogies, pairs of words in which you were supposed to find some sort of logical, semantic relationship—for example, "*Sunset* is to *nightfall* as _____ is to _____." And here you would be presented with a list of four possible pairs, one of which showed the same kind of relationship: *red* is to *stoplight*, *bus* is to *arrival*, *chills* is to *fever*, *yawn* is to *boring*. Well, I could never think that way. I knew what the tests were asking, but I could not block out of my mind the images already created by the first pair, "*sunset* is to *nightfall*"—and I would see a burst of colors against a darkening sky, the moon rising, the lowering of a curtain of stars. And all the other pairs of words—red, bus, stoplight, boring—just threw up a mass of confusing images, making it impossible for me to sort out something as logical as saying: "A sunset precedes nightfall" is the same as "a chill precedes a fever." The only way I would have gotten that answer right would have been to imagine an associative situation, for example, my being disobedient and staying out past sunset, catching a chill at night, which turns into feverish pneumonia as punishment, which indeed did happen to me.

I have been thinking about all this lately, about my mother's English, about achievement tests. Because lately I've been asked, as a writer, why there are not more Asian Americans represented in American literature. Why are there few Asian Americans enrolled in creative writing programs? Why do so many Chinese students go into engineering? Well, these are broad sociological questions I can't begin to answer. But I have noticed in

surveys—in fact, just last week—that Asian students, as a whole, always do significantly better on math achievement tests than in English. And this makes me think that there are other Asian-American students whose English spoken in the home might also be described as "broken" or "limited." And perhaps they also have teachers who are steering them away from writing and into math and science, which is what happened to me.

Fortunately, I happen to be rebellious in nature and enjoy the challenge of disproving assumptions made about me. I became an English major my first year in college, after being enrolled as pre-med. I started writing nonfiction as a freelancer the week after I was told by my former boss that writing was my worst skill and I should hone my talents toward account management.

But it wasn't until 1985 that I finally began to write fiction. And at first I wrote using what I thought to be wittily crafted sentences, sentences that would finally prove I had mastery over the English language. Here's an example from the first draft of a story that later made its way into *The Joy Luck Club*, but without this line: "That was my mental quandary in its nascent state." A terrible line, which I can barely pronounce.

Fortunately, for reasons I won't get into today, I later decided I should envision a reader for the stories I would write. And the reader I decided upon was my mother, because these were stories about mothers. So with this reader in mind—and in fact she did read my early drafts—I began to write stories using all the Englishes I grew up with: the English I spoke to my mother, which for lack of a better term might be described as "simple"; the English she used with me, which for lack of a better term might be described as "broken"; my translation of her Chinese, which could certainly be described as "watered down"; and what I imagined to be her translation of her Chinese if she could speak in perfect English, her internal language, and for that I sought to preserve the essence, but neither an English nor a Chinese structure. I wanted to capture what language ability tests can never reveal: her intent, her passion, her imagery, the rhythms of her speech and the nature of her thoughts.

Apart from what any critic had to say about my writing, I knew I had succeeded where it counted when my mother finished reading my book and gave me her verdict: "So easy to read."

How to write a reflection

These steps for the process of writing a reflection may not progress as neatly as this chart might suggest. Writing is not an assembly-line process. Writing about a remembered event, place, or person is, in itself, a powerful way to reflect. Be open to uncovering insights and understanding more broadly the significance.

1 CHOOSE A SUBJECT

- Analyze the assignment.
- Explore possible topics. Make lists of memories connected with your family, work, school, friends, and travels.
- Examine your lists for what might interest readers.
- Consider why this person, place, event, or object is significant to you.

2 DEVELOP A RESPONSE

- Generate details. Remember sounds, smells, tastes, and tactile feeling in addition to visual details.
- Make people come alive. Recreate conversations that reveal character. Record gestures and other details that make people unique.
- Think about the context. What was happening at the time for you and the larger community?
- Relate your experience to the experiences of others.

3
WRITE A DRAFT

- Select vivid details and dialogue. Describe people's mannerisms, gestures, and voices.

- Decide on an organization.

- Craft a strong beginning. Engage the reader with an incident or place that establishes a focus.

- Conclude by inviting further reflection, possibly by what you discovered or how you changed.

- Consider your voice and tone. Decide if you want to sound more conversational or more formal. Your tone reflects your attitude toward the subject.

- Choose a title that will interest readers.

4
REVISE, REVISE, REVISE

- Check that your paper or project fulfills the assignment.

- Make sure that the subject is focused.

- Add details, description, or dialog.

- Make sure your voice and tone will engage readers.

- Examine your organization and think of possible better ways to organize.

- Review the visual presentation.

- Proofread carefully.

5
SUBMITTED VERSION

- Make sure your finished writing meets all formatting requirements.

1: Find a reflective topic and a focus

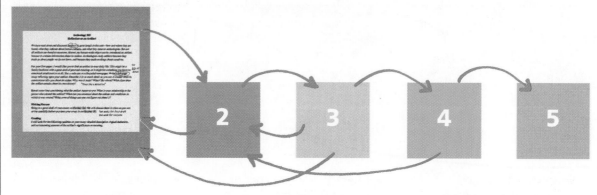

Analyze the assignment	• Read your assignment slowly and carefully. Look for key words like *reflect, reminisce,* or *contemplate.* These key words tell you that you are writing a reflective essay.
	• Identify any information about the length specified, date due, formatting, and other requirements. You can attend to this information later. At this point you want to give your attention to your topic and the focus of your reflection.
Explore possible topics	• Think about your family. What memories stand out about your parents? your brothers and sisters? your own child or children? your grandparents and other close relatives? your pets? your shared family experiences including vacations and holidays? Make a list of events and situations associated with your family.
	• Think about work experience. What was your first job? Did you ever have a great boss or a horrible boss? Do any other workers stand out? What important learning experiences did you have on the job? Make a list of events and situations associated with work.
	• Think about your school experience. What school memories stand out? Did a teacher have a strong influence on you? Did a coach make a difference in your life? What were the social groups in your school? Make a list of events and situations associated with school.
	• Think about friends and social relationships. What memories stand out about your friends? about people you've met? about people you've dated? Make a list of events and situations associated with friends and social relationships.
	• Review all of your lists and put a check beside any items that look like interesting possibilities for writing.

Remember places and objects	• Is a particular place important? Why is it critical? For example, how did you gain an understanding of your mother's attitudes when you visited the place where she grew up? • Is a particular object important? For example, can you describe the locket that belonged to your great-grandmother and was passed down to you?
Consider the significance	• Ask yourself: Why is this person, event, place, or object significant to me? • Think about why the person, place, event, or object seems more important now than in your initial experience. How did your view change? • How did you change as a result of being around this person, event, place, or object?
Analyze your potential readers	• What do your readers likely know about the subject? • What might you need to tell readers about your background? • How can you engage readers? • What will they gain from reading your reflection?

Write Now

Explore memories

- Select one of the items that you have checked on your lists.
- Write nonstop for five minutes to explore the event, situation, place, or object. What was your initial reaction? Who else was there? Did you share your reaction at the time?
- Write nonstop for five minutes to explore your current perspective. How did an experience change you? Why do you remember this person, event, place, or object so well? Looking back, what do you see now that you didn't recognize at the time?
- Stop and read what you have written. Do you see possibilities for writing at length about this person, event, or situation? If you do, then begin generating more content. If the idea seems limited, try writing nonstop about another person, event, place, or object.

Writer at work

Janine Carter received the following assignment in her Introduction to Archeology class.
She made notes on her assignment sheet as the class discussed the assignment.

Archeology 201
Reflection on an Artifact

We have read about and discussed (artifacts) at great length in this unit—how and where they are
found, what they indicate about human cultures, and what they mean to archeologists. But not
all artifacts are found in museums. Almost any human-made object can be considered an artifact,
because it contains information about its makers. Archeologists study artifacts because they
teach us about people we do not know, and because they teach us things about ourselves.

For your first paper, I would like you to find an artifact in your daily life. This might be a
family heirloom with a great deal of personal meaning, or it might be something you have no
emotional attachment to at all, like a soda can or a discarded newspaper. Write a 4-6 page
essay reflecting upon your artifact. Describe it in as much detail as you can. Consider what its
construction tells you about its maker. Why was it made? When? By whom? What clues does
the artifact contain about its own history?   *"Think like a detective"*

Use lots of detail

Spend some time considering what the artifact means to you. What is your relationship to the
person who created the artifact? What can you construct about the culture and conditions in
which it was created? What sorts of things can you not figure out about it?

Writing Process
Bring in a good draft of your essay on October 3rd. We will discuss them in class so you can
revise carefully before you turn your essay in on October 10.   *Two weeks for first draft*
                                                                  One week for revision

Grading
I will look for the following qualities in your essay: detailed description, logical deduction,
and an interesting account of the artifact's significance or meaning.

Then Janine made a list of possible objects to write about.

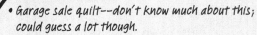

HEIRLOOMS/EMOTIONAL CONNECTION
- Aunt Marie's tulip quilt--shows my connection to
  a long line of quilters
- ~~Sea shells from Girl Scout camp~~ NOT MAN-MADE
- Bracelet from graduation
- Terry's photo
- Stuffed elephant--shows how much I have grown up.
  Where was it made?
✓ • Garage sale quilt--don't know much about this;
  could guess a lot though.
- Diploma

LESS IMPORTANT OBJECTS
- Cereal box--ingredients show lack of
  nutrition. Pictures show how kids are
  bombarded with cartoons and colorful images.
  Expiration date and other clues to where it was
  made.
- Desk in dorm room--Must have been used by
  dozens of people like me (?)
- Old calendar
- Old cookbook
- A floppy disk--Could talk about how fast
  technology is changing. Do I have one?

2: Develop a response

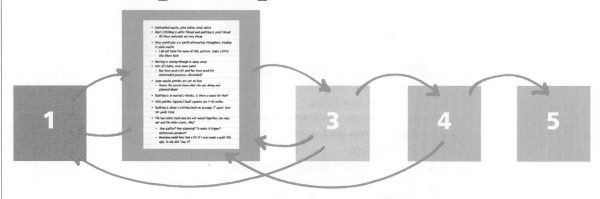

1	**3**	**4**	**5**

Generate details

- Write down all the sights, sounds, smells, tastes, and tactile sensations you associate with your topic.
- If you are using a photograph or other object, write a detailed description of it.
- If you are remembering a past event, write down everything that happened: what people said and did, how you felt as things happened, and anything else you remember or feel is significant.

Make people come alive

- Use dialog to let readers hear people talk, which reveals much about character.
- Record the little mannerisms, gestures, clothing, and personal habits that distinguish people.
- Don't forget to make yourself come alive. If you are reflecting on an incident from your childhood, how old were you? What do you remember about yourself at that age?

Think about the context

- How does your memory compare with similar experiences you have read or heard about from others?
- Does your memory connect to any larger trends or events going on at the time?

Relate your experience to the experiences of others

- The very fact that you find the topic memorable means there is something there you can share with others. Think about how to make it obvious to them.
- How is your subject particular to you? What do you notice, as you reflect, that other people might not notice? This is the "added value" that will make your reflection more than a mere description or memory.

Writer at work

Janine Carter sat down with her garage-sale quilt and a pen and paper. She observed it carefully and made a list of detailed observations about its physical appearance. Then, she added her conclusions and guesses about the quilt, its history, and its maker, based on these clues.

Janine thought about her relationship to the quilt. She jotted down, in no particular order, what she remembered about buying the quilt, conversations she had had with her grandmother about quilting, and ideas that occurred to her.

- Unbleached muslin, pink calico, coral calico
- Most stitching is white thread and quilting is pink thread
    - All these materials are very cheap
- Nine-patch plus a 5-patch alternating throughout; binding is plain muslin
    - I do not know the name of this pattern. Looks a little like Churn Dash.
- Batting is coming through in many areas
- Lots of stains, even some paint
    - Has been used a lot and has been used for unintended purposes—discarded?
- Large muslin patches are cut on bias
    - Means the person knew what she was doing and planned ahead
- Quilting is in nested L-blocks. Is there a name for that?
- 1372 patches (approx.) Small squares are 1-1/2 inches
- Quilting is about 5 stitches/inch on average, 1" apart. Over 100 yards total.
- The two colors clash and are not mixed together; one runs out and the other starts. Why?
    - New quilter? Poor planning? To make it bigger? Unforeseen accident?
    - Grandma would have had a fit if I ever made a quilt this ugly. So why did I buy it?

3: Write a draft

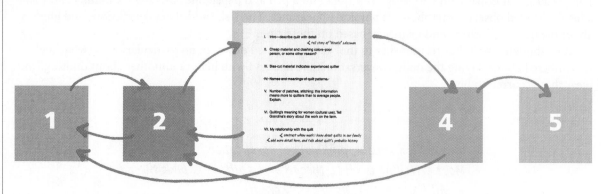

Select vivid details and dialog	• Don't rely solely on visual memory. Include sounds, smells, tastes, and tactile feelings. • Describe people's mannerisms, gestures, and voices. • Use dialog to reveal character.
Decide on an organization	• Use chronological order to help readers relive events with you. • Use conceptual order to show connections and links between ideas.
Craft a strong beginning	• Start with an incident or a place that is the focus.
Conclude by inviting further reflection	• Have you discovered anything new in the process of writing the reflection to share in your conclusion? • A conclusion can sometimes change the entire tone of a reflection. Do you want to surprise your readers? • Above all, your conclusion should help readers make sense of your reflection.
Consider your voice and tone	• Do you want to sound informal and conversational? Or do you want to sound more distanced and objective? • What is your attitude toward your subject? Serious or humorous? Positive or negative?
Choose a title that will interest readers in your essay	• Your title should suggest the direction or the significance of your reflection.

Writer at work

Janine Carter tried several organizational patterns for her essay. Because she knew so little about the quilt's history, she did not feel chronological organization would be a good strategy. However, as she worked through her draft she realized that readers would appreciate a firsthand account of her purchase of the quilt. She decided to include this story near the beginning of her essay, after describing the quilt. She organized the rest of her essay around the questions that occurred to her as she considered the quilt's appearance. As she worked, she referred back to her assignment frequently to make sure she was fulfilling all its terms. She decided to cut one section, about the names of various quilt patterns, because it was too general and distracted from the main focus of her essay. Here is the original outline Janine began working from, along with revisions she made.

I. Intro—describe quilt with detail

< *tell story of "Miracle" salesman*

II. Cheap material and clashing colors–poor person, or some other reason?

III. Bias-cut material indicates experienced quilter

~~IV. Names and meanings of quilt patterns.~~

V. Number of patches, stitching: this information means more to quilters than to average people. Explain.

VI. Quilting's meaning for women (cultural use). Tell Grandma's story about the work on the farm.

VII. My relationship with the quilt

< *contrast w/how much I know about quilts in our family*
< *add more detail here, and talk about quilt's probable history*

4: Revise, revise, revise

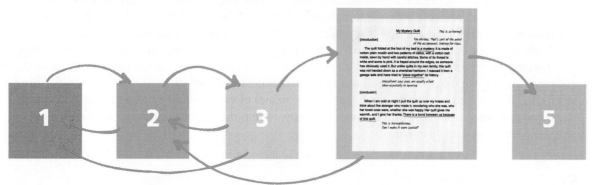

Skilled writers know that the secret to writing well is rewriting. Even the best writers often have to revise several times to get the result they want. You also must have effective strategies for revising if you're going to be successful. The biggest trap you can fall into is starting off with correcting errors. Leave the small stuff for last.

Does your paper or project meet the assignment?	• Look again at the assignment for specific guidelines, including length, format, and amount of research. Does your work meet these guidelines?
Is the subject focused?	• Will readers find your subject early on? • Is the significance evident?
Can you add dialog, description, and other details?	• Can you make events and memories from the past more concrete?
Is your tone engaging?	• Will readers sympathize and identify with you, or will they find your tone too negative, angry, or intensely personal? • Does your tone fit your topic? Some intensely personal topics may not be suited to humorous treatment.
Is your organization effective?	• Are links between concepts and ideas clear? • Are there any places where you find abrupt shifts or gaps? • Are there sections or paragraphs that could be rearranged to make your draft more effective?
Is the writing project visually effective?	• Is the font attractive and readable? • Are the headings and visuals effective? • If you have included an image associated with your reflection, where should it be placed for maximum impact?
Save the editing for last.	• When you have finished revising, edit and proofread carefully.

A peer review guide is on page 27.

Writer at work

Janine Carter was not satisfied with her opening paragraph, or her title. After talking to a consultant at her campus writing center, she worked on ending her opening paragraph with a surprising twist that would engage readers. She also realized that she could draw out the concept of "miracles" from within her essay to tie together the beginning and end. Here are the first drafts of Janine's opening and concluding paragraphs, with her notes.

My Mystery Quilt   *This is so boring!*

[introduction]   *Too obvious. That's sort of the point of the assignment, looking for clues.*

The quilt folded at the foot of my bed is a mystery. It is made of cotton: plain muslin and two patterns of calico, with a cotton batt inside, sewn by hand with careful stitches. Some of its thread is white and some is pink. It is frayed around the edges, so someone has obviously used it. But unlike quilts in my own family, this quilt was not handed down as a cherished heirloom. I rescued it from a garage sale and have tried to "piece together" its history.

consultant says puns are usually a bad idea—especially in opening

[conclusion]

When I am cold at night I pull the quilt up over my knees and think about the stranger who made it, wondering who she was, who her loved ones were, whether she was happy. Her quilt gives me warmth, and I give her thanks. There is a bond between us because of this quilt.

This is boring/obvious. Can I make it more special?

5: Submitted version

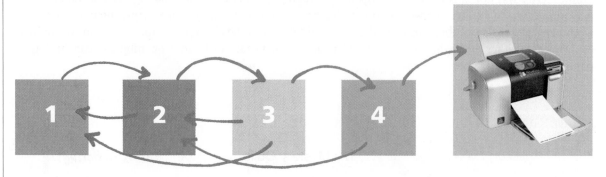

Janine Carter
Dr. Shapiro
Archeology 201
10 October 2008

The Miracle Quilt

The quilt folded at the foot of my bed has a long history. It is made of cotton: plain muslin and two patterns of calico, with a cotton batt inside, sewn by hand with careful stitches. Some of its thread is white and some is pink. It is frayed around the edges and has obviously lived a long, useful life. It is steeped in memories. Unfortunately, I don't know what any of them are.

I found the quilt at a city-wide garage sale. At the end of the auditorium, taking up half of the bleachers, was a vendor's booth called "Miracles by the Pound." The gentleman who ran the booth went around buying up vintage fabrics in bad condition. He would dump huge piles of them on the bleachers for people to pick through. When you had found what you wanted, he would weigh it on a scale and tell you how much it cost. Everything was five dollars per pound. As he weighed your purchase, he would call out the price so everyone at the garage sale could hear what a good deal you were getting. My quilt weighed three pounds. "Fifteen dollar miracle!" the vendor sang out as I opened my purse.

My quilt had already been dug out of the pile and discarded by another woman at the garage sale, who had two or three other vintage quilts in her

Fig. 1. Detail of the miracle quilt.

arms. She told me she bought old, damaged quilts and cut them up to make sofa pillows. My quilt didn't interest her because it wasn't in very good shape, and the blocks were the wrong size for the pillow forms she used. I come from a family of quilters, so when I saw the quilt I felt it needed a good home. I didn't like the idea of someone using it to wrap around furniture in a moving van, or even cutting it up for pillows. I took it home and washed it, and put it on my bed, and took a good look at it.

The quilt was probably made by someone poor, or at least very frugal, I decided. The muslin, which provides the background, is the cheapest unbleached kind. Even the binding around the edges, which in most quilts is a bright, contrasting color, is plain muslin. Whoever pieced the quilt—and it was almost certainly a woman, because quilting has always been women's work—started out using a coral-toned calico. But before she finished, she ran out and had to switch to a rose-colored calico. The effect is jarring, as the colors do not complement each other. The coral marches two-thirds of the way across the quilt, and then stumbles into rose. I do not know why the quiltmaker did not work the two colors evenly throughout the quilt; this is what my own grandmother taught me to do when I didn't have enough of

one color. Perhaps she was inexperienced; perhaps this was her first quilt, or perhaps she hadn't intended to make the quilt as large as it is. The coral would have been sufficient to cover a single bed; maybe, I think to myself, someone proposed to her while she was making it, and she ended up enlarging it to fit a double bed after she got married.

But there are other clues that suggest experience and planning. The octagon-shaped patches of muslin that center the five-patch blocks are cut so that the lines of quilting cross them on the bias—that is, diagonally across the up-and-down and side-to-side warp and woof threads of the fabric. Fabric is more flexible on the bias (this, my grandmother once explained to me, is why clothing cut on the bias fits and looks better, and is more expensive). A needle slips in and out between the threads more easily, so a quilter is wise to arrange pieces so as to maximize bias quilting. The quilting itself (that is the stitching through all the layers of the quilt) is respectable enough, about five stitches per inch. No fancy 12-stitch-per-inch quilting like you would see in a showpiece quilt, but quite firm and straight, in neat pink rows spaced an inch apart. The quilting pattern is in L-shaped blocks, which I have never seen before. There must be over one hundred yards of quilting all together; the length of a football field, taken one stitch at a time.

The quilt's pattern looks like a variation of wagon tracks, but it uses an octagonal block like a "churn-dash" pattern that sets it apart from a more straightforward Irish chain. Nine-patch and five-patch blocks alternate across it. By my count it contains 1,372 separate pieces, all cut, sewn, and quilted by hand. The nine-patch blocks use 1-1/2-inch patches. These may seem like insignificant details to most people, but to quilters they are important. They tell you how much work went into the quilt. The first nine-patch quilt I made with my grandmother contained a grand total of 675 patches, and I thought it would take forever to sew it (even using a sewing machine!). I remember asking my grandmother how she ever made her more complicated quilts: the flower garden with its thousands of tiny hexagons; the Dutchman's puzzle that was so mesmerizing you could hardly stop your eyes from running over it, trying to pick out the "real" pattern. "Doesn't quilting drive you crazy sometimes?" I asked her. She thought that was pretty funny. "Quilting was how we used to keep from going crazy," she told me.

When she first married my grandfather and moved to a farm in the Brazos River bottom over sixty years ago, there was no television and no neighbors for miles. In the spring, rain would turn the roads to thick clay mud and no one could get off their property for days at a time. Quilting was the way women dealt with the isolation. "That is what the pioneer women did too," she told me. Stuck out alone on the prairies and in the mountains, they kept their sanity by cutting and arranging hundreds of pieces of cloth in different patterns, methodically assembling quilts to bring some order into their own bleak lives.

"It looks like hard work to you now," my grandmother explained, "but for us it was like a vacation. So much of women's work was never done, but you could sit down after dinner in the evening and finish a quilt block and feel like you had done something that would last. You might have spent the whole day dirtying and washing the same set of dishes three times, feeding the same chickens and milking the same cows twice, and you knew you'd have to get up in the morning and do the same things all over again, from top to bottom. But quilt blocks added up to something. Nobody was going to take your finished quilt block and sit down at the breakfast table and pick it apart, and expect you to sew it back together again before lunch. It was done, and it stayed done. There wasn't much else you could say that about, on a farm."

In my family, quilts are heirlooms and are handed down with stories about who made them, who owned them, what they were used for, and what events they had been part of. Some were wedding presents, others were made for relatives when they were first born. I don't know the stories that go with my miracle quilt. It has had a hard life; that is easy to see. Most of the binding has frayed off and there are some spots where the quilt has holes worn straight through it—top, batting, and backing. There are stains that suggest coffee or tea or perhaps medicines from a sickbed spilled on it. There are some spots of dried paint. Evidently at some point it was used as a drop-cloth. But at least, I tell myself, it has found a home with someone who appreciates the work that went into it, and can guess at some of its history.

When I am cold at night I pull the quilt up over my knees and think about the stranger who made it, wondering who she was, who her loved ones were, whether she was happy. Her quilt gives me warmth, and I give her thanks. Though we will never meet, or even know each other's identity, there is a bond between us because of this quilt. And so it seems that the man who sold me this quilt was right: it is a sort of miracle.

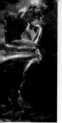

Projects

Reflections focus on people, places, events, and things—past and present—that have significance in the writer's life. Successful reflections engage readers in their subjects and convey the importance of the person, event, or place.

These projects are frequently written kinds of reflections.

Reflection on the past

List people, events, or places that have been significant in your life or in some way changed you. Many reflections focus on a conflict of some kind and how it was resolved. Look back over your list and check the items that seem especially vivid to you.

Take a few minutes to write first about the person, event, or place as you remember it, and then write about how you regard it today. What was your initial reaction? Did your initial reaction change over time? Why do you feel differently now?

Think about the significance of the person, event, or place in your life. What details best convey that significance? If conversations were involved, remember what was said and create dialog.

Organize your essay around the focus. Start fast to engage your readers. If there is a conflict in your reflection, get it up front.

Show the significance through describing, vivid details, and dialog. Make the characters and the places come to life.

Family photograph

Family photographs and cherished objects can be subjects for reflection. Try carefully observing (or picturing in your mind) an object or photograph that has special meaning for you. Write down all the details you can. What memories does each observation evoke? Do you find that different aspects of the photograph make you feel different ways?

Choose as a topic something that is significant to you, and which you can recall with a reasonable amount of detail. But also consider how interesting this topic will be to others. Will an audience want to share in your experience?

Write a reflective essay about that photograph. What does the photograph convey that other similar snapshots do not? What does it hide or not show? What does it say about your family?

Literacy narrative

Think about a childhood memory of reading or writing that remains especially vivid. The memory may be of a particular book you read, of something you wrote, or a teacher who was important in teaching you to read or write. Or think of a more recent experience of reading and writing. What have you written lately that was especially difficult? Or especially rewarding? List as many possibilities as you can think of.

Look over the items on the list and pick one that remains significant to you. Begin writing by describing the experience in as much detail as you can remember. Describe who was involved and recall what was said. Describe the setting of the experience: where exactly were you and what difference did it make? Remember key passages from what you either read or wrote. How did you understand the experience at the time? How do you understand it now? What makes it special?

Review what you have written and consider how to shape your raw material into an engaging essay. You may want to narrate the experience in the order it happened; you may want to start in the middle of the experience and give the background later; or you may want to start in the present as you look back. Above all, start fast. Somewhere along the way, you will need to convey why the experience was significant for you, but avoid the temptation to end with a moral. Don't forget to include a title that makes your readers want to read your literacy narrative.

8 Informative Essays

Successful informative writing begins with what the reader needs to know.

CHAPTER CONTENTS

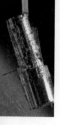

Reporting information

Whether reading the news, following a recipe, hooking up a new computer, deciding which course to take, or engaging in a multitude of other events in our daily lives, we depend on reliable and clear information. Reporting information takes many forms, ranging from newspaper articles and reports of experimental research to tables, charts, and simple lists of information.

In one sense, most kinds of writing, including writing to reflect and writing to persuade, also report information. The main difference is that the focus of a report and other informative kinds of writing is on the subject, not on the writer's reflections or on changing readers' minds or on getting them to take action.

Components of informative writing

Where do I find information?

Find information. Reports require research. Scientists make observations in the field and conduct experiments to create new knowledge. Journalists interview people for the information to include in articles. Accountants assemble financial information in order to write reports on the financial status of companies and organizations. Knowing where to find information and knowing how much you need is critical for writing reports.

What does it mean?

Interpret information. Writers not only report what they read and observe. They construct meaning through selecting what and what not to include and in organizing that information.

How can I explain it?

Explain information. Often what you know well is difficult to explain to others. In order to do so effectively, you will need to break down a process into steps that you can describe. Explaining a process sometimes requires you to think about something familiar in a new way.

What are the implications?

Explore questions and problems. Not all informative writing is about topics with which you are familiar or ones that you can bring to closure. Often college writing involves issues or problems that perplex us and for which we cannot come to a definitive conclusion. The goal in such writing is not the ending but the journey. Difficult issues often leave you conflicted; readers appreciate writers who deal honestly with those conflicts.

Keys to informative writing

Narrow the topic	A central difficulty in writing to inform is knowing where to stop. For any large subject, a lifetime may be insufficient. The key to success is limiting your topic to one you can cover adequately.
Start fast	The title and introduction should entice readers to want to read the rest. Dull generic titles and vague, general introductory paragraphs discourage further reading. Offer a new viewpoint that challenges the usual, commonplace viewpoint.
Keep readers interested	Readers become bored quickly if they have heard it all before. Once you have made your readers curious to know more about your subject, don't disappoint them.
Define key terms	Writers should define clearly any key terms and concepts that might be unfamiliar.
Provide relevant examples, illustrations, and details	The examples, illustrations, and details make or break informative writing, whether it is a news article, a profile, or even a set of instructions or a cookbook. Select them carefully.
Remain objective	Writers whose purpose is to inform usually stay in the background, taking the stance of an impartial, objective observer. An objective tone and the absence of bias help readers to believe the information is accurate and the writer is trustworthy.
Document the sources of information	If you use sources in a college assignment, you will be expected to document those sources. Lakshmi Kotra's essay at the end of this chapter (see pages 140–147) follows an academic format for citing sources.
Conclude with strength	Besides just stopping, a plain summary is the weakest possible conclusion. Leave your readers with something to think about— a memorable example, an anecdote that illustrates a key point, implications of the information you have provided, a quotation that expresses a main point vividly, or a projection into the future.
Explain with charts and graphs	Charts and graphs show facts and relationships that are often difficult to communicate using words alone. A good chart makes the significance of the data clear at a glance.

Explain with images

Pictures don't always tell a thousand words; indeed, we need words to understand what is represented in pictures. Nevertheless, photographs, drawings, maps, and other graphics can provide concrete evidence to support what is being explained in words.

Satellite photography helped the world to understand the damage caused by the tsunami that struck Indonesia on December 28, 2004.

Working Together

Explain a concept or activity

In a group of three or four students

First select a concept or activity that you know a great deal about (through your courses, your work experience, or your personal interests) but your classmates likely do not. Subjects might range from the second law of thermodynamics and postmodern architecture to competitive ballroom dancing and growing your own herbs. In your group give each person five minutes to explain the concept or activity.

Listen carefully to each classmate, and when each finishes, stop for a minute to note

• what you knew already
• what you found engaging
• what you wanted to know more about
• what you didn't understand

After the last person finishes, share your notes with the group. You'll have an immediate audience response to your explanation.

Effective informative writing

Informative writing succeeds when readers can connect new facts and concepts to what they know already.

The Emperor's Giraffe
Samuel M. Wilson

Samuel Wilson, a professor of anthropology, wrote "The Emperor's Giraffe" for the magazine *Natural History* in 1992. It was later collected with other essays and published in a book with the same title. Wilson had the challenge of writing about a subject unfamiliar to most of his readers, and moreover, he wanted to make a larger point. Notice how he leads his readers to his unexpected conclusion.

A HUGE FLEET LEFT PORT in 1414 and sailed westward on a voyage of trade and exploration. The undertaking far surpassed anything Columbus, Isabella, and Ferdinand could have envisioned. The fleet included at least sixty-two massive trading galleons, any of which could have held Columbus's three small ships on its decks. The largest galleons were more than 400 feet long and 150 feet wide (the *Santa Maria*, Columbus's largest vessel, was about 90 by 30 feet), and each could carry about 1,500 tons (Columbus's ships combined could carry about 400 tons). More than one hundred smaller vessels accompanied the galleons. All told, 30,000 people went on the voyage, compared with Columbus's crew of 90-some.

The commander's name was Zheng He (Cheng Ho), the Grand Eunuch of the Three Treasures and the most acclaimed admiral of the Ming dynasty. He was sailing from the South China Sea across the Indian Ocean, heading for the Persian Gulf and Africa. As the historian Philip Snow notes in his wonderful book *The Star Raft*, "Zheng He was the Chinese Columbus. He has become for China, as Columbus has for the West, the personification of maritime endeavour" (21). The flotilla was called the star raft after the luminous presence of the emperor's ambassadors on board.

Zheng He did not really set out to explore unknown lands— neither did Columbus, for that matter—for the Chinese were aware of most of the countries surrounding the Indian Ocean.

The 500th anniversary of Columbus's first trip to America was celebrated in 1992. Wilson uses the occasion to introduce his readers to a major Chinese voyage of discovery in 1414 that was massively larger in ships and personnel.

Wilson begins challenging commonly held views by pointing out that neither Zheng He nor Columbus was exploring unknown territory.

For centuries, China had been a principal producer and consumer of goods moving east and west from Mediterranean, African, and Middle Eastern trading centers. With this trade came cultural and ideological exchange.

Zheng He, like many Chinese of his time, was a Muslim, and his father and his father before him had made the pilgrimage to Mecca. But in Zheng He's day, the trade routes were controlled by Arabian, Persian, and Indian merchants. Private Chinese traders had been barred from traveling to the West for several centuries. China had been conquered by Ghengis Khan and his descendants in the 1200s, and the Mongol emperors of the subsequent Yuan dynasty were the first to impose these constraints. In 1368 the Chinese expelled the Mongol rulers and established the Ming dynasty, which was destined to rule for the next 300 years. (Thus, in 1492 Columbus was searching for a "Grand Khan" who had been put out of business 124 years earlier.)

After the period of Mongol rule, China became strongly isolationist, placing even more severe restrictions on Chinese traders. In 1402 an outward-looking emperor named Yong'le (Yung-lo) came to power. Seeking to reassert a Chinese presence on the Western seas and to enhance the prestige of his rule and dynasty, he began funding spectacular voyages by Zheng He. As sociologist Janet Abu-Lughod notes in *Before European Hegemony*, "The impressive show of force that paraded around the Indian Ocean during the first three decades of the fifteenth century was intended to signal the 'barbarian nations' that China had reassumed her rightful place in the firmament of nations—had once again become the 'Middle Kingdom' of the world" (343).

As Zheng He pressed westward in 1414, he sent part of his fleet north to Bengal, and there the Chinese travelers saw a wondrous creature. None like it had ever been seen in China, although it was not completely unheard of. In 1225 Zhao Rugua, a customs inspector at the city of Quanzhou, had recorded a secondhand description of such a beast in his

A parenthetical aside—that Columbus was looking for the "Grand Khan" who had long ceased to exist—speaks to the lack of knowledge of China among Europeans.

strange and wonderful *Gazetteer of Foreigners*. He said it had a leopard's hide, a cow's hoofs, a ten-foot-tall body, and a nine-foot neck towering above that. He called it a *zula*, possibly a corruption of zurafa, the Arabic word for giraffe.

The account of how a giraffe was described for those who had never seen one adds interest.

The giraffe the travelers saw in Bengal was already more than 5,000 miles from home. It had been brought there as a gift from the ruler of the prosperous African city-state of Malindi, one of the several trading centers lining the east coast of Africa (Malindi is midway along modern Kenya's coast, three degrees south of the equator). Zheng He's diplomats persuaded the Malindi ambassadors to offer the animal as a gift to the Chinese emperor. They also persuaded the Malindi ambassadors to send home for another giraffe. When Zheng He returned to Beijing, he was able to present the emperor with two of the exotic beasts.

A pair of giraffes in Beijing in 1415 was well worth the cost of the expedition. In China they thought the giraffe (despite its having one horn too many) was a unicorn (*ch'i-lin*), whose arrival, according to Confucian tradition, meant that a sage of the utmost wisdom and benevolence was in their presence. It was a great gift, therefore, to bring to the ambitious ruler of a young dynasty. The giraffes were presented to the emperor Yong'le by exotic envoys from the kingdom of Malindi, whom the Chinese treated royally. They and the marvelous gift so excited China's curiosity about Africa that Zheng He sent word to the kingdom of Mogadishu (then one of the most powerful trading states in East Africa and now the capital of modern Somalia) and to other African states, inviting them to send ambassadors to the Ming emperor.

Wilson explains why the giraffes took on great significance beyond their novelty.

The response of the African rulers was overwhelmingly generous, for China and Africa had been distant trading partners from the time of the Han dynasty (206 BC to AD 220). In the *Universal Christian Topography*, written about AD 525 by Kosmos, a Byzantine monk known as the Indian Traveler, Sri Lanka is described as a trading center frequented by both Chinese and Africans. Envoys from a place called

Wilson refutes another common view that sub-Saharan Africa was not engaged in international trade before Europeans arrived.

Zengdan—the name translates as "Land of Blacks"—visited China several times in the eleventh century. And a Chinese map compiled in the early fourteenth century shows Madagascar and the southern tip of Africa in remarkable detail, nearly two centuries before the Portuguese "discovered" the Cape of Good Hope. Archeologists find china (why the English word came to be synonymous with glazed pottery and porcelain, instead of silk or spices, is unclear) from the Han and later dynasties all along the east coast of Africa.

The African emissaries to the Ming throne came with fabulous gifts, including objects for which entrepreneurs had long before managed to create a market in the Far East: tortoise shell, elephant ivory, and rhinoceros-horn medicine. On their many visits they also brought zebras, ostriches, and other exotica. In return, the Ming court sent gold, spices, silk, and other presents. Zheng He was sent with his fleet of great ships on yet another voyage across the Indian Ocean to accompany some of the foreign emissaries home. This escort was the first of several imperially supported trips to Africa. According to official records, they went to Mogadishu, Brava, and perhaps Malindi; Snow (in *The Star Raft*) suggests that these Chinese expeditions may have gone farther—to Zanzibar, Madagascar, and southern Africa.

Meanwhile, as the Chinese were pushing down the east coast of Africa, Portuguese mariners were tentatively exploring the west coast. They had started the process in the early fifteenth century and were steadily working their way south. Bartolomeu Dias reached the Cape of Good Hope in 1488 and was the first of these mariners to see the Indian Ocean. Surely the Europeans and Chinese were poised to meet somewhere in southern Africa, where perhaps they would have set up trading depots for their mutual benefit.

This did not happen, however. Emperor Yong'le died in 1424, and by 1433 the Ming dynasty discontinued its efforts to secure tributary states and trading partners around the Indian Ocean. In Beijing, those favoring an isolationist foreign policy

That Chinese sailors might have met the Portuguese in Africa and established trade is a "what if?" that leads to Wilson's conclusion.

won out, and the massive funding needed to support Zheng He's fleet—difficult to sustain during what was a period of economic decline in China—was canceled. As Edwin Reischauer and John Fairbank note in *East Asia: The Great Tradition:*

> The voyages must be regarded as a spectacular demonstration of the capacity of early Ming China for maritime expansion, made all the more dramatic by the fact that Chinese ideas of government and official policies were fundamentally indifferent, if not actually opposed, to such an expansion. This contrast between capacity and performance, as viewed in retrospect from the vantage point of our modern world of trade and overseas expansion, is truly striking. (478)

Wilson uses the conclusion of other scholars to set up the point he makes in the following paragraph.

The contrast also refutes the argument that as soon as a country possesses the technology of overseas trade and conquest it will use it. Zheng He's fleet was 250 times the size of Columbus's, and the Ming navy was many times larger and more powerful than the combined maritime strength of all of Europe. Yet China perceived her greatest challenges and opportunities to be internal ones, and Yong'le's overseas agenda was forgotten. Restrictions on private trade were reimposed, and commercial and military ventures in the Indian Ocean and South China Sea in subsequent centuries were dominated by the Portuguese, Arabs, Indians, Spaniards, Japanese, Dutch, British, and Americans. Zheng He's magnificent ships finally rotted at their moorings.

Wilson concludes his essay by making a significant point. He refutes the idea that those who have the best technology necessarily will use it to conquer others. Had he started with this point, readers might have been skeptical, but he gives the impression that his conclusion logically follows from the data.

Works Cited

Abu-Lughod, Janet L. *Before European Hegemony: The World System AD 1250-1350*. New York: Oxford UP, 1989. Print.

Reischauer, Edwin O., and John K. Fairbank. *East Asia: The Great Tradition*. Boston: Houghton, 1958. Print.

Snow, Philip. *The Star Raft: China's Encounter with Africa*. London: Weidenfeld, 1988. Print.

Explore Current Issues

Is everybody an expert?

WikiHow was created in 2005 by Jack Herrick, one of the former owners of the professionally-authored online how-to manual eHow.com. Herrick used the wiki model—communal Web authorship with volunteer contributors—that made Wikipedia a household name. With a database of over 45,000 articles and in September 2008, over 13 million readers, wikiHow's mission is to build the world's largest how-to manual.

Write about it

1. Why do you think sites such as Wikipedia and wikiHow are so popular? Do you think wikis have changed the way people think about expertise? Why or why not?

2. Look at a few articles on wikiHow. What are the conventions of this kind of writing? Think about format, language, graphics, and tone. Using what you've observed, write a wikiHow-style article on how to write a wikiHow article.

3. Credibility and relevance are important for all types of informational writing. What other factors determine the success of a piece of informational writing?

? Help   RSS   Create an a

The How-to Manual That You Can Edit

Type in here

¡Hola! ¿Puedes ayudar a construir wikiH

Home > Categories > Arts and Entertainment > Performing Arts > Theater

Write an Article | R

Related wikiHows

- Mime
- Pose
- Pose for Portraits
- Be a Nude Art Model

| Article | Discuss | Edit | History | Bookmark |

How to Be a Living Statue

Human statues have a long history in the European street theater tradition. In Paris, you can see human statues in many a park and garden, busking for money in monochrome hues with physical patience and control that rivals most yogis or athletes. The costume is ninety percent of the battle, the physical control is the icing on the cake. Here's how to pull it off.

⊙ Steps

1. Choose a costume or character. This is the hardest part, but it's easy and fun if you're creative. Anything goes and your character/statue doesn't have to be anything or anyone specific. But go crazy. Make up a "realistic" bronze or white statue (à la something you would see in a park or museum) or come up with something fully fantastic. Monochrome is very helpful (all gold, all white, all blue) and metallic is great. The less skin you have to paint, the easier the makeup job and quicker the clean-up. Some props you can consider using are wings, broken umbrellas, boas, fans, bottles, scales, swords, strips of material, books, flowers, vines, and clocks.

How to read informative writing

Make notes as you read, either in the margins, if it is your copy, or on paper or a computer file. Circle any words or references that you don't know and look them up.

What is it?	• What kind of a text is it? An article? an essay? a profile? a set of instructions? a chart? a brochure? a Web site? an executive summary? What are your expectations for this kind of text? • What media are used? (Web sites, for example, often combine images, words, and sounds.)
Where did it come from?	• Who wrote this material? • Where did it first appear? In a book, newspaper, magazine, online, in a company, or in an organization?
What is the writer's thesis or main idea?	• Where is the thesis or main idea located? • If you cannot find a specific claim, what is the main focus? • What are the key ideas or concepts that the writer considers? • What are the key terms? Are they defined?
Who is the intended audience?	• What clues do you find about whom the writer had in mind as the readers? • What does the writer assume that the readers already know about the subject? • What new knowledge is the writer providing?
How is the piece of writing organized?	• Look for the main idea in each paragraph. It helps to write them down. Then examine how each paragraph connects to the others. • Where are the details and examples located? Do they support the main points?
What kinds of sources are cited?	• Are they from books, newspapers, periodicals, or the Web? • Are they completely documented?
How is it composed?	• How does the writer represent herself or himself? • How would you characterize the style? • How effective is the design? Is it easy to read? • If there are any photographs, charts, or other graphics, what information do they contribute?

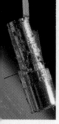

How Do I Love Thee?

(ESSAY)

Lori Gottlieb

Lori Gottlieb is the author of *Stick Figure* (2000) and a coauthor of *I Love You, Nice to Meet You* (2006). She is a regular commentator on NPR's *All Things Considered* and has written for many newspapers and magazines. A longer version of this essay appeared in *The Atlantic Monthly* in March 2006.

Return to these questions after you have finished reading.

Analyzing and Connecting

1. Why does Gottlieb begin with the story of her visit to Dr. Neil Clark Warren's office rather than her central question: can cold, hard science be a facilitator of romance?

2. How does Gottlieb answer her central question?

3. Buckwalter's studies and Warren's observations conclude that happy couples have many similarities. Think about happy and unhappy couples you know. Is their degree of happiness a result of what they have in common?

4. Online dating and relationship Web sites have become some of the fastest-growing businesses on the Internet. Compare eHarmony.com with Perfectmatch.com, Chemistry.com, Match.com, and others. What does each promise on the first page? What does each claim to distinguish it from other similar online dating sites?

Finding Ideas for Writing

Who is Gottlieb's audience? How do you know? Choose a new audience for the piece—of a different age range, gender, social class, and level of education—and write a memo advising the author how to change the piece for this audience. How should she change the level of formality? the language? the tone? the references?

HOW DO I LOVE THEE?

LORI GOTTLIEB

I'd been sitting in Dr. Neil Clark Warren's office for less than fifteen minutes when he told me he had a guy for me. It wasn't surprising that the avuncular seventy-one-year-old founder of eHarmony.com, one of the nation's most popular online dating services, had match-making on his mind. The odd thing was that he was eager to hook me up without having seen my eHarmony personality profile.

I'd come to the eHarmony headquarters in Pasadena, California, in early October to learn more about the site's "scientifically proven" and patented Compatibility Matching System. Apparently, the science wasn't working for me. The day before, after I'd taken the company's exhaustive (and exhausting) 436-question personality survey, the computer informed me that of the approximately 9 million eHarmony members, more than 40 percent of whom are men, I had zero matches. Not just in my city, state, region, or country, but in the entire world. So Warren, who looks like Orville Redenbacher and speaks with the folksy cadence of Garrison Keillor, suggested setting me up with one of his company's advisory board members, whom he described as brilliant, Jewish, and thirty-eight years old. According to Warren, this board member, like me, might have trouble finding a match on eHarmony.

"Let me tell you why you're such a difficult match," Warren said, facing me on one of his bright floral sofas. He started running down the backbone of eHarmony's predictive model of broad-based compatibility, the so-called twenty-nine dimensions (things like curiosity, humor, passion, intellect), and explaining why I and my prospective match were such outliers.

"I could take the nine million people on our site and show you dimension by dimension how we'd lose people for you," he began. "Just on IQ alone—people with an IQ lower than 120, say. Okay, we've eliminated people who are not intellectually adequate. We could do the same for people who aren't creative enough, or don't have your brilliant sense of humor. See, when you get on the tails of these dimensions, it's really hard to match you. You're too bright. You're too thoughtful. The biggest thing you've got to do when you're gifted like you are is to be patient."

After the over-the-top flattery wore off—and I'll admit, it took an embarrassingly long time—I told Warren that most people I know don't join online dating sites to be patient. Impatience with real-world dating, in fact, is precisely what drives many singles to the fast-paced digital meat market. From the moment Match.com, the first such site, appeared in 1995, single people suddenly had twenty-four-hour access to thousands of other singles who met their criteria in terms of race, religion, height, weight, even eye color and drinking habits.

Nearly overnight, it seemed, dozens of similar sites emerged, and online dating became almost de rigueur for busy singles looking for love. According to a recent Pew survey, 31 percent of all American adults (63 million people) know someone who has used a dating Web site, while 26 percent (53 million people) know someone who has gone out with a person he or she met through a dating Web site. But was checking off boxes in columns of desired traits, like an à la carte Chinese take-out menu, the best way to find a soul mate?

Enter eHarmony and the new generation of dating sites, among them PerfectMatch.com and Chemistry.com. All have staked their success on the idea that long-term romantic compatibility can be predicted according to scientific principles—and that they can discover those principles and use them to help their members find lasting love. To that end they've hired high-powered academics, devised special algorithms for relationship-matching, developed sophisticated personality questionnaires, and put into place mechanisms for the long-term tracking of data. Collectively, their efforts mark the early days of a social experiment of unprecedented proportions, involving millions of couples and possibly extending over the course of generations. The question at the heart of this grand trial is simple: In the subjective realm of love, can cold, hard science help?

Although eHarmony was the first dating site to offer science-based matching, Neil Clark Warren seems like an unlikely pioneer in the field. Even though he earned a Ph.D. in clinical psychology from the University of Chicago, in 1967, he never had much of a passion for academic research—or an interest in couples. "I was scared to death of adults," he told me. "So I did child therapy for a while." With a master's degree in divinity from Princeton Theological Seminary, he went on to Fuller Theological Seminary's Graduate School of Psychology, in southern California, where he taught and practiced humanistic psychology (what he calls "client-centered stuff") in the vein of his University of Chicago mentor, Carl Rogers. "I hated doing research," he admitted, before adding with a smile, "In fact, I was called 'Dr. Warm.'"

Fittingly, it was Warren's family, not academia, that piqued his interest in romantic compatibility. "When my daughters came along, that was a big pivot in my life in thinking about how do two people get together," he told me. "I started reading in the literature and realizing what a big chance they had of not having a satisfying marriage. I started trying to look into it."

Soon he began a private practice of couples therapy—with a twist. "People have always thought, wrongly, that psychotherapy is a place to go deal with problems," he said. "So when a couple would come in, I'd say, 'Tell me how you fell in love. Tell me the funniest thing that's happened in your marriage.' If you want to make a relationship work, don't talk about what you find missing in it! Talk about what you really like about it."

Warren is a big proponent of what he likes to call "folksy wisdom." One look at the shelves in his office confirms this. "I've been reading this little book about the Muppets—you know, Jim Henson," he said. "And I've been reading another book about Mister Rogers. I mean, Mister Rogers was brilliant beyond belief! He got a hold of concepts so thoroughly that he could transmit them to six-year-old kids! Do you know how much you have to get a hold of a concept to transmit it simply? His idea of simple-but-profound has had a profound influence on me."

The basis of eHarmony's matching system also sounds simple but profound. In successful relationships, Warren says, "similarities are like money in the bank. Differences are like debts you owe. It's all right to have a few differences, as long as you have plenty of equity in your account."

He leaned in and lowered his voice to a whisper. "Mister Rogers and Jim Henson," Warren continued, "they got a hold of the deep things of life and were able to put them out there. So that's what we want to do with our products. We want to put them out there in a way that you'd say, 'This is common sense. This seems right, this seems like it would work.' Our idea of broad-based compatibility, I put it out there in front of you. Does that seem right?"

Whether or not it seems right on an intuitive level is almost beside the point. After all, eHarmony's selling point, its very brand identity, is its scientific compatibility system. That's where Galen Buckwalter comes in.

A vice president of research and development for the company, Buckwalter is in charge of recruiting what he hopes will be twenty to twenty-five top relationship researchers away from academia—just as he was lured away by Warren nine years ago. A former psychology graduate student at Fuller Theological Seminary (his dissertation was titled "Neuropsychological Factors Affecting Survival in Malignant Glioma Patients Treated with Autologous Stimulated Lymphocytes"), Buckwalter had become an assistant professor at the University of Southern California, where he was studying the effects of hormones on cognition, when he got the call from Warren.

"Neil knew I lived and breathed research, and he had this idea to try to develop some empirically based model to match people," Buckwalter said when I visited him at his office at eHarmony. He wore a black T-shirt and wire-rimmed glasses, and had a hairstyle reminiscent of Einstein's. "He wasn't necessarily thinking, over the Internet—maybe a storefront operation like Great Expectations." Relationships weren't Buckwalter's area, but he welcomed the challenge. "A problem is a problem, and relationships are a good problem," he said. "In the research context, it's certainly an endlessly fascinating question."

With the help of a graduate student, Buckwalter reviewed the psychological literature to identify the areas that might be relevant in predicting success in long-term relationships. "Once we identified all those areas, then we put together a questionnaire— just a massively long questionnaire," he said.

"It was probably close to a thousand questions. Because if you don't ask it, you're never gonna know. So we had tons of questions on ability, even more on interest. Just every type of personality aspect that was ever measured, we were measuring it all."

Because it wasn't practical to execute a thirty-year longitudinal study, he and Warren decided to measure existing relationships, surveying people who were already married. The idea was to look for patterns that produce satisfaction in marriages, then try to reproduce them in the matching of singles.

Buckwalter's studies soon yielded data that confirmed one of Warren's longtime observations: namely, that the members of a happy couple are far more similar to each other than are the members of an unhappy couple. Compatibility, in other words, rests on shared traits. "I can't tell you how delighted I was," Warren said, "when the factor-analytic studies started bringing back the same stuff I'd seen for years."

But could this be true across the board? I told Warren that my most successful relationships have been with men who are far less obsessive than I am. Warren assured me that's not a similarity their system matches for. "You don't want two obsessives," he explained. "They'll drive each other crazy. You don't find two control freaks in a great marriage. So we try to tweak the model for that. Fifty percent of the ball game is finding two people who are stable."

For Warren, a big question remained: What should be done with these findings? Originally, he had partnered with his son-in-law, Greg Forgatch, a former real-estate developer, to launch the business. Their first thought was to produce educational videotapes on relationship compatibility. After all, Warren had recently written his book, *Finding the Love of Your Life*.

"We tried so hard to make videotapes and audiotapes," Warren said. "I went into the studio and made lists. We came up with a hundred things singles need. But singles don't want education; they want flesh! They want a person. So that's when, in 1997, we said, 'We've gotta help people find somebody who would be good for them. Some body?'"

To connect singles and create a data pool for more research, the Internet seemed the best option. Based on a study of 5,000 married couples, Warren put together the compatibility model that became the basis for eHarmony. "We got encouraged by everybody, 'Get out there, get out there! The first person to market is going to be the most successful,'" Warren recalled. But he insisted on getting the matching system right before launching the site—and that didn't happen until August of 2000, during the dot-com bust. By 2001 he was contemplating declaring bankruptcy.

"And then," Warren recalled, "we found an error in our matching formula, so a whole segment of our people were not getting matched. It was an error with all the Christian people on the site."

This is a sensitive topic for Warren, who bristles at the widely held opinion that eHarmony is a Christian dating site. The company's chief operating officer, he offered by way of rebuttal, is Jewish, and

Buckwalter, who became a quadriplegic at age sixteen after jumping into a river and breaking his neck, is agnostic. And while Warren describes himself as "a passionate Christian" and proudly declares, "I love Jesus," he worried about narrowing the site with too many questions about spiritual beliefs. Which is where the error came in.

"We had seven questions on religion," he explained, "and we eliminated four of them. But we forgot to enter that into the matching formula! These were seven-point questions. You needed twenty-eight points to get matched with a Christian person, but there was no way you could get them! We only had three questions! So every Christian person who had come to us had zero matches."

Fortunately, a wave of positive publicity, featuring married couples who'd met through eHarmony and the naturally charismatic Warren, turned things around. Still, Warren said of the innocent mistake, "you kind of wonder how many relationships fall apart for reasons like this—how many businesses?"

Today, eHarmony's business isn't just about using science to match singles online. Calling itself a "relationship-enhancement service," the company has recently created a venture-capital-funded think tank for relationship and marital research, headed up by Dr. Gian Gonzaga, a scientist from the well-known marriage-and-family lab at the University of California at Los Angeles. The effort, as Gonzaga put it to me recently, is "sort of like a Bell Labs or Microsoft for love."

An energetic, attractive thirty-five-year-old, Gonzaga thought twice about leaving the prestige of academia. "It seemed cheesy at first," he said. "I mean, this was a dating service." But after interviewing with Warren, he realized that conducting his research under the auspices of eHarmony would offer certain advantages. He'd be unfettered by teaching and grant-writing, and there would be no sitting on committees or worrying about tenure. More important, since his research would now be funded by business, he'd have the luxury of doing studies with large groups of ready subjects over many years—but without the constraints of having to produce a specific product.

"We're using science in an area most people think of as inherently unscientific," Gonzaga said. So far, the data are promising: a recent Harris Interactive poll found that between September of 2004 and September of 2005, eHarmony facilitated the marriages of more than 33,000 members—an average of forty-six marriages a day. And a 2004 in-house study of nearly 300 married couples showed that people who met through eHarmony report more marital satisfaction than those who met by other means. The company is now replicating that study in a larger sample.

"We have massive amounts of data!" Warren said. "Twelve thousand new people a day taking a 436-item questionnaire! Ultimately, our dream is to have the biggest group of relationship psychologists in the country. It's so easy to get people excited about coming here. We've got more data than they could collect in a thousand years."

But how useful is this sort of data for single people like me? Despite Warren's disclaimer about what a tough eHarmony match I am, I did finally get some profiles in my inbox. They included a bald man with a handlebar moustache, who was fourteen inches taller than me; a five-foot-four-inch attorney with no photos; and a film editor whose photo shows him wearing a kilt—and not in an ironic way. Was this the best science could do?

When I asked Galen Buckwalter about this, he laughed, indicating that he'd heard the question before. "The thing you have to remember about our system is we're matching on these algorithms for long-term compatibility," he said. "Long-term satisfaction is not the same as short-term attraction. A lot of people, when they see their initial matches, it's like, 'This is crap!' "

In ads and on his Web site, Warren talks about matching people "from the inside out." Was eHarmony suggesting that I overlook something as basic as romantic chemistry? "When we started out," Buckwalter said, "we were almost that naive." But now, he added, eHarmony is conducting research on the nature of physical attraction.

"We're trying to find out if we can predict physical chemistry with the same degree of statistical certainty that we've used to predict long-term satisfaction through our compatibility matching. In general, people seem to be attracted to people who share their physical attributes," Buckwalter explained, noting that he has found some exceptions, like height preference. "There's a lot of variability on that dimension," he

said. "A person's height, it turns out, is not a consistent predictor of short-term attraction." Meanwhile, Buckwalter's team is in the process of testing new hypotheses.

"We're still convinced that our compatibility-matching process is essential for long-term satisfaction, so we're not going to mess with that," he insisted. "But if we can fit a short-term attraction model on top of that, and it's also empirically driven, that's the Holy Grail."

Over at Chemistry.com, a new site launched by Match.com, short-term attraction is already built into the system. This competitor of eHarmony's was developed with help from Match.com's chief scientific adviser, Dr. Helen Fisher, an anthropologist at Rutgers University, whose research focuses on the brain physiology of romantic love and sexuality. Chemistry.com is currently assembling a multidisciplinary group of psychologists, relationship counselors, sociologists, neuroscientists, and sexologists to serve as consultants.

The company sought out Fisher precisely because its market research revealed that although a large segment of singles wanted a scientific approach, they didn't want it to come at the expense of romantic chemistry. "On most of the other sites, there's this notion of 'fitness matching,' " Fisher said from her office in New York City. "You may have the same goals, intelligence, good looks, political beliefs. But you can walk into a room, and every one of those boys might come from the same background, have the same level of intelligence, and so on, and maybe you'll talk to three but won't fall in love with any of them. And with the fourth one, you do. What creates that chemistry?"

It's a constellation of factors, Fisher told me. Sex drive, for instance, is associated with the hormone testosterone in both men and women. Romantic love is associated with elevated activity of the neurotransmitter dopamine and probably also another one, norepinephrine. And attachment is associated with the hormones oxytocin and vasopressin. "It turns out," she said, "that seminal fluid has all of these chemicals in it. So I tell my students, 'Don't have sex if you don't want to fall in love.' "

Romantic love, Fisher maintains, is a basic mating drive—more powerful than the sex drive. "If you ask someone to go to bed with you, and they reject you," she says, "you don't kill yourself. But if you're rejected in love, you might kill yourself."

For Chemistry.com's matching system, Fisher translated her work with neurotransmitters and hormones into discrete personality types. "I've always been extremely impressed with Myers-Briggs," she said, referring to the personality assessment tool that classifies people according to four pairs of traits: Introversion versus Extroversion, Sensing versus Intuition, Thinking versus Feeling, and Judging versus Perceiving. "They had me pinned to the wall when I took the test, and my sister, too. So when Chemistry.com approached me, I said to myself, I'm an anthropologist who studies brain chemistry, what do I know about personality?' "

The 146-item compatibility questionnaire on Chemistry.com correlates users' responses with evidence of their levels of these various chemicals. One question, for instance, offers drawings of a hand, then asks:

Which one of the following images most closely resembles your left hand?

The relevance of this question might baffle the average online dater accustomed to responding to platitudes like, "How would you describe your perfect first date?" But Fisher explains that elevated fetal testosterone determines the ratio of the second and fourth finger in a particular way as it simultaneously builds the male and female brain. So you can actually look at someone's hand and get a fair idea of the extent to which they are likely to be a Director type (ring finger longer than the index finger) or a Negotiator type (index finger longer or the same size).

Another question goes like this:

How often do you vividly imagine extreme life situations, such as being stranded on a desert island or winning the lottery?

Almost never
Sometimes
Most of the time
All the time

"Someone who answers 'All the time' is a definite Negotiator," Fisher said. "High estrogen activity is associated with extreme imagination."

While other sites gather data based on often unreliable self-reports ("How romantic do you consider yourself to be?"), many of the Chemistry.com questions are designed to translate visual interpretation into personality assessment, thus eliminating some of the unreliability. In one, the user is

presented with a book's jacket art. We see a woman in a sexy spaghetti-strapped dress gazing at a man several feet away in the background, where he leans on a stone railing. The sky is blue, and they're overlooking an open vista. "What is the best title for this book?" the questionnaire asks, and the choices are as follows:

A Spy in Rimini
Anatomy of Friendship:
     A Smart Guide for Smart People
A Scoundrel's Story
Things Left Unsaid

According to Fisher, each response is correlated with one of the four personality types: Choice A corresponds to Explorer, B to Builder, C to Director, and D to Negotiator.

Even sense of humor can be broken down by type, with questions like "Do you sometimes make faces at yourself in the mirror?" (people with a sense of humor do) and "At the zoo, which do you generally prefer to watch?" (the reply "monkeys and apes" indicates more of a funny bone than "lions and tigers"). According to Fisher, a Director likes people to laugh at his or her jokes; a Negotiator likes to be around someone funny so he or she can laugh at that person's jokes; an Explorer is spontaneous and laughs at just about anything; and a Builder, she suspects, generally isn't as funny as the others.

But how to match people up according to Fisher's four personality types, and under what circumstances, isn't so straightforward. Another question, for instance, presents four smiling faces and asks:

Take a look at the faces below. Are their smiles sincere?

Fisher says that people with high levels of estrogen—usually women—have better social skills, and are better at reading other people. So users who choose the correct "real" smiles (pictures two and three) will be the Negotiators. This, Fisher says, is an area where "complementarity" might be important. The problem with sites like eHarmony, she believes, is that they place too much emphasis on similarity, whereas, in her view, falling in love depends on two elements: similarity and complementarity. "We also want someone who masks our flaws," she explained. "For example, people with poor social skills sometimes gravitate toward people with good social skills. I'm an Explorer, so I don't really need a partner who is socially skilled. That's not essential to me. But it may be essential to a Director, who's generally less socially skilled."

Chemistry.com's compatibility questionnaire also examines secondary personality traits. To illustrate, Fisher cited her own relationship. "I'm currently going out with a man," she said, "and of course I made him take the test instantly. We're both Explorers and older. I'm not sure two Explorers want to raise a baby together, because nobody will be home. But in addition, I'm a Negotiator and he's a Director type. Our dominant personality is similar, but underneath, we're complementary."

Determining which works best—similarity or complementarity—may change with the circumstances. A young woman who's an Explorer, Fisher said, might be attracted to a Builder, someone who's more of a homebody, loyal, dependable, and protective. But the pair will be more compatible if their secondary personalities match—maybe they're both Negotiators underneath.

"Nobody is directly locked into any one of these temperament types," Fisher said. "That's why we provide each person with both a major and a minor personality profile. Do Explorers go well together? Do likes attract likes? Sometimes they do and sometimes they don't."

If this sounds a bit, well, unscientific, Fisher is the first to admit it. "I have theories about what personality type a person would be most ideally suited with," she told me, "but I also trust people to tell me what they are looking for. All throughout the questionnaire are checks and balances to what are just Helen Fisher's theories."

This is why she decided to include an item on the Chemistry.com questionnaire that asks about the traits of a person's partner in his or her most successful former relationship: Was that person an Explorer, a Builder, a Director, a Negotiator? "Anybody can match somebody for values. But I'm hoping to create a system so that five years later they still fascinate each other."

At the same time, Fisher wants couples to be fascinated by each other early on. In other words, why waste time e-mailing back and forth to get to know a potential match over the course of several weeks, as eHarmony encourages its users to do, if there won't be any chemistry when they finally meet? Chemistry.com's guided 1-2-3-Meet system provides a step-by-step

structure to get couples face to face as soon as possible for that all-important "vibe check." Then there's a post-meeting "chemistry check," where each person offers feedback about the date.

The goal is to incorporate this information into the algorithm to provide better matches, but it can also serve as an accuracy check of the data. Say, for instance, that Jack describes himself as a fashionable dresser, but Jill reports that he showed up for their date in flip-flops, cut-offs, and a do-rag. If the feedback from a number of Jack's first meetings indicates the same problem, Chemistry.com will send him an e-mail saying, "Jack, wear a pair of trousers."

Still, even a thoroughly researched biochemical model won't prevent glitches in the matching system. In Fisher's view, for example, no scientifically based site would pair her with the men she's dated, because, as she put it, "they're all better-looking than me."

"It would be preposterous for anyone to say they can create a formula that works perfectly," she said emphatically. "But I do believe that science can help us get close, and that there's a lot more to be learned."

Meanwhile, until these sites start sending me better dating prospects, I figured I'd take Neil Clark Warren up on his offer to introduce me to the thirty-eight-year-old single board member he thought would be such a good match for me. But when I asked a company spokesman about him, I was told that he had recently begun seeing someone. Did they meet through eHarmony? My potential soul mate declined to answer.

Affairs of the Lips: Why We Kiss

(ESSAY)

Chip Walter

Chip Walter is a former CNN bureau chief, filmmaker, science journalist, and author. His science books, written for a mainstream audience, cover subjects as diverse as astrophysics, cognitive psychology, and evolution and are devoted to exploring why humans do what we do. "Affairs of the Lips: Why We Kiss" was the cover story of the February 2008 edition of *Scientific American Mind*. In this article, Walters explores why humans kiss and the wealth of information transmitted in this small act.

Return to these questions after you have finished reading.

Analyzing and Connecting

1. Walter cites a variety of sources on the subject of kissing, from scientists and psychologists to the poet e. e. cummings and a character from the movie *Hitch*. Why do you think he uses such a range of sources?

2. Informative writing assumes that its audience has a certain amount of information about the subject already and then provides new information on that subject. What information does Walter assume his audience has about his subject? What new information is he presenting?

3. Walter ends the essay with the sentence: "But romance gives up its mysteries grudgingly. And in some ways, we like it like that." Why does he end the essay in this way?

4. Most people think humans kiss just because it is pleasurable. With so many different opinions, why is it important to study behaviors such as kissing?

Finding Ideas for Writing

Philematologists, scientists who study the behavior of kissing, disagree on whether it is an instinctual or learned behavior. Those in the instinctual camp cite evidence of kissing in primates, like the Bonobos that Walter mentions. Those who lean toward it being a learned behavior point out, as Walter also does, that not all cultures kiss. Nonetheless, these scientists do believe kissing does have to do with choosing a mate. Walters does not seem to be championing either position. Write a concluding paragraph that could shift this essay to persuade the audience to believe one or the other.

Affairs of the Lips:
Why We Kiss

When passion takes a grip, a kiss locks two humans together in an exchange of scents, tastes, textures, secrets and emotions. We kiss furtively, lasciviously, gently, shyly, hungrily and exuberantly. We kiss in broad daylight and in the dead of night. We give ceremonial kisses, affectionate kisses, Hollywood air kisses, kisses of death and, at least in fairytales, pecks that revive princesses.

Lips may have evolved first for food and later applied themselves to speech, but in kissing they satisfy different kinds of hungers. In the body, a kiss triggers a cascade of neural messages and chemicals that transmit tactile sensations, sexual excitement, feelings of closeness, motivation and even euphoria.

Not all the messages are internal. After all, kissing is a communal affair. The fusion of two bodies dispatches communiqués to your partner as powerful as the data you stream to yourself. Kisses can convey important information about the status and future of a relationship. So much, in fact, that, according to recent research, if a first kiss goes bad, it can stop an otherwise promising relationship dead in its tracks.

Some scientists believe that the fusing of lips evolved because it facilitates mate selection. "Kissing," said evolutionary psychologist Gordon G. Gallup of the University at Albany, State University of New York, last September in an interview with the BBC, "involves a very complicated exchange of information—olfactory information, tactile information and postural types of adjustments that may tap into underlying evolved and unconscious mechanisms that enable people to make determinations . . . about the degree to which they are genetically incompatible." Kissing may even reveal the extent to which a partner is willing to commit to raising children, a central issue in long-term relationships and crucial to the survival of our species.

SATISFYING HUNGER

Whatever else is going on when we kiss, our evolutionary history is embedded within this tender, tempestuous act. In the 1960s British zoologist and author

Desmond Morris first proposed that kissing might have evolved from the practice in which primate mothers chewed food for their young and then fed them mouth-to-mouth, lips puckered. Chimpanzees feed in this manner, so our hominid ancestors probably did, too. Pressing outturned lips against lips may have then later developed as a way to comfort hungry children when food was scarce and, in time, to express love and affection in general. The human species might eventually have taken these proto-parental kisses down other roads until we came up with the more passionate varieties we have today.

Silent chemical messengers called pheromones could have sped the evolution of the intimate kiss. Many animals and plants use pheromones to communicate with other members of the same species. Insects, in particular, are known to emit pheromones to signal alarm, for example, the presence of a food trail, or sexual attraction.

Whether humans sense pheromones is controversial. Unlike rats and pigs, people are not known to have a specialized pheromone detector, or vomeronasal organ, between their nose and mouth [see "Sex and the Secret Nerve," by R. Douglas Fields; *Scientific American Mind*, February/March 2007]. Nevertheless, biologist Sarah Woodley of Duquesne University suggests that we might be able to sense pheromones with our nose. And chemical communication could explain such curious findings as a tendency of the menstrual cycles of female dormitory mates to synchronize or the attraction of women to the scents of T-shirts worn by men whose immune systems are genetically compatible with theirs. Human pheromones could include androstenol, a chemical component of male sweat that may boost sexual arousal in women, and female vaginal hormones called copulins that some researchers have found raise testosterone levels and increase sexual appetite in men.

If pheromones do play a role in human courtship and procreation, then kissing would be an extremely effective way to pass them from one person to another. The behavior may have evolved because it helps humans find a suitable mate—making love, or at least attraction, quite literally blind.

We might also have inherited the intimate kiss from our primate ancestors. Bonobos, which are genetically very similar to us (although we are not their direct descendants), are a particularly passionate bunch, for example. Emory University primatologist Frans B. M. de Waal recalls a zookeeper who accepted what he thought would be a friendly kiss from one of the bonobos, until he felt the ape's tongue in his mouth!

GOOD CHEMISTRY

Since kissing evolved, the act seems to have become addictive. Human lips enjoy the slimmest layer of skin on the human body, and the lips are among the most densely populated with sensory neurons of any body region. When we kiss, these neurons, along with those in the tongue and mouth, rocket messages to the brain and body, setting off delightful sensations, intense emotions and physical reactions.

Of the 12 or 13 cranial nerves that affect cerebral function, five are at work when we kiss, shuttling messages from our lips, tongue, cheeks and nose to a brain that snatches information about the temperature, taste, smell and movements of the entire affair. Some of that information arrives in the somatosensory cortex, a swath of tissue on the surface of the brain that represents tactile information in a map of the body. In that map, the lips loom large because the size of each represented body region is proportional to the density of its nerve endings.

Kissing unleashes a cocktail of chemicals that govern human stress, motivation, social bonding and sexual stimulation. In a new study, psychologist Wendy L. Hill and her student Carey A. Wilson of Lafayette College compared the levels of two key hormones in 15 college male-female couples before and after they kissed and before and after they talked to each other while holding hands. One hormone, oxytocin, is involved in social bonding, and the other, cortisol, plays a role in stress. Hill and Wilson predicted that kissing would boost levels of oxytocin, which also influences social recognition, male and female orgasm, and childbirth. They expected this effect to be particularly pronounced in the study's females, who reported higher levels of intimacy in their relationships. They also forecast a dip in cortisol, because kissing is presumably a stress reliever.

But the researchers were surprised to find that oxytocin levels rose only in the males, whereas it decreased in the females, after either kissing or talking while holding hands. They concluded that females must require more than a kiss to feel emotionally connected or sexually excited during physical contact. Females might, for example, need a more romantic atmosphere than the experimental

setting provided, the authors speculate. The study, which Hill and Wilson reported in November 2007 at the annual meeting of the Society for Neuroscience, revealed that cortisol levels dropped for both sexes no matter the form of intimacy, a hint that kissing does in fact reduce stress.

To the extent that kissing is linked to love, the act may similarly boost brain chemicals associated with pleasure, euphoria and a motivation to connect with a certain someone. In 2005 anthropologist Helen Fisher of Rutgers University and her colleagues reported scanning the brains of 17 individuals as they gazed at pictures of people with whom they were deeply in love. The researchers found an unusual flurry of activity in two brain regions that govern pleasure, motivation and reward: the right ventral tegmental area and the right caudate nucleus. Addictive drugs such as cocaine similarly stimulate these reward centers, through the release of the neurotransmitter dopamine. Love, it seems, is a kind of drug for us humans.

Kissing has other primal effects on us as well. Visceral marching orders boost pulse and blood pressure. The pupils dilate, breathing deepens and rational thought retreats, as desire suppresses both prudence and self-consciousness. For their part, the participants are probably too enthralled to care. As poet e. e. cummings once observed: "Kisses are a better fate / than wisdom."

LITMUS TEST

Although a kiss may not be wise, it can be pivotal to a relationship. "One dance," Alex "Hitch" Hitchens says to his client and friend in the 2005 movie *Hitch*, "one look, one kiss, that's all we get . . . one shot, to make the difference between 'happily ever after' and, 'Oh? He's just some guy I went to some thing with once.' "

Can a kiss be that powerful? Some research indicates it can be. In a recent survey Gallup and his colleagues found that 59 percent of 58 men and 66 percent of 122 women admitted there had been times when they were attracted to someone only to find that their interest evaporated after their first kiss. The "bad" kisses had no particular flaws; they simply did not feel right—and they ended the romantic relationship then and there—a kiss of death for that coupling.

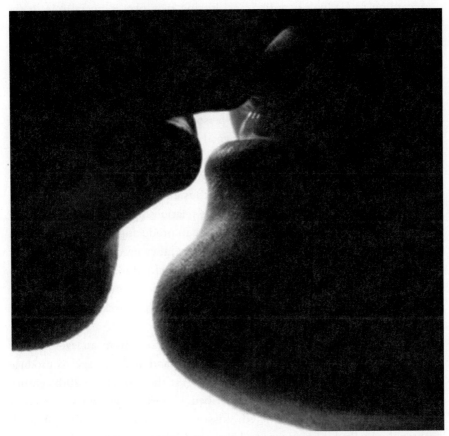

The reason a kiss carries such weight, Gallup theorizes, is that it conveys subconscious information about the genetic compatibility of a prospective mate. His hypothesis is consistent with the idea that kissing evolved as a courtship strategy because it helps us rate potential partners.

From a Darwinian perspective, sexual selection is the key to passing on your genes. For us humans, mate choice often involves falling in love. Fisher wrote in her 2005 paper that this "attraction mechanism" in humans "evolved to enable individuals to focus their mating energy on specific others, thereby conserving energy and facilitating mate choice—a primary aspect of reproduction."

According to Gallup's new findings, kissing may play a crucial role in the progression of a partnership but one that differs between men and women. In a study published in September 2007 Gallup and his colleagues surveyed 1,041 college undergraduates of both sexes about kissing. For most of the men, a deep kiss was largely a way of advancing to the next level sexually. But women were generally looking to take the relationship to the next stage emotionally, assessing not simply whether the other person would make a first-rate source of DNA but also whether he would be a good long-term partner.

"Females use [kissing] . . . to provide information about the level of commitment if they happen to be in a continuing relationship," Gallup told the BBC in September. The locking of lips is thus a kind of emotional barometer: the more enthusiastic it is, the healthier the relationship.

Because women need to invest more energy in producing children and have a shorter biological window in which to reproduce, they need to be pickier about whom they choose for a partner—and they cannot afford to get it wrong. So, at least for women, a passionate kiss may help them choose a mate who is not only good at fathering children but also committed enough to stick around and raise them.

That said, kissing is probably not strictly necessary from an evolutionary point of view. Most other animals do not neck and still manage to produce plenty of offspring. Not even all humans kiss. At the turn of the 20th century Danish scientist Kristoffer Nyrop described Finnish tribes whose members bathed together but considered kissing indecent. In 1897 French anthropologist Paul d'Enjoy reported that the Chinese regard mouth-to-mouth kissing to be as horrifying as many people deem cannibalism to be. In Mongolia some fathers do not kiss their sons. (They smell their heads instead.)

In fact, up to 10 percent of humanity does not touch lips, according to human ethology pioneer Irenäus Eibl-Eibesfeldt, now head of the Max-Planck-Society Film Archive of Human Ethology in Andechs, Germany, writing in his 1970 book, *Love and Hate: The Natural History of Behavior Patterns*. Fisher published a similar figure in 1992. Their findings suggest that some 650 million members of the human species have not mastered the art of osculation, the scientific term for kissing; that is more than the population of any nation on earth except for China and India.

LOPSIDED LOVE

For those cultures that do kiss, however, osculation conveys additional hidden messages. Psychologist Onur Güntürkün of the Ruhr-University of Bochum in Germany recently surveyed 124 couples kissing in public places in the U.S., Germany and Turkey and found that they tilted their heads to the right twice as often as to the left before their lips touched. Right-handedness cannot explain this tendency, because being right-handed is four times more common than is the act of kissing on the right. Instead Güntürkün suspects that right-tilted kissing results from a general preference that develops at the end of gestation and in infancy. This "behavioral asymmetry" is related to the lateralization of brain functions such as speech and spatial awareness.

Nurture may also influence our tendency to tilt to the right. Studies show that as many as 80 percent of mothers, whether right-handed or left-handed, cradle their infants on their left side. Infants cradled, face up, on the left must turn to the right to nurse or nuzzle. As a result, most of us may have learned to associate warmth and security with turning to the right.

Some scientists have proposed that those who tilt their heads to the left when they kiss may be showing less warmth and love than those who tilt to the right. In one theory, tilting right exposes the left cheek, which is controlled by the right, more emotional half of the brain. But a 2006 study by naturalist Julian Greenwood and his colleagues at Stranmillis University College in Belfast, Northern Ireland, counters this notion. The researchers found that 77 percent of 240 undergraduate students leaned right when kissing a doll on the cheek or lips. Tilting to the right with the doll, an impassive act, was nearly as prevalent among subjects as it was among 125 couples observed osculating in Belfast; they tilted right 80 percent of the time. The conclusion: right-kissing probably results from a motor preference, as Güntürkün hypothesized, rather than an emotional one.

Despite all these observations, a kiss continues to resist complete scientific dissection. Close scrutiny of couples has illuminated new complexities woven throughout this simplest and most natural of acts—and the quest to unmask the secrets of passion and love is not likely to end soon. But romance gives up its mysteries grudgingly. And in some ways, we like it like that.

How to write to inform

These steps for the process of informative writing may not progress as neatly as this chart might suggest. Writing is not an assembly-line process. As you write, you are constantly reading what you have written and rethinking.

Keep your readers in mind while you are writing, and if you don't know who your readers might be, imagine someone. What questions might that person have? Where would they appreciate a more detailed explanation?

1 ASSESS THE WRITING TASK

- Read the assignment, carefully noting key words.

- Determine what kind of writing is required. Who are the potential readers?

- Find the limits of your topic. What do you not need to cover? How far do you need to go in breaking down your explanations?

- Review class notes and textbooks; talk to instructor and peers.

- Search for topic ideas in Web subject directories and your library's online catalog.

2 CHOOSE A TOPIC AND WRITE A THESIS

- Within the scope of the assignment, explore what interests you.

- Ask yourself, "Who else will be interested in this topic?"

- Make a list of issues, questions, or problems associated with the topic area.

- Make idea maps about possible topics.

- Discuss possible choices with your peers, coworkers, or instructor.

- Ask questions:
  What happened? What do people need to know?

  Who is my audience?

  How can I connect with them on this topic?

- Narrow your topic. When you learn more about your topic, you should be able to identify one aspect or concept that you can cover thoroughly.

- Write a working thesis that describes what you plan to report or explain.

- If you are unsure if you can follow through with your thesis, do additional research and revise your thesis.

3 WRITE A DRAFT

- Write your revised thesis and main points.

- Think about how you will organize your main points.

- Make a working outline that lists the sections of your essay.

- Draft an introduction that will make readers interested in your subject.

- Build the organization by identifying the topic of each paragraph.

- Draft a conclusion that does more than summarize.

- Write an engaging title.

- If you have statistical information to present, consider using charts or graphs.

4 REVISE, REVISE, REVISE

- Reorganize your ideas for clarity.

- Add detail or further explanation where needed.

- Cut material that distracts from your thesis.

- Check that all key terms are defined.

- Frame your report with an introduction that interests readers and a conclusion that makes a point or raises an interesting question.

- Check that any sources are appropriately quoted or summarized and that they are documented correctly.

- Revise the title to be more accurate and to make readers more interested.

- Review the visual presentation of your report for readability and maximum impact.

5 SUBMITTED VERSION

- Make sure your finished writing meets all formatting requirements.

1: Assess the writing task

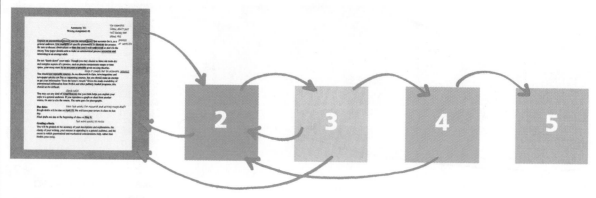

Analyze the assignment

Read your assignment slowly and carefully. Mark off any information about the length specified, date due, formatting, and other requirements. You can attend to this information later. At this point you want to zero in on the subject you will write about and how you will approach that subject.

What kind of writing is required?

Look for key words such as *analyze, compare and contrast, define, discuss,* or *explain.* Often these key words will help you in determining what direction to take. Highlight key words in all questions and commands.

Analyze
Find connections among a set of facts, events, or things, and make them meaningful.

Compare and contrast
Examine how two or more things are alike and how they differ.

Define
Make a claim about how something should be defined, according to features that you set out.

Discuss
Summarize what is known about a particular subject or issue, including research findings.

Explain
Go into detail about how something works or make an unfamiliar subject comprehensible.

Is the audience specified?

If the audience is mentioned in the assignment, how much will they know about your subject? How much background will you need to provide? What attitudes are they likely to have about your subject?

Find a topic

Sometimes you know immediately what you want to write about, but most often, it takes some time to find the right topic. Think first about what is most interesting to you.

What do you know about the general topic?

A good first step is to make an inventory of what you know. Make a list of possible ideas. After you write down as many ideas as you can, go back through the list and place a star beside the ideas that seem most promising.

What ideas can you find in your course notes, class discussions, and your textbooks?

Often you need to look no further than your course materials for possible topics. Think about subjects raised in lectures, in class discussions, or in your textbooks for potential ideas.

What can you find in a database or online library catalog?

Subject directories on databases and your library's online catalog can be valuable sources of potential topics. See Chapter 15.

What might you find on the Web?

Google searches and other search engines often turn up promising ideas to pursue. Yahoo has a subject directory that breaks down large topics into subtopics. See Chapter 15.

What might you find doing field research?

Sometimes the information you need cannot be found in libraries or on the Web, and you have to collect the information firsthand through interviews, surveys, or observations.

Write Now

Explore possible topics

1. Make a list of concepts in your courses. Textbooks usually highlight key concepts, so use them and your course notes to develop your list.

2. Put a check beside the concepts that look most interesting to write about or the ones that mean the most to you.

3. Put a question mark beside the concepts that you don't know much about. If you choose one of these concepts, you will probably have to do in-depth research—by talking to people, by using the Internet, or by going to the library.

4. Select a possible concept. Write nonstop for five minutes about why this concept is interesting to you and how it affects you and other people.

Writer at work

Astronomy 101
Writing Assignment #2

Use examples (Show, don't just tell) Galaxy 999 shows this

Explain an astronomical process, and the current theory that accounts for it, to a *process at work* general audience. Use examples of specific phenomena to illustrate the process. Be sure to discuss observations or data that aren't well understood or don't fit the theory. Your paper should seek to make an astronomical process accessible and ◄────── interesting to an average adult.

Do not "dumb down" your topic. Though you may choose to leave out more dry and complex aspects of a process, such as precise temperature ranges or time spans, your essay must be as accurate as possible given existing theories.

Keep it simple but be accurate. <u>Interest</u>

You should use reputable sources. As we discussed in class, newsmagazines and ◄────── newspaper articles are fine as supporting sources, but you should make an attempt to get your information "from the horse's mouth." Given the ready availability of astronomical information from NASA and other publicly funded programs, this should not be difficult.

Check NASA

You may use any kind of visual features that you think helps you explain your topic to a general audience. If you reproduce a graph or chart from another source, be sure to cite the source. The same goes for photographs.

Due dates   *Have two weeks for research and writing rough draft* ◄──────
Rough drafts will be due on April 22. We will have peer review in class on that day.
Final drafts are due at the beginning of class on May 6.

Two more weeks to revise

Grading criteria
You will be graded on the accuracy of your descriptions and explanations, the clarity of your writing, your success in appealing to a general audience, and the extent to which grammatical and mechanical considerations help, rather than hinder, your essay.

Assess the assignment

Lakshmi Kotra wrote a report in response to this assignment in her Introduction to Astronomy course. She made the following notes and observations to help determine what her essay needed to accomplish, and to explore how she might find a good topic.

Highlight key words

Lakshmi began by highlighting the words in the assignment that gave her specific information about the writing tasks she was to perform.

Identify goals

Then, she made notes on the assignment sheet to specify what she needed to do.

Note time frame

She also made notes about the time frame she has to work in.

Plan strategy

Lakshmi made notes about possible sources for her paper. Then she sketched out a brief time line to follow.

SOURCES
- Go back over lecture notes—Unit 3 was easiest for me to understand so may be best for a general audience?
- Review theories—what makes an idea a theory; who decides what is the accepted theory?
- See book also, esp. Table of contents, for topic ideas.
- Library subject index
- Online subject index
- Check NASA archives online for good pictures. Maybe categories there would help too.
- Ask Dr. Jenson if we can do something we haven't covered in class yet.

***Get to the library by _Friday_ so topic is ready over the weekend. See if Karen wants to go too. Check reference librarian hours first, just in case.

- Outline over the weekend so I have next week to ask Dr. Jenson for help with the rough draft, if I need it.
- Visuals will help make the essay interesting and appealing to a general audience, and also can help explain. So maybe pick two or three topics and then look at NASA images and other visuals to see what is available. This should help narrow down my choices.

2: Choose a topic and write a thesis

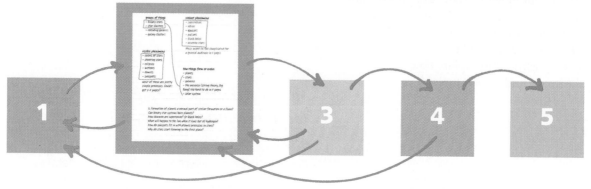

Connect your ideas

After you have done preliminary research and collected ideas, it's time to list possible topics and begin making connections. Circle the most interesting possibilities.

Choose a topic you will enjoy writing about

Writing is fun when you discover new things along the way. Choose a topic you want to explore. If your topic isn't interesting for you, it likely won't be for your readers either.

Choose a topic that your readers will enjoy reading about

Readers may ask, "Why are you telling me this?" Your subject should be interesting to your readers. If the subject isn't one that is immediately interesting, think about ways you can make it so.

Choose a topic that either you know something about or for which you can find the information you need

A central difficulty with writing to inform is determining where to stop. The key to success is to limit the topic. Choose a topic for which you can find the information you need and which you can cover thoroughly in the space you have. If you choose an unfamiliar topic, you must be strongly committed to learning much about it in a short time.

Narrow your topic and write a thesis

Look for ways of dividing large topics into smaller categories, and select one that is promising.

1. What is your topic exactly? (Try to state your answer in specific terms.)

2. What points do you want to make about your topic?

3. What exactly is your purpose in this project? To inform? explain? compare?

4. Develop a working thesis that draws on your answers to questions 1 and 2 and that reflects the purpose you described in your answer to question 3.

Staying on Track

Evaluate your thesis

Your thesis should fulfill the assignment

If your assignment is informative, your purpose is not to argue something is good or bad (see Chapter 11), not to argue for a position (see Chapter 12), and not to argue for change (see Chapter 13).

OFF TRACK

"The electoral college is an antiquated system that results in unfair election results."
(evaluates rather than informs)

ON TRACK

"Considering the huge impact the electoral college system has on American presidential elections, it is surprising that few people understand how it actually works."

Your thesis should be interesting

If your readers already know everything that you have to say, you will bore them. Likewise, your thesis should be significant. Readers will care little about what you have to say if they find your subject trivial.

OFF TRACK

"There are many steps involved before a bill becomes a law."
(vague, bland)

ON TRACK

"Only a tiny fraction of the bills proposed in Congress will ever become laws, and of those, most will accrue so many bizarre amendments and riders that they will barely resemble the original document."

Your thesis should be focused

You cannot tell the story of the Cold War in five pages. Narrow your thesis to a topic you can treat in depth.

OFF TRACK

"Many new products were developed in the 1950s to support the boom in housing construction."
(possibly interesting if particular products are described)

ON TRACK

"The rush to create new housing for returning WWII veterans in the 1950s resulted in many houses that are now extremely hazardous to live in."

Writer at work

groups of things
- binary stars
- star clusters
- colliding galaxies
- galaxy clusters

violent phenomena
- supernovae
- novae
- quasars
- pulsars
- black holes
- neutron stars

these might be too complicated for
a general audience in 7 pages

visible phenomena
- colors of stars
- shooting stars
- eclipses
- meteors
- comets
- sunspots

most of these are pretty
simple processes. Could I
get 5–7 pages?

How things form or evolve
- plants
- stars
- galaxies
- the universe (string theory, Big
Bang) too hard to do in 7 pages
- solar system

Is formation of planets a normal part of stellar formation or a fluke?
Can binary star systems have planets?
How common are supernovae? Or black holes?
What will happen to the Sun when it runs out of hydrogen?
How do sunspots fit in with atomic processes in stars?
Why do stars start forming in the first place?

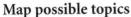

Map possible topics

Lakshmi Kotra began by reviewing her class notes and her textbooks. She also looked in the library's online catalog subject index and an online subject index. She listed all the possible topics she came across in these sources. Then she made an idea map of the topics that appealed to her, clustering types of theories, and adding new ones as they occurred to her. She made a few notes on some of her topic areas, describing how well they would meet the needs of her assignment. And she jotted down questions she had about some topics as well.

Narrow the search

Lakshmi narrowed her search by considering how complicated a topic she wanted to take on. Since she had to explain the theory to a general audience, she ruled out topics like black holes and string theory. She noticed that stellar processes showed up several times in her lists of interesting topics.

Identify the topic

Lakshmi settled on stellar formation as a theory that interested her and which she felt confident she could explain in layman's terms. Her preliminary research also indicated there was a wealth of observational data and photos that she could use in her report.

Find images and get source information

Lakshmi wanted to include photographs of star formation, and on NASA's Web site she located images that she could use legally. She carefully recorded all the information she would need to find the images again and to document the images in her paper.

AUTHOR: U.S. National Aeronautics and Space Administration

DATE: April 1, 1995

PAGE TITLE: The Eagle nebula.

SITE TITLE: Great Images in NASA

DATE OF RETRIEVAL: April 5, 2008

URL: http://grin.hq.nasa.gov/ABSTRACTS/GPN-000987.html

3: Write a draft

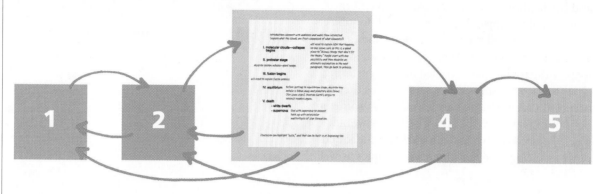

Organize your information

Gather your notes and other materials. Think about how you want to convey the information to your readers.

- If your subject matter occurs over time, you might want to use a chronological order.

- If you need to discuss several aspects, you likely will need to identify key concepts and think about how they relate to each other. An idea map can help you to determine these relationships.

- If you are comparing two or more things, you will want to think about how these things are similar and how they are different.

Make a working outline

A working outline is a tool that you can use as you write your first draft. The more detailed it is, the better. (If you would prefer to write a complete, formal outline before drafting your essay, by all means do so.) To make your outline, follow these steps:

1. List the sections of your essay, in the order that you expect them to appear.

2. Write two or three complete sentences describing the content and purpose of each section.

3. Now, review your outline. Does the project as you have described it here achieve the purpose you intend it to?

Think about a title

An effective title motivates your readers to want to read what you have written. Be as specific as you can.

Consider the use of visuals

Would a table or chart be helpful? photographs? a map? Do you need headings and subheadings?

Staying on Track

Write an effective introduction and conclusion

Write an effective introduction

Get off to a fast start. Cut to the chase: no empty sentences or big generalizations at the beginning.

OFF TRACK

"Because we all live such busy, hectic lives in these modern times, everyone wants to know why we must wait for hours and hours at the airport before boarding a flight."
(boring, predictable beginning—a signal that the paper will be dull)

ON TRACK

"It's a traveler's worst nightmare: the long line of people at the security gate, snaking back and forth across the waiting area. What exactly goes on in an airport screening area, and how does it help to keep us safe?"

Write an effective conclusion

Remember that a summary of what you have just written is the weakest way to conclude. Think of something interesting for your reader to take away such as an unexpected implication or a provocative example.

OFF TRACK

"In conclusion, we have seen how peer-to-peer file sharing works."
(ineffective; says only that the paper is finished)

ON TRACK

"The peer-to-peer file sharing process is relatively simple. Unfortunately, in many cases it is also illegal. It is ironic that a technology intended to help people has resulted in turning many of them into *de facto* criminals."
(ends with a significant point, which helps readers remember the paper)

Writer at work

Lakshmi Kotra began with the following rough outline of the process she planned to write about.

Introduction—connect with audience and make them interested
(explain what the clouds are first—composed of what elements?)

I. molecular clouds—collapse
   begins

will need to explain HOW that happens.
No one seems sure so this is a good
place to "discuss things that don't fit
the theory." Maybe start with one
possibility and then describe an
alternate explanation in the next
paragraph, then go back to process.

II. protostar stage

describe cocoon nebulae—good image

III. fusion begins

will need to explain fusion process

IV. equilibrium   Before getting to equilibrium stage, describe how
nebula is blown away and planetary disk forms
(for some stars). Mention Earth's origin to
interest readers again.

V. death

   - white dwarfs

   - supernova   End with supernova to connect
back up with interstellar
matter/cycle of star formation.

Conclusion can highlight "cycle," and that can be built in at beginning too.

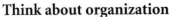

Think about organization

Lakshmi recognized that the process she was describing naturally lent itself to chronological, or time-order, organization, because one thing has to happen after another for a star to form. However, she found that she had to "break out" from the simple time line of stellar formation at some points, to explain in more detail or to trace multiple possibilities.

Make notes on how to develop the subject

She made notes on her outline indicating where she would step away from the chronological pattern to do this explaining. As she considered how she wanted to end her essay, she realized the idea of a "life cycle" for stars could point back toward the essay's beginning. This strategy helped her focus her thesis.

Connect with readers

Lakshmi realized that stellar formation would probably seem like a distant and forbidding topic to a general audience, so she thought carefully about making a connection with her readers. She began by trying out some different ways to introduce her essay. Here are some of her initial attempts and the comments she made on them. Lakshmi decided to work with the last of these openings and see how well she could integrate it with the rest of her essay.

> Stars have a complex and fascinating life cycle. Saying it's fascinating doesn't make it fascinating to readers.

> Have you ever looked up at the stars at night and wondered why they are there? Vague. Kind of sounds like I'm going to talk about religious or spiritual issues.

> Astronomers have spent many years studying the life cycle of stars. So? Anyway, I just want to talk about what they've found, not how long it took them.

> If "sunshine on your shoulders" makes you happy, you will be even happier to know that the sun will keep shining for at least another 8 billion years. Too corny. Does anyone even remember that song? Anyway, "happy" isn't the way I want readers to feel. But using a familiar phrase might be good.

> "Twinkle, twinkle little star. How I wonder what you are." Good—more personal than "Have you ever looked up at the stars and wondered . . ." Astronomers wonder too. That could be the connection between them and scientists' work. More familiar song, also.

4: Revise, revise, revise

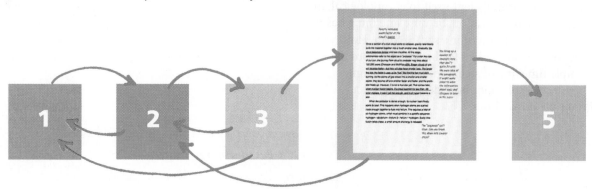

Skilled writers know that the secret to writing well is rewriting. Even the best writers often have to revise several times to get the result they want. You also must have effective strategies for revising if you're going to be successful. The biggest trap you can fall into is starting off with the little stuff first. Leave the small stuff for last.

Does your paper or project meet the assignment?	• Look again at your assignment. Does your paper or project do what the assignment asks?
	• Look again at the assignment for specific guidelines, including length, format, and amount of research. Does your work meet these guidelines?
Is your title specific?	• Vague titles suggest dull treatment of the topic. Can you make your title more accurate?
Does your writing have a clear focus?	• Does your project have an explicitly stated thesis? If not, is your thesis clearly implied?
	• Is each paragraph related to your thesis?
	• Do you get off the track at any point by introducing other topics?
	• Are your main points adequately developed?
	• Do you support your main points with reasons and evidence?
	• Can you add more examples and details that would help to explain your main points?
Is your organization effective?	• Is the order of your main points clear to your reader?
	• Are there any places where you find abrupt shifts or gaps?
	• Are there sections or paragraphs that could be rearranged to make your draft more effective?
Is your introduction effective?	• Do you have any general statements that you might cut to get off to a faster start?

- Can you think of a vivid example that might draw in readers?
- Can you use a striking fact to get readers interested?
- Does your introduction make clear where you are headed?

Is your conclusion effective?	• Conclusions that only summarize tend to bore readers. Does your conclusion add anything new to what you've said already?
	• Can you use the conclusion to discuss further implications?
	• Have you left your audience with a final provocative idea that might invite further discussion?
Do you represent yourself effectively?	• To the extent you can, forget for a moment that you wrote what you are reading. What impression do you have of you, the writer?
	• Does "the writer" create an appropriate tone?
	• Has "the writer" done his or her homework?
Is the writing project visually effective?	• Is the font attractive and readable?
	• Are the headings and visuals effective?
Save the editing for last.	When you have finished revising, edit and proofread carefully.

Staying on Track

Reviewing your draft

Give yourself plenty of time for reviewing your draft. For detailed information on how to participate in a peer review, how to review it yourself, and how to respond to comments from your classmates, your instructor, or a campus writing consultant, see pages 24–28.

Some good questions to ask yourself when reviewing informative writing

- Are the explanations in the essay easy to follow?
- Are there gaps or places where you feel you need more information?
- Are any unusual or discipline-specific words defined for readers?
- Can the reader construct a clear picture of what the essay describes?
- Is the essay interesting enough to catch readers' attention and keep them reading?

Writer at work

Density increases much faster at the cloud's <u>center</u> ←

Once a section of a dust cloud starts to collapse, gravity relentlessly pulls the material together into a much smaller area. Gradually, <u>the cloud becomes denser</u> and less cloudlike. At this stage, astronomers refer to the object as a "protostar." For a star the size of our sun, the journey from cloud to protostar may take about 100,000 years (Chaisson and McMillan 429). <u>Bigger clouds of gas will develop faster—but they will also have shorter lives. The larger the star, the faster it uses up its "fuel." But first the fuel must start burning.</u> As the atoms of gas crowd into a smaller and smaller space, they bounce off one another faster and faster, and the protostar heats up. However, it is not a true star yet. That comes later, when nuclear fusion begins. <u>If a cloud segment is less than .08 solar masses, it won't get hot enough, and it will never become a star.</u>

When the protostar is dense enough, its nuclear heart finally starts to beat. This happens when hydrogen atoms are pushed close enough together to fuse into helium. This requires a total of six hydrogen atoms, which must combine in a specific sequence: hydrogen—deuterium—helium 3—helium + hydrogen. Every time fusion takes place, a small amount of energy is released.

You bring up a number of concepts here that don''t quite fit with the main idea of the paragraph. It might make sense to move the information about mass and lifespan to later in the paper ←

The "sequence" isn't clear. Can you break this down into simpler steps?

Read carefully your instructor's comments

Lakshmi Kotra gave a copy of her first draft to her instructor for feedback. She used his comments to guide her revision of the essay.

Determine a plan for revision in light of your instructor's comments

Based on her instructor's comments, Lakshmi decided to shift some information on the rates at which stars burn nuclear fuel from an earlier section of the paper to her later discussion of the fates of stars with different masses. This strategy also allowed her to flesh out the description of "brown dwarfs"—starlike objects that do not develop into stars.

Act on specific comments

She also took her instructor's advice about simplifying her explanation of hydrogen fusion.

Read your paper aloud to catch mistakes and awkward phrasing

Lakshmi also read her essay aloud to help identify spelling errors and missing or poorly chosen words.

Visit your writing center

Finally, Lakshmi visited her school's writing center. She asked for specific help in making the paper accessible for an audience without a scientific background. Working with a consultant, she recognized the need to define scientific terms, like *nebulae, protostar,* and *equilibrium,* that might not be familiar to a general audience.

5: Submitted version

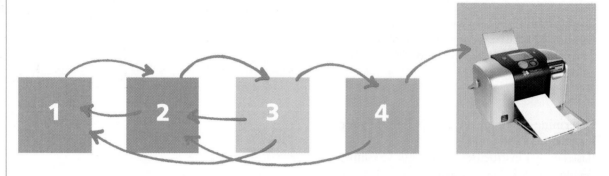

Kotra 1

Lakshmi Kotra
Professor Jenson
Astronomy 101
6 May 2008

The Life Cycle of Stars

"Twinkle, twinkle, little star; how I wonder what you are." This old nursery rhyme may not seem profound, but it echoes some of the biggest questions astronomers puzzle over: What are stars made of? How do they form? How are they born and how do they die? Current theories of star formation answer some of these questions, but not all of them. We do know that, even though stars are separated from one another by vast amounts of space, their life cycles are intertwined.

Twinkling stars are born in dark, cold clouds of dust and gas called nebulae. These clouds consist mainly of hydrogen, and may be as cold as 10 degrees Kelvin (Chaisson and McMillan 427). Nebulae are very dense compared to the near-vacuum of interstellar space. But something must concentrate this dust and gas even more if a star is to form. This first part of the star-forming process is not fully understood. Some force has to cause a portion of the nebula to begin collapsing. Magnetism and rotation are two forces already at work in most clouds, but astronomers have long thought that these forces are more likely to counteract the collapsing force of gravity (Chaisson and McMillan 427). However, new research may have found a solution to this problem. In some clouds, magnetic fields may cancel out some or all of the rotational force. This reorganization would allow gravity to begin collapsing the star (Farivar).

Another theory is that a shock wave from some outside event or object might trigger the collapse of a cloud. The Eagle Nebula provides a good illustration of this theory. Ultraviolet radiation from super-hot stars in the nebula has been observed bombarding the surrounding dust and gas. The radiation has stripped away a lot of dust but left dense columns of cloud where stars are believed to be forming. The impact of this "stellar wind" may have also triggered the star formation. Smaller clumps of denser gas are contracting within the columns, taking their first step on the journey to stardom (see fig. 1).

Once a section of a dust cloud starts to collapse, gravity relentlessly pulls the material together into a much smaller area. Gradually, the center of the cloud becomes denser and less cloudlike. At this stage, astronomers refer to the object as a "protostar." For a star the size of our sun, the journey from cloud to protostar may take about 100,000 years (Chaisson and McMillan 429). As the atoms of gas crowd into a smaller and smaller space, they bounce off one another faster and faster, and the protostar heats up. However, it is not a true star yet. That comes later, when nuclear fusion begins. For now,

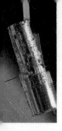

Fig. 1. Eagle Nebula
The columns of interstellar gas in the Eagle Nebula are incubators for
new stars (US, NASA, "Eagle").

the developing protostar is still surrounded by a shroud of dust that
hides it from view. This dust mantle is called a cocoon nebula. Some
protostars can be detected by the infrared glow of their cocoon nebulae
(Chaisson and McMillan 435-36).

Over millions of years, the protostar continues to grow and
change, like a butterfly in its cocoon. Gravity keeps compacting it, making
it smaller in size and denser. When the protostar is dense enough, its
nuclear heart finally starts to beat. This happens when hydrogen atoms
are pushed close enough together to fuse into helium. The fusion
process involves several steps. First, two hydrogen atoms will fuse to
form an atom of deuterium, or heavy hydrogen. When a third hydrogen
atom joins the deuterium atom, an isotope called helium 3 results. Finally,

when two helium 3 atoms fuse together, an atom of regular helium plus two of hydrogen are created. But the crucial part of this process is that, every time fusion takes place, a small amount of energy is released. The radiation emitted from the fusion of hydrogen into helium is what makes the majority of stars shine. Fusion radiation from the Sun lights our planet in the daytime, makes the moon shine at night—and gives you sunburn.

Hydrogen atoms must be moving at extremely high speeds in order to fuse. Another way to say this is that the temperature in the core of a protostar must be very high for fusion to take place: at least 10 million degrees Kelvin (Chaisson and McMillan 431). Now nuclear forces, not just gravity's grip, are controlling the star's development. In fact, these two forces will compete throughout the star's life. Gravity tries to collapse the star, while the pressure of its fast-moving, superheated atoms pushes it outward. As long as the two forces balance each other, the star will remain stable. Astronomers call this state "equilibrium."

During the intense heating at the end of the protostar stage, and when hydrogen fusion is beginning, intense radiation streams off the young star. The dust and gas that have surrounded the protostar are swept away by this energy bombardment, and the star emerges from its cocoon. This phenomenon can be observed visually in NGC 4214. Young stars in this nebula are pouring out radiation that has created "bubbles" in the surrounding gas. Brighter and older stars have pushed away more of the dust and gas. The bubbles around these stars are bigger than those around younger or cooler stars in the nebula (see fig. 2).

Sometimes, not all of a protostar's dust cocoon blows away. According to one theory, you can look around our own solar system and see the remnants of the dust that once surrounded our Sun. In fact, you are standing on some of it. The Earth and the rest of the planets in our solar system are believed to have formed from a disk of dust and gas left over after the sun formed. The reasons this happens are not entirely clear, but astronomers now think that many stellar systems have planetary disks around them. The Orion Nebula provides some confirmation of this theory. There, astronomers have observed many glowing disks of dust, called "proplyds." They think these disks are actually young stars surrounded by material that will eventually form a system of orbiting planets (see fig. 3).

Fig. 2. Star Formation
Clusters of new stars form from interstellar gas and dust in galaxy NGC 4214 (US, NASA, "Star").

The size of the original dust cloud a star is born from will also determine how it dies. Some protostars don't quite have what it takes to become a star. Clumps of dust and gas that are smaller than .08 solar masses never get hot enough to begin fusing hydrogen (Chaisson and McMillan 433). These "brown dwarfs" produce infrared radiation, but they never shine visibly.

True stars burn through their nuclear fuel at different rates. The larger the star, the faster its fuel is fused. Smaller stars, like our Sun, are called "dwarf stars." If they began life with less than eight times the mass of our Sun, they will quietly burn hydrogen for perhaps ten billion years. Toward the end of their lives, as they begin to run out of fuel,

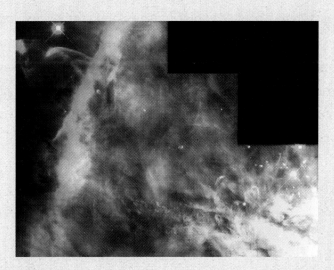

Fig. 3. Orion Nebula

This composite photo of the Orion nebula assembled from images taken by the Hubble Space Telescope shows the beginnings of new solar systems surrounding young stars (US, NASA, "Orion").

they will swell briefly into red giant stars, fusing their helium into carbon, and cooling substantially. Finally, they will subside into "white dwarf" stars, about the size of the planet earth. Provided they do not have nearby neighboring stars that might interact with them, white dwarfs gradually dim and cool, until they go dark altogether (Chaisson and McMillan 459). This cooling process is what astronomers predict will some day happen to our Sun.

A star of more than about eight solar masses has a shorter but much more spectacular life. It will fuse all its available fuel in well under one billion years—perhaps in as little as one million years. When a giant star has run through all its available nuclear fuel, it develops a core of iron atoms, which cannot be fused into anything else. When this core has grown to about 1.4 solar masses, the star will explode in a supernova. All that will be left of the original star is a dark neutron star or black hole (Chaisson and McMillan 475). But the shock wave from the supernova may go on to trigger new star formation in dust clouds nearby. In this way, dying stars contribute to the birth of new ones, and the life cycle of stars continues.

Kotra 8

Works Cited

Chaisson, Eric, and Steve McMillan. *Astronomy Today*. 6th ed. Upper
	Saddle River: Prentice, 2008. Print.

Farivar, Cyrus. "Galactic Map Aids Stellar Formation Theory." *Daily
	Californian*. Daily Californian, 23 Jan. 2002. Web. 8 Apr. 2008.

United States. National Aeronautics and Space Adm. "The Eagle
	Nebula." Photograph. *Great Images in NASA*. 1. Apr. 1995. Web. 8
	Apr. 2008.

---. ---. "Fireworks of Star Formation Light Up a Galaxy." Photograph.
	Great Images in NASA. 6 Jan. 2000. Web. 8 Apr. 2008.

---. ---. "The Orion Nebula." Photograph. *Great Images in NASA*. 20
	Nov. 1995. Web. 8 Apr. 2008.

Projects

No matter how diverse its forms, successful informative writing begins with the basics.

- What do readers already know about a subject?
- What do readers need to know about a subject?
- What kind of writing is best suited for particular readers? a Web site? a brochure? an article? or something else?

You'll do many kinds of informative writing in your life after college. The following projects are common informative writing tasks.

Instructions

Be aware that instructions are much harder to write than most people expect. They usually require a lot of detail, yet if they are too complex, people will be confused or intimidated. After all, how many times have you glanced at an instruction booklet for a new appliance, set it aside, and just started pushing buttons?

Think of a fairly simple device you have learned to use, like an iPod or a software application.

Imagine a friend who wants to learn to use the same device. How could you simply and accurately instruct him or her?

Write a one- or two-page set of instructions explaining how to perform a simple task, such as creating a play list on your iPod, using your school's Web-based email service, or changing the toner cartridge in your printer. When you are finished, have a friend volunteer to try out your instructions. How easy is it to follow them? Do they work?

Profile

Find several written profiles of people at your school—these might be your school president, a coach, and an award-winning student. Profiles often appear in school newspapers, on school Web sites, and in news reports about events on campus.

Read the profiles and note what information is included about each person, and what is left out.

• Are the profiles all written for the same audience?
• How does the information in each profile vary depending on the intended audience?

Choose someone else to write a profile about—a classmate, a staff member you have worked with, or even yourself— and interview that person. Choose someone you find interesting. A custodial worker or fellow student can be just as interesting as a college president, depending on the details you select to write about. Model your profile on the examples you have read.

Think carefully about the audience you wish to appeal to. How can you interest them in your subject?

Report

Think of a subject you know a great deal about but most other people, especially those who are your intended readers, do not.

Your subject might come from your life experience
• What's it like to grow up on a family farm?
• What's it like to be an immigrant to the United States?

Your hobbies
• What's the best way to train for a marathon?
• How can you avoid injuries in sports by stretching?

Your personal interests
• Why everyone over age 20 should pay attention to cholesterol

A place that you have found fascinating, or a subject you have studied in college
• The misunderstood nature of conceptual art
• Breakthroughs in nanotechnology in the near future.

Consider what will likely be most interesting about your subject to your readers.

Engage your readers with a provocative title and a thesis that will challenge them to think about your subject in new ways.

Aim for a report of 700–1000 words or about 3–5 double-spaced pages.

9 Rhetorical Analyses

Every piece of writing, every painting, every building, every movie, every new product, every advertisement, is a response to what came before it.

Writing to analyze

Critical reading and viewing are essential skills for all kinds of writing. Analysis is a more specific aim where those critical reading and viewing skills are applied to particular subjects. Analysis involves dividing a whole into parts that can be studied both as individual entities and as parts of the whole.

Rhetorical analysis is a kind of analysis that divides a whole into parts to understand how an act of speaking or writing conveys meaning. Thus the goal of a rhetorical analysis is to understand how a particular act of writing or speaking influenced particular people at a particular time.

Visual analysis is closely related to rhetorical analysis. The tools of rhetorical analysis have been applied to understanding how other human creations make meaning, including art, buildings, photographs, dance, memorials, advertisements— any kind of symbolic communication.

Literary analysis takes into account elements of literature such as plot, character, and setting, paying particular attention to language and metaphor. The goal of literary analysis is to interpret a literary text and support that interpretation with evidence or, more simply, to make a discovery about a text that you share with your readers.

Text and context

A rhetorical, visual, or literary analysis may be concerned with either text or context, but often it examines both. Textual analysis focuses on the features of a text—the words and evidence in a speech, the images and patterns in a picture, and so on. For a textual analysis, ask

- What is the subject?

- What is the author's claim or what are the main ideas?

- What is the medium of the text? a newspaper? a Web site? scholarly journal? a photograph? a short story?

- What appeals are used? What are the author's credentials, and how does he represent himself? What facts or evidence does he present? What values does he share with you and the rest of his audience? What emotions does he try to evoke?

- How is the text organized?

- What kind of style does the author use? Formal or informal, satirical or humorous? Are any metaphors used?

Contextual analysis reconstructs the cultural environment, or context, that existed when a particular rhetorical event took place, and then depends on that recreation to produce clues about persuasive tactics and appeals. For a contextual analysis, ask

- Who is the author? What else has she written or said on this subject? Who does she borrow from or quote? What motivated her to address this issue?

- Who is the audience? What are the occasion and forum for writing? Would the argument have been constructed differently if it had been presented in a different medium? What motivated the newspaper, magazine, or other venue to publish it?

- What is the larger conversation? When did the text appear? Why did it appear at that particular moment? Who or what might this text be responding to?

A contextual analysis focuses on the surroundings and the history of the statue. Legend has Castor and his twin brother Pollux, the mythical sons of Leda, assisting Romans in an early battle. Romans built a large temple in the Forum to honor them. The statues of Castor and Pollux were uncovered in sixteenth-century excavations and brought in 1583 to stand at the top of the Cordonata, a staircase designed by Michelangelo as part of a renovation of the Piazza del Campidoglio commissioned by Pope Paul III Farnese in 1536.

The statue of Castor stands at the entrance of the Piazza del Campidoglio in Rome. A textual analysis focuses on the statue itself. The size and realism of the statue makes it a masterpiece of classical Roman sculpture.

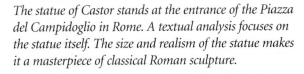

Working Together

Analyze text and context

In a group of three or four students

Find several examples of verbal and visual texts. These might be ads you have seen on television or heard on the radio, photos or editorials in the student newspaper, or Web sites.

• What is the context in which this text was produced?

• How was the creator of the text attempting to influence or persuade the audience? What appeals are made?

• In the visual texts, what connections or associations is the reader invited to create?

• In the verbal texts, what claims and reasons are explicitly stated?

Writing a rhetorical analysis

People often use the term *rhetoric* to describe empty language. "The Governor's speech was just a bunch of rhetoric," you might say, meaning that the Governor offered noble-sounding words but no real ideas. But rhetoric originated with a much more positive meaning. According to Aristotle, rhetoric is "the art of finding in any given case the available means of persuasion." Rhetoric is concerned with producing effective pieces of communication.

Rhetoric can also be used to interpret or analyze. Students of rhetoric know not only how to produce effective communication, but also how to understand communication. The two skills complement each other: Becoming a better writer makes you a better analyst, and becoming a better analyst makes you a better writer. For an example of rhetorical analysis, see pages 186–189.

Components of a rhetorical analysis

What is the author's purpose?	**Identify the purpose.** Some texts have an obvious purpose; for example, an ad wants you to buy something. But texts can have more than one purpose. A politician who accuses an opponent of being corrupt may also be making a case for her own honesty.
Who is the audience?	**Examine the audience.** The most effective texts are ones that are tailored specifically for an audience. What can you determine about the actual audience's values, attitudes, and beliefs? How does the author create an audience in the text by making assumptions about what the audience believes?
Who is the author of my text?	**Examine the author.** How did the author come to this subject? Is the author an expert or an outsider?
What is the background of my text?	**Examine the context.** What else has been said or written on this topic? What was going on at the time that influenced this text?
Which rhetorical appeals are used in my text?	**Analyze rhetorical appeals.** Aristotle set out three primary tactics of argument: appeals to the emotions and deepest held values of the audience (pathos), appeals based on the trustworthiness of the speaker (ethos), and appeals to good reasons (logos).
How does the language and style contribute to the purpose?	**Examine the language and style.** Is the style formal? informal? academic? Does the writer or speaker use humor or satire? What metaphors are used?

Keys to rhetorical analysis

Choose a text that you care about	Your paper will require close multiple readings of the text. Your interest (or lack of interest) in your text will come through in your paper.
Write a descriptive title	The title of your essay should indicate the focus of your analysis.
Check your thesis	Make sure your thesis is sensible and realistic as well as being supported by evidence and examples in the text.
Interrogate evidence	Look closely at the evidence supporting the writer's claims. Is it convincing? Are there gaps? Can it be interpreted in a different way? Is counterevidence acknowledged?
Examine underlying values, attitudes, and beliefs	When a writer or speaker neglects the audience's values, attitudes, and beliefs, the text is rarely persuasive.
Identify fallacies	Be aware when only one side of the story is being presented, when claims and accusations are grossly exaggerated, and when complex issues are oversimplified. See pages 14–15.
Identify relationships	An effective rhetorical analysis makes connections, showing how strategies in the text are responses to other texts and the larger context.
Recognize complexity	Many texts cannot be reduced to a sound bite. Successful rhetorical analyses often read between the lines to explain why a statement may be ironic or what is not being said. Readers appreciate being shown something they may not otherwise have noticed.

Writing a visual analysis

We are bombarded by images on a daily basis. They compete for our attention, urge us to buy things, and guide us on our way home from work. These visual texts frequently attempt to persuade us; to make us think, feel, or act a certain way. Yet we rarely stop to consider how they do their work.

Visual texts leave room for the audience to interpret to a greater degree than many verbal texts, which make them particularly rich subjects for analysis.

Components of a visual analysis

What kind of visual is it?	**Describe what you see.** Is it a single image, part of a series, a sign, a building, or something else? What are the conventions for this kind of visual?
What is the image about?	**Consider the subject.** What does the image depict? What is the setting? What is the purpose? Are words connected with the image?
How is the image arranged?	**Analyze the composition.** What elements are most prominent? Which are repeated? Which are balanced or in contrast to each other? Which details are important?
What is the context?	**Examine the context.** Who created the image? When and where did it first appear? Can you determine why it was created?
What visuals are like it?	**Look for connections.** What is the genre? What kind of visual is it? What elements have you seen before? Which remind you of other visuals?

Keys to visual analysis

Choose a visual text that you care about	If an image or other visual text means something to you, you will find it easier to analyze.
Pay close attention to details	Identify the key details that keep the viewer's attention and convey meaning. Also, examine the point of view—the viewer's perspective of the subject.
Provide a frame for understanding	You will need to provide a context for understanding a visual text, giving a sense of how it is a response to events and trends going on at the time and how it was initially understood.
Go beyond the obvious	A successful visual analysis gets readers to make connections and see aspects that they otherwise would not have noticed.

An effective analysis

A successful analysis can be generally textual or contextual in nature. But the two approaches are not mutually exclusive—in fact, most analysts consider the details of the text, but also attend to the particulars of context as well.

theguardian | ### Straight from the Heart
Tim Collins

On July 11, 2005, a woman named Marie Fatayi-Williams made an immensely moving speech in London at the site where her son Anthony had been killed in a terrorist bombing four days earlier. Her speech was reported in numerous media outlets. *The Guardian,* a British newspaper, printed Fatayi-Williams's speech on July 13, with an analysis and commentary by Tim Collins. Collins considers the factors that make Fatayi-Williams's speech so powerful, and places it in a larger context of responses to terrorism.

Caught in the spotlight of history, set on the stage of a very public event, Marie Fatayi-Williams, the mother of Anthony Fatayi-Williams, 26 and missing since Thursday, appeals for news of her son. Her words are a mixture of stirring rhetoric, heartfelt appeal and a stateswoman-like vision, and so speak on many levels to the nation and the world. Her appeal is a simple one—where is my son? If he has been killed, then why? Who has gained?

Marie has found herself, as I did on the eve of the invasion of Iraq, an unwitting voice, speaking amid momentous events. Her appeal, delivered on Monday not far from Tavistock Square, where she fears her son died in the bomb attack on the number 30 bus, gives a verbal form to the whirlpool of emotions that have engulfed society as the result of last week's bombings. I suspect Marie, like myself, had no idea that her words would find such wide recognition, have fed such an acute hunger for explanation, have slaked such a thirst for expression of the sheer horror of Thursday's events.

This kind of speech is normally the preserve of the great orators, statesmen and playwrights, of Shakespeare, Churchill or Lincoln. It is often a single speech, a soliloquy or address from the steps of the gallows, that explains, inspires, exhorts and challenges. But always such addresses are crafted for effect and consciously intended to sway and influence, and often, as in the case of Shakespeare's Henry V, they are set in the mouth

Collins points out the appeal to pathos—the beliefs and values of the audience—that lies at the heart of Fatayi-Williams's speech.

Collins identifies the genre of the speech, which is usually crafted for a specific occasion. Marie's speech is remarkable because it is spontaneous.

of a long dead hero or delivered by wordsmiths who are masters of their craft. It is rare in history that such oratory is the genuine article, springing from the heart and bursting forth to an unwitting audience. In Marie's case, her speech gains its power as a vehicle of grief and loss, and of the angst of a mother who yearns for her beloved son. In my case it was the opposite emotion from which I drew inspiration—an appeal to understand, to empathize, to give courage and purpose. I was motivated by a need to warn and teach as well as to encourage. Marie's motivation is a reflection on loss and that most powerful of all emotions, a mother's love.

The form the address takes is as poignant as the language used. There is an initial explanation of the extraordinary circumstances of the loss, a cri de coeur for the innocent blood lost, a rejection of the act by its comparison to the great liberators, and the assertion that her loss is all our loss in the family of humanity. It ends with her personal grief for her flesh and blood, her hopes and pride. The language echoes verses of the Bible as well as from the Koran. It has raw passion as well as heart-rending pathos.

Several rhetorical techniques used in the speech connect it to a larger historical tradition.

With only a photograph of her son and a sheet of paper as a prompt, Marie's words burst out with as much emotion as anger. Her speech stands in stark contrast to the pronouncements of politicians, prepared by aides and delivered from copious notes. It is indeed the raw originality and authentic angst that give the delivery such impact, the plea such effect. No knighted veteran of the Royal Shakespeare Company could deliver such an address without hours or even days of rehearsal. I know from my own experience that only momentous events can provoke such a moment, only raw emotion can inspire such a spontaneous plea. I am often asked how long it took me to write my speech, delivered to my regiment, the Royal Irish, on the eve of the invasion of Iraq on March 19, 2003, at Fort Blair Mayne camp in the Kuwaiti desert. My answer is simple—not one moment. There was no plan; I spoke without notes. For me there was only the looming specter of actual warfare and the certainty of loss and killing, and I was speaking to myself as well as to my men. I suspect for Marie there was only the yawning black void of loss, the cavern left behind in her life caused by the loss of a son who can never be replaced.

Collins's own experience informs his understanding of what Fatayi-Williams might have been feeling. His empathy helps assure his audience that he is qualified to comment on the meaning of her speech.

What, then, can we take from this? Marie's appeal is as important as it is momentous. Her words are as free from hatred as they are free from self-interest; it is clear that no man can give her her heart's desire—her son. I was also struck by the quiet dignity of her words, the clarity of her view and the weight of her convictions. She does not condemn, she appeals; her words act as an indictment of all war and violence, not just acts of terror but also the unnecessary aggression of nation states. Her message is simple: here is a human who only wanted to give, to succeed and to make his mother proud. Where is the victory in his death? Where is the progress in his destruction? In her own words: "What inspiration can senseless slaughter provide?"

Collins examines how Marie creates her ethos, which convinces her audience of her sincerity and lack of malice.

I am certain that Marie's appeal will go down as one of the great speeches of our new century. It will give comfort to the families and friends of the dead and injured, both of this act and no doubt, regrettably, of events still to come. It should act as a caution to statesmen and leaders, a focus for public grief and, ultimately, as a challenge to, as well as a condemnation of, the perpetrators.

Collins sees Fatayi-Williams's directness as perhaps the most important aspect of her speech. She responds to historic events in a way that personalizes them and shows their human cost.

Marie is already an icon of the loss of Thursday July 7. Having travelled from Africa to find a better life, Anthony Fatayi-Williams carried the hopes and pride of his family. Now, as his mother has traveled to London, arguably one of the most cosmopolitan and integrated cities in the world, and standing nearby a wrecked icon of that city, a red double-decker bus, she has made an appeal which is as haunting as it is relevant, as poignant as it is appealing. It is a fact that such oratory as both Marie and I produced is born of momentous events, and inspired by hope and fears in equal measure.

But Marie's appeal is also important on another level. I have long urged soldiers in conflict zones to keep communicating with the population in order to be seen as people—it is easier to kill uniforms than it is to kill people. On July 7 the suicide bombers attacked icons of a society that they hated more than they loved life, the red London bus and the tube. Marie's speech has stressed the real victims' identities. They are all of us.

Marie's speech

This is Anthony, Anthony Fatayi-Williams, 26 years old, he's missing and we fear that he was in the bus explosion ... on Thursday. We don't know. We do know from the witnesses that he left the Northern line in Euston. We know he made a call to his office at Amec at 9.41 from the NW1 area to say he could not make [it] by the tube but he would find alternative means to work.

Marie Fatayi-Williams

Since then he has not made any contact with any single person. Not New York, not Madrid, not London. There has been widespread slaughter of innocent people. There have been streams of tears, innocent tears. There have been rivers of blood, innocent blood. Death in the morning, people going to find their livelihood, death in the noontime on the highways and streets.

They are not warriors. Which cause has been served? Certainly not the cause of God, not the cause of Allah because God Almighty only gives life and is full of mercy. Anyone who has been misled, or is being misled to believe that by killing innocent people he or she is serving God should think again because it's not true. Terrorism is not the way, terrorism is not the way. It doesn't beget peace. We can't deliver peace by terrorism, never can we deliver peace by killing people. Throughout history, those people who have changed the world have done so without violence, they have won people to their cause through peaceful protest. Nelson Mandela, Martin Luther King, Mahatma Gandhi, their discipline, their self-sacrifice, their conviction made people turn towards them, to follow them. What inspiration can senseless slaughter provide? Death and destruction of young people in their prime as well as old and helpless can never be the foundations for building society.

My son Anthony is my first son, my only son, the head of my family. In African society, we hold on to sons. He has dreams and hopes and I, his mother, must fight to protect them. This is now the fifth day, five days on, and we are waiting to

know what happened to him and I, his mother, I need to know what happened to Anthony. His young sisters need to know what happened, his uncles and aunties need to know what happened to Anthony, his father needs to know what happened to Anthony. Millions of my friends back home in Nigeria need to know what happened to Anthony. His friends surrounding me here, who have put this together, need to know what has happened to Anthony. I need to know, I want to protect him. I'm his mother, I will fight till I die to protect him. To protect his values and to protect his memory.

Innocent blood will always cry to God Almighty for reparation. How much blood must be spilled? How many tears shall we cry? How many mothers' hearts must be maimed? My heart is maimed. I pray I will see my son, Anthony. Why? I need to know, Anthony needs to know, Anthony needs to know, so do many other unaccounted for innocent victims, they need to know.

It's time to stop and think. We cannot live in fear because we are surrounded by hatred. Look around us today. Anthony is a Nigerian, born in London, worked in London, he is a world citizen. Here today we have Christians, Muslims, Jews, Sikhs, Hindus, all of us united in love for Anthony. Hatred begets only hatred. It is time to stop this vicious cycle of killing. We must all stand together, for our common humanity. I need to know what happened to my Anthony. He's the love of my life. My first son, my first son, 26. He tells me one day, "Mummy, I don't want to die, I don't want to die. I want to live, I want to take care of you, I will do great things for you, I will look after you, you will see what I will achieve for you. I will make you happy." And he was making me happy. I am proud of him, I am still very proud of him but I need to now where he is, I need to know what happened to him. I grieve, I am sad, I am distraught, I am destroyed.

He didn't do anything to anybody, he loved everybody so much. If what I hear is true, even when he came out of the underground he was directing people to take buses, to be sure that they were OK. Then he called his office at the same time to tell them he was running late. He was a multi-purpose person, trying to save people, trying to call his office, trying to meet his appointments. What did he then do to deserve this? Where is he, someone tell me, where is he?

Explore Current Issues

Analyzing the rhetoric of the gay marriage debate

On May 15, 2008, the California Supreme Court handed down a decision that legalized gay marriage in the state, based on the ruling that denying same-sex couples the same rights as different-sex couples was unconstitutional. Conservative and religious groups called the judges activist and liberal and accused them of bending to social and political pressure in going against the intentions of the framers of the state constitution.

Andrew Sullivan, a gay, conservative political commentator argues instead that the law *had* to adapt—the judges' apparent change of mind was not ideological but instead "empirical…based on increased knowledge of who gay people are." He continues:

> Once you absorb this knowledge, this evidence, this truth, legislative schemes which arbitrarily separate gay people from straight people—and put gay relationships in a separate and unequal box—seem grossly unfair, and certainly a violation of the equality promised in various state constitutions. I think that's what has really happened in the two decades I've been arguing about this. We have altered our view of homosexuality. And the alteration is not one of degree but of kind. And so the law must adapt. Maybe it has happened too quickly for easy cultural digestion. But it is inevitable if we are not now to replace knowledge with fear, and inclusion with, yes, prejudice.

Write about it

1. What is Sullivan's position in the debate over whether or not the California Supreme Court was right to make same-sex marriage? What are the reasons he gives to support this position?

2. What strategies other than appeals to logic does he use to build his argument? In other words, how does he appeal to his audience's values? Their emotions? How does he present himself as a credible voice for this position?

3. Why is Sullivan making this argument? What is at stake for him? What is at stake for his audience?

4. Summarize the position that Sullivan is arguing against. What is at stake for those who support this position? Does Sullivan attempt to address these concerns?

How to read analyses

Make notes as you read, either in the margins, if it is your own copy, or on paper or a computer file. Circle any words or references that you don't know and look them up.

What kind of analysis is it?	• Is it a rhetorical analysis? a literary analysis? an analysis of a visual? an analysis of an object?
Where did it come from?	• Who wrote the analysis? • What do you know about the writer's background that might have influenced the analysis?
Who is the intended audience?	• What clues do you find about whom the writer had in mind as the readers? • What does the writer assume that the readers already know about the subject? • What new knowledge is the writer providing?
What is the focus of the analysis?	• What does the writer have to say about the context or background? • What does the writer have to say about how the text or object is composed?
What is the significance of the analysis?	• Does the writer make specific claims? • What did you learn or come to understand differently by reading the analysis?
How is it composed?	• How does the writer represent herself or himself? • How would you characterize the style? • If there are any photographs or other graphics, what information do they contribute?

The Collapse of Big Media: The Young and the Restless

(ESSAY)

David T. Z. Mindich

David T. Z. Mindich, a former assignment editor at CNN, is a professor of journalism and mass communication at St. Michael's College in Colchester, Vermont, and the author of *Tuned Out: Why Americans under 40 Don't Follow the News* (2005). "The Collapse of Big Media: The Young and the Restless" was published in the *Wilson Quarterly* in spring 2005.

Return to these questions after you have finished reading.

Analyzing and Connecting

1. Mindich's essay is an audience analysis in which he concludes that "Most of the young people I interviewed had almost no measurable interest in political news." First, from your experience do you agree with Mindich's claim? If you do agree, does having no measurable interest in political news mean that young people are not interested in news in general?

2. Make a log for one entire day on all the news you read, watch, or listen to: newspapers, radio, television news broadcasts, comedy reporting of news like *The Daily Show*, comic monologues commenting on events, news flashes at the bottom of other television programs, news on the Web, blogs, and personal news sources such as email. Make notes about what the news contained, and keep track of the time you spent reading, viewing, or listening. On the next day total the time for each category. Bring your analysis to class to compare with other students' totals. Do the results for the entire class surprise you in any way?

3. Mindich speaks of the decline in newspaper readership and television news viewing as a cultural crisis. Do you believe this trend is something to worry about? Why or why not?

4. In the next-to-last paragraph, Mindich makes proposals that news should be a part of the school curriculum, high school seniors should take a civics test, and broadcasters should be required to produce a certain amount of children's news programming. Do you support these proposals? What suggestions do you have to raise the civic awareness of young people?

Finding Ideas for Writing

Watch the NBC, CBS, or ABC evening news and make a list of the ads. Then watch *The Daily Show* or another comedy news program and make a list of the ads. Write a paragraph in which you compare the lists. What can you infer about the audiences for each program from the ads? What age group is being targeted? Are men or women being targeted? What income level?

The Collapse of Big Media:
The Young and the Restless

When news executives look at the decline over the past few decades in the number of people who read or watch the news, they're scared silly. But then they reassure themselves that the kids will come around. Conventional wisdom runs that as young men and women gain the trappings of adulthood—a job, a spouse, children, and a house—they tend to pick up the news habit, too. As CBS News president Andrew Heyward declared in 2002, "Time is on our side in that as you get older, you tend to get more interested in the world around you." Unfortunately for Heyward and other news executives, the evidence suggests that young people are not picking up the news habit—not in their teens, not in their twenties, not even in their thirties.

When they aren't reassuring themselves, editors and publishers are lying awake at night thinking about the dismaying trends of recent decades. In 1972, nearly half of 18-to-22-year-olds read a newspaper every day, according to research conducted by Wolfram Peiser, a scholar who studies newspaper readership. Today, less than a quarter do. That younger people are less likely to read than their elders is of grave concern, but perhaps not surprising. In fact, the baby boomers who came of age in the 1970s are less avid news consumers than their parents were. More ominous for the future of the news media, however, is Peiser's research showing that a particular age cohort's reading habits do not change much with time; in other words, as people age, they continue the news habits of their younger days. Thus, the real danger, Peiser says, is that cohort replacement builds in a general decline in newspaper reading. The deleterious effects of this phenomenon are clearly evident: In 1972, nearly three-quarters of the 34-to-37 age group read a paper daily. Those thirtysomethings have been replaced by successive crops of thirtysomethings, each reading less than its predecessor. Today, only about a third of this group reads a newspaper every day. This means that fewer parents are bringing home a newspaper or discussing current events over dinner. And fewer kids are growing up in households in which newspapers matter.

A similar decline is evident in television news viewership. In the past decade, the median age of network television news viewers has crept up from about 50 to about 60.

Tune in to any network news show or CNN, and note the products hawked in the commercials: The pitches for Viagra, Metamucil, Depends, and Fixodent are not aimed at teenyboppers. Compounding the problem of a graying news audience is the proliferation of televisions within the typical household, which diminishes adult influence over what's watched. In 1970, six percent of all sixth graders had TVs in their bedrooms; today that number is an astonishing 77 percent. If you are in sixth grade and sitting alone in your room, you're probably not watching Peter Jennings.

One of the clearest signs of the sea change in news viewing habits was the uproar following the appearance last fall by Jon Stewart, host of *The Daily Show*, a parody of a news program, on CNN's *Crossfire*, a real one. With a median age of 34, *The Daily Show*'s audience is the envy of CNN, so when Stewart told *Crossfire*'s hosts that their show's predictable left/right approach to debates of current issues was "hurting America," one could have guessed that CNN bigwigs would pay attention. But who could have foreseen that CNN president Jonathan Klein would cancel *Crossfire*? "I agree wholeheartedly with Jon Stewart's overall premise," he told the *New York Times*. News executives are so desperate to get to consumers before the AARP does that they're willing to heed the advice of a comedian.

If the young (and not so young) are not reading newspapers or watching network television news, many assume that they are getting news online. Not so. Only 18 percent of Americans listed the Internet as a "primary news source" in a survey released earlier this year by the Pew Internet and American Life Project and the Pew Research Center for the People and the Press. And the theory that younger people are more reliant on the Internet for news than their elders doesn't hold up. Certainly an engaged minority of young people use the Net to get a lot of news, but studies show that most use it primarily for e-mailing, instant messaging, games, and other diversions. You only need to wander into a computer lab at your local college or high school and see what the students have on their screens for the dismal confirmation of these choices.

The entertainment options competing with the news for the attention of the youth audience have multiplied exponentially. In the 1960s, there were only a handful of television stations in any given market. When Walter Cronkite shook the nation by declaring in a February 1968 report on the Vietnam War that the United States was "mired in

stalemate," he spoke to a captive audience. New York City, for example, had only seven broadcast stations. At 10:30 p.m. on the night of Cronkite's remarks, channels 4 and 11 ran movies, channels 5 and 9 had discussion shows, and channel 7 was showing *N. Y. P. D.*, a cop show. In this media universe of limited competition, nearly 80 percent of all television viewers watched the nightly news, and from the late 1960s on, Cronkite won the lion's share of the total news audience. Today, young people can choose from hundreds of stations, less than a tenth of which are devoted to news. And that's not to mention the many competing diversions that weren't available in 1968, from video games to iPods. Amid this entertainment cornucopia, the combined network news viewership has shrunk significantly—from some 50 million nightly in the 1960s to about 25 million today. (In comparison, CNN's audience is minuscule, typically no more than a million or so viewers, while public television's *NewsHour with Jim Lehrer* generally reaches fewer than three million viewers.)

The effects of this diet are evident in how little Americans know about current events. True, Americans have been extremely uninformed for a long time. Most follow public affairs only in a vague way, and many don't bother to engage at all. In the 1950s and 1960s, at the height of the Cold War, a poll revealed that only 55 percent of Americans knew that East Germany was a communist country, and less than half knew that the Soviet Union was not part of NATO, report political scientists Michael X. Delli Carpini and Scott Keeter in *What Americans Know about Politics and Why It Matters* (1996). In short, there was never a golden age of informed citizenry. But in recent decades, Americans' ignorance has reached truly stupefying levels, particularly among young adults. A series of reports published over the past two decades by the Pew Research Center for the People and the Press (and its predecessor, the Times Mirror Center) suggest that young adults were once nearly as informed as their elders on a range of political issues. From 1944 to 1968, the interest of younger people in the news as reported in opinion surveys was less than five percent below that of the population at large. Political debates and elections in the 1940s, the Army-McCarthy hearings of the 1950s, and the Vietnam War in the 1960s generated as much interest among the young as among older people. But Watergate in the 1970s was the last in this series of defining events to draw general public attention. (Decades later, in 2001, the bombing of the World Trade Center towers revived general public engagement, at least for a few weeks.) Soon after Watergate, surveys began to show flagging interest in current affairs among younger people.

There is no single explanation for this sudden break. Many of the young people I spoke with in doing my research were disaffected with the political process and believed that it was completely insulated from public pressure. Why, in that case, keep up with public affairs? The blurring line between entertainment and journalism, along with corporate consolidation of big media companies, has also bred in some minds a deep skepticism about the news media's offerings. At bottom, however, the sense of community has declined as Americans are able to live increasingly isolated lives, spending long hours commuting to work and holing up in suburban homes cocooned from the rest of the world.

The failing health of the nation's news media is not only a symptom of Americans' low levels of engagement in political life. It is a threat to political life itself. "The role of the press," writes news media critic James W. Carey, "is simply to make sure that in the short run we don't get screwed." Independent, fair, and accurate reporting is what gives "We the People" our check on power. Reporters dig up corruption and confront power; they focus the public's attention on government policies and actions that are unwise, unjust, or simply ineffective. It was the news media that exposed the Watergate burglary and cover-up engineered by Richard Nixon, sparked the investigation of the Iran-Contra affair during the watch of Ronald Reagan and George H. W. Bush, ferreted out Bill Clinton's Whitewater dealings, and turned a searchlight on George W. Bush's extrajudicial arrests of American citizens suspected of terrorism.

A shrinking audience impairs the news media's ability to carry out their watchdog role. It also permits the powers that be to undermine journalism's legitimate functions. Where was the public outrage when it was revealed that the current Bush administration had secretly paid journalists to carry its water, or when the White House denied a press pass to a real journalist, Maureen Dowd of the *New York Times*, and gave one to a political hack who wrote for purely partisan outlets using a fake identity? The whole notion of the news media as the public's watchdog, once an unquestioned article of the American civic faith, is now in jeopardy. A recent study commissioned by the John S. and James L. Knight Foundation showed that more than a third of high school students feel that newspaper articles should be vetted by the federal government before publication.

If we are entering a post-journalism age—in which the majority of Americans, young and old, have little interaction with mainstream news media—the most valuable thing we are losing is the marketplace of ideas that newspapers and news broadcasts uniquely provide, that place where views clash and the full range of democratic choices is debated. You usually don't get that on a blog. You don't get that in the left-leaning *Nation* or on right-wing talk shows. But any newspaper worth its salt, and there are plenty, presents a variety of views, including ones antithetical to its editorial page positions. These papers are hardly immune from criticism—they sometimes err, get sloppy, or succumb to partisan or ideological bias—but they do strive to be accurate and independent sources of fact and opinion, and more often than not they fulfill that indispensable public function.

America's newspapers and television news divisions aren't going to save themselves by competing with reality shows and soap operas. The appetite for news, and for engagement with civic life itself, must be nurtured and promoted, and it's very much in the public interest to undertake the task. It's not the impossible assignment it may seem. During the course of my research, I met a group of boys in New Orleans who were very unlikely consumers of news: They were saturated with television programs and video games, they were poor, and they were in eighth grade. Yet they were all reading the *New York Times* online. Why? Because one of their teachers had assigned the newspaper to them to read when they were in sixth grade, and the habit stuck. There's no reason why print and broadcast news shouldn't be a bigger part of the school curriculum, or why there shouldn't be a short civics/current affairs section on the SAT for college-bound students, or why all high school seniors shouldn't have to take a nonbinding version of the civics test given to immigrants who want to become U.S. citizens. And why shouldn't broadcasters be required to produce a certain amount of children's news programming in return for their access to the public airwaves? These are only the most obvious possibilities.

Reporters, editors, producers, and media business executives will all need to make their own adjustments to meet the demands of new times and new audiences, but only by reaching a collective judgment about the value and necessity of vigorous news media in American democracy can we hope to keep our public watchdogs on guard and in good health.

Volkswagen Beetle

(PRODUCT DESIGN)

The Volkswagen Type 1, better known as the Beetle or Bug, is the most produced car in history. From 1938 until the last original Beetle came off an assembly line in Puebla, Mexico, over twenty-one million were built. The Beetle began in Nazi Germany, when Adolf Hitler commissioned Ferdinand Porsche to produce a car for common people. Only a handful were produced before World War II started in 1939. Volkswagen was soon back in production after the war, and by 1954, the number of Beetles passed a million. Volkswagen began shipping cars to the United States at a time when American cars were big and boxy. The VW Beetle was just the opposite—small and rounded, inexpensive, and three times as fuel efficient. Beetles dominated the small-car market until Japanese imports showed up in large numbers in the mid-1970s.

More than the story of a car, however, the Beetle demonstrates how what we buy reflects cultural attitudes and values.

Return to these questions after you have finished reading.

Analyzing and Connecting

1. Volkswagen ads in the United States in the 1960s appealed to simplicity—simple shape, simple technology—which grew out of long-standing American values of honesty, economy, and lack of pretense. Look at automobile ads today, both in print and on television. What values do they appeal to?

2. Your campus may have a building that is better known by a nickname than its official name. Is the building liked or disliked by students? How does the nickname change the image of the building? For example, is it more friendly or less friendly?

3. Look up the word *bug* in the *Oxford English Dictionary*, which traces the histories of words. Your library has the print OED and may allow access through the library's Web site. How has the meaning of *bug* changed over time? Think about how *bug* is used today. For example, a common saying among computer programmers is "It's not a bug, it's a feature." Identify examples of other words such as *pimp* that have changed meanings in recent years.

4. Think of other products that we find cute and lovable. What makes them cute and lovable? Does advertising promote these associations?

Finding Ideas for Writing

The Volkswagen Beetle has a complicated and dark history. What values from the car's conceptualization were carried over into the advertising you see here? How were the negative historical associations downplayed or erased? How do today's advertisements for Volkswagen cars compare? Write a paragraph describing the associations the brand has now, and how these relate (or not relate) to the car's history.

VOLKSWAGEN BEETLE

When Adolf Hitler became Chancellor of Germany in 1933, he declared that a centerpiece of Nazism would be the motorization of the country. He asked Ferdinand Porsche to design a car that would be affordable for everyone.

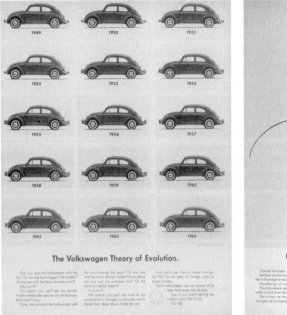

Clever advertising helped make the Beetle a hit in the 1960s. The American advertising firm Doyle Dane Bernbach (DDB) began a campaign in 1959 that emphasized the differences between the Beetle and bulky American cars that changed designs yearly.

In 1968, Walt Disney's *The Love Bug* created a new generation of Beetle fans and led to a series of *Herbie* sequels.

Beetles became part of the counterculture of the 1960s. Many were hand-painted and customized in various ways, even adding fins that mocked American cars.

Misery has enough company.
Dare to be happy.

In 1998 Volkswagen launched the New Beetle, which benefited from the lovable image of the original Beetle.

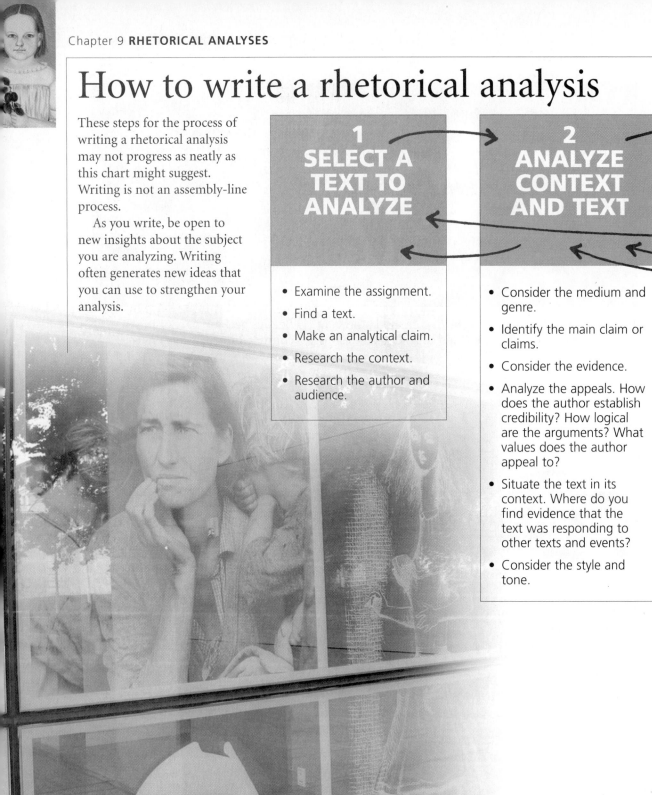

How to write a rhetorical analysis

These steps for the process of writing a rhetorical analysis may not progress as neatly as this chart might suggest. Writing is not an assembly-line process.

As you write, be open to new insights about the subject you are analyzing. Writing often generates new ideas that you can use to strengthen your analysis.

1 SELECT A TEXT TO ANALYZE

- Examine the assignment.
- Find a text.
- Make an analytical claim.
- Research the context.
- Research the author and audience.

2 ANALYZE CONTEXT AND TEXT

- Consider the medium and genre.
- Identify the main claim or claims.
- Consider the evidence.
- Analyze the appeals. How does the author establish credibility? How logical are the arguments? What values does the author appeal to?
- Situate the text in its context. Where do you find evidence that the text was responding to other texts and events?
- Consider the style and tone.

3 WRITE A DRAFT

- Briefly describe the text you are analyzing. Name the author and give information about when and where the text was published or delivered.

- Make a claim about the text.

- Analyze the context. Discuss what motivated the author to write and the author's purpose. Describe the original audience and their attitudes. Place the text in the larger "conversation" that was occurring at the time.

- Analyze the text. Identify the main claim. Analyze appeals to ethos, logos, and pathos.

- Consider your voice and tone.

- Choose a title that will interest readers.

4 REVISE, REVISE, REVISE

- Check that your paper or project fulfills the assignment.

- Make sure your analysis has a clear focus and claim.

- Check that each point of your analysis is supported with evidence.

- Make sure your voice and tone will engage readers.

- Examine your organization and think of possible better ways to organize.

5 SUBMITTED VERSION

- Make sure your finished writing meets all formatting requirements.

1: Select a text to analyze

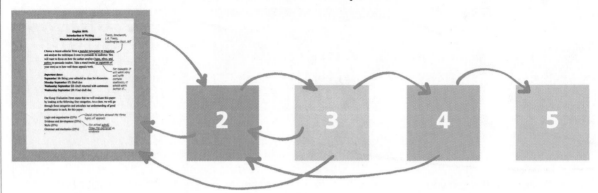

Examine the assignment	• Read your assignment slowly and carefully. Look for the key words *analyze* or *critique*. These key words tell you that you are writing an analysis.
	• Make a note of any information about the length specified, date due, formatting, and other requirements. You can attend to this information later. At this point you want to zero in on the subject and your analytical claim.
Find a text to analyze	• Look for a text or image that offers an argument or opinion—one that tries to influence the thoughts, feelings, or actions of its audience.
	• Newspaper editorials, activist Web sites, speeches, art, and advertisements are all good sources of texts for analysis.
Make an analytical claim	• Ask: What will my analysis reveal for readers that they might not otherwise have realized about the text?
	• Think about the evidence you will need to support your claim. It may come from the text itself, or from your research into the piece's context.
Research the context	• What else was being written and said about this subject at the time the text was written?
	• What events were taking place that might have influenced the author?
Research the author and audience	• Who is the author? What else has he or she said on this subject? What motivated him or her to produce this text?
	• Who is the audience? Where did the text first appear (or, why was this image made or created)? Why did it appear at that particular moment?

Find a verbal text to analyze

Find at least three examples of verbal texts that intend to persuade you in some way. They may ask you to do something specific such as buy a product or vote for a candidate or else they may aim at changing your attitude. Note what makes each text interesting and make a tentative claim.

Text	Deadspin.com blog
What makes it interesting	Takes a humorous look at sports, exposing the pretensions and lack of honesty among sports figures.
Claim	Deadspin.com represents the spirit of many blogs in going for the truth underneath layers of hype and having fun along the way.

Find a visual text to analyze

Identify at least three visual texts for possible analysis. Look for a visual text that in some way attempts to influence the viewer—an advertisement, a public building, a statue, a controversial work of art, a dramatic photograph, a television commercial, a corporate logo, and so on. Note what makes it interesting and make a tentative claim.

Text	Logos of competing political candidates
What makes it interesting	Candidate X's logo appears much better than candidate Y's logo among people I have asked, but they cannot explain why.
Claim	Candidate X has a better logo than candidate Y because the type-face and colors of X's logo express strength, energy, and movement while those on Y's logo suggest indecision and weakness.

Writer at work

Kelsey Turner was asked to write a rhetorical analysis for her composition class. She made the following notes and observations on her assignment sheet:

English 1010:

Introduction to Writing

Rhetorical Analysis of an Argument

Times, Newsweek, L.A. Times, Washington Post, NYT

Choose a recent editorial from a popular newspaper or magazine and analyze the techniques it uses to persuade its audience. You will want to focus on how the author employs logos, ethos, and pathos to persuade readers. Take a stand (make an argument of your own) as to how well these appeals work.

For example: It will work very well with certain audience; it would work better if...

Important dates:

September 10: Bring your editorial to class for discussion.

Monday September 17: Draft due

Wednesday September 22: Draft returned with comments

Wednesday September 29: Final draft due

Our Essay Evaluation Form states that we will evaluate this paper by looking at the following four categories. As a class, we will go through these categories and articulate our understanding of good performance in each, for this paper:

Logic and organization (25%)

Evidence and development (25%)

Style (25%)

Grammar and mechanics (25%)

Could structure around the three types of appeals

Use actual words from the editorial as evidence

Kelsey found a *Washington Post* opinion piece on food banks and poverty that interested her (see pages 305–309 to read the full essay). She began by asking the questions she would need to answer to write a good rhetorical analysis (see page 154). Here are the questions and her responses:

<u>What is the author's purpose?</u>
—To make readers re-think their "generous" donations to food banks, and look at causes of hunger.

<u>Who is the audience?</u>
— Readers of Washington Post (nationwide distribution). People concerned with hunger and poverty. People who usually make gestures rather than really working for change?

<u>Who is the author?</u>
— He worked at a food bank, was very successful, became disillusioned. He understands the problem better than most people.

<u>What is the background?</u>
— It was published right before Thanksgiving, when people are thinking about having enough food as an American tradition.

<u>Which rhetorical appeals are used?</u>
— All three:

- Pathos—Appeals to readers' sympathy for those who are hungry. Describes fatigue of donors and volunteers with current system. Makes volunteering and donating seem foolish and possibly harmful.

- Ethos—His background. He assumes readers will agree that it is better to empower people and that we shouldn't patronize them just to make ourselves feel generous.

- Logos— Paints the bigger picture of poverty, of which hunger is just one part. But he goes back and forth between saying maybe food is given to people who don't need it, and then saying the more food we give, the more people need it. It seems like the meaning of "need" changes.

The pathos appeals are the strongest and most noticeable, but the ethos of the author probably works the best to persuade people.
<u>How does the language and style contribute to the purpose?</u>
— Words like "play," and "pep rally," are associated with frivolous activities. They belittle the actions of food pantry workers and donors. Author makes food-givers feel kind of stupid or self-interested and short-sighted. Like they are making the problem worse. Blaming them, almost.

2: Analyze context and text

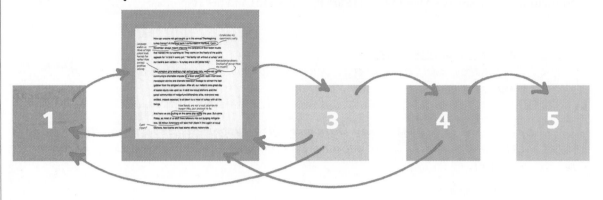

Consider the medium and genre	• What is the medium? • What is the genre of the piece? Is it an editorial? a speech? an advertisement?
Consider the main claim or claims	• Summarize the claim, or describe the subject.
Consider the evidence	• Note all the reasons and evidence given to support the claim.
Analyze the appeals	• How is the author presented? As a credible, trustworthy person? • How logical are the arguments? Are there any logical fallacies? • What emotions, if any, does the author appeal to? • How effective is each one of these appeals and techniques? How effective are they all together? Why are they effective or not effective?
Situate the text in its context	• Where do you find evidence that this text was responding to other texts and events? • What does this text contribute to the ongoing conversation of which it is part?
Consider the style and tone	• How would you characterize the style? Is the style formal? informal? academic? • How would you characterize the tone? Does the writer or speaker use humor or satire? • How is language used to influence the audience? repetition? contrast? particular word choices? What metaphors are used?

Writer at work

Kelsey Turner read her chosen editorial carefully several times, making notes in the margins about the rhetorical appeals she saw being used.

Establishes his experiences early.

How can anyone not get caught up in the annual Thanksgiving turkey frenzy? At the food bank I co-founded in Hartford, Conn.,

Language makes us think of high school kids having fun rather than serious problem solving.

November always meant cheering the caravans of fowl-laden trucks that roared into our parking lot. They came on the heels of the public appeals for "A bird in every pot," "No family left without a turkey" and our bank's own version -- "A turkey and a 20 [dollar bill]."

Manipulating donors (Instead of giving them the truth?)

Like pompom girls leading a high school pep rally, we revved up the community's charitable impulse to a fever pitch with radio interviews, newspaper stories and dramatic television footage to extract the last gobbler from the stingiest citizen. After all, our nation's one great day of social equity was upon us. In skid row soup kitchens and the gated communities of hedge-fund billionaires alike, everyone was entitled, indeed expected, to sit down to a meal of turkey with all the fixings.

Food banks are not a real solution to hunger—they just pretend to be.

And here we are, putting on the same play again this year. But come Friday, as most of us stuff more leftovers into our bulging refrigerators, 35 million Americans will take their place in line again at soup

Exact figure?

kitchens, food banks and food stamp offices nationwide.

Finally, Kelsey developed a position that could serve as a working thesis for her paper:

Mark Winne's essay gives good reasons for readers to stop supporting the food banking industry, but the belittling tone he uses to describe food bank donors and workers may insult or offend readers, making them less likely to agree with him.

3: Write a draft

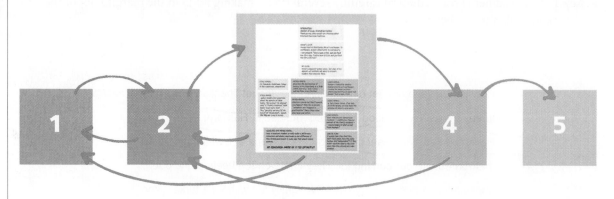

Briefly describe the text you are analyzing	• Describe the medium and genre (newspaper editorial, blog on the Web, radio interview, and so on). • Who produced it? Where and when did it first appear?
Make a claim	• Analysis adds a new dimension to a text; what will your analysis reveal for readers? Be sure your claim is not an over-generalization and can be supported by textual and contextual evidence.
Analyze the context	• Through research find out what else was being said about the subject your text discusses. • Track down any references to other texts or events.
Analyze the text	• Select the most important parts of the text to focus on. Choose elements that will show a pattern or illustrate specific techniques you want to talk about. However, be honest: do not leave out evidence that might undercut your claims. • Build a critical mass of evidence. Supply the evidence and examples to support your claim. • Make larger patterns or contrasts visible for your readers. For example, does an author seem to be appealing to two different audiences in a single essay? What parts of the work appeal to one audience? What parts appeal to the other?
Build a strong conclusion	• Don't merely summarize what you have already said. Ask yourself "Have I learned anything new in this analysis?" A conclusion can be a good place to succinctly describe a larger pattern you have been tracing in a work. Or, it may be a good place to make conjectures about other works by the same artist, about the motivations of a school or movement, or to tie your analysis of this text to other texts.

Writer at work

Kelsey used sticky notes to determine the best structure for her paper. She grouped them in different categories and changed their order until she was satisfied with the basic structure for her first draft.

INTRODUCTION
Context of essay: Printed just before Thanksgiving, when people are thinking about food and American tradition.

WINNE'S CLAIM:
Giving food to food banks doesn't end hunger. To end hunger, people should work to end poverty.

- Use proverb: " Give a man a fish, and you feed him for a day. Teach a man to fish, and you feed him for a lifetime."

MY CLAIM:
Winne's argument makes sense, but some of his appeals will probably do more to alienate readers than convince them.

ETHOS APPEAL:
Co-founded a food bank (shows he has experience, compassion)

ETHOS APPEAL:
makes readers feel suspicious about the motives of food banks. The system's "co-dependency" is "frankly troubling." Food banks "must curry favor . . ." They "carefully nurture [d] the belief" of "doing good"— sounds like they are lying to people.

PATHOS APPEAL:
describes the distribution of turkeys at his food bank as a "high school pep rally," and a "play," making them seem frivolous

PATHOS APPEAL:
volunteers giving out food "seemed even happier" than the recipients. . . Volunteers are "trapped in . . . gratification." Makes them seem delusional and selfish.

LOGOS APPEAL:
Hunger is caused by poverty. Ending poverty will end hunger. Feeding the hungry without addressing poverty will never end hunger. "Give a man a fish . . .

LOGOS APPEAL:
In fact, Winne claims, if we only feed the hungry, we may make the problem of poverty even worse.

LOGOS APPEAL:
"more than 275,000 Connecticut residents -- slightly less than 8.6 percent of the state's residents -- remain hungry or what we call 'food insecure.'"

CONCLUDES WITH PATHOS APPEAL:
tries to motivate readers to really make a difference. Volunteers and donors could make a real difference if they forced government to make laws that would reduce poverty.

MY CONCLUSION: MAYBE HE IS TOO OPTIMISTIC?

LOGICAL FLAW:
If people take free food they don't really need, have they really become less "independent"? If they didn't need the food in the first place then they already are independent.

4: Revise, revise, revise

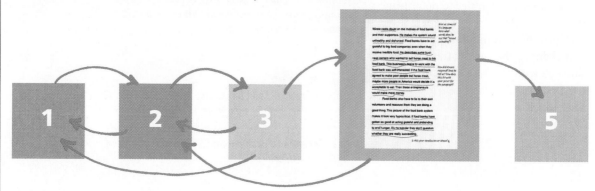

Skilled writers know that the secret to writing well is rewriting. Leave correcting errors for last.

Does your paper or project meet the assignment?	• Look again at your assignment. Does your paper or project do what the assignment asks? • Check the assignment for specific guidelines, including length, format, and amount of research. Does your work meet these guidelines?
Does your analysis have a clear purpose?	• Does it tell readers something they would not have otherwise noticed? • Do you make some kind of claim about the work you are analyzing? Is it a debatable claim?
Do you support your analysis with evidence?	• Do you provide a background about the author, intended audience, and the larger conversation surrounding the text you are analyzing? • Can you provide additional analysis to support your claims?
Is your organization effective?	• Is the order of your main points clear to your reader? • Are there any places where you find abrupt shifts or gaps? • Are there sections or paragraphs that could be rearranged to make your draft more effective?
Is the writing project visually effective?	• Is the font attractive and readable? • Are the headings and visuals effective?
Save the editing for last.	• When you have finished revising, edit and proofread carefully.

A peer review guide is on page 27.

Writer at work

Kelsey Turner received comments from her instructor on her draft. She used these comments to revise her draft.

Kelsey's instructor encouraged her to use Winne's own words instead of summarizing them

Kelsey found several points in her paper where she had included information that did not directly advance her argument. Some of these points could be moved to other sections of the paper where they fit better; others she removed entirely

Kelsey received specific feedback on an important aspect of her analysis: the shifts back and forth between her voice and Winne's. To see how she distinguished her ideas from Winne's see her submitted draft on page 328.

Winne casts doubt on the motives of food banks and their supporters. He makes the system sound unhealthy and dishonest. Food banks have to act grateful to big food companies even when they receive inedible food. He describes some business owners who wanted to sell horse meat to his food bank. This business's desire to work with the food bank was self-interested: if the food bank agreed to make poor people eat horse meat, maybe more people in America would decide it is acceptable to eat. Then these entrepreneurs would make more money.

Food banks also have to lie to their own volunteers and reassure them they are doing a good thing. This picture of the food bank system makes it look very hypocritical. If food banks have gotten so good at acting grateful and pretending to end hunger, it's no wonder they don't question whether they are really succeeding.

Give us some of his language here—what words does he use that "sound unhealthy"?

How did Winnie respond? Does he tell us? How does this fit with your point for the paragraph?

Is this your conclusion or Winne's?

5: Submitted version

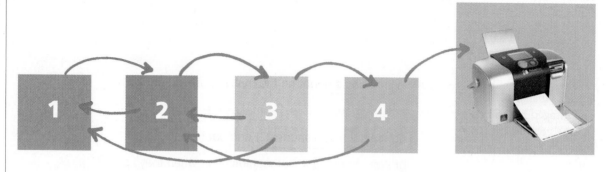

Kelsey Turner

Turner 1

Professor Perez

English 1010

29 September 2008

Biting the Hands That Feed America

Mark Winne's Thanksgiving 2007 article in the *Washington Post*, "When Handouts Keep Coming, the Food Line Never Ends," makes readers re-think their "generous" donations to food banks and pantries. Winne calls our attention instead to poverty, which causes hunger, and challenges us to end hunger by ending poverty. This challenge makes sense. After all, most of us have heard the proverb, "Give a man a fish, and you feed him for a day. Teach a man to fish, and you feed him for a lifetime." However, Winne's tone in his essay works against the logic of his argument. Even though he is a compassionate person who has spent much of his life working to feed the poor, the language he uses belittles the people who want to help. He tries to motivate readers, but he does this partly by making them feel ashamed of themselves. His frustration with the food bank system is understandable, but taking it out on casual readers diminishes sympathy for him and his cause.

Winne begins by mentioning that he co-founded a food bank in Hartford, Connecticut, which establishes a strong ethos for his argument, letting his readers

know that Winne has experience with the system he is going to criticize. If anyone should know what works and doesn't work in food-banking, it is the people who structure and run the food banks. He also establishes his compassion for the plight of the poor and hungry. Furthermore, Winne says he wants to empower the poor, not just feed them. Because America has a long tradition of self-reliant citizens who can take care of themselves, promoting self-reliance should sound like a worthy goal to most readers. Because we are a democracy, we want our citizens to be strong and self-supporting, not just well-fed.

Winne makes a simple, logical argument: Hunger is caused by poverty. Ending poverty will end hunger. Feeding the hungry without addressing poverty will never end hunger. In fact, Winne claims, if we only feed the hungry, we may make the problem of poverty even worse.

Winne uses statistics to support his case. Despite his best efforts, and those of other food bank workers, he tells us, "more than 275,000 Connecticut residents—slightly less than 8.6 percent of the state's residents—remain hungry or what we call 'food insecure.'" After Thanksgiving, "35 million Americans will take their place in line again at soup kitchens, food banks and food stamp offices nationwide." We learn that families on food stamps only receive three dollars per person per day. These numbers make a compelling appeal to our sense of logic and reason. The problem is not going away. The government's response to hunger is inadequate. Anyone who can read the *Washington Post* is smart enough to know that a three-dollar food budget might buy enough French fries to keep you alive, but it wouldn't keep you healthy for very long.

A flaw undercuts his argument, however, when he describes a scene which made him realize the "futility" of food banks: "No one made any attempt to determine whether the recipients actually needed the food, nor to encourage the recipients to seek other forms of assistance, such as food stamps." Winne implies that some of the people taking the food didn't really need it, but just took it because it was free. The lines of people grew longer, leading Winne to observe, "It may have been that a donor-recipient co-dependency had developed. Both parties were trapped in an ever-expanding web of

immediate gratification that offered the recipients no long-term hope of eventually achieving independence and self-reliance." If people take free food even though they don't need it, have they really become less "independent"? The fact that they didn't need the food in the first place means they already *are* independent.

Most people accept free things from time to time, but doing so doesn't automatically make us less self-reliant. Winne explains what he sees as a cause-and-effect problem—too much free food causing people to depend upon more free food—by quoting another food bank director: "The more you provide, the more demand there is." However, demand isn't the same thing as need. People may want free food, and take it when it is offered. They may even "demand" more of it when they don't get what they are expecting. But that's not the same as really needing it. Winne uses "demand" and "need" interchangeably, but he doesn't explain how people go from accepting free food they don't need, to needing free food. Do they get so used to receiving free food that they quit their jobs on the assumption that they don't need to earn money for food? Does free food make them eat more? Maybe there is some way free food can cause dependence, but Winne doesn't explain this process, and it's clearly not logical to assume that free food always makes people less self-reliant.

Winne's article was published on the Sunday before Thanksgiving when readers would be reminded of the American tradition of plentiful food. Likely many would feel sympathy for the hungry and possibly want to do something to help; however, Winne belittles and insults the generous impulses of donors and volunteers. He describes the distribution of turkeys at his food bank as a "high school pep rally" and a "play," making them seem like frivolous activities that make no real difference. This language is sure to make readers think twice before they give a turkey to their local food bank. Winne even makes them feel selfish for wanting to help. He says the volunteers giving out food "seemed even happier" than the recipients. He describes their charity as an "act of faith," and says they are "fortified by the belief that their act of benevolence was at least mildly appreciated." Like the recipients of the food, Winne says, the volunteers are "trapped in an ever-expanding web of immediate gratification." Winne makes feeding the hungry seem like a selfish act rather than an act of charity.

Winne attempts to make readers suspicious about the motives of food banks and their supporters. He says the system's "co-dependency" is "frankly troubling." Food banks "must curry favor with the nation's food industry, which often regards food banks as a waste-management tool." Food banks keep their own volunteers "dependent on carefully nurtured belief that they are 'doing good' by 'feeding the hungry.'" This assertion renders volunteers as dupes for large corporations who have their own motives for supporting food banks. The hypocrisy of the food bank system is what prevents people who want to help from asking "if this is the best way to end hunger, food insecurity and their root cause, poverty."

Winne concludes by trying to motivate readers to really make a difference. All the energy poured into food banks by volunteers and donors could make a real difference, he feels, if it were used to force government to make policies that would reduce poverty. One the one hand, Winne's call to action appears unrealistic given that politicians largely ignore poverty because it is not an issue that stirs voters. On the other hand, Winne does effectively contrast the power of volunteers, who could "dismantle the Connecticut state capitol brick by brick " with his earlier descriptions of the fatigue and frustration of the current system. He at least gets us to think about food banks in a way other than a feel-good story on the evening news at Thanksgiving.

Work Cited

Winne, Mark. "When Handouts Keep Coming, the Food Line Never Ends." *Washington Post* 18 Nov. 2007. late ed.: B1. Print.

Projects

Analyzing is valuable for clarifying and developing your own thinking as well as for giving your readers a broader understanding.

These projects are frequently written kinds of analyses.

Rhetorical analysis

Select a text to analyze—a speech, a sermon, an editorial, a persuasive letter, an essay, a Web site, a pamphlet, a brochure, or another kind of text.

Explain briefly what kind of text it is, when and where it was first published or spoken, and its main argument.

Make a claim about the text, which you support with close analysis.

Analyze the context. Is the text part of a larger debate? What other texts or events does it respond to? Who is the author? What motivated the author to write this text? What can you infer about the intended audience?

Analyze the appeals. What appeals to values and emotions are used? What appeals to logic are used? Do you find any logical fallacies (see pages 14–15)? Do you trust the writer?

Analyze the organization and style. What are the major parts and how are they arranged? Is the style formal, informal, satirical, or something else? Are any metaphors used?

Visual analysis

Find a visual text to analyze. You might analyze a popular consumer product, a public building, advertising, art, or a map.

Make a claim about the visual text. Support your claim with close analysis. Describe key features.

Analyze the context. Where and when was the visual created? What was the purpose? Who created it? What can you infer about the intended audience?

Analyze the visual text. What kind of visual is it? What is the medium? How is it arranged? How would you characterize the style? Are any words connected?

Critical literary analysis

Read carefully a short story or other literary text. Map out the plot. What is the conflict and how is it resolved?

Examine the characterization, including the major and minor characters. Characters are not real people, but instead they are constructed for a purpose. What role does each character perform? The setting too is a character. What role does the setting play in the story?

Consider the point of view. Does a character tell the story? Or is the narrator an all-knowing observer? Describe the language, style, and tone of the story. Identify any important images, symbols, and metaphors.

Identify the story's central theme. How does the title of the story relate to the theme?

Write an arguable thesis that connects one or more elements—characters, setting, language, metaphors, and so on—to the overall theme. A paper that begins with an engaging thesis arouses the reader's interest. Support your thesis with evidence from the text. A successful paper shares a discovery with the reader.

10 Causal Analyses

An effective causal analysis moves beyond the obvious to examine complex underlying causes.

CHAPTER CONTENTS

Writing to analyze causes

Have you ever wondered why your car is hard to start on a cold morning? Why all the shoppers in the supermarket seem to converge on the checkout stands at the same time? Why a company's stock price rises when it announces hundreds of layoffs?

Questions of causation confront us all the time. We spend much of our daily lives puzzling over them—trying to start the car, pick the best time to visit the supermarket, or buy the most valuable stock. Causal investigation also drives scientists, as they search for cures to diseases, to try to explain certain behaviors in people and animals, and attempt to predict the weather.

Answering these kinds of questions requires a causal analysis, which typically takes the form "SOMETHING causes (or does not cause) SOMETHING ELSE."

Understand how causal arguments work

Causal arguments take three basic forms.

FORM 1

One cause leads to **one or more effects.**

EXAMPLE

The invention of the telegraph led to the commodities market, the establishment of standard time zones, and news reporting as we know it today.

FORM 2

One effect has **several causes.**

EXAMPLE

Hurricanes are becoming more financially destructive to the United States because of the greater intensity of recent storms, an increase in the commercial and residential development of coastal areas, and a reluctance to enforce certain construction standards in coastal residential areas.

FORM 3

Something causes something to happen, which in turn causes something else to happen.

EXAMPLE

Making the HPV vaccination mandatory for adolescent girls will make unprotected sex seem safer, leading to greater promiscuity and resulting in more teenage pregnancies.

Methods of analyzing causes

Causal analyses can be challenging to write because any topic worth writing about is likely to be complex. Causes can be hard to identify, and there may be more than one cause behind any given phenomenon. The philosopher John Stuart Mill (1806–1873) developed four different methods for finding causes.

1 The Common Factor Method	If you look at all the cases of a phenomenon, and find a single factor that is common to all of them, that common factor is probably the cause. For example, if a number of people in your dormitory all develop symptoms of food poisoning, and it turns out they all ate the potato salad from the cafeteria salad bar the night before, the potato salad is probably the cause of their illness.
2 The Single Difference Method	This method is useful when you have two similar situations, with only one leading to an effect. Look for something that was present in one case and not the other. It is commonly used in scientific experiments under controlled conditions. You might grow a group of identical soybean plants, for example, giving them all equal amounts of light and water, but only feeding fertilizer to half of them. If the fertilized plants grow faster, the fertilizer is probably the cause.
3 Concomitant Variation	This method is also frequently used by scientists, especially when they cannot completely control the conditions they are observing. Investigators look for a similar pattern of variation between a possible cause and a possible effect. If you give different amounts of fertilizer to each soybean plant in the example, and the plants getting the most fertilizer grow the tallest, while the ones getting the least stay the smallest, a causal relationship between fertilizer and accelerated growth is likely.
4 The Process of Elimination	The more complex the set of causes behind a phenomenon, the more likely you are to use the process of elimination. Let's return to the soybean plants from the earlier example. You are fairly certain that adding fertilizer to the plants causes them to grow faster. Yet you notice that some plants have developed spots on their leaves. Some of the spotted plants get a lot of fertilizer, and some only get a little, but they all have a similar number of leaf spots, so the fertilizer is probably not the cause. Upon further investigation, you find that an absentminded professor has been emptying the remains of his diet soda into the spotted plants' pots every evening. Even though conditions among the spotted plants are not identical, it is reasonable to infer that the soda is causing the spotting. It is the only factor "left over" after you have accounted for all the others' impact on the plants.

Which method should I use?

You can use more than one of Mill's methods to evaluate possible causes. For example, the common factor and single difference methods are often combined: If everyone in your dorm who got sick had eaten the potato salad and the fruit cocktail, you would have to find someone who ate the fruit cocktail, but not the potato salad, to determine which food was the cause of illness. If anyone who ate fruit cocktail stayed healthy, you can eliminate it as a possible cause and focus on the potato salad.

Keys to causal analysis

Pay attention to effects

It's not enough to simply identify causes. In order for a causal analysis to matter, you must make clear why the effects are important. Otherwise, readers are apt to ask, "So what?" We often look for causes so that we can prevent something bad from happening, or facilitate something good. You may make the case that the film versions of *101 Dalmatians* led to an increase in the popularity of Dalmatian dogs, but your analysis gains more stature if you further explore that effect: many of the puppies bred and sold to people who saw the movie ended up in animal shelters because their new owners were not prepared for such high-energy pets.

Identify what is at stake

Because a strong causal claim may inspire people to change policies or behaviors or take other action, you will find that some members of your audience hold different stakes in the outcome of your analysis. Their stakes can influence the ways, and the degree to which, they oppose your claim. For example, although the causal link between cigarette smoke and cancer was widely accepted in scientific circles for many years, tobacco companies argued vociferously that no such link existed.

Move beyond the obvious to identify underlying causes

When people are involved, you can expect causes to be complex. Perhaps the cause you are seeking to link to an effect is only one of several causes. You'll need to address all the contributing causes, not just the one you are focusing on. A well-thought-out causal analysis will trace multiple causes and consider their cumulative effect.

Avoid mistaking correlation for causations

A common pitfall of causal analysis is confusing causation with correlation. Events can be correlated, or mutually related in some way, without one being the cause of the other. Deaths by drowning and baseball games are correlated. But does one cause the other? Or is it because both occur most frequently in the summer?

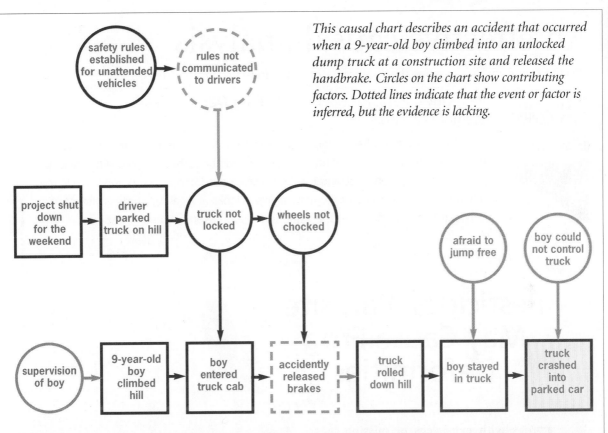

This causal chart describes an accident that occurred when a 9-year-old boy climbed into an unlocked dump truck at a construction site and released the handbrake. Circles on the chart show contributing factors. Dotted lines indicate that the event or factor is inferred, but the evidence is lacking.

Working Together

Find causes

In a group of three or four students

Brainstorm to create a list of "Why?" questions about causes. Your list might include questions such as "Why is the sky blue?" or "Why do music CDs cost $15 when DVDs of entire films, with director's cuts, outtakes, and other extras only cost $19?" Try to come up with at least ten or fifteen questions.

Working together, come up with as many possible causes for each phenomenon as you can. Use your imagination, but stay within the realm of possibility. You might want to arrange your responses from the most plausible to the least plausible.

An effective causal analysis

Effective causal analyses examine the significance of cause-and-effect relationships.

Pesticides, Parasite May Cause Frog Deformities
Stentor Danielson

Over the past ten to fifteen years, more and more frogs have been discovered with deformed, missing, or extra hind legs. Concerned about these abnormalities, scientists worldwide have been searching for the cause. In this *National Geographic* article from July 2002, science journalist Stentor Danielson looks at a careful study of the interplay between two potential causes: a waterborne parasite and common pesticides.

Pesticides, Parasite May Cause Frog Deformities

Frogs with extra legs or missing legs have been showing up with greater frequency over the past decade, and scientists have been baffled by the cause.

Some researchers have concluded that pesticide runoff from farms is to blame; others say a common parasite is the culprit. Now, a new study suggests that both these factors in combination have disturbed normal development in many frogs, leading to the abnormalities.

The study, published today in the *Proceedings of the National Academy of Sciences*, was based on tests in both the laboratory and the field that were designed to examine the interaction of parasites and pesticides. The research team, led by Joseph Kiesecker, found that only frogs infected by the larvae of a parasite, the trematode worm, developed deformities, but infected frogs exposed to pesticide runoff experienced much higher levels of deformities.

Danielson begins by briefly laying out the problem and by explaining how his article will add to previous discussions: new research indicates that two potential causes need to be considered together in order to get a clear picture of what is happening.

"It is not uncommon now for 20 to 30 percent of the frogs at many locations to have limb deformities," said Kiesecker, an assistant professor of biology at Penn State University.

Abnormalities have been documented in 52 species of amphibians, mainly frogs, in 46 U.S. states and four Canadian provinces, according to the U.S. Geological Survey. Reports of deformed frogs have been particularly common in New England and the Upper Midwest and on the Pacific coast.

Although there is some disagreement about what levels of deformities occur naturally in frog populations, most researchers agree that current levels are above normal.

Kiesecker and other researchers have warned that the physiological problems seen in frogs may foreshadow similar effects on humans.

Statistics provide a sense of the scope of the phenomenon. Notice the use of a government source for this information—sources which are usually credible and respected by readers.

Infected by Trematodes

During its life cycle, the parasitic trematode depends on several hosts, including pond snails. Tadpoles in ponds with snails pick up trematode larvae, called cercariae. In some cases the cercariae develop into hard cysts, which interfere with the tadpole's metamorphosis into a frog. When the cysts occur in tissue that later develops into legs, the cysts disrupt the animal's normal development and cause duplicate or missing legs.

At the end of this introductory section, Danielson places an important point about the issue: it could directly affect humans.

The trematode also affects people—although not so dramatically as in developing frogs. It's the same parasite that causes "swimmer's itch," a common ailment in people who swim in ponds and lakes. Eventually, the human immune system defeats the cercariae, leaving the victim with just a rash.

Details about one of the causes are explained step-by-step.

Pesticides, Parasite May Cause Frog Deformities

In tropical climates trematodes cause schistosomiasis, a disease that kills millions of people. The World Health Organization estimates that 120 million people worldwide suffer from schistosomiasis.

Kiesecker's team took tadpoles from Centre County, Pennsylvania, and placed them in six local ponds—three affected by pesticide runoff and three pesticide-free. In each pond, the tadpoles were separated into two groups. One group was placed inside a fine mesh that kept out cercariae.

Only the tadpoles that were exposed to cercariae developed deformities. "We learned from the first field experiment that tadpoles have to be exposed to trematode infection for limb deformities to develop," Kiesecker said.

Danielson explains how an experiment was designed to isolate possible causes of the limb mutations.

Pesticide Problems

Kiesecker's team then compared the rate of infection between trematode-exposed tadpoles in the different ponds. The team discovered that rates of infection were much higher in the ponds that received pesticide runoff.

This result parallels the finding of a study in 2000 in which frogs from the same pond—that is, those experiencing the same environmental conditions—were found to have similar deformities.

To examine the effects of pesticides on cercariae development, the team conducted lab experiments on four groups of tadpoles—three groups exposed to three common pesticides and a control group. The pesticides were Atrazine, the most commonly used pesticide in North America; Malathion, a common household pesticide that also is used to control insect pests in agricultural fields; and Esfenvalerate, a synthetic pyrethroid pesticide. The tadpoles were all exposed to cercariae.

Scientists repeated the pond test under controlled laboratory conditions and got similar results, with more detailed findings. In scientific causal analysis, repeatability of results strengthens the case for causality.

When they counted the number of cysts that formed in the tadpoles, the researchers found much higher levels in the tadpoles exposed to pesticides. The team also took blood samples before and after the experiments to determine whether the tadpoles' white blood cell count—a measure of immune system health—was affected.

"The tadpoles that we exposed to pesticides had fewer of this particular kind of white blood cell compared to the tadpoles that we did not expose to pesticides, suggesting that pesticides make these animals more susceptible to parasitic infections," Kiesecker said.

Pesticides have been found to have additional harmful effects on frogs. A study published in April in the *Proceedings of the National Academy of Sciences* found that Atrazine interfered with the sexual development of male frogs in the Midwest, reducing their levels of testosterone to below the levels found in female frogs.

"Atrazine-exposed frogs don't have normal reproductive systems," said Tyrone Hayes, the leader of a team from the University of California at Berkeley. "The males have ovaries in their testes and much smaller vocal organs."

Human Impacts?

Kiesecker said society can learn a lot from the experiments because "amphibians are particularly sensitive to environmental changes that appear to be associated with the recent emergence of new diseases and resurgence of old diseases that infect humans."

Especially disturbing, he added, is that the concentrations of two of the pesticides that caused the deformities in frogs, Esfenvalerate and Atrazine, were low enough for the water to be considered safe for human consumption under Environmental Protection Agency standards.

"Frogs may be a sentinel species that is warning us about the interplay between human-caused environmental change and disease susceptibility," he said, adding: "Hopefully, people will listen."

In other recent research on this problem, a study published in the July 1 issue of *Environmental Science & Technology* indicates that frog deformities may also occur as a result of exposure to ultraviolet (UV) radiation. At levels close to 60 percent of normal sunlight, frogs experienced deformities.

A survey of ponds in the Duluth, Minnesota, area showed that frogs in only three of 26 ponds were at risk of UV-induced deformities, because wetlands absorb a significant portion of the radiation. However, Steve Diamond of the Environmental Protection Agency's Duluth office and leader of the UV study said there may be cause for concern if human activities cause UV levels to rise.

Danielson closes by reminding readers of the possibility that the cause-and-effect relationship at work in frogs might have parallels for humans.

Explore Current Issues

Is fast-food marketing contributing to childhood obesity?

Over the past few years, the connection between fast food and obesity—especially childhood obesity—has also become a part of the public's consciousness. Many chain restaurants, theme parks, and even cities such as New York have banned the use of trans fats in commercial food preparation. However, popular family movies continue to have marketing tie-ins to fast food restaurants. In 2008, for example, Burger King joined forces with two summer blockbusters, *Iron Man* and *Indiana Jones and the Kingdom of the Crystal Skull*. In *Iron Man*, a Burger King cheeseburger is the ultimate comfort food to Robert Downey Jr.'s Tony Stark.

In an open letter to George Lucas and Steven Speilberg published on Slate.com, pediatrician Rahul K. Parikh, M.D. argues that this common marketing strategy is feeding the obesity epidemic:

> Each week American kids spend a full-time job's worth of time in front of the TV, on the Web and playing video games. They will see about 40,000 ads per year, and two-thirds of those ads are for junk food and fast food. Studies show that what kids see on TV is what they tell their parents they want for supper. No doubt the Indy Double Whopper—with bacon!—will be flying off the greasy grill in short order.

Parikh ultimately blames power players in the entertainment world such as Lucas and Spielberg for this irresponsible and greedy use of their influence.

Write about it

1. Do you think marketing tie-ins of movies with fast food such as the ones Parikh criticizes are responsible for exacerbating the childhood obesity epidemic? Why or why not?

2. Who do you think is most responsible for the childhood obesity epidemic? Why? Do you think anyone in the entertainment industry is to blame for aggravating the problem? Why?

3. Which of the following might also be factors in the cause-and-effect relationship Parikh sets up? Rate these in order of relevance.
   - Increasing cost of living
   - Workers working more hours
   - Single parents
   - Food shortages
   - Increasing food costs
   - Associations people have with certain brands

Are there any you would add?

How to read causal analyses

Make notes as you read, either in the margins, if it is your copy, or on paper or a computer file. Circle any words or references that you don't know and look them up.

What is it?	• What kind of a text is it? An article? an essay? a chart? a scientific report? a Web site? an executive summary? What are your expectations for this kind of text? • What media are used? (Web sites, for example, often combine images, words, and sounds.)
Where did it come from?	• Who wrote the analysis? • Where did it first appear? In a book, newspaper, magazine, online, in a company, or in an organization?
What is the writer's thesis or main idea?	• What is the writer's topic? What effect is he or she trying to determine the cause of? • Why is this topic important? • What are the key ideas or concepts that the writer considers? • What are the key terms? How does the writer define those terms?
Who is the intended audience?	• What clues do you find about whom the writer had in mind as the readers? • What does the writer assume that the readers already know about the subject? • What new knowledge is the writer providing?
How are causes analyzed?	• What methods does the writer use to determine causation? • Does the writer consider multiple causes? • How complex is the analysis? Does the writer examine relationships between causes, or look at how one cause may arise from another? • Can you think of other causes that the writer doesn't consider?
What kinds of evidence are given?	• Is the evidence from books, newspapers, periodicals, the Web, or field research? • Is the evidence convincing that the causes given are the actual causes?
How is it composed?	• How does the writer represent herself or himself? • How would you characterize the style? • How effective is the design? Is it easy to read? • If there are any photographs, charts, or other graphics, what information do they contribute?

The Future of Marriage

(ESSAY)

Stephanie Coontz

Stephanie Coontz teaches history and family studies at Evergreen State College in Olympia, Washington, and is Director of Research and Public Education for the Council on Contemporary Families. She is most recently the author of *Marriage, A History: From Obedience to Intimacy, or How Love Conquered Marriage* (2005). "The Future of Marriage" appeared January 14, 2008, on *Cato Unbound*, an online magazine-blog hybrid that presents the ideas of key thinkers and encourages public discourse.

Return to these questions after you have finished reading.

Analyzing and Connecting

1. Given the mission of *Cato Unbound*, what is the purpose of this article? Does Coontz ever state this purpose directly?

2. In her first paragraph, Coontz states: "Many people who hope to 're-institutionalize' marriage misunderstand the reasons that marriage was once more stable and played a stronger role in regulating social life." What does the phrase "re-institutionalize" mean? Why do some people want to "re-institutionalize" marriage?

3. Coontz concludes with the assertion that we need to let go of an idealized and mythical view of marriage in order to help people forge better relationships and be better parents. What other "institutions" might this philosophy apply to?

4. Think about the marriages with which you are familiar. What seems to be the greatest reason for a marriage's success? How about a marriage's failure?

Finding Ideas for Writing

This article was published on a site dedicated to public discourse. Write a paragraph response to Coontz's ideas on marriage that might appear on this site.

The Future of Marriage

Any serious discussion of the future of marriage requires a clear understanding of how marriage evolved over the ages, along with the causes of its most recent transformations. Many people who hope to "re-institutionalize" marriage misunderstand the reasons that marriage was once more stable and played a stronger role in regulating social life.

For most of history, marriage was more about getting the right in-laws than picking the right partner to love and live with. In the small-scale, band-level societies of our distant ancestors, marriage alliances turned strangers into relatives, creating interdependencies among groups that might otherwise meet as enemies. But as large wealth and status differentials developed in the ancient world, marriage became more exclusionary and coercive. People maneuvered to orchestrate advantageous marriage connections with some families and avoid incurring obligations to others. Marriage became the main way that the upper classes consolidated wealth, forged military coalitions, finalized peace treaties, and bolstered claims to social status or political authority. Getting "well-connected" in-laws was a preoccupation of the middle classes as well, while the dowry a man received at marriage was often the biggest economic stake he would acquire before his parents died. Peasants, farmers, and craftsmen acquired new workers for the family enterprise and forged cooperative bonds with neighbors through their marriages.

Because of marriage's vital economic and political functions, few societies in history believed that individuals should freely choose their own marriage partners, especially on such fragile grounds as love. Indeed, for millennia, marriage was much more about regulating economic, political, and gender hierarchies than nourishing the well-being of adults and their children. Until the late 18th century, parents took for granted their right to arrange their children's marriages and even, in many regions, to dissolve a marriage made without their permission. In Anglo-American law, a child born outside an approved marriage was a "fillius nullius"—a child of no one, entitled to nothing. In

fact, through most of history, the precondition for maintaining a strong institution of marriage was the existence of an equally strong institution of illegitimacy, which denied such children any claim on their families.

Even legally-recognized wives and children received few of the protections we now associate with marriage. Until the late 19th century, European and American husbands had the right to physically restrain, imprison, or "punish" their wives and children. Marriage gave husbands sole ownership over all property a wife brought to the marriage and any income she earned afterward. Parents put their children to work to accumulate resources for their own old age, enforcing obedience by periodic beatings.

Many people managed to develop loving families over the ages despite these laws and customs, but until very recently, this was not the main point of entering or staying in a union. It was just 250 years ago, when the Enlightenment challenged the right of the older generation and the state to dictate to the young, that free choice based on love and compatibility emerged as the social ideal for mate selection. Only in the early 19th century did the success of a marriage begin to be defined by how well it cared for its members, both adults and children.

These new marital ideals appalled many social conservatives of the day. "How will we get the right people to marry each other, if they can refuse on such trivial grounds as lack of love?" they asked. "Just as important, how will we prevent the wrong ones, such as paupers and servants, from marrying?" What would compel people to stay in marriages where love had died? What would prevent wives from challenging their husbands' authority?

They were right to worry. In the late 18th century, new ideas about the "pursuit of happiness" led many countries to make divorce more accessible, and some even repealed the penalties for homosexual love. The French revolutionaries abolished the legal category of illegitimacy, according a "love child" equal rights with a "legal" one. In the mid-19th century, women challenged husbands' sole ownership of wives' property, earnings, and behavior. Moralists predicted that such female economic independence would "destroy domestic tranquility," producing "infidelity in

HOW TO READ CAUSAL ANALYSES

the marriage bed, a high rate of divorce, and increased female criminality." And in some regards, they seemed correct. Divorce rates rose so steadily that in 1891 a Cornell University professor predicted, with stunning accuracy, that if divorce continued rising at its current rate, more marriages would end in divorce than death by the 1980s.

But until the late 1960s, most of the destabilizing aspects of the love revolution were held in check by several forces that prevented people from building successful lives outside marriage: the continued legal subordination of women to men; the ability of local elites to penalize employees and other community members for then-stigmatized behaviors such as remaining single, cohabiting, or getting a divorce; the unreliability of birth control, combined with the harsh treatment of illegitimate children; and above all, the dependence of women upon men's wage earning.

In the 1970s, however, these constraints were swept away or seriously eroded. The result has been to create a paradox with which many Americans have yet to come to terms. Today, when a marriage works, it delivers more benefits to its members—adults and children—than ever before. A good marriage is fairer and more fulfilling for both men and women than couples of the past could ever have imagined. Domestic violence and sexual coercion have fallen sharply. More couples share decision-making and housework than ever before. Parents devote unprecedented time and resources to their children. And men in stable marriages are far less likely to cheat on their wives than in the past.

But the same things that have made so many modern marriages more intimate, fair, and protective have simultaneously made marriage itself more optional and more contingent on successful negotiation. They have also made marriage seem less bearable when it doesn't live up to its potential. The forces that have strengthened marriage as a personal relationship between freely-consenting adults have weakened marriage as a regulatory social institution.

In the 1970s and 1980s, the collapse of the conditions that had forced most people to get and stay married led to dramatic—and often traumatic—upheavals in marriage. This was exacerbated by an

SEARCH

About Cato Unbound
Archived Issues

economic climate that made the 1950s ideal of the male breadwinner unattainable for many families. Divorce rates soared. Unwed teen motherhood shot up. Since then, some of these destabilizing trends have leveled off or receded. The divorce rate has fallen, especially for college-educated couples, over the past 20 years. When divorce does occur, more couples work to resolve it amicably, and fewer men walk away from contact with their children. Although there was a small uptick in teen births last year, they are still almost 30 percent lower than in 1991.

Still, there is no chance that we can restore marriage to its former supremacy in coordinating social and interpersonal relationships. Even as the divorce rate has dropped, the incidence of cohabitation, delayed marriage and non-marriage has risen steadily. With half of all Americans aged 25-29 unmarried, marriage no longer organizes the transition into regular sexual activity or long-term partnerships the way it used to. Although teen births are lower than a decade ago, births to unwed mothers aged 25 and older continue to climb. Almost 40 percent of America's children are born to unmarried parents. And gay and lesbian families are permanently out of the closet.

The decline in marriage's dominating role in organizing social and personal life is not unique to America. It is occurring across the industrial world, even in countries with less "permissive" values and laws. In predominantly Catholic Ireland, where polls in the 1980s found near-universal disapproval of premarital sex, one child in three today is born outside marriage. China's divorce rate has soared more than 700 percent since 1980. Until 2005, Chile was the only country in the Western Hemisphere that still prohibited divorce. But in today's world, prohibiting divorce has very different consequences than in the past, because people no longer feel compelled to marry in the first place. Between 1990 and 2003, the number of marriages in Chile fell from 100,000 to 60,000 a year, and nearly half of all children born in Chile in the early years of the 21st century were born to unmarried couples. In Italy, Singapore, and Japan, divorce, cohabitation, and out-of wedlock births remain low by American standards, but a much larger percentage of women avoid marriage and childbearing altogether. This suggests that

CATO | UNBOUND

SEARCH »

About Cato Unbound
Archived Issues
Cato Institute

EARTH & FIRE
EROWID

we are experiencing a massive historical current that, if blocked in one area, simply flows over traditional paths of family life at a different spot.

The late 20th-century revolution in the role and function of marriage has been as far-reaching—and as wrenching—as the replacement of local craft production and exchange by wage labor and ndustrialization. Like the Industrial Revolution, the family diversity revolution has undercut old ways of organizing work, leisure, caregiving, and redistribution to dependents. It has liberated some people from restrictive, socially-imposed statuses, but stripped others of customary support systems and rules for behavior, without putting clearly defined new ones in place. There have been winners and losers in the arriage revolution, just as there were in the Industrial Revolution. But we will not meet the challenges of this transformation by trying to turn back the clock. Instead we must take two lessons away from these historical changes.

First, marriage is not on the verge of extinction. Most cohabiting couples eventually do get married, either to each other or to someone else. New groups, such as gays and lesbians, are now demanding access to marriage—a demand that many pro-marriage advocates oddly interpret as an attack on the institution. And a well-functioning marriage is still an especially useful and effective method of organizing interpersonal commitments and improving people's well-being. But in today's climate of gender equality and personal choice, we must realize that successful marriages require different traits, skills, and behaviors than in the past.

Marriages used to depend upon a clear division of labor and authority, and couples who rejected those rules had less stable marriages than those who abided by them. In the 1950s, a woman's best bet for a lasting marriage was to marry a man who believed firmly in the male breadwinner ideal. Women who wanted a "MRS degree" were often advised to avoid the "bachelor's" degree, since as late as 1967 men told pollsters they valued a woman's cooking and housekeeping skills above her intelligence or education. Women who hadn't married by age 25 were less likely to ever marry than their more traditional counterparts, and studies in the 1960s suggested that if they did marry at an older

age than average they were more likely to divorce. When a wife took a job outside the home, this raised the risk of marital dissolution.

All that has changed today. Today, men rank intelligence and education way above cooking and housekeeping as a desirable trait in a partner. A recent study by Paul Amato *et al.* found that the chance of divorce recedes with each year that a woman postpones marriage, with the least divorce-prone marriages being those where the couples got married at age 35 or higher. Educated and high-earning women are now less likely to divorce than other women. When a wife takes a job today, it works to stabilize the marriage. Couples who share housework and productive work have more stable marriages than couples who do not, according to sociologist Lynn Prince Cooke. And the Amato study found that husbands and wives who hold egalitarian views about gender have higher marital quality and fewer marital problems than couples who cling to more traditional views.

The second lesson of history is that the time has passed when we can construct our social policies, work schedules, health insurance systems, sex education programs—or even our moral and ethical beliefs about who owes what to whom—on the assumption that all long-term commitments and care-giving obligations should or can be organized through marriage. Of course we must seek ways to make marriage more possible for couples and to strengthen the marriages they contract. But we must be equally concerned to help couples who don't marry become better co-parents, to help single parents and cohabiting couples meet their obligations, and to teach divorced parents how to minimize their conflicts and improve their parenting.

The right research and policy question today is not "what kind of family do we wish people lived in?" Instead, we must ask "what do we know about how to help every family build on its strengths, minimize its weaknesses, and raise children more successfully?" Much recent hysteria to the contrary, we know a lot about how to do that. We should devote more of our energies to getting that research out and less to fantasizing about a return to a mythical Golden Age of marriage of the past.

Why Should I Be Nice To You? Coffee Shops and the Politics of Good Service

(ESSAY)

Emily Raine

Emily Raine recently received a Masters degree in Communication Studies at McGill University in Montreal. She also writes about graffiti and street art. This essay appeared in the online journal *Bad Subjects* in 2005.

Return to these questions after you have finished reading.

Analyzing and Connecting

1. What exactly is Raine's causal argument about why work in coffee chains is worse than in other kinds of service jobs?

2. Raine mixes technical terms with informal language. For example, she says "café labor is heavily grounded in the rationalism of Fordist manufacturing principles," which is the technical term for the method of assembly-line production developed by Henry Ford. But she says she "felt like an aproned Coke machine." Look for other examples of technical and informal language. Why does she mix them?

3. Why is it important that coffee shop employees not act like individuals from the employer's perspective?

4. Have you ever worked in a restaurant, coffee shop, retail store, or another service industry? If so, how was your experience similar to or different from Raine's? If not, think about your experiences as a customer in coffee shops and similar businesses. How did the employees behave?

5. Look at the last paragraph. Raine makes a new claim that rudeness allows workers to retain their individuality. Why does she put this claim in the conclusion? Does it lead to a strong conclusion?

Finding Ideas for Writing

Think about the causal argument that Raine presents and your own experiences as an employee or as a customer at a coffee shop, restaurant, store, or other service-oriented establishment. Are there any factors she's neglecting that may change the nature of the causal relationship she's setting up? Write a one-paragraph rebuttal based on this overlooked factor.

eserver » bad home » bad editorials » 2006 » raza/race: why support immigrants?

Bad Subjects

home   about   articles   authors   books   contact us   **editorials**   links   news   reviews

Why Should I Be Nice To You?
Coffee Shops and the Politics of Good Service

"There is no more precious commodity than the relationship of trust and confidence a company has with its employees."

–Starbucks Coffee Company Chairman Howard Schultz

I actually like to serve. I'm not sure if this comes from some innate inclination to mother and fuss over strangers, or if it's because the movement and sociability of service work provides a much-needed antidote to the solitude of academic research, but I've always found something about service industry work satisfying. I've done the gamut of service jobs, from fine dining to cocktail waitressing to hip euro-bistro counter work, and the only job where I've ever felt truly whipped was working as a barista at one of the now-ubiquitous specialty coffee chains, those bastions of jazz and public solitude that have spread through urban landscapes over the last ten years or so. The pay was poor, the shifts long and oddly dispersed, the work boring and monotonous, the managers demanding, and the customers regularly displayed that unique spleen that emerges in even the most pleasant people before they've had the morning's first coffee. I often felt like an aproned Coke machine, such was the effect my sparkling personality had on the clientele. And yet, some combination of service professionalism, fear of termination and an imperative to be "nice" allowed me to suck it up, smile and continue to provide that intangible trait that the industry holds above all else, good service.

Bad Subjects

home   about   articles   authors   books   contact us   **editorials**   links   news   reviews

Good service in coffee shops doesn't amount to much. Unlike table service, where interaction with customers spans a minimum of half an hour, the average contact with a café customer lasts less than ten seconds. Consider how specialty cafés are laid out: the customer service counter is arranged in a long line that clients move along to "use" the café. The linear coffee bar resembles an assembly line, and indeed, café labor is heavily grounded in the rationalism of Fordist manufacturing principles, which had already been tested for use in hospitality services by fast food chains. Each of the café workers is assigned a specific stage in the service process to perform exclusively, such as taking orders, using the cash registers, or handing clients cups of brewed coffee.

The specialization of tasks increases the speed of transactions and limits the duration of any one employee's interaction with the clientele. This means that in a given visit a customer might order from one worker, receive food from the next, then brewed coffee or tea from yet another, then pay a cashier before proceeding down the line of the counter, finishing the trip at the espresso machine which is always situated at its end. Ultimately, each of the café's products is processed and served by a different employee, who repeats the same preparation task for hours and attends to each customer only as they receive that one product.

Needless to say, the productive work in cafés is dreary and repetitive. Further, this style of service severely curtails interaction with the clientele, and the very brevity of each transaction precludes much chance for authentic friendliness or conversation—even asking about someone's day would slow the entire operation. The one aspect of service work that can be unpredictable—people—becomes redundant, and interaction with customers is reduced to a fatiguing eight-hour-long smile and the repetition of sentiments that allude to good service, such as injunctions to enjoy their purchases or to have a nice day. Rather than friendly exchanges with customers, barista workers' good service is reduced to a quick rictus in the customer's direction between a great deal of friendly interaction with the espresso machine.

eserver » bad home » bad editorials » 2006 » raza/race: why support immigrants?

Bad Subjects

home   about   articles   authors   books   contact us   **editorials**   links   news   reviews

As the hospitality industry really took off in the sixties, good service became one of the trademarks of its advertising claims, a way for brands to distinguish themselves from the rest of the pack. One needn't think too hard to come up with a litany of service slogans that holler the good graces of their personnel—at Starbucks where the baristas make the magic, at PSA where smiles aren't just painted on, or at McDonald's where smiles are free. Employee friendliness emerged as one of the chief distinguishing brand features of personal services, which means that the workers themselves become an aspect of the product for sale.

Our notions of good service revolve around a series of platitudes about professionalism—we're at your service, with a smile, where the customer's always right—each bragging the centrality of the customer to everything "we" do. Such claims imply an easy and equal exchange between two parties: the "we" that gladly serves and the "you" that happily receives. There is, however, always a third party involved in the service exchange, and that's whoever has hired the server, the body that ultimately decides just what the dimensions of good service will be.

Like most employees, a service worker sells labor to an employer at a set rate, often minimum wage, and the employer sells the product of that labor, the service itself, at market values. In many hospitality services, where gratuities make up the majority of employment revenue, the worker directly benefits from giving good service, which of course translates to good tips. But for the vast majority of service staff, and particularly those employed in venues yielding little or no gratuities—fast food outlets, café chains, cleaning and maintenance operations—this promises many workers little more than a unilateral imperative to be perpetually bright and amenable.

The vast majority of service personnel do not spontaneously produce an unaffected display of cheer and good will continuously for the duration of a shift. When a company markets its products on servers' friendliness, they must then monitor and control employees' friendliness, so good service is defined and enforced from above. Particularly in chains, which are premised

Bad Subjects

home   about   articles   authors   books   contact us   **editorials**   links   news   reviews

upon their consistent reproduction of the same experience in numerous locations, organizations are obliged to impose systems to manage employees' interaction with their customers. In some chains, namely the fast food giants such as McDonald's and Burger King, employee banter is scripted into cash registers, so that as soon as a customer orders, workers are cued to offer, "would you like a dessert with that?" (an offer of dubious benefit to the customer) and to wish them a nice day. Ultimately, this has allowed corporations to be able to assimilate "good service"—or, friendly workers—into their overall brand image.

While cafés genuflect toward the notion of good service, their layouts and management styles preclude much possibility of creating the warmth that this would entail. Good service is, of course, important, but not if it interferes with throughput. What's more, these cafés have been at the forefront of a new wave of organizations that not only market themselves on service quality but also describe employees' job satisfaction as the seed from which this flowers.

Perhaps the most glaring example of this is Starbucks, where cheerful young workers are displayed behind elevated counters as they banter back and forth, calling out fancy Italian drink names and creating theatre out of their productive labor. Starbucks' corporate literature gushes not only about the good service its customers will receive, but about the great joy that its "partners" take in providing it, given the company's unique ability to "provide a great work environment and treat each other with respect and dignity," and where its partners are "emotionally and intellectually committed to Starbucks success." In the epigraph to this essay, Starbucks' chairman even describes the company's relationship with its workers as a commodity. Not only does Starbucks offer good service, but it attempts to guarantee something even better: good service provided by employees that are genuinely happy to give it.

Starbucks has branded a new kind of worker, the happy, wholesome, perfume-free barista. The company offers unusual benefits for service

eserver » bad home » bad editorials » 2006 » raza/race: why support immigrants?

Bad Subjects

home   about   articles   authors   books   contact us   **editorials**   links   news   reviews

workers, including stock options, health insurance, dental plans and other perks such as product discounts and giveaways. Further, they do so very, very publicly, and the company's promotional materials are filled with moving accounts of workers who never dreamed that corporate America could care so much. With the other hand, though, the company has smashed unionization drives in New York, Vancouver and at its Seattle roaster; it schedules workers at oddly timed shifts that never quite add up to full-time hours; the company pays only nominally more than minimum wage, and their staffs are still unable to subsist schlepping lattes alone.

Starbucks is not alone in marketing itself as an enlightened employer. When General Motors introduced its Saturn line, the new brand was promoted almost entirely on the company's good relations with its staff. The company's advertising spots often featured pictures of and quotes from the union contract, describing their unique partnership between manufacturer, workers and union, which allowed blue-collar personnel to have a say in everything from automobile designs to what would be served for lunch. The company rightly guessed that this strategy would go over well with liberal consumers concerned about the ethics of their purchases. Better yet, Saturn could market its cars based on workers' happiness whether personnel were satisfied or not, because very few consumers would ever have the chance to interact with them.

At the specialty coffee chains, however, consumers have to talk to employees, yet nobody ever really asks. The café service counter runs like a smooth piece of machinery, and I found that most people preferred to pretend that they were interacting with an appliance. In such short transactions, it is exceedingly difficult for customers to remember the humanity of each of the four to seven people they might interact with to get their coffees. Even fast food counters have one server who processes each customer's order, yet in cafés the workers just become another gadget in the well-oiled café machine. This is a definite downside for the employees—clients are much ruder to café staff than in any other sector of the industry I ever worked in. I found that

Bad Subjects

home   about   articles   authors   books   contact us   **editorials**   links   news   reviews

people were more likely to be annoyed than touched by any reference to my having a personality, and it took no small amount of thought on my part to realize why.

Barista workers are hired to represent an abstract category of worker, not to act as individuals. Because of the service system marked by short customer interaction periods and a homogenous staff, the services rendered are linked in the consumer imagination to the company and not to any one individual worker. Workers' assimilation into the company image makes employees in chain service as branded as the products they serve. The chain gang, the workers who hold these eminently collegiate after-school jobs, are proscribed sales scripts and drilled on customer service scenarios to standardize interactions with customers. The company issues protocols for hair length, color and maintenance, visible piercings and tattoos as well as personal hygiene and acceptable odorific products. Workers are made more interchangeable by the use of uniforms, which, of course, serve to make the staff just that. The organization is a constant intermediary in every transaction, interjecting its presence in every detail of the service experience, and this standardization amounts to an absorption of individuals' personalities into the corporate image.

Many of the measures that chains take to secure the homogeneity of their employees do not strike us as particularly alarming, likely because similar restrictions have been in place for several hundred years. Good service today has inherited many of the trappings of the good servant of yore, including prohibitions against eating, drinking, sitting or relaxing in front the served, entering and exiting through back doors and wearing uniforms to visually mark workers' status. These measures almost completely efface the social identities of staff during work hours, providing few clues to workers' status in their free time. Contact between service workers and their customers is thus limited to purely functional relations, so that the public only see them as workers, as makers of quality coffee, and never as possible peers.

eserver » bad home » bad editorials » 2006 » raza/race: why support immigrants?

Bad Subjects

home   about   articles   authors   books   contact us   **editorials**   links   news   reviews

Maintaining such divisions is integral to good service because this display of class distinctions ultimately underlies our notions of service quality. Good service means not only serving well, but also allowing customers to feel justified in issuing orders, to feel okay about being served—which, in turn, requires demonstrations of class difference and the smiles that suggest servers' comfort with having a subordinate role in the service exchange.

Unlike the penguin-suited household servant staffs whose class status was clearly defined, service industry workers today often have much more in common from a class perspective with those that they serve. This not only creates an imperative for them to wear their class otherness on their sleeves, as it were, but also to accept their subordinate role to those they serve by being unshakably tractable and polite.

Faith Popcorn has rather famously referred to the four-dollar latte as a "small indulgence," noting that while this is a lot to pay for a glass of hot milk, it is quite inexpensive for the feeling of luxury that can accompany it. In this service climate, the class status of the server and the served—anyone who can justify spending this much on a coffee—is blurry, indeed. Coffee shops that market themselves on employee satisfaction assert the same happy servant that allows politically conscientious consumers who are in many cases the workers' own age and class peers, to feel justified in receiving good service. Good service—as both an apparent affirmation of subordinate classes' desire to serve and as an enforced one-sided politeness—reproduces the class distinctions that have historically characterized servant-served relationships so that these are perpetuated within the contemporary service market.

The specialty coffee companies are large corporations, and for the twenty-somethings who stock their counters, barista work is too temporary to bother fighting the system. Mostly, people simply quit. Dissatisfied workers are stuck with engaging in tactics that will change nothing but allow them to make the best of their lot. These include minor infractions such as taking liberties with the uniforms or grabbing little bits of company time for their own pleasure,

Bad Subjects

home   about   articles   authors   books   contact us   **editorials**   links   news   reviews

what Michel de Certeau calls *la perruque* and the companies themselves call "time theft." As my time in the chain gang wore on, I developed my own tactic, the only one I found that jostled the customers out of their complacency and allowed me to be a barista and a person.

There is no easy way to serve without being a servant, and I have always found that the best way to do so is to show my actual emotions rather than affecting a smooth display of interminable patience and good will. For café customers, bettering baristas' lots can be as simple as asking about their day, addressing them by name—any little gesture to show that you noticed the person behind the service that they can provide. My tactic as a worker is equally simple, but it is simultaneously an assertion of individual identity at work, a refusal of the class distinctions that characterize the service environment and a rebuttal to the companies that would promote my satisfaction with their system: be rude. Not arbitrarily rude, of course— customers are people, too, and nobody gains anything by spreading bad will. But on those occasions when customer or management behavior warranted a zinging comeback, I would give it.

Rudeness, when it is demanded, undermines companies' claims on workers' personal warmth and allows them to retain their individuality by expressing genuine rather than affected feelings in at-work interpersonal exchanges. It is a refusal of the class distinctions that underlie consumers' unilateral prerogative of rudeness and servers' unilateral imperative to be nice. It runs contrary to everything that we have been taught, not only about service but about interrelating with others. But this seems to be the only method of asserting one's person-hood in the service environment, where workers' personalities are all too easily reduced to a space-time, conflated with the drinks they serve. Baristas of the world, if you want to avoid becoming a green-aproned coffee dispensary, you're just going to have to tell people off about it.

How to write a causal analysis

These steps for the process of writing a causal analysis may not progress as neatly as this chart might suggest. Writing is not an assembly-line process. As you write, you are constantly reading what you have written and rethinking.

Continue thinking about causation as you write and revise. The process of writing may lead you to additional causal relationships.

1 MAKE A CAUSAL CLAIM

- Examine a social trend, law, or policy.

- Analyze problems in your neighborhood or at your school.

- Investigate natural phenomena.

- Investigate the impact of human activity on the environment.

- Think about what is at stake. What could or should change if the cause is known?

- Put your claim in the form "_____ causes (or does not cause) _____."

2 THINK ABOUT THE POSSIBLE CAUSES

- What are the obvious causes?

- What are the underlying causes?

- What causes might be hidden?

- What are the causes that most people have not recognized before?

- Who is affected by what you are investigating? Do your readers have a stake in what you are analyzing?

- Look for disagreement among your sources. If they all agree on the cause, probably you won't have much to add.

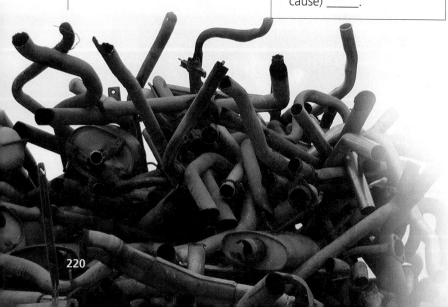

3 WRITE A DRAFT

- Describe the trend, event, or phenomenon.
- Give the background your readers will need.
- If the trend or event you are analyzing is unfamiliar to your readers, explain the cause or the chain of causation.
- Another way to organize the body of your analysis is to set out the causes that have already been offered and reject them one by one. Then you can present the cause or causes that you think are the right ones.
- A third method is to look at a series of causes one by one, analyzing the importance of each.
- Do more than simply summarize in your conclusion. You might consider additional effects beyond those you have previously noted, or explain to readers any action you think should be taken based on your conclusions.
- Choose a title that will interest readers in your essay.
- Include any necessary images or tables.

4 REVISE, REVISE, REVISE

- Check that your causal analysis fulfills the assignment.
- Make sure that your claim is clear and that you have sufficient evidence to convince readers.
- Look at additional potential causes, if necessary.
- Reconsider how multiple causes might interact.
- Go further back in the causal chain, if necessary, showing how the causes you examine have their roots in other events.
- Examine the organization of your analysis and think of possible better ways to organize.
- Review the visual presentation of your analysis for readability and maximum impact.
- Proofread carefully.

5 SUBMITTED VERSION

- Make sure your finished writing meets all formatting requirements.

1: Make a causal claim

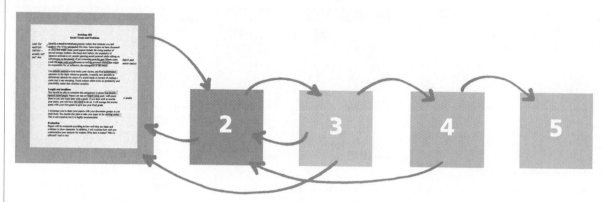

Analyze the assignment	• Read your assignment slowly and carefully. Look for key words like *causes, effect, result, impact, why,* and *influence.* These key words tell you that you are writing a causal analysis.
	• Highlight any information about the length specified, date due, formatting, and other requirements. You can attend to this information later. At this point you want to give your attention to the topic and criteria you will use in your analysis.
Explore possible topics	• Make a list of fashion trends including cars, clothing, hairstyles, food, tattoos, and piercing. Look at your list and think about where and why a particular trend originates. Make notes about the origins of trends on your list.
	• Make a list of social trends including music, television shows, movies, sports, exercising, childrearing, and leisure. Look at your list and think about where and why a particular trend originates. Make notes about the origins of trends on your list.
	• Make a list of important historical events or discoveries that changed the course of civilization. Make notes about what led to these events or discoveries and how people's lives were changed by them.
Think about what's at stake	• Remember that people often have a stake in the outcome of a causal claim. Ask: Who will agree with me? Who will disagree, and why?
	• Think about why your analysis matters. If people accept your causal claim, will anything change?

222

Make a claim that matters

Make an arguable claim

Easy answers generally make bad arguments. If all the sources you consult agree about the cause of the effect you are interested in, there is probably no need for you to make another argument saying the same thing. Look for a phenomenon that hasn't been explained to everyone's satisfaction.

OFF TRACK
Cigarette smoke is a leading cause of lung cancer.

ON TRACK
New research indicates that childhood asthma may be linked to exposure to cockroaches.

Explain why it matters

Readers need to know why this cause-and-effect relationship is important. If we determine the cause of this phenomenon, what will change? What can we do? What might happen?

OFF TRACK
This paper will investigate the most common causes of foundation failure in U.S. residential housing.

ON TRACK
Foundation failure, especially cracked slabs, can cost anywhere from a few thousand to tens of thousands of dollars to repair. Determining the primary causes of foundation failure can help homeowners and insurers protect themselves against economic loss and inconvenience.

Write Now

Think about causal factors

1. Consider trends or problems you are familiar with—in your daily life, or in the larger world.
2. List these trends and problems on the right side of a piece of paper. On the left side, write down what you think some of the causes of the problems might be. Underline the causes that you are confident about.
3. Look over your two lists. Which topics seem most interesting to you? If an entry has many underlined causes or effects, it may be too obvious to write about.

Writer at work

Sean Booker was asked to write a paper analyzing the causes of a current trend in popular culture for a course in Social Trends and Problems. He made the following notes on his assignment sheet while his class was discussing the assignment.

Sociology 032
Social Trends and Problems

Look for multiple factors – usually not just one

Identify a trend in American popular culture that interests you and analyze why it has emerged at this time. Some topics we have discussed in class that might make good papers include the rising number of unwed teenage mothers who keep their babies; the popularity of Japanese animation art; people ignoring social protocol while talking on cell phones; or the growth of pet ownership over the past fifteen years. Look for large scale social causes as well as personal causes that might be responsible for, or influence, the emergence of this trend.

Macro and micro causes

Use outside sources to help make your claims, and find authoritative opinions on the topic whenever possible. It usually isn't possible to definitively identify the cause of a social trend, so beware of making a claim that is too sweeping. Social science often relies on probability and plausibility rather than absolute certainty.

Length and deadlines
You should be able to complete this assignment in about four double-spaced, typed pages. Papers are due on March 22nd, and I will return them to you one week later with a grade. If you then wish to rewrite your paper, you will have one week to do so. I will average the rewrite grade with your first grade to give you your final grade.

2 weeks

I encourage you to share your papers with your discussion groups as you draft them. You should also plan to take your paper to the writing center. This is not required, but it is highly recommended.

Evaluation
Papers will be evaluated according to how well they use logic and evidence to show causation. In addition, I will consider how well you contextualize your analysis for readers (Why does it matter? Who is affected? And so on).

Read the assignment closely
Sean Booker began by circling the words and phrases that indicated his analytical task. Then he highlighted information about dates and processes for the project.

Choose a topic
Sean Booker made a list of trends he might write about. After each item on his list, he made notes about why the topic would matter, and to whom. He also made preliminary observations about where he might find "authoritative opinions" on each topic, wrote down any possible causes that occurred to him at the time, and noted any other observations or questions he had about that topic. Finally, he chose one trend for further research.

POPULARITY OF ANIME
- Is it more popular with certain age groups or other demographic groups?
- Is there any scholarly/authoritative research on it? Maybe in Art History?
- I've seen tons of magazines devoted to it at the bookstore.
- Could interview Sarah about the collection she has.

POPULARITY OF RAP MUSIC ** Best research possibilities **
(especially among white teenagers)
- What percentage of sales of rap music are to white kids?
- Is it any different from white teenagers liking rock n' roll in the 50s?
- Because it annoys parents?
- Does it indicate racial tolerance?
- I know there has been research on this from an economic viewpoint.

SUV SALES
- Why do people want to drive "off-roading" cars to work every day?
- Are sales declining with rising gas prices?
- Is this even a trend any more? People are buying VWs and Mini Coopers now.

"ILLEGAL" FILE SHARING
- Why do so many people do it if it is "illegal"? (Because you get something for free.)
- What are the arguments saying that it is or isn't illegal?
- Easy answer: people are willing to "steal" in this case because there is still significant disagreement over whether it is really stealing.

2: Think about possible causes

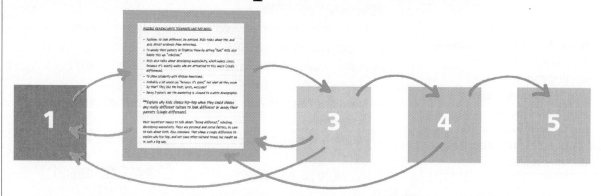

Find the obvious causes, and then dig deeper	• **What causal factors might be hidden from the general observer, and why?** Use your imagination; hidden causes require new thinking if they are to be uncovered.
	• **How do various causal factors interact?** Several causes together might contribute to an effect, rather than any single cause being the determining factor.
	• **What "causes the cause" that you have identified?** What prior conditions does each cause arise from? If poor attendance is a factor in drop-out rates, what causes some students to have poor attendance in the first place?
Analyze your audience	• **Think about who is affected by the phenomenon you are investigating.** Who is in a position to react to your claims, and make changes?
	• **If you don't know who your audience is, do some research to find out who is interested in your topic.** Who has offered opinions or responded to previous causal claims on this topic?
Research your analysis	• **Look for some disagreement among your sources.** If they all agree on the cause, your analysis won't matter much.
	• **When your sources disagree, ask why.** Does one give more weight to some pieces of evidence than to others? Do they draw different conclusions from the same evidence? Do they use Mill's methods of determining causation in different ways?
	• **Be on the lookout for new potential causes, or new findings that could help you rule out potential causes.**

Writer at work

Sean Booker began his analysis by brainstorming for all the possible causes he could think of. Then, he researched the topic to find information on the causes he had listed and also to learn about other potential causes that had been put forward.

Sean Booker thought about his own experience with the trend to help define his audience. He also noted the types of audiences his sources appeared to be writing for. Finally, Sean Booker identified what he thought were the most likely causes of rap's popularity with white teenagers. He did this analysis by applying Mill's methods of determining causation and by weighing the opinions of the authoritative sources he had read.

POSSIBLE REASONS WHITE TEENAGERS LIKE RAP MUSIC:

- Fashion: to look different, be noticed. Mills talks about this and uses direct evidence from interviews.

- To annoy their parents or frighten them by acting "bad." Mills also backs this up: "rebellion."

- Mills also talks about developing masculinity, which makes sense, because it's mostly males who are attracted to this music (single difference).

- To show solidarity with African Americans.

- Probably a lot would say "Because it's good," but what do they mean by that? They like the beat, lyrics, message?

- Davey D points out the marketing is skewed to a white demographic.

**Explain why kids choose hip-hop when they could choose any really different culture to look different or annoy their parents (single difference).

Most important causes to talk about: "being different," rebelling, developing masculinity. These mix personal and social factors; be sure to talk about both. Also, economic. That shows a single difference to explain why hip-hop, and not some other cultural trend, has caught on in such a big way.

3: Write a draft

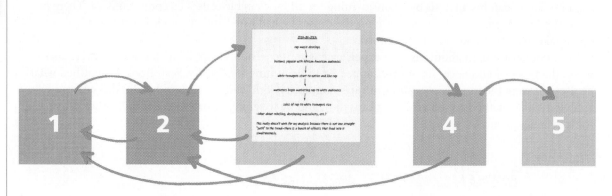

Introduce what you will be analyzing	• Describe the trend, event, or phenomenon you will be analyzing. • Give your readers any background information they will need. • Explain why it is important to determine the cause of this phenomenon (you can save this for the conclusion if you wish).
Describe the causal relationship	• Explain how the chain of causation works to produce the effect in question. Break down each step so readers can follow the process. • Alternatively, set out the causes offered by other people and show how they can be ruled out. Then, introduce your own claim and demonstrate why it is superior to others'. • A third method is to look at a series of possible causes one at a time, analyzing each and making a claim about its relative impact on a phenomenon.
Anticipate and address opposing viewpoints	• Acknowledge other stakeholders in the analysis, and consider their claims. • Demonstrate why your claim is preferable.
Conclude by doing more than summarizing	• Spell out the importance of the analysis, if you haven't already done so. • Consider additional effects you haven't previously discussed. • Explain any action you think needs to be taken based on your conclusion.

Staying on Track

Look at the big picture

Don't confuse correlation with causation

Mill's method of concomitant variation might lead you to conclude that any mutual relationship between two events is causal. Remember that concomitant variation only determines cause when all other variables are accounted for.

OFF TRACK

The drop in the number of Americans living in poverty during the Clinton administration was due to a number of factors, the Welfare Reform Act being chief among them.

ON TRACK

The lower number of Americans living in poverty during the Clinton administration was due to a number of factors. How much did the Welfare Reform Act contribute to this trend? The general economic prosperity experienced by the entire country during that time probably had a greater impact. Statistics show that the primary effect of the Welfare Reform Act was to simply remove people from welfare rolls, not actually lift them out of poverty.

Identify the stakeholders in your analysis

Be especially alert for opinions about your topic from people who would be adversely affected by a different causal outcome.

OFF TRACK

Can mega-doses of vitamin C prevent colds, flu, and other illnesses? Good health is important to everyone, so we should all be interested in the news that vitamin C has many important health benefits.

ON TRACK

Can mega-doses of vitamin C prevent colds, flu, and other illnesses? The supplements industry has spent millions of dollars to convince consumers that this is the case. The industry stands to make hundreds of millions more if people believe them. But evidence from independent researchers casts some doubt on the effectiveness of mega-doses of vitamin C in preventing illness.

Writer at work

Sean Booker tested three organizational patterns for his analysis. First he looked at how describing a chain of causation could illuminate his analysis. Next, he considered examining causes one by one and eliminating them before describing the cause he thought was correct. Finally, he structured his analysis as an examination of possible causes, one by one, with accompanying discussion of each cause's relative contribution to the overall effect. This seemed to Sean Booker like the best method for making his analysis, so he used it to write his draft.

STEP-BY-STEP:

rap music develops

↓

becomes popular with African American audiences

↓

white teenagers start to notice and like rap

↓

marketers begin marketing rap to white audiences

↓

sales of rap to white teenagers rise

—What about rebelling, developing masculinity, etc.?

This really doesn't work for my analysis because there is not one straight "path" to the trend—there is a bunch of effects that feed into it simultaneously.

<u>DISPROVING ALTERNATE CAUSES:</u>

White kids like rap just because "it is good" and they are colorblind about music.
- Actually, they are acutely aware of the racial difference between themselves and the performers; that's part of why they like it.

White kids like rap because they feel sympathy with African American culture.

- I'm the only person who even thought of this reason. A lot of people I know who listen to rap know next to nothing about African American culture, so this is pretty clearly wrong. But what good does it do to bring it up and refute it if no one else would have even considered it as a possibility?

I guess the problem here is that there isn't a big controversy over which causes are "right." That kind of controversy would work better with this structure. It's more a question of how many different causes there might be, and how they might work together.

<u>ONE CAUSE AT A TIME:</u>

- Appeal of the fashion and style is one possible cause. Explain how it fills a need for white teenagers.
- Rebellion against social expectations. Explain why white kids need to do this.
- Developing masculinity. Explain how social pressures lead white male teenagers to think rap's message makes them more masculine.
- Marketing. Look at how rap is marketed to white kids, amplifying all the causes above.

This strategy is the best approach because it lets me look at all the possible causes in detail and finish with the one that sort of gathers up and amplifies the first three.

4: Revise, revise, revise

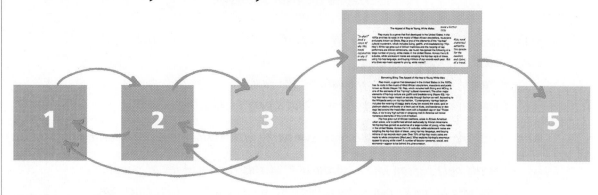

Skilled writers know that the secret to writing well is rewriting. Even the best writers often have to revise several times to get the result they want. You also must have effective strategies for revising if you're going to be successful. The biggest trap you can fall into is starting off with the little stuff first. Leave the small stuff for last.

Does your paper or project meet the assignment?	• Look again at your assignment. Does your paper or project do what the assignment asks? • Look again at the assignment for specific guidelines, including length, format, and amount of research. Does your work meet these guidelines?
Is your causal claim arguable?	• Do enough people disagree with you to make the evaluation worthwhile? • Who cares about this topic? Do you explain to readers why it is important?
Do you use logical means of determining causation?	• Do you examine common factors, single differences, and concomitant variations? • Do you use more than one method whenever possible? • Do you avoid confusing correlation with causation?
Is your evidence authoritative and convincing?	• Have you found the most accurate available information about your topic? • Have you identified stakeholders in your analysis? • Have you carefully examined the analysis and conclusions of people who have already expressed an opinion on this topic?

Do you address opposing views?	• Have you acknowledged the opinions of people who disagree with your claim? • Have you shown how your causal claim is preferable?
Is the writing project visually effective?	• Is the font attractive and readable? • Are the headings and visuals effective? • If you use images or tables as part of your analysis, are they legible and appropriately placed?
Save the editing for last.	When you have finished revising, edit and proofread carefully.

A peer review guide is on page 27.

Writer at work

Sean Booker talked with his peer group about his analysis, and took his draft to the writing center for a consultation. He wrote notes on the draft to help him revise, and then he made some changes to the draft. His peers particularly urged him to focus his introduction. Here is the draft of Sean Booker's introduction as he originally wrote it, with notes he made, and as he revised it for his final draft.

The Appeal of Rap to Young, White Males   *Need a better title*

"So what?" Need a sense of why this needs explanation or why it matters

Rap music is a genre that first developed in the United States in the 1970s and has its roots in the music of West African storytellers, musicians and poets known as Griots. Rap is one of the elements of the "hip-hop" cultural movement, which includes DJing, graffiti, and breakdancing ("Hip-Hop"). While rap grew out of African traditions and the majority of rap performers are African Americans, rap music has gained the following of a large number of young, white males in the United States. Across the U.S. suburbs, white adolescent males are adopting the hip-hop style of dress, using hip-hop language, and buying millions of rap records each year. But why does rap music appeal to young, white males?

Also, need statistics/ authoritative opinion for the numbers and claims of a trend.

Borrowing Bling: The Appeal of Hip-hop to Young White Men

Rap music, a genre that developed in the United States in the 1970s, has its roots in the music of West African storytellers, musicians and poets known as Griots (Keyes 19). Rap, which includes both DJing and MCing, is one of the elements of the "hip-hop" cultural movement. The other major elements of hip-hop culture are graffiti and breakdancing (Keyes 63). Hip-hop has had a major impact on society through fashion as well. According to the Wikipedia entry on hip-hop fashion, "Contemporary hip-hop fashion includes the wearing of baggy jeans slung low around the waist, gold or platinum chains and boots or a fresh pair of kicks, and bandanas or doo rags tied around the head often worn with a baseball cap on top." These days, a trip to any high school or shopping mall in America will reveal numerous examples of this kind of fashion.

Hip-hop grew out of African traditions, arose in African American urban areas, and is performed almost exclusively by African Americans. Yet hip-hop has gained an audience of a large number of young, white males in the United States. Across the U.S. suburbs, white adolescent males are adopting the hip-hop style of dress, using hip-hop language, and buying millions of rap records each year. Over 70% of hip-hop music sales are made to white consumers (MacLean). What explains hip-hop's enormous appeal to young white men? A number of factors—personal, social, and economic—appear to be behind this phenomenon.

Reviewing your draft

Give yourself plenty of time for reviewing your draft. For detailed information on how to participate in a peer review, how to review it yourself, and how to respond to comments from your classmates, your instructor, or a campus writing consultant, see pages 24–28.

Some good questions to ask yourself when reviewing causal analysis

- Is my causal claim clear? Have I avoided oversimplifying?

- Will my audience understand why this issue is important?

- Have I accounted for the various stakeholders in this analysis?

- Have I considered all possible causes? Have I used sound logic to evaluate them?

- Have I provided evidence to support my claim?

5: Submitted version

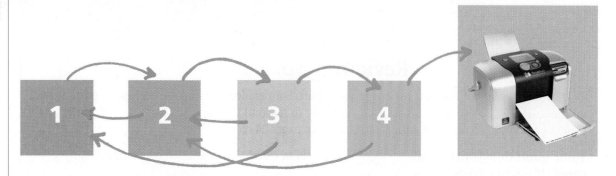

Booker 1

Sean Booker
Professor Martinez
SOC 032
22 March 2008

Borrowing Bling: The Appeal of Hip-hop to Young White Men

Rap music, a genre that developed in the United States in the 1970s, has its roots in the music of West African storytellers, musicians and poets known as Griots (Keyes 19). Rap, which includes both DJing and MCing, is one of the elements of the "Hip-Hop" cultural movement. The other major elements of hip-hop culture are graffiti and breakdancing (Keyes 63). Hip-hop has had a major impact on society through fashion as well. According to the Wikipedia entry on hip-hop, "Contemporary hip-hop fashion includes the wearing of baggy jeans slung low around the waist, gold or platinum chains and boots or a fresh pair of kicks, and bandanas or doo rags tied around the head often worn with a baseball cap on top." These days, a trip to any high school or shopping mall in America will reveal numerous examples of this kind of fashion.

Hip-hop grew out of African traditions, arose in African American urban areas, and is performed almost exclusively by African Americans. Yet hip-hop has gained an audience of a large number of young, white males in the United States. Across the U.S. suburbs, white adolescent males are adopting the hip-hop style of dress, using hip-hop

language, and downloading millions of rap records each year. Over seventy percent of hip-hop music sales are made to white consumers (MacLean). What explains hip-hop's enormous appeal to young white men? A number of factors—personal, social, and economic—appear to be behind this phenomenon.

On a personal level, hip-hop appeals to young, white males because it allows them to escape from the constraints of white society and experience the world of the rapper. Rap music details the life of the African American, sometimes describing a violent and gritty life on the street, or alternatively, a life filled with the glamour of flashy jewelry, nice cars, women, and money. Both of these world views differ vastly from the often insulated, predictable world of the young white adolescent. Professor Fiona Mills interviewed young white rap listeners for her essay "Rap and Young, White Males: Masculinity, Masking and Denial." She found that "young, white men are drawn to the escapist and exotic aspects of rap."

But hip-hop is more than an outlet for personal fantasy. It can also provide a highly defined alternative culture which appeals to the young, white man who may have trouble finding himself within white culture, or who may consciously reject white culture. The fact that hip-hop especially appeals to young men at a time in their lives when they are seeking to define themselves as adults supports this theory. For a white teenager trying desperately to establish himself as a unique person, hip-hop style may appeal because it is something he can easily recognize and emulate, and something which then sets him apart from his white peers. It is a means for situating himself in society.

Additionally, Mills explains that rap music, with its focus on sex, money, drugs and violence, builds a "hyper-masculine aura" that white adolescent males are drawn to because it gives them a model for establishing their masculinity. As Mills revealed in her study, white males often begin listening to music around age twelve or thirteen, just as they are entering adolescence and beginning to establish their masculine identities. In contrast, Mills found that African American males reported listening to rap music from a very young age. Mills suggests that the white adolescents she interviewed saw rap music "as a way of asserting their manhood by associating themselves with an overtly masculine culture—one in which femininity had no place."

Rap music also appeals to young white men because it is a way to rebel against their parents and white society in general. By associating themselves with a musical

culture that involves heavy use of profane language and often centers on violence and drugs, white males establish their rebellion against societal standards. Many teens may like rap for the simple fact that their parents do not approve of its foul language, portrayal of violence, and treatment of women.

These factors all help explain why young white men might be drawn to hip-hop and rap music and what they might gain from adopting its cultural markers. But do these factors alone explain hip-hop's enormous popularity with white consumers? There are many other types of music and culture that might appeal to white adolescents on the same grounds as hip-hop. Why has hip-hop become such a huge cultural phenomenon?

Marketing may well be the answer. Hip-hop historian and journalist Davey D has chronicled the economic pressures that led to hip-hop being marketed directly to white audiences. Historically, advertisers and record companies have cared little about young African American consumers, who typically have less disposable income than white consumers. Young white males, on the other hand, are a key demographic that all marketers pursue. As Davey D puts it, "As major corporations saw lots of white kids getting down with hip-hop, they decided to do whatever it took to appeal to what is considered a lucrative demographic. . . . What this all boiled down to was there was a premium placed on white/more affluent listeners. Many corporations simply did not want to attract a young African American clientele." To attract a white clientele, Davey D argues, record companies and promoters began putting out hip-hop acts that fed white stereotypes about African Americans. As a result, "in 2003 you have a genre of music that was born in the harshest ghettos outselling any other music and now attracting the desired Holy Grail for corporate advertisers—white folks 18-34 [translation: Generation X]."

If Davey D's argument is correct, then the popularity of hip-hop among young white men is cause for concern. While cultural crossover is in many ways a good thing and can help promote understanding among people, some feel that hip-hop is being used to manipulate consumers and even promote racial stereotypes. If true, this would be a sad statement about today's white hip-hop fans. Like white audiences at a 1920s vaudeville show, they could be exposed to a parody of African American culture and think it was the real thing.

Works Cited

D, Davey. "Hip Hop's Ultimate Battle: Race and the Politics of Divide and Conquer." *Davey D's Hip Hop Daily News.* N.p., 10 Jan. 2003. Web. 13 Mar. 2008.

Keyes, Cheryl Lynette. *Rap Music and Street Consciousness.* Champaign: U of Illinois P., 2002. Print.

MacLean, Natalie. "Bring on the Bling—Rappers Give Cristal and Hennessy Street Cred." *San Francisco Chronicle.* San Francisco Chronicle, 16 Dec. 2004. Web. 10 Mar. 2008.

Mills, Fiona. "Rap and Young, White Males: Masculinity, Masking and Denial." *Magazine Americana.* Americana: The Institute for the Study of American Popular Culture, Dec. 2001. Web. 13 Mar. 2008.

Projects

A causal analysis answers the question: How did something get that way? They first have to identify what that something is: an event, an object, a phenomenon, or a trend. Once they have identified the **what,** then they move to the **how** and **why**.

Causal analyses have several different purposes. Sometimes we are just curious about why something happened. In some cases, we may want to repeat something, such as the successful sales of a product. In other cases, we may want to prevent potentially bad effects from occurring. And in still other cases, we might want to forecast the future.

The following projects give you a range of opportunities for causal analysis.

Causal analysis of a trend

Identify a significant change in human behavior over a period of months or years. Why have mega-churches grown rapidly? Why has reality television become popular? Why have the wealthiest one percent of Americans grown significantly richer over the past twenty years? Why have homicide rates dropped to levels not seen since the 1960s? Why are children increasingly obese?

Determine the time span of the trend. When did it start? When did it stop? Is it still going on? You likely will need to do research.

Analyze the possible causes of the trend, arguing for the ones you think are most likely the true causes. Look for underlying and hidden causes.

Remember that providing facts is not the same thing as establishing causes, even though facts can help support your causal analysis.

Analyzing claims and stakeholders

Identify a causal relationship that is now generally accepted but was once in doubt, such as Galileo's explanation of the phases of the moon, the link between DDT and the decline of bald eagle populations, or the effects of vitamin B12 on developing fetuses.

Research the arguments that were made for and against these causal relationships. Who initially proposed the cause? What was the reaction? Who argued against them, and why? How did the causal relationship come to be accepted as real? Write a short essay outlining the stakeholders in the issue you have chosen.

Explain the arguments made for and against the now-accepted cause, and the evidence presented. Which of Mill's methods of determining causation did each party use (see page 195)? Why were the arguments of the now-accepted cause more effective?

Causal analysis of a human-influenced natural phenomenon

Find a natural phenomenon or trend that is (or may be) the result of human activity. Is the growing hole in the earth's ozone layer the result of human-produced chemicals in the atmosphere? Why have populations of American alligators rebounded in the southern United States? Are sinkholes in a Kentucky town the result of new mining activity in the area? Why are more and more bacteria developing resistance to antibiotics? Choose a topic that interests you and which you feel is important. If you think the topic is important, it will be easier to convince your audience that your analysis is important.

Research the possible causes of the phenomenon, focusing on the ones you think are most likely the true causes. Remember to look at underlying and hidden causes.

Think about possible alternative causes. Do you need to incorporate them? If you don't think they are valid causes, then you need to refute them.

Recognize that causal relationships between humans and the natural world are so complex and large in scale that it is often difficult to prove them definitively. Don't oversimplify or make sweeping claims that can't be proven.

11 Evaluations

Convincing evaluations rely on selecting criteria and supporting
a claim with reasons and evidence.

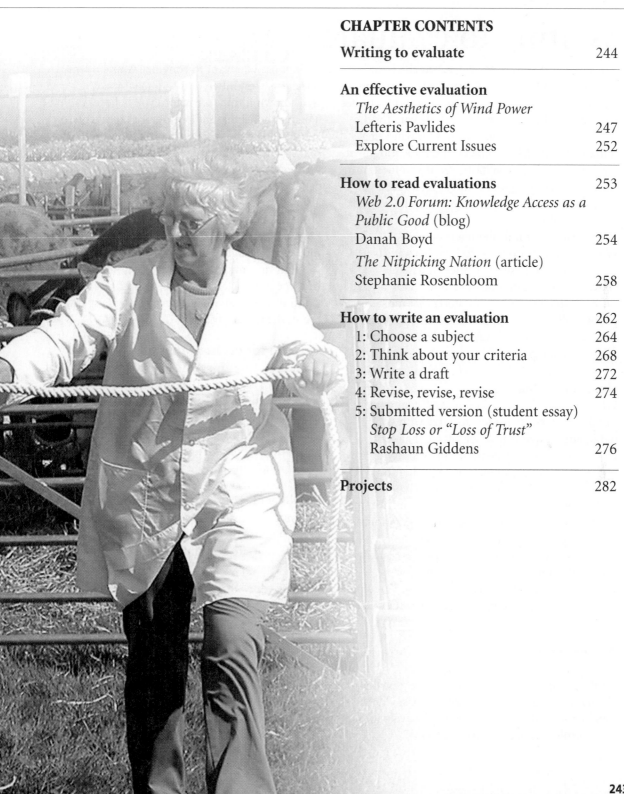

Writing to evaluate

You make evaluations every day. You choose a favorite CD, a favorite restaurant, a favorite ring tone on your cell phone. Newspapers and Web sites feature "best of" polls that let people vote for the restaurant, movie, television show, or band they think is the "best." To some extent, these judgments are a matter of personal taste. Yet, if you look into the reasons people give for their preferences, you often find that different people use similar criteria to make evaluations.

For example, think about a restaurant you like. What are your reasons for feeling this way? Is it clean? The food fresh? The prices low? Is it convenient to your home or campus? Do you like the atmosphere? These are criteria that most people will use to judge a restaurant. That's why some restaurants are always crowded, while many others quickly go out of business.

Goals of evaluation

When you write an evaluation, your goal is usually to convince readers to agree with your judgment. Convincing other people that your judgment is sound depends on the validity of the criteria you will use to make your evaluation. Will the criteria you're using as the basis of your evaluation be convincing to other people? You may think a movie is good because it has exceptional cinematography, but an action-movie fan is less likely to go see a movie just because it is visually beautiful. Sometimes you must argue for the validity of your criteria before readers will accept them. If they don't accept your criteria, they won't agree with your conclusions.

An evaluative claim

An evaluation can be stated in the form "SOMETHING is good (or bad, the best or the worst) if measured by these criteria." Usually, the most important task when writing an evaluation is to determine the kind of criteria to use.

Suppose you want to convince your student Speakers' Committee to host a talk by a well-known filmmaker whom you believe would be a better choice than other potential speakers. You could argue that, because she is famous, the filmmaker will draw many students to her talk, thus raising the profile of the Speakers' Program, and generating more money in ticket sales. You could also argue that the filmmaker's talk would be a culturally enriching experience for students because she has made many critically acclaimed movies. You might argue that a large number of students on campus have expressed their desire to hear the filmmaker, and that the Speakers' Committee has an obligation to provide speakers the students want to hear.

Criteria for evaluation

Each of these arguments uses a different kind of criteria. An argument that the filmmaker will draw students and make money is based on **practical criteria**. An argument that her artistic achievement makes her a worthwhile speaker is based on **aesthetic criteria**. An argument that the committee is bound to consider the wishes of students is based on **ethical criteria**. These are the three basic categories of criteria for all evaluative arguments.

Things are usually judged to be good (or bad) either because they work well (practicality), because they are beautiful (aesthetics), or because they are morally fair or just (ethics). An evaluative argument may use any or all of these types of criteria, and can emphasize them in different ways. For example, if you want to convince your roommate to go to an expensive sushi restaurant, you would probably emphasize the aesthetic experience of enjoying fresh sushi in a fashionable atmosphere. You would want to downplay practical criteria like cost, especially if your roommate's budget requires that he usually dine on Ramen noodles instead of sushi.

Understand how evaluation arguments work

Evaluation arguments set out criteria and then judge something to be good or bad or best or worst according to those criteria.

> # Something is a good (bad, the best, the worst)_____if measured by certain criteria (practicality, aesthetics, ethics).

EXAMPLE

Google Maps is the best mapping program **because** it is easy to use, it is accurate, **and** it provides entertaining and educational features such as Google Earth.

Components of evaluations

What will make a good subject to evaluate?	**Find something to evaluate.** Listing is one way to identify possible subjects for evaluation. You might list restaurants, buildings, cars, computers, and other objects. You might evaluate a film, a book, a TV show, a presidential speech, or certain policies or courses at your school.
What is my working thesis?	**Write a working thesis.** Your thesis should argue that something is good/better/best or bad/worst, successful or unsuccessful on the basis of criteria that you name.
What values are most important for my readers?	**Consider your readers**. How interesting will this topic be to your readers? What criteria will be most convincing to them?
What are the appropriate criteria for my subject?	**Choose the appropriate criteria. Practical criteria** will demand that the thing being evaluated work efficiently or lead to good outcomes (profits, satisfied customers, improved conditions, lower costs, and so on). **Aesthetic criteria** hinge on the importance and value of beauty, image, or tradition. **Ethical criteria** are used to evaluate whether something is morally right, consistent with the law and with rules of fair play.
Who would disagree with me?	**Consider other views.** Has anyone evaluated your subject before? What criteria did they use? For example, you might hate horror movies because they give you bad dreams, but many other people love them. You should consider why they have such a strong following.
What is the most engaging way to begin?	**Start fast.** You may have to give some background but get quickly to your subject.
What is the most effective way to end?	**Finish strong.** If you have not announced your stance, then you can make your summary evaluation. If your readers know where you stand, you might end with a compelling example.

Keys to evaluations

Describe briefly your subject	Your readers may be unfamiliar with what you are evaluating. Give your readers a brief description.
Explain your criteria	The importance of many criteria may not be evident to your readers. You may need to state explicitly each criterion you use and explain why it is relevant.
Be fair	Be honest about the strengths and weaknesses of what you are evaluating. Rarely is anything perfectly good or absolutely bad. Your credibility will increase if you give a balanced view.
Support your judgments with evidence	Back up your claims with specific evidence. If you write that a restaurant serves inedible food, describe examples in detail.
Define criteria for visual evaluations	Criteria for visual evaluations may require additional work to define and explain.

Working Together

What makes an effective review?

In a group of three or four students

- Look at a selection of short, amateur online reviews, such as customer book reviews at Amazon.com, consumer reviews on a site like Epinions.com, or user comments on a film at www.imdb.com.

- Select several examples of reviews that you think are persuasive and several that are not (see if you can find some persuasive reviews that you don't necessarily agree with). Share these with the rest of your group.

- As a group, discuss the following: What criteria do reviewers of similar products share? What types of criteria do the persuasive reviews use? What types do the less persuasive reviews use? Do you see any patterns that make reviews persuasive?

An effective evaluation

A successful evaluation makes a claim about the value of something. It supports its main claim with criteria that the audience will agree are important.

The Providence Journal

The Aesthetics of Wind Power
Lefteris Pavlides

People argue that wind turbines are good or bad depending on the criteria they select. Proponents of wind power argue that they produce energy without creating pollution and reduce dependence on foreign oil (practical criteria). Opponents argue that they drive down real estate values (a practical criterion), are ugly (an aesthetic criterion), and kill birds (an ethical criterion). The proposed Cape Wind project on Nantucket Sound in Massachusetts has provoked an especially contentious debate. Lefteris Pavlides, who is a professor of architecture at Roger Williams University, published this evaluation in the *Providence Journal* in March 2005.

The Aesthetics of
Wind Power

by Lefteris Pavlides

"Wind turbines are not pretty," said Massachusetts Governor Romney late last year, to the applause of about half of the emotional crowd at an Army Corps of Engineers public hearing on Cape Wind Park.

Yet the Corps's 3,800-page report was an overwhelmingly positive evaluation of the 130 modern windmills proposed for Horseshoe Shoal, in Nantucket Sound. And despite the governor's attempt to speak for the public's aesthetic, the truth is that most people love the elegance of slow-moving giants that quietly turn wind into electricity.

The author assumes his readers are familiar with the controversy, so the evaluation begins with an opposing view—that wind turbines are bad because they are ugly.

Whose visual judgment matters on this issue? And how do we know that most people see modern windmills as visual assets?

Blind impartial market indicators provide indirect evidence that modern windmills are seen as beautiful. Surveys on real-estate prices and on tourism cited in the Army Corps's draft Environmental Impact Study (section 5) clearly show the strong visual appeal of modern windmills in many places around the world.

Pavlides questions the opposing view, claiming that most people find wind turbines elegant.

A boon to real estate values and tourism

And a study of 29,000 real-estate transactions in America found that the property values of homes with views of wind turbines rose faster than those of nearby homes with no such views.

Pavlides challenges the assertions that wind turbines lower the value of surrounding homes and harm tourism.

The Corps's report also examined surveys of visitors to sites around the globe where wind energy is well established—modern windmills in such places as Scotland, Australia and California, and off Denmark and Sweden. Installation of wind turbines increases tourism, it was found, providing evidence that most people see them as attractive additions to land- and seascapes. From Scotland to New Zealand, and from California to the Greek Isles, people pay to visit wind turbines and be photographed with them.

As a professor of architecture, I understand the visual logic of this phenomenon. I teach that forms made to move in wind—such as sailboats and Porsches—are inherently beautiful. Experts discuss the artistic qualities of aerodynamic lines and the kinetic grace of modern windmills, using such terms as proportion, contrast, rhythm and movement to express what we all experience.

The author builds his credibility as an authority.

The aesthetics of wind power

From an abstract view, the graceful modern windmills are even more beautiful than their ancient

He returns to aesthetic criteria and offers more evidence of the beauty of modern windmills.

counterparts. A Cape Cod sculptor recently wrote to me, "[T]he beauty of modern windmills is a joyous scene to behold. As sail boats provide visual delight while transforming air into propulsion, so will windmills that catch ambient breezes for essential power."

Non-experts in aesthetics also discuss the delight of watching windmills. An engineer with no artistic training sent me his unsolicited opinion that the Danish Horns Rev offshore wind park was "one of the most inspiring and thrilling sights seen from the Blavaand lighthouse observatory deck."

To adapt an adage, beauty is in the eye and also the mind of the beholder. Our judgment of what is beautiful is based not just on abstract qualities of form. Modern windmills, for instance, have acquired a broad range of connotations.

For some, they are worse than ugly, evoking deep fear in their enormous scale. For others, they are beyond magnificent, evoking deep religious feelings.

More common associations with modern windmills include economic benefits or threats to market share (for fossil-fuel interests); reduction of disease in the reduction of polluting emissions; and real or bogus environmental threats.

Visual delight accompanies connotations of:

- Economic benefits, such as fixed energy prices for years to come. The Army Corps reported that Cape Wind would have a significant positive impact on the local economy.
- Health benefits from reduced pollution, including fewer people with asthma and bronchitis, and fewer premature deaths. The Corps reported a probable $53 million in health savings.

The strongest arguments for wind turbines are based on practical criteria. They provide a dependable, pollution-free source of energy.

Visual blight is an impression that accompanies connotations of:

- Loss of market share. Modern windmills are a constant reminder of eroding market share for executives of coal and oil companies, such as Douglas Yearly, a former chairman of Phelps Dodge who is on the board of Marathon Oil. Mr. Yearly, who has a summer place in Cape Cod's Osterville, has spearheaded opposition to Cape Wind.

Pavlides questions the motives of some critics of wind power.

The Army Corps's report indicates that Cape Wind would produce three-quarters of the electricity needed by Cape Cod and the Islands.

Regarding wildlife, when people are told that modern windmills offer protections to animals, they see them as beautiful, while those who believe widespread misinformation about dangers to birds have reservations.

The Corps's exhaustive avian studies conclude that there is no basis for concern. Further scientific studies show that wind energy is hugely beneficial to birds and other wildlife, in that it reduces:

- acid rain, which causes regional bird extinctions by killing the snails that are critical to bird diets;
- mercury contamination, which has caused extinction of loons on the Great Lakes;
- oil spills, which kill all manner of wildlife;
- and global warming, the biggest threat of all

He counters the ethical argument of harm to birds by pointing to benefits to wildlife from reduced pollution.

There is every indication that the opposition to Cape Wind will evolve much the way public attitudes toward the Statue of Liberty evolved over a century ago. The statue's installation was resisted and delayed because, as newspapers declared, it "was neither an object of art [n]or beauty." Now an adored icon, the statue significantly raises the value of properties with views of it. It is seen as beautiful because of its sculptural qualities and also because of the freedom and human rights that it represents.

He ends with the analogy to the Statue of Liberty, which many people initially found ugly when it was installed in New York Harbor but soon grew to love.

As an architect who has been studying public perception of wind turbines, I predict that most people would similarly come to see Cape Wind's turbines as breath-givingly beautiful.

The vast majority of people around Nantucket Sound would see Cape Wind as a magnificent addition to the sound—making visible the reduction of invisible toxic gases that despoil the region's environment.

And the windmills would visually communicate, now and to future generations, our commitment to energy freedom and a disease-free environment.

New Englanders have a responsibility to express their support for this project.

Explore Current Issues

What makes a video game "smart"?

Both fans and detractors of the "Grand Theft Auto" game series know it to be extremely violent; the goal of each game in the series is essentially to use any means necessary to rise to the top of the criminal underworld of a familiar, yet fictional futuristic city. Critics of the game argue that the game flaunts crime, racial conflict, and sexual violence. Perhaps most shocking is the amorality of the game: innocent citizens as well as hardened criminals are mown down not just indiscriminately, but gleefully.

The latest installment in the series, "Grand Theft Auto IV" set sales records when it was released in late April of 2008 and garnered critical praise for its superior playability and graphics. More interestingly, however, is that "GTA IV" is being called "smart." *Salon.com* writer Farhad Manjoo argues that the richness of the story (so rich, in fact, that engaged players might be less inclined to kill random bystanders), the depth and realism of the world, the dimensionality and quirkiness of the characters, the wry humor, and the more interactive and socially based tasks and puzzles of the game will make players it call it "the smartest video game ever created."

Write about it

1. How do you think Manjoo defines the word "smart"? Why do you think this? Do you agree with this definition? Why or why not? What other word could he use instead of "smart"?

2. Which of the following criteria are useful for evaluating the content of a video game? Why?

   • Richness of story line
   • Realism
   • Violence
   • Complexity of characters
   • Types of puzzles and tasks
   • Representation of gender, class, ethnicity, and disability
   • Morality
   • Humor

3. Are any of the criteria more important than the others? If so, how would you rank them? Are there any criteria you would add?

How to read evaluations

Make notes as you read, either in the margins or on paper or a computer file. Circle any words or references that you don't know and look them up.

What is it?	• What kind of a text is it? A review? an essay? a blog? an editorial? What are your expectations for this kind of text? • What media are used? (Web sites, for example, often combine images, words, and sounds.)
Where did it come from?	• Who wrote the evaluation? • What do you know about the writer's background that might have influenced the evaluation?
What is the writer's thesis or main idea?	• What clues do you find about whom the writer had in mind as the readers? • What does the writer assume that the readers already know about the subject? • What new knowledge is the writer providing?
Who is the intended audience?	• What clues do you find about whom the writer had in mind as the readers? • What does the writer assume that the readers already know about the subject? • What new knowledge is the writer providing?
Does the writer make a clear evaluative claim?	• What exactly is the writer's evaluative claim?
What are the criteria used in the evaluation?	• Does the writer use practical criteria? aesthetic criteria? ethical criteria? (See pages 244–245.) • Does the writer argue for how these criteria apply to the subject? • Does the writer acknowledge opposing views?
How is it composed?	• How does the writer represent herself or himself? • How would you characterize the style? • If there are any photographs or other graphics, what information do they contribute?

Web 2.0 Forum: Knowledge Access as a Public Good
(BLOG)
Danah Boyd

Danah Boyd researches and writes on how teens present themselves and socialize within mediated environments, especially social networking sites on the Internet such as MySpace, YouTube, and Facebook. She also maintains a blog on social media, called *Apophenia*. In this blog, she responds to Michael Gorman's argument in the same forum that Web 2.0 is damaging to intellectual life. "Knowledge Access as a Public Good" was published in an online forum sponsored by the Encyclopedia Britannica on June 27, 2007.

Return to these questions after you have finished reading.

Analyzing and Connecting

1. Examine the language, tone, and cultural references in Boyd's argument. How do they affect the appeal of the argument?

2. Much like Stephpanie Rosenbloom's "The Nitpicking Nation" (see pages 258–261) is not so much a straightforward evaluation of Craigslist but instead a look at how people make evaluations on Craigslist, so too does Boyd's response evaluate Gorman's response to Web 2.0. Where exactly does she find strengths and weaknesses in Gorman's argument?

3. Thinking about the positive and negative aspects of Web 2.0 you gleaned from Boyd's argument, what does she consider an effective response? Does this response address both the positive negative aspects of Web 2.0 effectively? Why or why not?

4. Boyd begins her concluding paragraph with the historic phrase "I hold these truths to be self-evident." Why do you think she chooses this phrase for her conclusion? What kind of appeal does it make? Is it appropriate for her argument? Why or why not?

Finding Ideas for Writing

Boyd's argument proceeds from two large claims in the seventh paragraph. She writes:

> I want to help people gain access to information in the hopes that they can create knowledge that is valuable for everyone. I have lost faith in traditional organizations leading the way to mass access and am thus always on the lookout for innovative models to produce and distribute knowledge.

Do you agree that if people have broad access to information, they will create knowledge that is valuable to everyone? And do you agree with her claim that traditional organizations have failed in giving people mass access to information?

KNOWLEDGE ACCESS AS A PUBLIC GOOD

As a child, I believed that all educated people were wise. In particular, I placed educators and authorities on a high pedestal and I entered the academy both to seek their wisdom and to become one of them. Unfortunately, eleven years of higher education has taught me that parts of the academy are rife with many of the same problems that plague society as a whole: greed, self-absorbtion, addiction to power, and an overwhelming desire to be validated, praised, and rewarded. As Dr. Gorman laments the ills of contemporary society, I find myself nodding along. Doing ethnographic work in the United States often leaves me feeling disillusioned and numb. It breaks my heart every time a teenager tells me that s/he is more talented than Sanjaya and thus is guaranteed a slot on the next "American Idol."

The pervasive view that American society is a meritocracy makes me want to scream, but I fear as though my screams fall on deaf ears.

To cope with my frustration, I often return to my bubble. My friends all seem to come from Lake Wobegon where "the women are strong, the men are good looking, and all of the children are above average." I have consciously surrounded myself with people who think like me, share my values, and are generally quite overeducated. I feel very privileged to live in such an environment, but like all intellectuals who were educated in the era of identity politics, I am regularly racked with guilt over said privilege.

The Internet is a funny thing, especially now that those online are not just the connected elite. It mirrors and magnifies the offline world—all of the good, bad, and ugly. I don't need to travel to Idaho to face neo-Nazis. I don't need to go to Colorado Springs to hear religious views that contradict my worldview. And I don't need to go to Capitol Hill to witness the costs of power for power's sake.

If I am willing to look, there are places on the Internet that will expose me to every view on this planet, even those that I'd prefer to pretend did not exist. Most of the privileged people that I know prefer to live like ostriches, ignoring the realities of everyday life in order to sustain their privileges. I am trying not to be that person, although I find it to be a challenge.

In the 16th century, Sir Francis Bacon famously wrote that "knowledge is power." Not surprisingly, institutions that profit off of knowledge trade in power. In an era of capitalism, this equation often gets tainted by questions of profitability. Books are not published simply because they contain valued and valid information; they are published if and when the publisher can profit off of the sale of those books. Paris Hilton stands a far better chance of getting a publishing deal than most astute and thought-provoking academics. Even a higher education is becoming more inaccessible to more people at a time when a college degree is necessary to work in a cafe. $140,000 for a college education is a scary proposition, even if you want to enter

the ratrace of the white collar mega-corporations where you expect to make a decent salary. Amidst this environment, it frustrates me to hear librarians speak about information dissemination while they create digital firewalls that lock people out of accessing knowledge unless they have the right academic credentials.

I entered the academy because I believe in knowledge production and dissemination. I am a hopeless Marxist. I want to equal the playing field; I want to help people gain access to information in the hopes that they can create knowledge that is valuable for everyone. I have lost faith in traditional organizations leading the way to mass access and am thus always on the lookout for innovative models to produce and distribute knowledge.

Unlike Dr. Gorman, Wikipedia brings me great joy. I see it as a fantastic example of how knowledge can be distributed outside of elite institutions. I have watched stubs of articles turn into rich homes for information about all sorts of subjects. What I like most about Wikipedia is the self-recognition that it is always a work-in-progress. The encyclopedia that I had as a kid was a hand-me-down; it stated that one day we would go to the moon. Today, curious poor youth have access to information in an unprecedented way. It may not be perfect, but it is far better than a privilege-only model of access.

Knowledge is not static, but traditional publishing models assume that it can be captured and frozen for consumption. What does that teach children about knowledge? Captured knowledge makes sense when the only opportunity for dissemination is through distributing physical artifacts, but this is no longer the case. Now that we can get information to people faster, why should we support the erection of barriers?

In middle school, I was sent to the principal's office for correcting a teacher's math. The issue was not whether or not I was correct—I was; I was ejected from class for having the gall to challenge authority. Would Galileo have been allowed to write an encyclopedia article? The "authorities" of his day rejected his scientific claims. History has many examples of how the vetting process has failed us. Imagine all of the knowledge that was produced that was more successfully suppressed by authorities. In the era of the Internet, gatekeepers have less power. I don't think that this is always a bad thing.

Like paper, the Internet is a medium. People express a lot of crap through both mediums. Yet, should we denounce paper as inherently flawed? The Internet—and Wikipedia—change the rules for distribution and production. It means that those with knowledge do not have to retreat to the ivory towers to share what they know. It means that individuals who know something can easily share it, even when they are not formally declared as experts. It means that those with editing skills can help the information become accessible, even if they only edit occasionally. It means that multi-lingual individuals can help get information to people who speak languages that publishers do not consider worth their time. It means that anyone with an Internet connection can get access to information traditionally locked behind the gates of institutions (and currently locked in digital vaults).

Don't get me wrong—Wikipedia is not perfect. But why do purported experts spend so much time arguing against it rather than helping make it a better resource? It is free! It is accessible! Is it really worth that much prestige to write an encyclopedia article instead of writing a Wikipedia entry? While there are certainly errors there, imagine what would happen if all of those who view themselves as experts took the time to make certain that the greatest and most broad-reaching resource was as accurate as possible.

I believe that academics are not just the producers of knowledge—they are also teachers. As teachers, we have an ethical responsibility to help distribute knowledge. We have a responsibility to help not just the 30 people in our classroom, but the millions of people globally who will never have the opportunity to sit in one of our classes. The Internet gives us the tool to do this. Why are we throwing this opportunity away? Like Dr. Gorman, I don't believe that all crowds are inherently wise. But I also don't believe that all authorities are inherently wise. Especially not when they are vying for tenure.

Why are we telling our students not to use Wikipedia rather than educating them about how Wikipedia works? Sitting in front of us is an ideal opportunity to talk about how knowledge is produced, how information is disseminated, how ideas are shared. Imagine if we taught the "history" feature so that students would have the ability to track how a Wikipedia entry is produced and assess for themselves what the authority of the author is. You can't do this with an encyclopedia. Imagine if we taught students how to fact check claims in Wikipedia and, better yet, to add valuable sources to a Wikipedia entry so that their work becomes part of the public good.

Herein lies a missing piece in Dr. Gorman's puzzle. The society that he laments has lost faith in the public good. Elitism and greed have gotten in the way. By upholding the values of the elite, Dr. Gorman is perpetuating views that are destroying efforts to make knowledge a public good. Wikipedia is a public-good project. It is the belief that division of labor has value and that everyone has something to contribute, if only a spelling correction. It is the belief that all people have the inalienable right to knowledge, not just those who have academic chairs. It is the belief that the powerful have no right to hoard the knowledge. And it is the belief that people can and should collectively help others gain access to information and knowledge.

Personally, I hold these truths to be self-evident, and I'd rather see us put in the effort to make Wikipedia an astounding resource that can be used by all people than to try to dismantle it simply because it means change.

The Nitpicking Nation
(ARTICLE)
Stephanie Rosenbloom

In addition to being a journalist for the *New York Times*, 1997 Colgate graduate Stephanie Rosenbloom began acting at a young age and has directed plays since she was a senior in high school. She writes articles about real estate and about how people adapt new technologies for their own purposes. "The Nitpicking Nation" appeared in the *New York Times* in May 2006.

Return to these questions after you have finished reading.

Analyzing and Connecting

1. In one way "The Nitpicking Nation" is not a classic evaluation but rather a look at how people make evaluations on Craigslist. But it also indirectly evaluates Craigslist. What positives and negatives of Craigslist are given?

2. Visit Craigslist.org, and compare housing and roommate ads for a city in the United States with those in a city in another country. Make a list of what is desirable and undesirable in roommates or house-sharing partners for both cities. Which criteria are the same on both lists? Which are different?

3. What criteria do you use to evaluate roommates? What makes an ideal roommate in your view?

4. Think of a product that you already own or would like to own. Enter the name of the product on Google followed by the word *review*. If you don't find many reviews, try consumersearch.com. Read several reviews and make a list of the most frequent criteria used to evaluate the product.

Finding Ideas for Writing

Rosenbloom cites Craig Newmark's belief that Craigslist operates in a "culture of trust," inspiring users to be honest. How does this culture work? Does it always work? Write a paragraph to insert into Rosenbloom's article explaining how and why this culture of trust works (or doesn't). Use your own or others' experiences with listing sites such as Craigslist, eBay, and others to provide support for your explanation.

THE NITPICKING NATION

THEY are single, gay, straight, biracial, conservative, liberal and tattooed—and they have as many preferences for a potential roommate as an online dater has for a potential lover. They are bankers, fetishists, self-declared nerds and drug users. They have old wounds and new hopes, and are willing to barter their cooking and sexual expertise for free or discounted rent.

They are all seeking and selling housing on Craigslist.org, the electronic listing service with sites in all 50 states and more than 200 worldwide. And because users pay nothing (for now) and are able to go on at length about who they are and what they want, their postings provide a sociological window into housing trends and desires across the country, from the neon cityscape of the Las Vegas Strip to the wheat fields of Wichita, Kan.

Myriad other sites provide roommate-matching services, but in the last decade Craigslist has emerged as the gold standard. It is easy to navigate, has an extensive number of listings and does not require people to complete an online sign-up sheet to view postings in their entirety. And the intimate and sometimes politically incorrect nature of Craigslist postings can make them fun to read—amusing, frank and even kinky.

Perhaps the most eyebrow-raising thing about the housing listings is the abundance of users—even young, savvy residents of anything-goes metropolises like Los Angeles and Miami—who want mellow, nonpartying roommates. Las Vegas sounds more like Snore City if you judge it by its housing listings. And New Yorkers can come off sounding square. "No parties" and "no drama" are common refrains.

There are exceptions, but even club-hopping Paris Hilton hopefuls seem to have their limits. As four women (ages 19 to 22) seeking a fifth roommate in Boston wrote, "We want a partier, not a puker."

People in their 20's often list their alma maters and request a roommate in their own age group. Cleanliness is a must, or at least "clean-ish," "decently clean" or "clean in public spaces." And spending life with a "professional" appears to be just as important to users of Craigslist's housing listings as it is to users of Match.com.

Some listings have stirred up trouble, however, and the Chicago Lawyers' Committee for Civil Rights Under Law, a nonprofit group, has filed a lawsuit in federal court against Craigslist for "publishing housing advertisements which exclude prospective tenants on the basis of race, gender, family status, marital status, national origin and religion."

A news release issued by the organization said that the Craigslist postings contained such language as "no minorities," "African-Americans and Arabians tend to clash with me so that won't work out," "ladies, please rent from me," "requirements: clean godly Christian male," "will allow only single occupancy," and "no children."

The suit is addressed on Craigslist: "Although in all likelihood this suit will be dismissed on the grounds that Internet sites cannot legally be held liable for content posted by users, Craigslist has no need to hide behind this well-established immunity."

The statement also says that Craigslist respects constitutionally protected free speech rights and that "discriminatory postings are

exceedingly uncommon, and those few that do reach the site are typically removed quickly by our users through the flagging system that accompanies each ad."

Craig Newmark, the founder of Craigslist, said that its "culture of trust" inspires users to be straightforward. In fact, some users do not even feel compelled to embellish the descriptions of their spaces, as housing advertisements commonly do. Rather, they take a certain pride in the gritty crudeness of their offerings. A small room for rent in the East Village is described as "definitely a young person's apartment" with "two small junky TV's that we have cheap antennas on, but we get the normal channels, and that is enough for us."

"There is no window," the listing says, "but you have a full-sized door."

And where else do you find housing listings that include candid photographs of the owner or leaseholder instead of the property they are advertising? (A man in Fort Lauderdale, Fla., compromised and included images of his bare room and his bare chest.)

Indeed, Craigslist is where sex and real estate can truly merge. Near Dallas, a married couple are looking for a female roommate "with benefits." A listing for Astoria, Queens, reads: "I am offering a free room for up to three months for any females who are ticklish." A single man in Los Angeles is offering foot massages and free rent to women with comely feet.

Those are some of the tamer overtures, though the majority of roommate listings are not suggestive.

But just who are the most desirable roommates?

Many people prefer women to men. There are women who feel more comfortable sharing a home with someone of the same sex, men who say they get along better with female housemates, and a few cyberspace Casanovas who want to take a shot at turning a roommate into a bedmate. Interns are also desirable, apparently because they are thought to be hard-working, responsible and willing to pay good money for cramped rooms.

But couples are sometimes lumped into a list of the unacceptable, like cigarette smoking. Over all, Democrats are more vocal than Republicans in expressing a desire not to live with the opposing party, though two "hip professional guys" found elusive harmony on Capitol Hill: "One guy is straight, and one is gay. One is a Republican, and the other is a Democrat," they wrote in a listing for a third roommate. "We appreciate and welcome diversity."

Users in the San Francisco Bay Area appear to be among the least interested in rooming with a pet. This area had the highest percentage of "no pets" listings during a key-word search last Thursday (slightly more than 16 percent of 32,295 housing listings). In Boston, about 14 percent of 45,880 listings said "no pets."

Dallas, Wyoming and Birmingham, Ala., seemed quite pet-friendly by comparison: only about 1 percent of the housing listings in each location said "no pets." But Wichita, Kan., emerged as one of the most accepting places, with less than 1 percent of the listings snubbing pets.

In some parts of the country Craigslist housing postings are an essential part of the real estate biosphere. New York is by far the leader in this regard (it had some 180,245 housing listings last Thursday).

Mr. Newmark said there were two reasons for that. "New York real estate is kind of a blood sport," he said, "and also, because our site is free, brokers tend to post a lot of redundant ads."

He said he hoped to address that problem in a matter of weeks by beginning to charge a fee.

Although Mr. Newmark has not studied how the number of housing listings fluctuates day to day, he believes they remain fairly steady on weekdays and drop off on weekends.

Boston had 45,880 housing listings last Thursday, and the San Francisco Bay Area had 32,295. In other places like Montana and Louisville, Ky., there were just a few hundred postings, and North Dakota had fewer than 100.

The New York listings include some of the most expensive, precarious sleeping arrangements in the country. A sofa bed in the living room/kitchen of a one-bedroom apartment on 55th Street between Eighth and Ninth Avenues is $683 a month. You could get a 780-square-foot one-bedroom cottage in Savannah, Ga., for $665 a month. A couch on the West Coast, in a Los Angeles apartment belonging to three actors, is merely $400 a month and includes utilities, cable, Netflix membership, Starbucks wireless membership and wireless Internet, as well as household staples like toothpaste and shampoo.

New Yorkers are also adept at constructing what the military calls a zone of separation. A woman with an apartment at Union Square posted a photograph, not of the bedroom she wanted to rent out for $1,150 a month, but of a large divider she planned to use to create the bedroom from part of her living room.

Near Columbus Circle, a "very small, but cozy space enclosed by tall bookshelves and bamboo screens" is listed for $1,700 a month.

Potential occupants are advised that they must be older than 30 and cannot wear shoes inside the apartment, smoke, consume alcohol, invite guests over or have "sleepovers."

A plethora of "no smokers" statements in the New York housing listings make it appear that the public smoking ban has infiltrated private spaces, too.

But while cigarettes are a deal breaker for some, a number of Craigslist users across the country (Denver and Boulder, Colo.; San Francisco; Boston; and Portland, Ore., to name but a few) say that they are "420 friendly," slang for marijuana use. References to 420 were nonexistent in other cities, including Little Rock, Ark.; Santa Fe, N.M.; and Boise, Idaho.

There are also myriad references to amenities, everything from the use of old record collections and video games to a trapeze suspended in a Brooklyn loft. A posting for a room for rent in Detroit lacks images of the property, though there is a photograph of the L.C.D. television.

And if nothing else, Craigslist housing postings in the United States confirm the zaniness of the hunt and provide a taste of the free-spirited, random connections that have always been part of the experience.

A posting in Asheville, N.C., says that two 21-year-old women are planning to drive almost 20 hours to Austin, Tex., this summer, where they will rent a two-bedroom apartment for $550 a month. "We are looking for one or two (yeah, you can bring a buddy) cool people to ride out there and split an apartment with us," the listing reads. "Are you up for being spontaneous?"

Would-be Jack Kerouacs, take note: they hit the road at the end of the month.

How to write an evaluation

These steps for the process of writing an evaluation may not progress as neatly as this chart might suggest. Writing is not an assembly-line process.

As you write and revise, think about how you might sharpen your criteria and better explain how they apply to what you are evaluating. Your instructor and fellow students may give you comments that help you to rethink your argument from the beginning.

1 CHOOSE A SUBJECT

- Analyze the assignment.

- Explore possible subjects by making lists. Consider which items on your list you might evaluate.

- Analyze a subject by thinking about other things like it.

- Make an evaluative claim that something is good, bad, best, or worst if measured by certain criteria.

- Think about what's at stake. If nearly everyone agrees with you, your claim probably isn't important. Why would some people disagree with you?

2 THINK ABOUT YOUR CRITERIA

- List the criteria that makes something good or bad.

- Which criteria are the most important?

- Which criteria are fairly obvious, and which will you have to argue for?

- How familiar will your readers be with what you are evaluating?

- Which criteria will they accept with little explanation, and which will they possibly disagree with?

- Research your argument by finding evidence and reliable sources.

3 WRITE A DRAFT

- Introduce the issue and give the necesary background.

- Describe each criterion and then analyze how well what you are evaluating meets that criterion.

- If you are making an evaluation according to the effects of something, describe those effects in detail.

- Anticipate where readers might question your criteria and address possible objections.

- Anticipate and address opposing viewpoints by acknowledging how others' evaluations might differ.

- Conclude with either your position, a compelling example, or what is at stake.

- Choose a title that will interest readers in your essay.

4 REVISE, REVISE, REVISE

- Check that your paper or project fulfills the assignment.

- Is your evaluative claim arguable?

- Are your criteria reasonable, and will your audience accept them?

- Is your evidence convincing and sufficient?

- Do you address opposing views?

- Review the visual presentation of your paper or project.

- Proofread carefully.

5 SUBMITTED VERSION

- Make sure your finished writing meets all formatting requirements.

1: Choose a subject

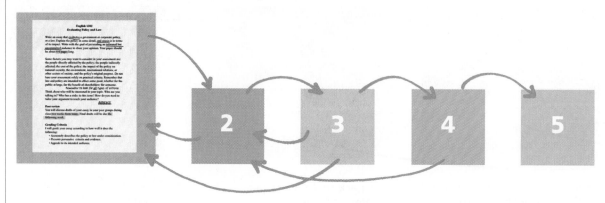

Analyze the assignment	• Read your assignment slowly and carefully. Look for key words like *evaluate, rank, review,* and *assess.* These key words tell you that you are writing an evaluative essay.
	• Mark off any information about the length specified, date due, formatting, and other requirements. You can attend to this information later.
Explore possible subjects by making lists	• Make a list of goods and services you consume; sports, entertainment, or hobbies you enjoy; books you have read recently; films you have seen; speeches you have heard; or policies and laws that affect you or concern you.
	• Consider which items on your list you might evaluate. Which are interesting to you? Which would likely interest your readers? Put checkmarks by these items.
	• Choose something to evaluate that is potentially controversial. You will learn the most, and interest readers most, if you build a strong evaluation that persuades your opponents to rethink their position.
Analyze a subject	• What does your subject attempt to achieve? What do other similar subjects attempt to achieve? (For example, a mountain bike is designed to climb and descend trails, but a good mountain bike will be lightweight, durable, and have good suspension.)
	• Who is the audience for your subject? (Mountain bikes appeal to people who prefer to ride on trails rather than pavement.)
Think about what's at stake	• Who will agree with you? Who will disagree, and why?
	• Think about why your evaluation matters.

Staying on Track

Make an arguable claim

A claim that is too obvious or too general will not produce an interesting evaluation.
Don't waste your time—or your readers'.

OFF TRACK
Michael Jordan was a great basketball player.
ON TRACK
Bill Russell was the best clutch player in the history of professional basketball.

OFF TRACK
Running is great exercise and a great way to lose weight.
ON TRACK
If you start running to lose weight, be aware of the risks: your body running exerts eight times its weight on your feet, ankles, legs, hips, and lower back, often causing injury to your joints. Swimming, biking, or exercise machines might be the better choice.

Write Now

Finding a subject to evaluate

1. Make a list of possible subjects to evaluate, and select the one that appears most promising.

2. Write nonstop for five minutes about what you like and dislike about this particular subject.

3. Write nonstop for five minutes about what you like and dislike about things in the same category (Mexican restaurants, world leaders, horror movies, mountain bikes, and so on).

4. Write nonstop for five minutes about what people in general like and dislike about things in this category.

5. Underline the likes and dislikes in all three freewrites. You should gain a sense of how your evaluation stacks up against those of others. You may discover a way you can write against the grain, showing others a good or bad aspect of this subject that they may not have observed.

Writer at work

Rashaun Giddens began by underlining the words and phrases that indicated his evaluative task and highlighting information about dates and processes for the project. He then made notes and list of possible subjects. He selected the military's stop loss policy, which he knew about first hand.

English 1302
Evaluating Policy and Law

Write an essay that evaluates a government or corporate policy, or a law. Explain the policy in some detail, and assess it in terms of its impact. Write with the goal of persuading an informed but uncommitted audience to share your opinion. Your paper should be about 4-6 pages long.

Some factors you may want to consider in your assessment are: the people directly affected by the policy; the people indirectly affected; the cost of the policy; the impact of the policy on national security, the environment, international relations, or other sectors of society; and the policy's original purpose. Do not base your assessment solely on practical criteria. Remember that law and policy are intended to effect some good, whether for the public at large, for the benefit of shareholders–for someone.
Remember to look for all types of criteria.
Think about who will be interested in your topic. Who are you talking to? Who has a stake in this issue? How do you need to tailor your argument to reach your audience?
AUDIENCE

Peer review
You will discuss drafts of your essay in your peer groups during class two weeks from today. Final drafts will be due the following week.

Grading Criteria
I will grade your essay according to how well it does the following:
- Accurately describes the policy or law under consideration.
- Presents persuasive criteria and evidence.
- Appeals to its intended audience.

<u>CLAIMS COULD BE:</u>

1. The "don't ask, don't tell" policy in the military is ineffective and discriminatory.

2. The Washington, DC, Metro is one of the best subway systems in the world.

3. <u>The "stop loss" policy that forbids thousands of soldiers from leaving the military when their volunteer commitment ends is not an effective policy.</u>

4. The movie <u>War of the Worlds</u> does not hold up to the original radio broadcast.

5. The current policy regarding steroid use in professional sports does not effectively deter steroid use.

<u>FREEWRITE:</u>

I remember the Army recruiter who came to my high school during my last year. He made a really good pitch about joining the reserves. He said it was a chance to serve our country and get a start on paying for college. That was a big one at my school because most of us had jobs in high school to pay for food and clothes. That's one thing people don't think about--even when you get a scholarship that pays tuition, you still have to eat and have a place to stay. Anyway, my cousin jumped at the chance to join. The recruiter told us 15 months of active duty, but my cousin now knows the Army can keep him much longer.

2: Think about your criteria

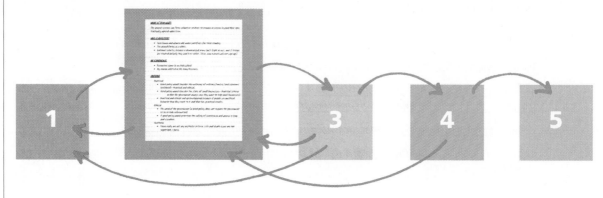

Find the obvious criteria, and then dig deeper

- Write down the criteria you already know you will use in your evaluation. For example, a good study location is quiet, well-lit, safe, and easy to get to.

- Consider other criteria you might not be aware you're using. Perhaps you gravitate toward the student union rather than the library because you are allowed to drink coffee there. Maybe you began avoiding the library when its blue and orange carpet started to hurt your eyes.

- Think about whether these criteria are practical, aesthetic, or ethical. It isn't that important for you to classify each criterion exactly; there is often overlap between these categories. But you may run into trouble with your audience if you rely too much on one type of criteria, such as aesthetics, and neglect others, like practicality, such as a beautiful chair that hurts your back.

Research your argument

- Find evidence to show how the thing you are evaluating meets or doesn't meet your criteria. If you claim that a symphony has a compelling melodic theme in the first movement, describe the passage in detail.

- Go to reliable sources to find out how others have evaluated the same thing. Do other reviewers tend to agree or disagree with you? Do they use criteria that you don't? Are they addressing the same audience you are?

Analyze your audience

- Consider which of your criteria are most likely to appeal to your audience. Which criteria might they find unconvincing or unimportant?

- How familiar will readers be with your topic? How much background information will they need?

Staying on Track

Specify and argue for your criteria

Specify your criteria
Show exactly how your criteria apply to what you are evaluating.

OFF TRACK
Border collies make the best pets because they are smart, friendly, and easy to train. *[Vague; many pets are smart, friendly, and easy to train]*

ON TRACK
Border collies are ideal family pets because their intelligence and trainability enable them to fit into almost any household, no matter how crowded.

Support your criteria
Give evidence to demonstrate why your criteria are valid.

OFF TRACK
Swimming is better exercise than running because you get a better workout. *[How so?]*

ON TRACK
Health professionals maintain that for those who have access to pools or lakes, swimming is the best workout because it exercises all major muscle groups and it's not prone to causing injuries.

Don't assume your audience shares your criteria
It's easy to forget that other people have different concerns and priorities. Your challenge as a writer is finding common ground with people who think differently.

OFF TRACK
Coach X is a bad coach who should be fired because he has lost to our rival school three years in a row. *[For some fans beating the big rival is the only criterion, but not all fans.]*

ON TRACK
While coach X hasn't beaten our big rival in three years, he has succeeded in increasing attendance by 50%, adding a new sports complex built by donations, and raising the players' graduation rate to 80%.

Writer at work

Rashaun Giddens made the following notes about his evaluative claim.

WHAT IS "STOP LOSS"?

The armed services can force volunteer soldiers to remain in service beyond their contractually agreed-upon term.

WHO IS AFFECTED?

- Servicemen and women who make sacrifices for their country.
- The armed forces as a whole.
- National security, because a demoralized army can't fight as well, and if troops are treated unfairly they won't re-enlist. (Also, new recruits will not sign up.)

MY EXPERIENCE

- Recruiters came to my high school.
- My cousin enlisted in the Army Reserves.

CRITERIA

Practical

- Good policy would consider the well-being of military families (and economic livelihood)--Practical and ethical.
- Good policy would consider the state of small businesses--Practical (ethical in that the government always says they want to help small businesses).
- Practical and ethical end up overlapping because if people see unethical behavior then they react to it and that has practical results.

Ethical

- The word of the government (a good policy does not require the government to lie or hide information).
- A good policy would prioritize the safety of servicemen and women in Iraq and elsewhere.

Aesthetic

- There really are not any aesthetic criteria. Life and death issues are too important, I guess.

AUDIENCE

Who has a stake in this issue? What do they know about it? How should I appeal to them?

Military families

- Families feel direct effect.
- Military families will probably have a strong sense of duty. They are likely to feel upset if the government does not treat them fairly.

All citizens

- Citizens are responsible for the way our government treats our soldiers. Appeal to people's sense of fair play.
- Citizens have concerns on moral or ideological grounds.
- All citizens need to feel a sense of empathy with the military families; that "This could be me or my child."

BACKGROUND

People may or may not have basic knowledge of policy. Perhaps don't know the specifics or the origin (bring in the history to ground it). May not be aware of how bad it can be in the details.

TO RESEARCH

- Need to get info on how stop loss originated, when it has been used, and what impact it had. Were situations in the past comparable to now?
- Find evidence of hardships for troops. Personal anecdotes from news articles and figures about effects on enlistment.
- Find evidence and testimony about effects on families and small businesses.

3: Write a draft

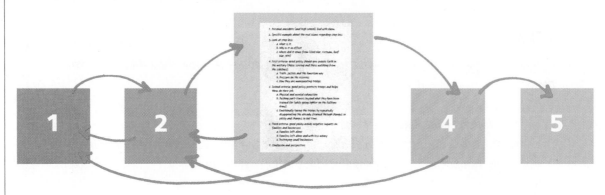

Introduce the issue

- Give your readers any background information they will need.
- State your stance up front, if you wish. Some evaluations work better if the writer's judgment is issued at the beginning; sometimes, it is more effective to build up a mass of evidence and then issue your verdict at the end.

Describe your criteria and offer evidence

- Organize the criteria you present to be as effective as possible. Do you want to start with the most important one, or build up to it? Try both ways, and see which seems more convincing.
- Explain each criterion and give reasons to support its use, if readers are unlikely to automatically accept it.
- Analyze how well the thing you are evaluating meets each criterion. Provide specific examples.

Anticipate and address opposing viewpoints

- Acknowledge why others may have a different opinion than you do.
- Demonstrate why your evaluation is better by pointing out either why your criteria are better or why you have better evidence and reasons.

Conclude with strength

- State your position at the end of your argument if you haven't done so previously.
- Offer a compelling example or analogy to end your essay.
- State explicitly what is at stake in your evaluation, especially if you are evaluating a policy or issue that affects many people.

Choose a title that will interest readers in your essay

- A bland, generic title like "An Evaluation of X" gives little incentive to want to read the paper.

Writer at work

Based on his lists of criteria, his conclusions about his audience, and his research, Rashaun Giddens
sketched out a rough outline for his essay.

1. Personal anecdote (and high school). End with claim.

2. Specific example about the real issues regarding stop loss

3. Look at stop loss
   a. What is it
   b. Why is it in effect
   c. Where did it come from (Civil War, Vietnam, Gulf
      War, 9/11)

4. First criteria: good policy should give people faith in
   the military (those serving and those watching from
   the sidelines).
   a. Truth, justice and the American way
   b. Pressure on the reserves
   c. How they are manipulating troops

5. Second criteria: good policy protects troops and helps
   them do their job.
   a. Physical and mental exhaustion
   b. Pushing part-timers beyond what they have been
      trained for (while going lighter on the fulltime
      Army).
   c. Emotionally taxing the troops by repeatedly
      disappointing the already strained through changes in
      policy and changes in out time.

6. Third criteria: good policy avoids negative impacts on
   families and businesses
   a. Families left alone
   b. Families left alone and with less money
   c. Destroying small businesses

7. Conclusion and perspective

4: Revise, revise, revise

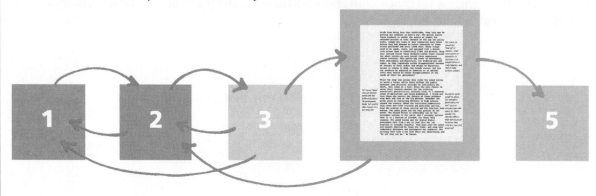

Skilled writers know that the secret to writing well is rewriting. Leave correcting errors for last.

Does your paper or project meet the assignment?	• Look again at your assignment. Does your paper or project do what the assignment asks? • Look again at the assignment for specific guidelines, including length, format, and amount of research. Does your work meet these guidelines?
Is your evaluative claim arguable?	• Do enough people disagree with you to make the evaluation worthwhile? • Does anyone but you care about this topic?
Are your criteria reasonable, and will your audience accept them?	• Do you provide compelling reasons for readers to accept your criteria for evaluation, if they weren't predisposed to do so? • Do you weight criteria appropriately, balancing aesthetic, ethical, and practical considerations in a way likely to appeal to your audience?
Is your evidence convincing and sufficient?	• Will readers believe what you say about the thing you are evaluating? What proof do you offer that it does or doesn't meet your criteria? • Are your descriptions clear and accurate?
Do you address opposing views?	• Have you acknowledged the opinions of people who disagree with you? • Where do you show why your evaluation is better?
Is the writing project visually effective?	• Is the font attractive and readable? • Are the headings and visuals effective? • If you use images or tables as part of your evaluation, are they legible and appropriately placed?
Save the editing for last.	• See guidelines for editing and proofreading on pages 24–28.

Writer at work

Working with a group of his fellow students, Rashaun Giddens made comments on his rough draft, and used them to help produce a final draft.

Aside from being less than forthright, stop loss may be putting our soldiers in harm's way. The policy forces these soldiers to suffer the strain of combat for extended periods of time. Because of the way the policy works, troops may learn of tour extensions mere hours before they had planned to return stateside to lower stress positions and their loved ones. These troops need to be ready, alert, and equipped with a morale with allows them to effectively fight and protect. Stop loss instead forces these soldiers—often those trained for short stints—to work beyond their experience and/or training. This policy may prove to overextend, both emotionally and physically, our fighting men and women. As they repeatedly suffer disappointment because of changes in their orders and delays of departure, morale is likely to drop. War breeds stress, but how can soldiers be expected to function at an optimal level when forced to suffer disappointments at the hands of their own government?

> *This starts to sound like "hearsay" or rumors--find some quotes or anecdotes to illustrate it so people believe it really happens, and that it really bothers soldiers.*

> *"Us" versus "them" tone will alienate people who feel differently about the government. Maybe "we" need to show respect–it is our army too*

While the stop loss policy does allow the armed forces to build a larger active force without the public backlash (and political suicide) of instituting the draft, this comes at a cost. Those who have chosen to serve their country–whether for the training, educational possibilities, economic need, or a personal sense of patriotism—are being bamboozled. I would ask that those who control the futures of these soldiers step back and look at the big picture. Remember the pitch given by recruiting officers in high schools around the country. Watch the television commercials that—even now—tout training and part-time service. Read the stories of those serving and the families left behind. The sales pitch and the real picture do not match. The United States is undeniably one of the strongest nations in the world, and I strongly believe that it is a bastion of freedom. For these very reasons, the armed forces and the United States government must find a way to lead this war (or conflict or crusade) honestly. They must show the honor and respect deserved by those who fight, and stop loss undeniably dishonors and disrespects our soldiers. The military must take a cue from their own advertising and "be all they can be." Be honest.

> *Giving too much weight to ethics, not enough to practicality. We can't just let everyone leave who wants to; there wouldn't be enough soldiers. What option would be better than stop loss, but still practical?*

5: Submitted version

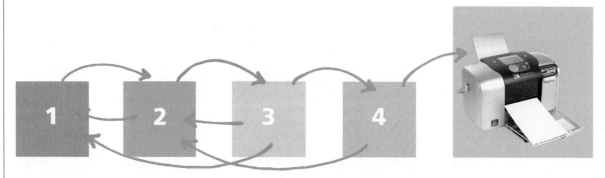

Giddens 1

Rashaun Giddens

Professor Chen

English 1302

21 April 2008

Stop Loss or "Loss of Trust"

Looking back on my high school career, my social and extracurricular lives were filled with countless highs: hanging out with my friends, prom, and varsity track to name a few. My academic career, however, was a bit shakier. So busy with what I saw then as the important things in life, I often procrastinated or altogether avoided my schoolwork. My senior year, the recruiter from the U.S. Army Reserves spoke at a school assembly. He asked that we as seniors consider the prospect of becoming "weekend warriors." In the wake of September 11, we could help protect our country and simultaneously work toward paying for a college education, which seemed like a great idea to many students. For those who could not otherwise afford college, the prospect of receiving a higher education in return for patriotism and some good hard work sounded fair enough. My life, however, took a different turn. When I received my track scholarship, I decided to head off to college right away. Many of my friends, however, heeded the call to service. So far, their realities have been far from the lives that were pitched to them; rather, this was the beginning of a path to broken dreams and broken promises.

My cousin, moved to action by a charismatic recruiter, an Army announcement of fifteen-month active tours, and the prospect of a paid college education, chose to join the United States Army Reserves. The Army, suffering from a recruitment shortfall, had recently announced a policy that would allow recruits to serve in active duty for a mere fifteen months. For serving for just over a year, my cousin could do his national duty and put himself on a path to self-improvement. The recruiter did not, however, highlight the fine print to this new program. No one told my cousin that he could be called back to active duty for up to eight years under the government's stop loss policy. Further, no one told him that just one day after the Army announced the incentive program, an appeals court ruled that the Army could, under "stop loss," compel soldiers to remain beyond the initial eight-year obligation (Wickham).

The "stop loss" policy forces thousands of soldiers to serve beyond their volunteer enlistment contracts. The all-volunteer army—on which the government prides itself—is slowly developing into a disgruntled mass of men and women being held against their wills. These men and women wanted to serve their country and they signed what they believed were binding agreements with a trustworthy employer—the United States government—only to find that their government didn't bargain in good faith.

As far back as the Civil War, the government needed incentives to retain its troops. (Although we all want freedom, fewer actually want to put our own lives on the line in the pursuit of that goal.) Both the Union and the Confederacy needed to make tough decisions to maintain strong armed forces when soldiers' contracts were expiring. The Union chose to offer financial incentives to keep its young men in uniform, while the Confederacy instituted a series of (not so) "voluntary" reenlistment policies (Robertson). During World War II all soldiers were forced to remain active until they reached a designated number of "points." Vietnam saw the last stage of a mandatory draft, with soldiers serving one-year tours (Hockstader). Today's military relies on "stop loss," making soldiers stay in the military after their commitment ends. Congress first gave the military the authority to retain soldiers after the Vietnam War when new volunteers were too few to replace departing soldiers. In November 2002 the Pentagon gave stop-loss orders for Reserve and National Guard units activated to fight terrorism (Robertson).

This policy is neither forthcoming, safe, nor compassionate toward those most directly impacted—the soldiers and their families. As the United States became more and more entrenched in the conflict in Iraq, the military was stretched thinner and thinner. By 2004, approximately 40% of those serving in Iraq and Afghanistan came from the ranks of the part-time soldiers: the Reserves and the National Guard (Gerard). While these individuals did know that their country could call if they enlisted, they continue to bear an inordinate burden of actual combat time, and this new policy continues to create situations further removed from the job for which they had enlisted. Recruiters often pitch the military—including the Reserves and the Guard—to young, impressionable, and often underprivileged kids. I have experienced this pitch firsthand and seen the eyes of my classmates as the recruiter promised them a better and richer tomorrow. Seeing a golden opportunity for self-respect and achievement, young men and women sign on the dotted line. Today, other young men and women are buying a bill of goods. These recruits—and those who came before them—deserve to have an honest relationship with the government they protect. As policymakers tout the all-volunteer Army, those who serve find their rights threatened. The military claims to teach soldiers respect and honor. Is misleading your employees honest?

Aside from being less than forthright, stop loss may be putting our soldiers in harm's way. The policy forces these soldiers to suffer the strain of combat for extended periods of time. Because of the way the policy works, troops may learn of

tour extensions mere hours before they had planned to return stateside to lower stress positions and their loved ones. These troops need to be ready, alert, and equipped with a morale with allows them to fight effectively. Stop loss instead forces these soldiers—often those trained for short stints—to work beyond their experience and training. This policy may prove to overextend, both emotionally and physically, our fighting men and women. As they repeatedly suffer disappointment because of changes in their orders and delays of departure, morale is likely to drop. Based on reports from families, this practice has been devastating to their soldiers. Nancy Durst, wife of United States Reservist Staff Sergeant Scott Durst, told *Talk of the Nation's* Neal Conan that the military detained her husband's unit just thirty minutes before it was to board the bus scheduled to deliver it to a stateside flight. The unit was later informed that tours had been extended for another four months (Durst). War breeds stress, but how can soldiers be expected to function at an optimal level when forced to suffer disappointments at the hands of their own government?

Finally, this policy simply runs contrary to the current administration's stated interest in the preservation of family and the bolstering of small businesses. First (and most obviously), this less-than-forthright policy keeps families separated. Husbands, wives, and children find themselves separated for longer periods of time, left with uncertainty and ambiguity for comfort. How does this aid in preserving the family? Second, when the government deploys reservists, soldiers often take a severe pay cut. Forced to leave their regular jobs, soldiers—and their families—must survive on often a much smaller government wage. Stop loss extends tours of duty and consequently the economic struggles of the families in question. Third, the policy has proven detrimental to the small business owner. Men and women have used their military experience, discipline, and training to further themselves economically. America prides itself on the power of the small businessman; however, individuals such as Chief Warrant Officer Ronald Eagle have been hurt by this policy. After

twenty years of service, Eagle was set to retire from the Army and focus on his aircraft-maintenance business. Instead, the Army has indefinitely moved his retirement date. As a consequence, Eagle has taken a $45,000 pay cut and wonders whether his business will survive his hiatus (Hockstader). Is this the way the government and military fight to preserve the family—emotionally and economically?

Because American men and women risk their lives in the name of bettering those of Iraqis, the military should think about how their policy affects the lives of their soldiers and those back home. While the stop loss policy does allow the armed forces to build a larger active force without the public backlash (and political suicide) of instituting the draft, this policy comes at a cost. Those who have chosen to serve their country—whether for the training, educational possibilities, economic need, or a personal sense of patriotism—are being bamboozled.

Watch the television commercials that, even now, tout training and part-time service. Read the stories of those serving and the families left behind. The sales pitch and the real picture do not match. The United States is undeniably one of the strongest nations in the world and a bastion of freedom. For these very reasons, the armed forces and the United States government, which represents all citizens, must find a way to lead this war (or conflict or crusade) honestly. If we have to pay soldiers double what they currently make in order to get them to re-enlist, we should do so. Even a draft would at least be aboveboard and honest. But we cannot continue to trick people into risking their lives for our national security. Our country must show the honor and respect deserved by those who fight, and stop loss undeniably dishonors and disrespects our soldiers. The military must take a cue from their own advertising and "be all they can be." Be honest.

Works Cited

Durst, Nancy. Interview by Neal Conan. *Talk of the Nation*. Natl. Public Radio.
   WNYC, New York. 19 Apr. 2004. Radio.

Gerard, Philip. "When the Cry Was 'Over the Hill in October.'" *Charleston Gazette* 16
   May 2004: 1E. *LexisNexis Academic*. Web. 6 Apr. 2008.

Hockstader, Lee. "Army Stops Many Soldiers From Quitting; Orders Extend
   Enlistments to Curtail Troop Shortages." *Washington Post* 29 Dec. 2003: A01.
   LexisNexis Academic. Web. 8 Apr. 2008.

Robertson, John. "The Folly of Stop Loss." *Pittsburgh Post-Gazette* 19 Dec. 2004: J1.
   LexisNexis Academic. Web. 7 Apr. 2008.

Wickham, DeWayne. "A 15-Month Enlistment? Check Army's Fine Print." *USA
   Today* 17 May 2005: 13A. *LexisNexis Academic*. Web. 6 Apr. 2008.

Projects

You likely have a great deal of experience making consumer evaluations, and when you have time to do your homework to compare features, quality, and price, probably you will make a good decision. For other evaluations, however, the criteria may not be obvious. Often the keys are finding the right criteria and convincing your readers that these criteria are the best ones to use.

These projects are frequently written kinds of evaluations.

Evaluate a controversial subject

Think of controversial subjects on your campus or in your community for which you can find recent articles in your campus or local newspaper. For example, is your mayor or city manager an effective leader? Is your campus recreational sports facility adequate? Is a new condominium complex built on city land that was used as a park good or bad?.

Identify what is at stake in the evaluation. Who thinks it is good or effective? Who thinks it is bad or ineffective? Why does it matter?

List the criteria that make something or someone good or bad. Which criteria are the most important? Which will you have to argue for?

Analyze your potential readers. How familiar will they be with what you are evaluating? Which criteria will they likely accept and which might they disagree with?

Write a draft. Introduce your subject and give the necessary background. Make your evaluative claim either at the beginning or as your conclusion. Describe each criterion and evaluate your subject on each criterion. Be sure to address opposing viewpoints by acknowledging how their evaluations might be different.

Evaluate a campus policy

Identify a policy on your campus that affects you. Examples include the way your school schedules classes and has students register, the way parking spaces are allotted on campus, the library's late fee and returns policy, housing or admissions policies, or rules regulating student organizations.

Consider your target audience as the readers of your campus newspaper. Who else besides you does this issue affect? What office or division of the school is responsible for the program? Who implemented it in the first place? Keep in mind that your school's administration is part of your audience.

Determine the criteria for your evaluation. Which criteria will be most important for other students? for the faculty and staff? for the administration?

Take a clear position about the policy. If you think the policy is unfair or ineffective, acknowledge why it was put into place. Sometimes good intentions lead to bad results. If you think the policy is fair or effective, explain why according to the criteria you set out. In either case, give reasons and examples to support your judgment.

Film review

Select a film to review. Choose a specific magazine, newspaper, or online publication as the place where you would publish the review. Read some reviews in that publication and notice the criteria that they use. You will need to keep the audience in mind.

Watch the film more than once and take notes. Analyze the film's genre. What makes a good horror movie? a good action-adventure movie? a good documentary? a good comedy? These will be your criteria for evaluation.

Find information on the film. The Internet Movie Database (**www.imdb.com**) is a good place to start. Look at the director's credits to find other films that he or she has done. Look at the information about the actors and locations.

Write a thesis that makes an evaluative claim: the film is a successful or unsuccessful example of its genre. Go beyond the obvious in selecting criteria. A comedy is supposed to make you laugh, but movies that are only gags tend to wear thin. Comedies that have engaging characters keep your interest. Acting often makes the difference between a good and great movie. Use evidence from the film to support your claim.

12 Arguments for a Position

Position arguments aim to change readers' attitudes and beliefs.

CHAPTER CONTENTS

Writing a position argument

Many people think of the term *argument* as a synonym for *debate*. College courses and professional careers, however, require a different kind of argument—one that, most of the time, is cooler in emotion and more elaborate in detail than oral debate. In college it is not sufficient simply to write that "I believe this" or "It's just my opinion." Readers in college assume that if you make a claim in writing, you believe that claim. More important, a claim is rarely *only* your opinion. Because most beliefs and assumptions are shared by many people, responsible readers will consider your position seriously.

Readers in college expect the following of an argument.

• A **claim** that is interesting and makes them want to find out more about what you have to say

• At least one **good reason** that makes your claim worth taking seriously

• Some **evidence** that the good reason or reasons are valid

• Some acknowledgment of the **opposing views** and **limitations** of the claim

Working Together

Identify reasons that support conflicting claims

In a group of three or four students

Select a controversial issue for which there are multiple points of view. You can find a list of issues at **www.dir.yahoo.com/ Society_and_Culture/Issues_and_Causes/**. Explore the links for one of the issues to get a sense of the range of opinion. Then decide which Web sites will give your group a range of views on the issue.

Each member of your group will analyze two Web sites. Write down the following for each site.

• What is the main claim of the Web site?

• What reason or reasons are given?

• What evidence (facts, examples, statistics, and the testimony of authorities) is offered?

Bring your answers to class and compare them with other members of your group. How do the reasons differ for opposing claims? What assumptions underlie the reasons? How does the evidence differ?

Components of position arguments

What exactly is my issue?	**Define the issue.** Your subject should be clear to your readers. If readers are unfamiliar with the issue, you should give enough examples so they understand the issue in concrete terms.
Who are the stakeholders?	**Identify the stakeholders.** Who is immediately affected by this issue? Who is affected indirectly?
What has been written about the issue?	**Read about the issue.** Every significant issue has an extensive history of discussion involving many people and various points of view. Before you formulate a claim about an issue, become familiar with the conversation about that issue by reading.
What exactly is my stand on the issue?	**State your position.** You may want to state your thesis in the opening paragraph to let readers know your position immediately. If your issue is unfamiliar, you may want to find out more before you state your position. In any case, you should take a definite position on the issue.
What are the reasons for my position?	**Find one or more reasons.** You need to give one or more reasons for your position. List as many reasons as you can think of. Use the ones that are most convincing.
Where can I find evidence?	**Provide evidence.** In support of your reasons, provide evidence—in the form of examples, statistics, and testimony of experts—that the reasons are valid. When the issue is unfamiliar, more evidence than usual is required.
Who disagrees with my position?	**Acknowledge opposing views and limitations of the claim.** If everybody thinks the same way, then there is no need to write a position argument. Anticipate what objections might be made to your position. You can answer possible objections in two ways: that the objections are not valid or that the objections have some validity but your argument is stronger.

Understand how position arguments work

Position arguments often take two forms—definition arguments and rebuttal arguments.

Definition arguments

The continuing controversies about what art is, free speech, pornography, and hate crimes (to name just a few) illustrate why definitions often matter more than we might think. People argue about definitions because of the consequences of something being defined in a certain way.

People make definitions that benefit their interests. Early in life you learned the importance of defining actions as "accidents." Windows can be broken through carelessness, especially when you are tossing a ball against the side of the house, but if it's an accident, well, accidents just happen (and don't require punishment). Your mother or father probably didn't think breaking the window was an accident, so you had to convince Mom or Dad that you were really being careful, and the ball just slipped out of your hand. If you can get your audience to accept your definition, then usually you succeed. For this reason, definition arguments are the most powerful arguments.

For example, is graffiti vandalism? Or is it art? If you claim at least some forms of graffiti should be considered art, you need to set out criteria to define art and argue that graffiti meets those criteria.

Something = or ≠ _____
>
> **Criteria A**
>
> **Criteria B**
>
> **Criteria C**

EXAMPLE

Graffiti is art because it is a means of self expression, it shows an understanding of design pinciples, and it stimulates both the senses and the mind.

Rebuttal arguments

Rebuttal arguments take the opposite position. You can challenge the criteria a writer uses to make a definition or you can challenge the evidence that supports a claim. Sometimes the evidence presented is incomplete or simply wrong. Sometimes you can find counterevidence. Often when you rebut an argument, you identify one or more fallacies in that argument (see pages 14–15).

Opposing claim
>
> **Bad reason 1**
>
> **Bad reason 2**

EXAMPLE

The great white shark gained a reputation as a "man eater" from the 1975 movie *Jaws,* but in fact attacks on humans are rare and most bites have been "test bites," which is a common shark behavior with unfamiliar objects.

Keys to position arguments

Understand your goal	A well-written and well-reasoned position argument may not change minds entirely, but it can convince readers that a reasonable person can hold this point of view. Position arguments do not necessarily have winners and losers. Your goal is to invite a response that creates a dialogue.
Be sensitive to the context	Even position arguments that have become classics and in a sense "timeless" frequently were written in response to a historical event; for example, Martin Luther King, Jr. wrote his powerful argument for civil disobedience, "Letter from Birmingham Jail," in response to a published statement by eight Birmingham clergymen. A careful analysis of a recent or historical event often provides your argument with a sense of immediacy.
Rely on careful definitions	What exactly does *freedom of speech* mean? What exactly does *privacy* mean? What exactly does *animal rights* mean? Getting readers to accept a definition is often the key to a position argument. For example, torturing animals is against the law. Animal rights activists argue that raising and slaughtering animals for food is torture and thus would extend the definition. If you can get readers to accept your definition, then they will agree with your position.
Use quality sources	Find the highest-quality sources for citing evidence. Recent sources are critical for current topics, such as the relationship of certain diets to disease.
Create credibility	You have probably noticed that many times in the course of reading, you get a strong sense of the writer's character, even if you know nothing about the person. Be honest about strengths and weaknesses and about what you don't know, and avoid easy labels. If readers trust you are sincere, they will take you seriously.
Cultivate a sense of humor and a distinctive voice	A reasonable voice doesn't have to be a dull one. Humor is a legitimate tool of argument, especially when the stakes are high and tempers are flaring.
Argue responsibly	When you begin an argument by stating "in my opinion," you are not arguing responsibly. If you don't like broccoli, it is a matter of personal taste. But if you are for or against universal health care, then it is not just your opinion. Millions of other Americans hold views similar to yours on this contested issue.

An effective position argument

Position arguments succeed when readers consider the writer's position as one to take seriously.

Take My Privacy, Please!
Ted Koppel

Ted Koppel joined ABC News in 1963 and served from 1980 until 2005 as the anchor and managing editor of *Nightline,* the first late-night network news program. He has had a major reporting role in every presidential campaign since 1964. "Take My Privacy, Please!" which appeared in June 2005 in the *New York Times,* is an example of a position argument that doesn't begin with a thesis but first gives a series of examples.

Take My Privacy, Please!

by Ted Koppel

THE PATRIOT ACT—brilliant! Its critics would have preferred a less stirring title, perhaps something along the lines of the Enhanced Snooping, Library and Hospital Database Seizure Act. But then who, even right after 9/11, would have voted for that?

Precisely. He who names it and frames it, claims it. The Patriot Act, however, may turn out to be among the lesser threats to our individual and collective privacy.

There is no end to what we will endure, support, pay for and promote if only it makes our lives easier, promises to save us money, appears to enhance our security and comes to us in a warm, cuddly and altogether nonthreatening package. To wit: OnStar, the subscription vehicle tracking and assistance system.

Koppel announces his stance and his subject in the first two paragraphs. He questions the Patriot Act and then suggests that there may be bigger threats to privacy.

Part of its mission statement, as found on the OnStar Web site, is the creation of "safety, security and peace of mind for drivers and passengers with thoughtful wireless services that are always there, always ready." You've surely seen or heard their commercials, one of which goes like this:

ANNOUNCER -- The following is an OnStar conversation. (Ring)

ONSTAR -- OnStar emergency, this is Dwight.

DRIVER -- (crying) Yes, yes??!

ONSTAR -- Are there any injuries, ma'am?

DRIVER -- My leg hurts, my arm hurts.

ONSTAR -- O.K. I do understand. I will be contacting emergency services.

ANNOUNCER -- If your airbags deploy, OnStar receives a signal and calls to check on you. (Ring)

EMERGENCY SERVICES -- Police.

ONSTAR -- This is Dwight with OnStar. I'd like to report a vehicle crash with airbag deployment on West 106th Street.

EMERGENCY SERVICES -- We'll send police and E.M.S. out there.

DRIVER -- (crying) I'm so scared!

ONSTAR -- O.K., I'm here with you, ma'am; you needn't be scared.

The OnStar commercial provides a concrete example.

In the ad, OnStar is portrayed as a technology that can save lives.

Well, maybe just a little scared. Tell us again how Dwight knows just where the accident took place. Oh, right! It's those thoughtful wireless services that are always there. Always, as in any time a driver gets into an OnStar-equipped vehicle. OnStar insists that it would disclose the whereabouts of a subscriber's vehicle only after being presented with a criminal court order or after the vehicle has been reported stolen. That's certainly a relief. I wouldn't want to think that anyone but Dwight knows where I am whenever I'm traveling in my car.

Of course, E-ZPass and most other toll-collecting systems already know whenever a customer passes through one of their scanners. That's because of radio frequency identification technology. In return for the convenience of zipping through toll booths, you need to have in your car a wireless device. This tag contains information about your account, permitting E-ZPass to deduct the necessary toll—and to note when your car whisked through that particular toll booth. They wouldn't share that information with anyone, either; that is, unless they had to.

Radio frequency identification technology has been used for about 15 years now to reunite lost pets with their owners. Applied Digital Solutions, for example, manufactures the VeriChip, a tiny, implantable device that holds a small amount of data. Animal shelters can scan the chip for the name and phone number of the lost pet's owner. The product is now referred to as the HomeAgain Microchip Identification System.

Useful? Sure. Indeed, it's not much of a leap to suggest that one day, the VeriChip might be routinely implanted under the skin of, let's say, an Alzheimer's patient. The Food and Drug Administration approved the VeriChip for use in people last October. An Applied Digital Solutions spokesman estimates that about 1,000 people have already had a VeriChip implanted, usually in the right triceps. At the moment, it doesn't carry much information, just an identification number

Koppel uses critical thinking to question the main assumption of the ad: Is it necessarily good that OnStar always knows where you are while driving?

Convenient technologies also keep track of our movements. Koppel gets his readers to think about what happens to personal information that is passively collected.

that health care providers can use to tap into a patient's medical history. A Barcelona nightclub also uses it to admit customers with a qualifying code to enter a V.I.P. room where drinks are automatically put on their bill. Possible variations on the theme are staggering.

Technologies used to track pets can also track people.

And how about all the information collected by popular devices like TiVo, the digital video recorder that enables you to watch and store an entire season's worth of favorite programs at your own convenience? It also lets you electronically mark the programs you favor, allowing TiVo to suggest similar programs for your viewing pleasure. In February, TiVo announced the most frequently played and replayed commercial moment during the Super Bowl (it involves a wardrobe malfunction, but believe me, you don't want to know), drawing on aggregated data from a sample of 10,000 anonymous TiVo households. No one is suggesting that TiVo tracks what each subscriber records and replays. But could they, if they needed to? That's unclear, although TiVo does have a privacy policy. "Your privacy," it says in part, "is very important to us. Due to factors beyond our control, however, we cannot fully ensure that your user information will not be disclosed to third parties."

The popular TiVo service admits that it does not fully protect the privacy of its subscribers.

Unexpected and unfortunate things happen, of course, even to the most reputable and best-run organizations. Only last February, the Bank of America Corporation notified federal investigators that it had lost computer backup tapes containing personal information about 1.2 million federal government employees, including some senators. In April, LexisNexis unintentionally gave outsiders access to the personal files (addresses, Social Security numbers, drivers license information) of as many as 310,000 people. In May, Time Warner revealed that an outside storage company had misplaced data stored on computer backup tapes on 600,000 current and former employees. That same month, United Parcel Service picked up a box of computer tapes in New Jersey from CitiFinancial, the consumer finance subsidiary of

Numerous accidents and data thefts have given private information to unauthorized people.

KOPPEL: TAKE MY PRIVACY, PLEASE!

Citigroup, that contained the names, addresses, Social Security numbers, account numbers, payment histories and other details on small personal loans made to an estimated 3.9 million customers. The box is still missing.

Whoops!

CitiFinancial correctly informed its own customers and, inevitably, the rest of the world about the security breach. Would they have done so entirely on their own? That is less clear. In July 2003, California started requiring companies to inform customers living in the state of any breach in security that compromises personally identifiable information. Six other states have passed similar legislation.

No such legislation exists on the federal stage, however—only discretionary guidelines for financial institutions about whether and how they should inform their customers with respect to breaches in the security of their personal information.

Both the House and Senate are now considering federal legislation similar to the California law. It's a start but not nearly enough. We need mandatory clarity and transparency; not just with regard to the services that these miracles of microchip and satellite technology offer but also the degree to which companies share and exchange their harvest of private data.

We cannot even begin to control the growing army of businesses and industries that monitor what we buy, what we watch on television, where we drive, the debts we pay or fail to pay, our marriages and divorces, our litigations, our health and tax records and all else that may or may not yet exist on some computer tape, if we don't fully understand everything we're signing up for when we avail ourselves of one of these services.

Koppel hopes by this point he has raised concerns about privacy for his readers. He now gives his thesis: The public has the right to know what is being done with private information they give to companies and services.

Explore Current Issues

Can pennies really solve the world's problems?

On World Water Day, March 22, 2007, UNICEF kicked off their Tap Project, in which diners at restaurants in select cities can donate $1 for every glass of tap water they order. The money goes to clean drinking water programs around the world. A video on the Tap Project Web site promotes the program, segueing from images of people living in areas with poor drinking water to a question: "But what if . . . you could change these lives without making a change to yours?"

Pushing the convenience of giving in small amounts has long been a strategy of charitable organizations. The refrain "for only pennies a day" has inspired people of many generations to sponsor starving children and house homeless pets. However, are small monetary donations as effective as people believe? According to Larry Brilliant, writing for Slate.com's 2008 special philanthropy issue, less than one-third of the funds donated to nonprofits in 2005 actually reached the people for whom they were intended.

Write about it

1. The effectiveness of small monetary donations, or the effectiveness of monetary donations in comparison to donations of time, skills, or goods are only two issues surrounding charitable donations. Think about other issues on which people might hold different positions, such as how charitable organizations advertise, how kids are getting involved in charitable giving, and how organizations are using new technologies to raise donations.

2. What is at stake in making arguments about charitable organizations? Choose one of the issues you listed for the first question. Who is involved with this issue? What is at stake for each individual or group? Which position might each of these groups hold?

3. Think about your own patterns of charitable giving. What inspires you to give to an organization? Are you more likely to donate your time or money? Why? Write a paragraph explaining your position.

How to read position arguments

Make notes as you read, either in the margins or on paper or a computer file. Circle any words or references that you don't know and look them up.

What is it?
- What kind of a text is it? An article? an essay? a chart? a scientific report? a Web site? an executive summary? What are your expectations for this kind of text?
- What media are used? (Web sites, for example, often combine images, words, and sounds.)

Where did it come from?
- Who wrote the analysis?
- Where did it first appear? In a book, newspaper, magazine, online, in a company, or in an organization?

What is the writer's thesis or main idea?
- What is the writer's topic? What effect is he or she trying to determine the cause of?
- Why is this topic important?
- What are the key ideas or concepts that the writer considers?
- What are the key terms? How does the writer define those terms?

Who is the intended audience?
- What clues do you find about whom the writer had in mind as readers?
- What does the writer assume that the readers already know about the subject?
- What new knowledge is the writer providing?

What are the reasons that support the claim?
- Is there one primary reason?
- Are multiple reasons given?
- Do you find any fallacies in the reasons (see pages 14–15)?

What kinds of evidence are given?
- Is the evidence from books, newspapers, periodicals, the Web, or field research?
- Is the evidence convincing that the causes given are the actual causes?

How is it composed?
- How does the writer represent himself or herself?
- How would you characterize the style?
- How effective is the design? Is it easy to read?
- If there are any photographs, charts, or other graphics, what information do they contribute?

What to the Slave Is the Fourth of July?

(SPEECH)

Frederick Douglass

On the fifth of July, 1852, former slave Frederick Douglass spoke at a meeting of the Ladies' Anti-Slavery Society in Rochester, New York. In this series of excerpts from his lengthy oration (published shortly thereafter as a pamphlet), Douglass reminds his audience of the irony of celebrating freedom and liberty in a land where much of the population was enslaved.

Return to these questions after you have finished reading.

Analyzing and Connecting

1. Douglass spends considerable time telling his audience what points do *not* need to be argued: that a slave is human, that man is entitled to liberty, and so on. If in fact these points are agreed upon by all, why do you think Douglass spends so much time talking about them?

2. Douglass was speaking in the last few years before the American Civil War began. How did the vivid imagery in this speech likely affect listeners? Read carefully through Douglass's descriptions of the slave trade and its impact on individuals and families. What values is he appealing to?

3. What impact does Douglass's personal history have on his credibility? Would the argument in this speech have been as compelling if it had been made by someone who had never experienced slavery firsthand?

4. What words would you use to describe the overall tone of Douglass's speech? Is it angry? threatening? hopeful? pessimistic? Why do you think Douglass chose the tone he used in this argument?

Finding Ideas for Writing

Imagine you were at Douglass's speech. Write a brief newspaper article describing the event and summarizing Douglass's argument. Make sure to also describe how the audience might have reacted to Douglass as a speaker and particular passages, especially the last paragraph. What appeals was he using and how did the audience respond?

DOUGLASS: WHAT TO THE SLAVE IS THE FOURTH OF JULY?

Fellow-citizens, pardon me, allow me to ask, why am I called upon to speak here to-day? What have I, or those I represent, to do with your national independence? Are the great principles of political freedom and of natural justice, embodied in that Declaration of Independence, extended to us? And am I, therefore, called upon to bring our humble offering to the national altar, and to confess the benefits and express devout gratitude for the blessings resulting from your independence to us?

But, such is not the state of the case. I say it with a sad sense of the disparity between us. I am not included within the pale of this glorious anniversary! Your high independence only reveals the immeasurable distance between us. The blessings in which you, this day, rejoice, are not enjoyed in common. The rich inheritance of justice, liberty, prosperity, and independence, bequeathed by your fathers, is shared by you, not by me. The sunlight that brought life and healing to you has brought stripes and death to me. This Fourth [of] July is yours, not mine. You may rejoice, I must mourn. To drag a man in fetters into the grand illuminated temple of liberty, and call upon him to join you in joyous anthems is inhuman mockery and sacrilegious irony. Do you mean, citizens, to mock me, by asking me to speak to-day?

Fellow-citizens, above your national, tumultuous joy, I hear the mournful wail of millions whose chains, heavy and grievous yesterday, are, to-day, rendered more intolerable by the jubilee shouts that reach them. To forget them, to pass lightly over their wrongs, and to chime in with the popular theme, would be treason most scandalous and

shocking, and would make me a reproach before God and the world. My subject, then fellow citizens, is AMERICAN SLAVERY. I shall see, this day, and its popular characteristics, from the slave's point of view. Standing, there, identified with the American bondman, making his wrongs mine, I do not hesitate to declare, with all my soul, that the character and conduct of this nation never looked blacker to me than on this 4th of July! Whether we turn to the declarations of the past, or to the professions of the present, the conduct of the nation seems equally hideous and revolting. America is false to the past, false to the present, and solemnly binds herself to be false to the future. Standing with God and the crushed and bleeding slave on this occasion, I will, in the name of humanity which is outraged, in the name of liberty which is fettered, in the name of the constitution and the Bible, which are disregarded and trampled upon, dare to call in question and to denounce, with all the emphasis I can command, everything that serves to perpetuate slavery—the great sin and shame of America! "I will not equivocate; I will not excuse"; I will use the severest language I can command; and yet not one word shall escape me that any man, whose judgment is not blinded by prejudice, or who is not at heart a slaveholder, shall not confess to be right and just.

But I fancy I hear some one of my audience say, it is just in this circumstance that you and your brother abolitionists fail to make a favorable impression on the public mind. Would you argue more, and denounce less, would you persuade more, and rebuke less, your cause would be much more likely to succeed. But, I submit, where all is plain there is nothing to be argued. What point in the anti-slavery creed would you have me argue? On what branch of the subject do the people of this country need light? Must I undertake to prove that the slave is a man? That point is conceded already. Nobody doubts it. The slaveholders

themselves acknowledge it in the enactment of laws for their government. They acknowledge it when they punish disobedience on the part of the slave. There are seventy-two crimes in the State of Virginia, which, if committed by a black man, (no matter how ignorant he be), subject him to the punishment of death; while only two of the same crimes will subject a white man to the like punishment. What is this but the acknowledgement that the slave is a moral, intellectual and responsible being? The manhood of the slave is conceded. It is admitted in the fact that Southern statute books are covered with enactments forbidding, under severe fines and penalties, the teaching of the slave to read or to write. When you can point to any such laws, in reference to the beasts of the field, then I may consent to argue the manhood of the slave. When the dogs in your streets, when the fowls of the air, when the cattle on your hills, when the fish of the sea, and the reptiles that crawl, shall be unable to distinguish the slave from a brute, there will I argue with you that the slave is a man!

For the present, it is enough to affirm the equal manhood of the negro race. Is it not astonishing that, while we are ploughing, planting and reaping, using all kinds of mechanical tools, erecting houses, constructing bridges, building ships, working in metals of brass, iron, copper, silver and gold; that, while we are reading, writing and ciphering, acting as clerks, merchants and secretaries, having among us lawyers, doctors, ministers, poets, authors, editors, orators and teachers; that, while we are engaged in all manner of enterprises common to other men, digging gold in California, capturing the whale in the Pacific, feeding sheep and cattle on the hillside, living, moving, acting, thinking, planning, living in families as husbands, wives and children, and, above all, confessing and worshipping the Christian's God, and looking hopefully for life and immortality beyond the grave, we are called upon to prove that we are men!

Would you have me argue that man is entitled to liberty? That he is the rightful owner of his own body? You have already declared it. Must I argue the wrongfulness of slavery? Is it to be settled by the rules of logic and argumentation, as a matter beset with great difficulty, involving a doubtful application of the principle of justice, hard to be understood? How should I look to-day, in the presence of Americans, dividing, and subdividing a discourse, to show that men have a natural right to freedom? speaking of it relatively, and positively, negatively, and affirmatively. To do so would be to make myself ridiculous and offer an insult to your understanding. There is not a man beneath the canopy of heaven that does not know that slavery is wrong for him.

What, am I to argue that it is wrong to make men brutes, to rob them of their liberty, to work them without wages, to keep them ignorant of their relations to their fellow men, to beat them with sticks, to flay their flesh with the lash, to load their limbs with irons, to hunt them with dogs, to sell them at auction, to sunder their families, to knock out their teeth, to burn their flesh, to starve them into obedience and submission to their masters? Must I argue that a system thus marked with blood, and stained with pollution, is wrong? No! I will not. I have better employments for my time and strength, than such arguments would imply.

What, then, remains to be argued? Is it that slavery is not divine; that God did not establish it; that our doctors of divinity are mistaken? There is blasphemy in the thought. That which is inhuman, cannot be divine! Who can reason on such a proposition? They that can, may; I cannot. The time for such argument is past.

What, to the American slave, is your 4th of July? I answer: a day that reveals to him, more than all other days in the year, the gross injustice

and cruelty to which he is the constant victim. To him, your celebration is a sham; your boasted liberty, an unholy license; your national greatness, swelling vanity; your sounds of rejoicing are empty and heartless; your denunciations of tyrants, brass fronted impudence; your shouts of liberty and equality, hollow mockery; your prayers and hymns, your sermons and thanksgivings, with all your religious parade, and solemnity, are, to him, mere bombast, fraud, deception, impiety, and hypocrisy—a thin veil to cover up crimes which would disgrace a nation of savages. There is not a nation on the earth guilty of practices, more shocking and bloody, than are the people of these United States, at this very hour.

Behold the practical operation of this internal slave-trade, the American slave-trade, sustained by American politics and American religion. Here you will see men and women reared like swine for the market. You know what is a swine-drover? I will show you a man-drover. They inhabit all our Southern States. They perambulate the country and crowd the highways of the nation, with droves of human stock. You will see one of these human flesh-jobbers, armed with pistol, whip and Bowie-knife, driving a company of a hundred men, women, and children from the Potomac to the slave market at New Orleans. These wretched people are to be sold singly, or in lots, to suit purchasers. They are food for the cotton-field, and the deadly sugar-mill. Mark the sad procession, as it moves wearily along, and the inhuman wretch who drives them. Hear his savage yells and his blood-chilling oaths, as he hurries on his affrighted captives! There, see the old man, with locks thinned and gray. Cast one glance, if you please, upon that young mother, whose shoulders are bare to the scorching sun, her briny tears falling on the brow of the babe in her arms. See, too, that girl of thirteen, weeping, yes! weeping, as she thinks of the mother from whom she has been torn! The drove moves tardily. Heat

and sorrow have nearly consumed their strength; suddenly you hear a quick snap, like the discharge of a rifle; the fetters clank, and the chain rattles simultaneously; your ears are saluted with a scream, that seems to have torn its way to the centre of your soul! The crack you heard, was the sound of the slave-whip; the scream you heard, was from the woman you saw with the babe. Her speed had faltered under the weight of her child and her chains! that gash on her shoulder tells her to move on. Follow this drove to New Orleans. Attend the auction; see men examined like horses; see the forms of women rudely and brutally exposed to the shocking gaze of American slave-buyers. See this drove sold and separated forever; and never forget the deep, sad sobs that arose from that scattered multitude. Tell me citizens, WHERE, under the sun, you can witness a spectacle more fiendish and shocking. Yet this is but a glance at the American slave-trade, as it exists, at this moment, in the ruling part of the United States.

I was born amid such sights and scenes. To me the American slave-trade is a terrible reality. When a child, my soul was often pierced with a sense of its horrors. I lived on Philpot Street, Fell's Point, Baltimore, and have watched from the wharves, the slave ships in the Basin, anchored from the shore, with their cargoes of human flesh, waiting for favorable winds to waft them down the Chesapeake. There was, at that time, a grand slave mart kept at the head of Pratt Street, by Austin Woldfolk. His agents were sent into every town and county in Maryland, announcing their arrival, through the papers, and on flaming "hand-bills," headed CASH FOR NEGROES. These men were generally well dressed men, and very captivating in their manners. Ever ready to drink, to treat, and to gamble. The fate of many a slave has depended upon the turn of a single card; and many a child has been snatched from the arms of its mother by bargains arranged in a state of brutal drunkenness.

Allow me to say, in conclusion, notwithstanding the dark picture I have this day presented of the state of the nation, I do not despair of this country. There are forces in operation, which must inevitably work the downfall of slavery. "The arm of the Lord is not shortened," and the doom of slavery is certain. I, therefore, leave off where I began, with hope. While drawing encouragement from the Declaration of Independence, the great principles it contains, and the genius of American Institutions, my spirit is also cheered by the obvious tendencies of the age. Nations do not now stand in the same relation to each other that they did ages ago. No nation can now shut itself up from the surrounding world, and trot round in the same old path of its fathers without interference. The time was when such could be done. Long established customs of hurtful character could formerly fence themselves in, and do their evil work with social impunity. Knowledge was then confined and enjoyed by the privileged few, and the multitude walked on in mental darkness. But a change has now come over the affairs of mankind. Walled cities and empires have become unfashionable. The arm of commerce has borne away the gates of the strong city. Intelligence is penetrating the darkest corners of the globe. It makes its pathway over and under the sea, as well as on the earth. Wind, steam, and lightning are its chartered agents. Oceans no longer divide, but link nations together. From Boston to London is now a holiday excursion. Space is comparatively annihilated. Thoughts expressed on one side of the Atlantic are distinctly heard on the other. The far off and almost fabulous Pacific rolls in grandeur at our feet. The Celestial Empire, the mystery of ages, is being solved. The fiat of the Almighty, "Let there be Light," has not yet spent its force. No abuse, no outrage whether in taste, sport or avarice, can now hide itself from the all-pervading light.

When Handouts Keep Coming, the Food Line Never Ends
(OPINION)

Mark Winne

Mark Winne was the director of Connecticut's Hartford Food System from 1979 to 2003. He is the author of *Closing the Food Gap: Resetting the Table in the Land of Plenty* (2008), which examines how people from all classes obtain food: from lower income people at food pantries and convenience stores to more affluent people who tend to seek out organic and local products. Instead of the term *hunger*, Winne uses the phrase *food insecure*, which refers to a lack of access at all times to enough food for an active, healthy life. According to the USDA, 10.9% of households in the United States were food insecure at least some time during 2006. "When Handouts Keep Coming, the Food Line Never Ends" was published in the *Washington Post* on November 18, 2007.

Return to these questions after you have finished reading.

Analyzing and Connecting

1. Winne begins his article by talking about the flurry of giving that occurs during Thanksgiving. Why do you think people are more likely to make donations and volunteer during the holiday season?

2. In this article, Winne explains his position on the government's methods of dealing with poverty. In doing so, he sets up several causal relationships, the most clearly stated: "We know hunger's cause—poverty. We know its solution—end poverty." What are the others?

3. Winne is making a controversial claim—that we need to rethink our devotion to food donation. What is at stake in this claim for donors, food banks, and the poor? What is at stake for Winne in making this argument?

4. In this article, Winne provides many details—some of them potentially surprising to his audience—about the operations of food banks and of public food services. Why do you think he does this? How do these details affect his argument? his credibility?

Finding Ideas for Writing

As Winne points out, certain kinds of philanthropy continue—even though a change in policy might be more effective—because donors, whether corporations, organizations, or individuals, gain some benefit such as good public relations or even just feeling good. Write about an experience of volunteering, even if it was only an act of helping a stranger. Has this experience affected the way you feel about philanthropy? public services?

When Handouts Keep Coming, the Food Line Never Ends

How can anyone not get caught up in the annual Thanksgiving turkey frenzy? At the food bank I co-founded in Hartford, Conn., November always meant cheering the caravans of fowl-laden trucks that roared into our parking lot. They came on the heels of the public appeals for "A bird in every pot," "No family left without a turkey" and our bank's own version—"A turkey and a 20 [dollar bill]."

Like pompom girls leading a high school pep rally, we revved up the community's charitable impulse to a fever pitch with radio interviews, newspaper stories and dramatic television footage to extract the last gobbler from the stingiest citizen. After all, our nation's one great day of social equity was upon us. In skid row soup kitchens and the gated communities of hedge-fund billionaires alike, everyone was entitled, indeed expected, to sit down to a meal of turkey with all the fixings.

And here we are, putting on the same play again this year. But come Friday, as most of us stuff more leftovers into our bulging refrigerators, 35 million Americans will take their place in line again at soup kitchens, food banks and food stamp offices nationwide. The good souls who staff America's tens of thousands of emergency food sites will renew their pleas to donors fatigued by their burst of holiday philanthropy. Food stamp workers will return to their desks and try to convince mothers that they can feed their families on the $3 per person per day that the government allots them. The cycle of need—always present, rarely sated, never resolved—will continue.

Unless we rethink our devotion to food donation.

America's far-flung network of emergency food programs—from Second Harvest to tens of thousands of neighborhood food pantries—constitutes one of the largest charitable institutions in the nation. Its vast base of volunteers and donors and its ever-expanding distribution infrastructure have made it a powerful force in shaping popular perceptions of domestic hunger and other forms of need. But in the end, one of its most lasting effects has been to sidetrack efforts to eradicate hunger and its root cause, poverty.

As sociologist Janet Poppendieck made clear in her book *Sweet Charity,* there is something in the food-banking culture and its relationship with donors that dampens the desire to empower the poor and take a more muscular, public stand against hunger.

It used to be my job to scour every nook and cranny of Hartford for food resources, and I've known the desperation of workers who saw the lines of the poor grow longer while the food bank's inventory shrank. The cutback in federal support for social welfare programs triggered by the Reagan administration in the 1980s unleashed a wave of charitable innovation and growth not seen since the Great Depression. As demand for food rose unabated—as it does to this day—our food bank's staff became increasingly adept at securing sustenance from previously unimaginable sources.

No food donation was too small, too strange or too nutritionally unsound to be refused.

I remember the load of nearly rotten potatoes that we "gratefully" accepted at the warehouse loading dock and then promptly shoveled into the dumpster once the donor was safely out of sight. One of our early food bank meetings included a cooking demonstration by a group of local entrepreneurs who were trying to develop a market for horse meat. The product's name was Cheva-lean, taken from "cheval," the French word for horse. The promoters reminded us that the French, the world's leading authorities on food, ate horse meat, implying that therefore our poor clients could certainly do the same. The only thing that topped that was when we had to secure recipes from the University of Maine to help us use the moose parts proudly presented by representatives of the Connecticut Fish and Game Division who'd been forced to put down the disoriented Bullwinkle found wandering through suburban back yards.

We did our job well, and everything grew: Over 25 years, the food bank leapfrogged five times from warehouse to ever-vaster warehouse, finally landing in a state-of-the-art facility that's the equal of most commercial food distribution centers in the country. The volunteers multiplied to 3,000 because the donations of food, much of it unfit for human consumption, required many hands for sorting and discarding. The number of food distribution sites skyrocketed from five in 1982 to 360 today.

But in spite of all the outward signs of progress, more than 275,000 Connecticut residents—slightly less than 8.6 percent of the state's

residents—remain hungry or what we call "food insecure." The Department of Agriculture puts 11 percent of the U.S. population in this category. (The department also provides state-by-state breakdowns.)

The overall futility of the effort became evident to me one summer day in 2003 when I observed a food bank truck pull up to a low-income housing project in Hartford. The residents had known when and where the truck would arrive, and they were already lined up at the edge of the parking lot to receive handouts. Staff members and volunteers set up folding tables and proceeded to stack them with produce, boxed cereal and other food items. People stood quietly in line until it was their turn to receive a bag of pre-selected food.

No one made any attempt to determine whether the recipients actually needed the food, nor to encourage the recipients to seek other forms of assistance, such as food stamps. The food distribution was an unequivocal act of faith based on generally accepted knowledge that this was a known area of need. The recipients seemed reasonably grateful, but the staff members and volunteers seemed even happier, having been fortified by the belief that their act of benevolence was at least mildly appreciated.

As word spread, the lines got longer until finally the truck was empty. The following week, it returned at the same time, and once again the people were waiting. Only this time there were more of them. It may have been that a donor-recipient co-dependency had developed. Both parties were trapped in an ever-expanding web of immediate gratification that offered the recipients no long-term hope of eventually achieving independence and self-reliance. As the food bank's director told me later, "The more you provide, the more demand there is."

My experience of 25 years in food banking has led me to conclude that co-dependency within the system is multifaceted and frankly troubling. As a system that depends on donated goods, it must curry favor with the nation's food industry, which often regards food banks as a waste-management tool. As an operation that must sort through billions of pounds of damaged and partially salvageable food, it requires an army of volunteers who themselves are dependent on the carefully nurtured belief that they are "doing good" by "feeding the

hungry." And as a charity that lives from one multimillion-dollar capital campaign to the next (most recently, the Hartford food bank raised $4.5 million), it must maintain a ready supply of well-heeled philanthropists and captains of industry to raise the dollars and public awareness necessary to make the next warehouse expansion possible.

Food banks are a dominant institution in this country, and they assert their power at the local and state levels by commanding the attention of people of good will who want to address hunger. Their ability to attract volunteers and to raise money approaches that of major hospitals and universities. While none of this is inherently wrong, it does distract the public and policymakers from the task of harnessing the political will needed to end hunger in the United States.

The risk is that the multibillion-dollar system of food banking has become such a pervasive force in the anti-hunger world, and so tied to its donors and its volunteers, that it cannot step back and ask if this is the best way to end hunger, food insecurity and their root cause, poverty.

During my tenure in Hartford, I often wondered what would happen if the collective energy that went into soliciting and distributing food were put into ending hunger and poverty instead. Surely it would have a sizable impact if 3,000 Hartford-area volunteers, led by some of Connecticut's most privileged and respected citizens, showed up one day at the state legislature, demanding enough resources to end hunger and poverty. Multiply those volunteers by three or four—the number of volunteers in the state's other food banks and hundreds of emergency food sites—and you would have enough people to dismantle the Connecticut state capitol brick by brick. Put all the emergency food volunteers and staff and board members from across the country on buses to Washington, to tell Congress to mandate a living wage, health care for all and adequate employment and child-care programs, and you would have a convoy that might stretch from New York City to our nation's capital.

But what we have done instead is to continue down a road that never comes to an end. Like transportation planners who add more lanes to already clogged highways, we add more space to our food banks in the futile hope of relieving the congestion.

We know hunger's cause—poverty. We know its solution—end poverty. Let this Thanksgiving remind us of that task.

How to write a position argument

These steps for the process of writing a position argument may not progress as neatly as this chart might suggest. Writing is not an assembly-line process.

As you write and revise you may think of additional reasons to support your position. Your instructor and fellow students may give you comments that help you to rethink your argument. Use their comments to work through your paper or project again, strengthening your content and making your writing better organized and more readable.

1 FIND AN ISSUE

- Read your assignment slowly and carefully. Note key words like *argue for* and *take a stand* that indicate the assignment requires a position argument.

- Make a list of possible issues.

- Select a possible issue.

- Read about your issue.

- Analyze your potential readers. What do your readers likely know about the issue? Where are they most likely to disagree with you?

2 DEVELOP REASONS AND A THESIS

- Take a definite position.

- Develop reasons by considering whether you can argue from a definition, compare or contrast, consider good and bad effects, or refute objections.

- Support your reasons by making observations and finding facts, statistics, and statements from authorities.

- Write a working thesis.

3
WRITE A DRAFT

- Introduce the issue and give the necessary background. Explain why the issue is important.

- Think about how readers will view you, the writer.

- If you argue from a definition, set out the criteria.

- Avoid fallacies.

- Provide evidence to support your main points.

- Address opposing views. Summarize opposing positions and explain why your position is preferable.

- Make counterarguments if necessary. Examine the facts and assumptions on which competing claims are based.

- Conclude with strength. Avoid merely summarizing. Emphasize the importance of your argument and possibly make an additional point or draw implications.

- Choose a title that will interest readers.

4
REVISE, REVISE, REVISE

- Check that your position argument fulfills the assignment.

- Make sure that your claim is arguable and focused.

- Check your reasons and add more if you can.

- Add additional evidence where reasons need more support.

- Examine the organization.

- Review the visual presentation.

- Proofread carefully.

5
SUBMITTED VERSION

- Make sure your finished writing meets all formatting requirements.

1: Find an issue

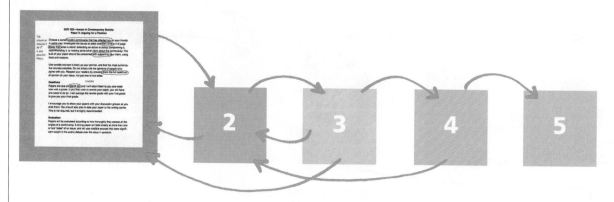

Analyze the assignment

- Read your assignment slowly and carefully. Look for key words like *argue for, take a stand,* and *write on a controversial issue.* These key words tell you that you are writing a position argument.

- Note any information about the length specified, date due, formatting, and other requirements. You can attend to this information later. At this point you want to give your attention to finding an issue if one is not specified.

Make a list of possible campus issues

Think about issues that are debated on your campus such as these.

- Should smoking be banned on campus?
- Should varsity athletes get paid for playing sports that bring in revenue?
- Should admissions decisions be based exclusively on academic achievement?
- Should knowledge of a foreign language be required for all degree plans?
- Should fraternities be banned from campuses if they are caught encouraging alcohol abuse?

Make a list of possible community issues

Think about issues that are debated in your community such as these.

- Should people who ride bicycles and motorcycles be required to wear helmets?
- Should high schools be allowed to search students for drugs at any time?
- Should bilingual education programs be eliminated?
- Should bike lanes be built throughout your community to encourage more people to ride bicycles?
- Should more tax dollars be shifted from building highways to public transportation?

Make a list of possible national and international issues

Think about national and international issues such as these.

- Should advertising be banned on television shows aimed at preschool children?
- Should the Internet be censored?
- Should the government be allowed to monitor all phone calls and all email to combat terrorism?
- Should handguns be outlawed?
- Should people who are terminally ill be allowed to end their lives?
- Should the United States punish nations with poor human rights records?

Read about your issue

- What are the major points of view on your issue?
- Who are the experts on this issue? What do they have to say?
- What major claims are being offered?
- What reasons are given to support the claims?
- What kinds of evidence are used to support the reasons?

Analyze your potential readers

- For whom does this issue matter? Whose interests are at stake?
- What attitudes and beliefs will your readers likely have about this issue?
- What key terms will you need to define or explain?
- What assumptions do you have in common with your readers?
- Where will your readers most likely disagree with you?

Write Now

Choose an issue that you care about

1. Make a list of issues that fulfill your assignment.
2. Put a checkmark beside the issues that look most interesting to write about or the ones that mean the most to you.
3. Put a question mark beside the issues that you don't know very much about. If you choose one of these issues, you will probably have to do in-depth research—by talking to people, by using the Internet, or by going to the library.
4. Select a possible issue. What is your stand on this issue? Write nonstop for five minutes about why this issue is important and how it affects you.

Writer at work

Chris Nguyen received a writing assignment in her government class, and made the following notes on her assignment sheet.

GOV 322—Issues in Contemporary Society
Paper 3: Arguing for a Position

"We should or shouldn't do X" is one possible thesis.

Choose a current public controversy that has affected you or your friends in some way. Investigate the issues at stake and then write a 4–6 page essay that takes a stand: defending an action or policy, condemning it, recommending it, or making some other claim about the controversy. The bulk of your paper should be concerned with supporting your claim, using facts and reasons.

Use outside sources to back up your opinion, and find the most authoritative sources possible. Do not simply cite the opinions of people who agree with you. Respect your readers by showing them the full spectrum of opinion on your issue, not just one or two sides.

Deadlines

2 weeks

Papers are due on March 24, and I will return them to you one week later with a grade. If you then wish to rewrite your paper, you will have one week to do so. I will average the rewrite grade with your first grade to give you your final grade.

I encourage you to share your papers with your discussion groups as you draft them. You should also plan to take your paper to the writing center. This is not required, but it is highly recommended.

Evaluation

Papers will be evaluated according to how thoroughly they assess all the angles of a controversy. A strong paper will look closely at more than one or two "sides" of an issue, and will use credible sources that carry significant weight in the public debate over the issue in question.

Read the assignment closely

Chris Nguyen began by marking information about due dates and requirements. She noted her instructor's suggestion that students might phrase their thesis in a particular way. She also wrote down her teacher's advice to avoid oversimplifying the controversy.

Choose a topic

Chris made a list of potential topics for her paper. She began by thinking of controversies she had talked about with her friends in the recent past. She chose to write about a recent event on campus, in which a number of students had been ejected from a public talk because they were wearing T-shirts critical of the speaker.

Explore the issue

Chris looked for news articles about similar events, and court proceedings that followed. As she researched, she made a list of events she wanted to compare to the event at her school. She also found references to a number of court cases, which she researched as well.

Identify key terms

Chris compiled a list of key terms to help her think about her issue.

POSSIBLE TOPICS

Should military recruiting on campus be allowed if the military discriminates against gays? What is college's responsibility to students/country?

Peer-to-peer music downloading—should it be legal?

Students thrown out of speech for wearing T-shirts—violation of free speech?

NOTES

Two people wearing anti-Bush T-shirts at a rally at the West Virginia Capitol were arrested for trespassing, but charges were dropped.

High school student sent home from school for wearing a T-shirt with the word "redneck" was vindicated by court ruling.

A man is arrested for trespassing in a mall for wearing a shirt he had bought there reading "Give peace a chance."

1969 Tinker v. Des Moines ISD
Supreme Court: In order to censor, a high school must show evidence of substantial disruption as a result of speech, or invasion of others' rights.

1969 Brandenburg v. Ohio
Supreme Court: to prohibit speech, it must be "directed at inciting or producing imminent lawless action" or "likely to incite or produce such action."

1986 Bethel v. Fraser
Supreme Court: vulgar speech can be prohibited at a school assembly.

1988 Hazelwood School District v. Kuhlmeier
Supreme Court: school-sponsored speech (like school papers) can be censored.

What is free speech?
What is an invasion of someone else's rights?
What is a "substantial disruption"?
What is vulgar speech?
What is school-sponsored speech? [what about protest of it?]
What is "socially inappropriate behavior"?

2: Develop reasons and a thesis

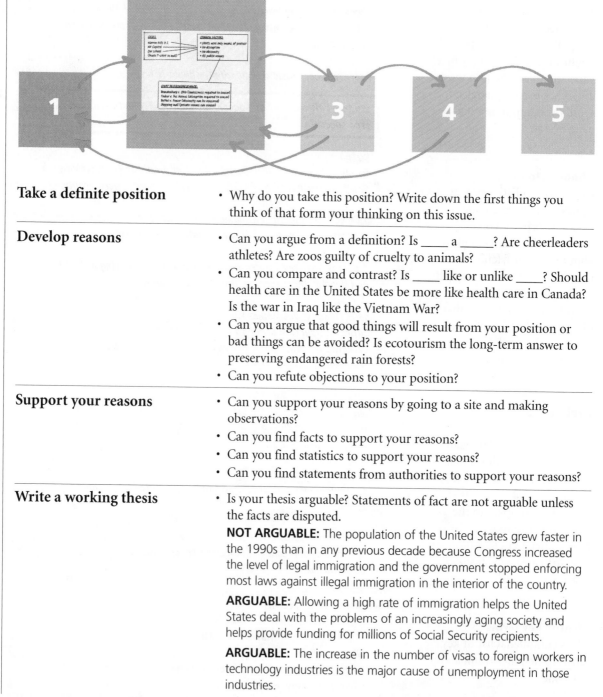

Take a definite position	• Why do you take this position? Write down the first things you think of that form your thinking on this issue.
Develop reasons	• Can you argue from a definition? Is _____ a _____? Are cheerleaders athletes? Are zoos guilty of cruelty to animals? • Can you compare and contrast? Is _____ like or unlike _____? Should health care in the United States be more like health care in Canada? Is the war in Iraq like the Vietnam War? • Can you argue that good things will result from your position or bad things can be avoided? Is ecotourism the long-term answer to preserving endangered rain forests? • Can you refute objections to your position?
Support your reasons	• Can you support your reasons by going to a site and making observations? • Can you find facts to support your reasons? • Can you find statistics to support your reasons? • Can you find statements from authorities to support your reasons?
Write a working thesis	• Is your thesis arguable? Statements of fact are not arguable unless the facts are disputed. **NOT ARGUABLE:** The population of the United States grew faster in the 1990s than in any previous decade because Congress increased the level of legal immigration and the government stopped enforcing most laws against illegal immigration in the interior of the country. **ARGUABLE:** Allowing a high rate of immigration helps the United States deal with the problems of an increasingly aging society and helps provide funding for millions of Social Security recipients. **ARGUABLE:** The increase in the number of visas to foreign workers in technology industries is the major cause of unemployment in those industries.

- Is your thesis specific? A thesis may be arguable but too broad to be treated adequately in a short paper.

ARGUABLE, BUT TOO BROAD: We should take action to resolve the serious traffic problem in our city.

ARGUABLE AND FOCUSED: The existing freight railway that runs through the center of the city should be converted to a passenger railway because it is the cheapest and most quickly implemented way to decrease traffic congestion downtown.

Staying on Track

Evaluate your thesis

Once you have a working thesis, ask these questions:

1. Is it arguable?
2. Is it specific?
3. Is it manageable in the length and time you have?
4. Is it interesting to your intended readers?

OFF TRACK Over 60% of Americans play video games on a regular basis.	**ARGUABLE?** The thesis states a commonly acknowledged fact. **SPECIFIC?** The thesis is a bland general statement. **MANAGEABLE?** A known fact is stated in the thesis, so there is little to research. Several surveys report this finding. **INTERESTING?** Video games are interesting as a cultural trend, but nearly everyone is aware of the trend.
ON TRACK Video games are valuable because they improve children's visual attention skills, their literacy skills, and their computer literacy skills.	**ARGUABLE?** The thesis takes a position contrary to the usual view of video games. **SPECIFIC?** The thesis gives specific reasons for the claim. **MANAGEABLE?** The thesis is manageable if research can be located and observations of game playing included. **INTERESTING?** The topic is interesting because it challenges conventional wisdom.

Writer at work

*I believe school administrators were wrong to eject
the students wearing T-shirts.*

HOW TO ARGUE?????

Chris Nguyen knew how she felt, but she didn't know at first how to make a convincing case. She read more about events similar to the one that happened on her campus, and she became convinced that her school's administrators had acted improperly, and perhaps illegally, in ejecting the students. She examined the cases she had researched and drew an idea map.

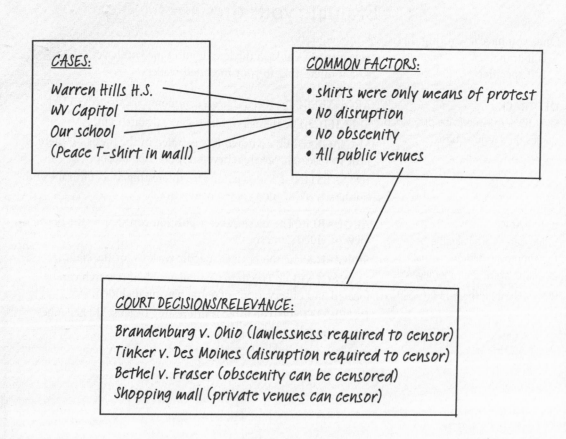

CASES:

Warren Hills H.S.
WV Capitol
Our school
(Peace T-shirt in mall)

COMMON FACTORS:

• shirts were only means of protest
• No disruption
• No obscenity
• All public venues

COURT DECISIONS/RELEVANCE:

Brandenburg v. Ohio (lawlessness required to censor)
Tinker v. Des Moines (disruption required to censor)
Bethel v. Fraser (obscenity can be censored)
Shopping mall (private venues can censor)

Chris used the idea map to define the conditions in which speech can be restricted.

CRITERIA FOR FREE SPEECH
- Cannot incite violence
- Cannot threaten violence
- Cannot be obscene (although what exactly is obscene isn't clear)
- Only on public property
- Only for adults

Ejecting students would be justified if
- The students were doing something "directed to and likely to incite imminent lawless action" NO
- They used vulgar or obscene language NO
- They were in a private venue NO
- They were minors NO

WORKING THESIS
The college was wrong to eject the six protesting students from last month's speakers' event because the students were not inciting lawless action, did not use vulgar or obscene language, were in a public venue, and were not minors.

Chris's research supported a more specific claim than the one she initially made: that the college was "wrong" to remove the students. She revised her thesis to focus on this stronger and, she thought, more interesting claim. In addition to claiming the students' right to free speech was violated, she argued that her school should apologize to the students involved. Here is the final working thesis Chris used to begin drafting her essay:

The University administration should drop trespassing charges against the six students arrested last month and offer them a formal apology, because their ejection and arrest was a violation of the students' constitutionally protected right to free speech.

3: Write a draft

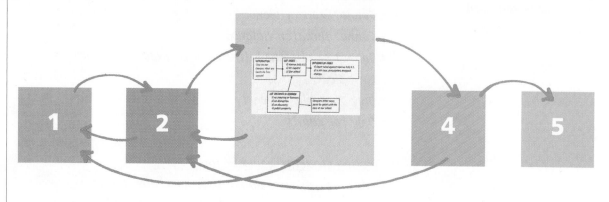

| **1** | **2** | | **4** | **5** |

Introduce the issue
- Describe the trend, event, or phenomenon you will be analyzing.
- Give your readers any background information they will need.

Think about how readers will view you, the writer
- What group or group will readers consider you a part of? At the very least, they will consider you as a college student. What assumptions will they have about you?
- Think about how you can connect with your readers as you write by appealing to their sense of fairness, their core beliefs, and their sense of logic.

If you argue from a definition, set out the criteria
- Which criteria are necessary for _____ to be a _____?
- Which are not necessary?
- Which are most important?
- Does your case in point meet all the necessary criteria?

Avoid fallacies
- Fallacies generally arise from a lack of evidence or faulty evidence.
- You can find a list of fallacies on pages 14–15.

Anticipate and address opposing viewpoints
- Acknowledge other stakeholders for the issue, and consider their positions.
- Explain why your position is preferable.

Make counterarguments if necessary
- Examine the facts on which a competing claim is based. Are the facts accurate, current, and a representative sample? Are sources treated fairly or taken out of context?
- Examine the primary assumption of a claim that you are rejecting. Is the assumption flawed? What other assumptions are involved?

Conclude with strength

- Avoid summarizing what you have just said.
- Spell out the importance of the analysis, if you haven't already done so.
- Consider additional effects you haven't previously discussed.
- Explain any action you think needs to be taken based on your conclusion.

Choose a title that will interest readers

- Make your title specific.
- Engage your readers with the issue.

Staying on Track

Facts vs. your opinion

Distinguish facts from opinions

Find facts to support what you think. You may be surprised to find that the facts are not what you anticipated.

OFF TRACK
I believe that Americans have the best medical care in the world.

ON TRACK
On one of the most trusted indicators of health—life expectancy at birth—in 2005 the United States ranks 48th behind nearly all of Europe, Japan, Singapore, Hong Kong, and even countries like Jordan, Cuba, and Costa Rica.

OFF TRACK
It is obvious from watching television news that violent crime is on the rise.

ON TRACK
While violent crime remains the staple of local news, FBI statistics show a 24% drop in violent crimes in the United States between 1995 and 2004.

Writer at work

Chris mapped the ideas she would need to include in her paper.

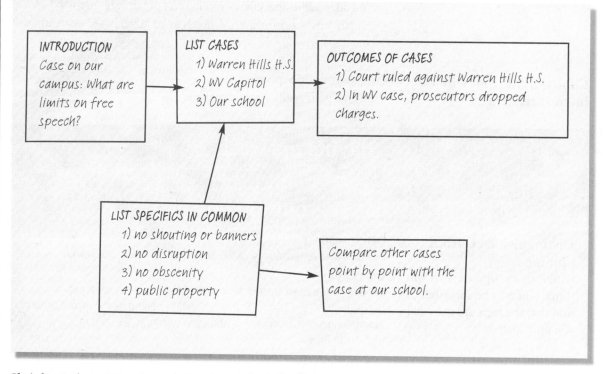

INTRODUCTION
Case on our campus: What are limits on free speech?

LIST CASES
1) Warren Hills H.S.
2) WV Capitol
3) Our school

OUTCOMES OF CASES
1) Court ruled against Warren Hills H.S.
2) In WV case, prosecutors dropped charges.

LIST SPECIFICS IN COMMON
1) no shouting or banners
2) no disruption
3) no obscenity
4) public property

Compare other cases point by point with the case at our school.

Chris began by writing the common factors in the cases because they would be the core of her paper. She would build the rest of the paper around these four factors.

These are the factors the three cases have in common:

1) In each case, the wearers of the shirts did not express themselves in any way other than by wearing the shirts. They did not speak, shout, hold up banners or signs, or call attention to themselves in any way.

2) None of the events were disrupted by the shirts. Any disruption that occurred was due to the removal of the wearers by authority figures.

3) None of the T-shirts featured obscene language or imagery.

4) All took place in government-funded venues: a public school, a state capitol, and a state-funded university.

Chris next made a working outline, which she used to write her paper.

1) start with a brief mention of our case where students were ejected

2) describe limits on free speech

3) introduce the three T-shirt cases; end with claim that ejection at our school was unconstitutional

4) list factors that the cases have in common

5) introduce standard of lawless action for restricting free speech

6) discuss the Warren Hills High School case

7) discuss the West Virginia Capitol case

8) discuss the issue of what is offensive or considered obscene

9) compare the West Virginia Capitol incident to our campus because both involve political speech

10) make the distinction between public and private venues

11) point out that all cases were at public venues

12) raise the issue of minors and point out that college students are of legal age

13) conclude with a call for an apology

4: Revise, revise, revise

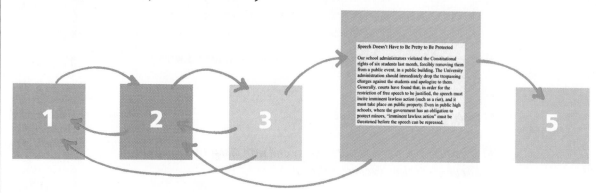

Speech Doesn't Have to Be Pretty to Be Protected

Our school administrators violated the Constitutional rights of six students last month, forcibly removing them from a public event, in a public building. The University administration should immediately drop the trespassing charges against the students and apologize to them. Generally, courts have found that, in order for the restriction of free speech to be justified, the speech must incite imminent lawless action (such as a riot), and it must take place on public property. Even in public high schools, where the government has an obligation to protect minors, "imminent lawless action" must be threatened before the speech can be repressed.

Skilled writers know that the secret to writing well is rewriting. Even the best writers often have to revise several times to get the result they want. You also must have effective strategies for revising if you're going to be successful. The biggest trap you can fall into is starting off with the little stuff first. Leave the small stuff for last.

Does your position argument fulfill the assignment?	• Look again at your assignment. Does your paper or project do what the assignment asks? • Look again at the assignment for specific guidelines, including length, format, and amount of research. Does your work meet these guidelines?
Is your claim arguable and focused?	• Is your position arguable? Statements of fact and statements of religious belief are not arguable. • Can you make your claim more specific to avoid ambiguous language and situations where your claim may not apply?
Are your reasons adequate?	• Are your reasons clear to your readers? • Can you add additional reasons to strengthen your argument? • Have you acknowledged the views of people who disagree with your position? • Have you shown how your position is preferable?
Are your reasons supported with evidence?	• Have you found the most accurate information available about your issue? • Can you find additional evidence in the form of examples, quotations from experts, statistics, comparisons, and on-site observations?

Is your organization effective?	• Are your reasons in the best possible order?
	• Do you get off to a fast start with your title and introduction? Can you do more to gain and keep the reader's interest?
	• Is your conclusion only a summary of what you have said? If so, can you think of an implication or an example that gets at the heart of the issue?
Is the writing project visually effective?	• Is the font attractive and readable?
	• Are the headings and visuals effective?
	• If you use images or tables as part of your analysis, are they legible and appropriately placed? Do you have captions for each?
Save the editing for last.	When you have finished revising, edit and proofread carefully.

A peer review guide is on page 27.

Writer at work

Chris Nguyen took her first draft of the essay to her school's writing center. In particular, she asked to discuss the paper's opening, which she felt was too abrupt. The consultant at the writing center suggested that one possible strategy was to move the thesis statement to the end of the introductory section. Chris found this change worked well for her essay, giving her claim more weight.

Chris had her thesis in the second sentence in her first draft. Moving it to the end of the introductory section allowed her to explain the issue of restricting free speech before announcing her position. Her revised paper begins on the next page.

Speech Doesn't Have to Be Pretty to Be Protected

Our school administrators violated the Constitutional rights of six students last month, forcibly removing them from a public event, in a public building. The University administration should immediately drop the trespassing charges against the students and apologize to them. Generally, courts have found that, in order for the restriction of free speech to be justified, the speech must incite imminent lawless action (such as a riot), and it must take place on public property. Even in public high schools, where the government has an obligation to protect minors, "imminent lawless action" must be threatened before the speech can be repressed.

325

5: Submitted version

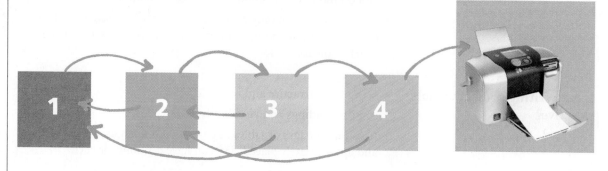

Chris Nguyen
Professor Conley
GOV 322
24 March 2008

Speech Doesn't Have to Be Pretty to Be Protected

Last month six students on our campus were ejected from a university auditorium for wearing T-shirts with "war criminal" on the front. Was the university justified in removing our fellow students who were not disruptive in any other way?

The First Amendment to the Constitution of the United States of America guarantees the right to freedom of expression. This important right is one of the foundations of our democracy. Yet many Americans do not understand what the right to free speech really means. Free speech is your right to say what you think—within limits. It is not the right to cause mayhem, or to threaten violence, or to incite others to violence. Authority figures also need to understand the limits on free speech. Generally, courts have found that, in order for the restriction of free speech to be justified, the speech must incite imminent lawless action (such as a riot), and it must take place on public property. Even in public high schools, where the government has an obligation to protect minors, "imminent lawless action" must be threatened before the speech can be repressed.

Clearly, it's not always easy to tell when restriction of free speech is justified. Consider these recent controversies over free speech:

- A student at Warren Hills Regional High School in New Jersey was suspended for wearing a T-shirt that featured the word "redneck" ("Federal Court").
- Jeff and Nicole Rank attended an official visit by President Bush at the West Virginia Capitol and were charged with trespassing when they refused to remove T-shirts that read "Love America, Hate Bush" (Bundy).
- Six students were removed from a university auditorium and charged with trespassing during a speech by former U.S. Secretary of State, Henry Kissinger, for wearing T-shirts that referred to the speaker as a "war criminal."

In the first two cases, it has been established that authorities did not have the right to curtail the speech of the people involved: a federal appeals court decided the first case in favor of the student, and the prosecutor in the second case dropped the charges, admitting that no law had been broken. If we examine the similarities and differences among these three cases, it becomes clear that in the third case, which happened on our own campus last month, the administration's ejection of the students was unconstitutional.

These are the factors the three cases have in common:

1. In each case, the wearers of the shirts did not express themselves in any way other than by wearing the shirts. They did not speak, shout, hold up banners or signs, or call attention to themselves in any way.
2. None of the events where the shirts were worn were disrupted by the shirts. Any disruption that occurred was due to the removal of the wearers by authority figures.
3. None of the T-shirts featured obscene language or imagery.
4. All took place in government-funded venues: a public school, a state capitol, and a state-funded university.

These similarities are important because they show how, in each case, the T-shirt wearers acted within their constitutionally protected right to free expression.

The first two factors above show how each of these cases fails to meet the standard of "imminent lawless action," set in the 1969 case of Brandenburg v. Ohio. In that case, the Supreme Court ruled that in order to ban forms of expression, the government had to prove the expression was "directed to and likely to incite imminent lawless action." If the act of expression did not seem likely to cause a riot, for example, it could not be restricted. Simply making people angry or uncomfortable is not justification for censorship.

In the first case, at Warren Hills High School, the only person who objected to the "redneck" T-shirt was a vice principal, who claimed the term "redneck" was offensive to minority students and violated the school's racial harassment policy ("Federal Court"). The U.S. Court of Appeals for the Third Circuit, however, ruled that the school failed to prove "that the shirt might genuinely threaten disruption or, indeed, that it violated any of the particular provisions of the harassment policy." This decision followed the precedent of another landmark case, Tinker v. Des Moines, in which the Supreme Court ruled that, even in public schools, the government must provide evidence that the speech would cause "(a.) a substantial disruption of the school environment, or (b.) an invasion of the rights of others" (Haynes).

In the second case, the government never even made a claim that the T-shirts worn by Jeff and Nicole Rank were inciting lawlessness. The only people who were upset by the Ranks' T-shirts were two Secret Service officers, who ordered the couple to remove the shirts. When they refused, the officers ordered Charleston city police to arrest them, which the police did. The Ranks were charged with trespassing ("Secret Service"). The irony of arresting U.S. citizens for standing peacefully on public, state-owned property was even clear to the prosecutor, who dropped the charges (Bundy).

Moreover, none of the cases met the test for "vulgar or obscene" language. Vulgar and obscene language can be regulated, to some extent, without violating the First Amendment. In 1986, the Supreme Court ruled in the case of Bethel v. Fraser that public school officials could prohibit vulgar speech at a school assembly. The court said that "[T]he undoubted freedom to advocate unpopular and controversial views in schools and classrooms must be balanced against the society's countervailing interest in teaching students the boundaries of socially appropriate behavior." The vice principal in the Warren Hills Case was the only one who thought "redneck" was offensive, and the fact that the word is used constantly on television and other media shows that it is not considered obscene by society at large.

The Ranks' arrest is a better comparison to the situation at our school, because their shirts were clearly singled out for their political content, not for vulgarity. They carried a message that might have been offensive to some of the supporters of the president who were present, but under no circumstances could the content of the shirts be considered obscene. The same is true of the shirts that got my fellow students kicked out of a public event. Calling someone a war criminal is a serious accusation, but it is not obscene.

Finally, public versus private venue is an important factor in the protection of free speech. The Constitution guarantees that the state will not infringe the right to free expression. Private entities are free to do so, however. For example, protestors can be thrown out of a private meeting of club members. Even a shopping mall owner can deny entry to protesters or even people without shoes. Of course, anyone with private property also has to consider the economic impact of limiting speech. Recently a shopping mall owner had police arrest a man wearing a "Give Peace a Chance" T-shirt ("Man Arrested") that he had just bought in the mall. Not surprisingly, the mall owner received a great deal of bad publicity about this decision. Concerned citizens who felt this action by the mall owner went too far wrote letters to newspapers publicizing the act. They even wrote letters to the police who arrested the man ("Big Support"). The trespassing charges against the man were dropped. This incident illustrates how free speech is negotiated in the marketplace.

In the Ranks' case, the trespassing charges against them were dropped because they were on the statehouse grounds. How can a citizen trespass on public property? In the same vein, how can students be trespassing on their own campus? The six people arrested at our school were students, whose tuition and fees helped pay for the building they were in. What's more, the event was advertised in flyers and

newspaper ads as "free and open to the public." How can anyone be charged with trespassing at a public event?

The Warren Hills case was decided in favor of the student, even though the expression took place in a public school. As Bethel v. Fraser shows, courts generally feel that schools can take special steps to protect minors: vulgar or obscene speech can be censored, and school-sponsored forms of expression, like newspapers, can be censored. But these actions are justified because the students are minors. Presumably, they need more guidance as they learn about the boundaries of socially acceptable behavior. But most if not all college students are legally adults, so it does not make sense to say our school was "teaching students the boundaries of socially appropriate behavior" by throwing them out of a public event because of their shirts. It is not the job of a college administration to teach manners.

Our school administrators violated the Constitutional rights of six students last month. They forcibly removed them from a public event, in a public building. The students were not causing a commotion in any way before their arrests; there was no indication whatsoever that "imminent lawless action" might be provoked by their T-shirts. Because the students in this case were clearly exercising their Constitutional right to free speech, the university administration should immediately drop the trespassing charges against the students. Evidence from prior cases indicates the charges will not stand up in court in any case, so the legal battle will be a waste of money for the college. Furthermore, as an institution of learning that supposedly safeguards the free exchange of ideas, the college should offer a sincere apology to the arrested students. The administrators would send an important message to all students by doing this: Your right to free speech is respected at this school.

Works Cited

Bethel School Dist. v. Fraser. 478 US 675. Supreme Court of the US. 1986.
    Supreme Court Collection. Legal Information Inst., Cornell U Law School, n.d.
    Web. 7 Mar. 2008.

"Big Support for 'Peace' T-shirt Arrestees." *The Smoking Gun.* Turner Entertainment
    Digital Network, 25 Mar. 2003. Web. 10 Mar. 2008.

Brandenburg v. Ohio. 395 US 444. Supreme Court of the US. 1969. *Supreme
    Court Collection.* Legal Information Inst., Cornell U Law School, n.d. Web.
    7 Mar. 2008.

Bundy, Jennifer. "Trespass Charges Dropped Against Bush Protesters."
    CommonDreams.org Newscenter. CommonDreams.org, 15 Jul. 2004. Web.
    18 Mar. 2008.

"Federal Court Says NJ School Can't Ban Redneck T-shirt." *Center for Individual
    Rights.* Center for Individual Rights, 6 Nov. 2003. Web. 11 Mar. 2008.

Haynes, Charles C. "T-shirt Rebellion in the Land of the Free." *First Amendment.*
    First Amendment Center, 14 Mar. 2004. Web. 18 Mar. 2008.

"Man Arrested for 'Peace' T-shirt." *CNN.com.* Cable News Network, 4 Mar. 2003.
    Web. 15 Mar. 2008.

"Secret Service and White House Charged with Violating Free Speech Rights in
    ACLU Lawsuit." *ACLU.* American Civil Liberties Union, 14 Sep. 2004. Web.
    19 Mar. 2008.

Projects

Much of what passes for position arguments on television talk shows and on talk radio is little more than shouted assertions and name calling. Arguments in writing are different in character. They are not merely statements of someone's opinion, but are reasoned arguments backed by evidence. They aim not to get in the last word but rather to advance the discussion on an issue so that all benefit from hearing different points of view. These projects are frequently written kinds of position arguments.

Position argument

Make a position claim on a controversial issue. See pages 312–313 for help on identifying an issue.

Think about what's at stake. Would everyone agree with you? Then your claim probably isn't interesting or important. If you can think of people who would disagree, then something is at stake.

Identify the key term. Often position arguments depend on the definition of the key term. What criteria are necessary for something to meet this definition? How would others benefit from a different definition?

Analyze your potential readers. How does the claim you are making affect them? How familiar are they with the issue? How likely will they be to accept your claim or the definition that underlies your claim?

Write an essay on a controversial issue that takes a stand supported by developed reasons.

Rebuttal argument

Identify a position argument to argue against. What is its main claim or claims? A fair summary of your opponent's position should be included in your finished rebuttal.

↓

Examine the facts on which the claim is based. Are the facts accurate? Are the facts current? Can the statistics be interpreted differently? How reliable are the author's sources?

↓

Analyze the assumptions on which the claim is based. What is the primary assumption of the claim you are rejecting? What are the secondary assumptions? How are these assumptions flawed? What fallacies does the author commit (see pages 14–15)?

↓

Consider your readers. To what extent do your potential readers support the claim you are rejecting? If they strongly support that claim, then how do you get them to change their minds? What beliefs and assumptions do you share with them?

↓

Write a rebuttal. Make your aim clear in your thesis statement. Identify the issue you are writing about and give background information if the issue is likely to be unfamiliar to your readers. Question the evidence and show the flaws in the argument you are rejecting. Conclude on a strong note with your counterargument or counterproposal.

Narrative position argument

Think about an experience you have had that makes an implicit causal argument. Have you ever experienced being stereotyped? Have you ever had to jump through many unnecessary bureaucratic hoops? Have you ever been treated differently because of your perceived level of income? Have you ever experienced unfair application of laws and law enforcement?

↓

How common is your experience? If other people have similar experiences, probably what happened to you will ring true.

↓

Describe the experience in detail. When did it happen? How old were you? Why were you there? Who else was there? Where did it happen? If the place is important, describe what it looked like.

↓

Reflect on the significance of the event. How did you feel about the experience when it happened? How do you feel about the experience now? What long-term effects has it had on your life?

↓

Write an essay. You might need to give some background, but if the story is compelling, often it is best to jump right in. Let the story do most of the work. Avoid drawing a simple moral lesson. Your readers should feel the same way you do if you tell your story well.

13 Proposal Arguments

Proposal arguments aim to convince others to take action for change
(or not to take action).

CHAPTER CONTENTS

Making a proposal argument

Every day we hear and read arguments that some action should be taken. We even make these arguments to ourselves: We should exercise more; we should change our work habits. We can make many changes in our lives if we convince ourselves that the effort is worth it.

Convincing others to take action for change is always harder. Other people might not see the same problem that you see or they might not think that the problem is important. And even if they do see the same problem and think it is important, they may not want to commit the time and resources to do something about it. In the short term, at least, doing nothing is the easy choice. Nevertheless, most people aren't satisfied with doing nothing about a problem they think is important. We are impatient when we believe something is wrong or something could be improved. We expect things to change; indeed, we have even designed our political system to guarantee a new president of the nation at least every eight years. The problem we face in persuading others is not so much that people are resistant to change but that the change we propose is the right one and worthy of their effort to make it happen.

Every major construction project, every large-scale product, every major scientific endeavor starts with an argument for change—an argument to do something that we are not currently doing and to take action. Arguments for change can even involve changing an entire government (think of the Declaration of Independence). These kinds of arguments are called proposal arguments, and they take the classic form: *We should (or should not) do SOMETHING.*

Working Together

Make a list of problems to solve

In a group of three or four students

First make a list of all the things you can think of that are problems: your library closes too early for late-night study, there is too little work-study aid on your campus, your roommate is a slob, the weather stays too hot or too cold for too long, store clerks are rude, and on and on. Share your list with the group. Then discuss the following.

• Which items turned up on more than one list?

• Which problems are the most important?

• Which are possible to solve?

• Which problems are the most interesting to your group?

• Which problems are the least interesting to your group?

Understand how proposal arguments work

Proposal arguments call for some action to be taken (or not taken). The challenge for writers is to convince readers that they should take action, which usually involves their commitment of effort or money.

Someone should (or should not) do something because _____.

EXAMPLE

We should convert existing train tracks in the downtown area to a light-rail system and build a new freight track around the city because we need to relieve traffic and parking congestion downtown.

Components of proposal arguments

What exactly is the problem?	**Identify the problem.** Sometimes, problems are evident to your intended readers. If your city is constantly tearing up the streets and then leaving them for months without doing anything to repair them, then you shouldn't have much trouble convincing the citizens of your city that streets should be repaired more quickly. But if you raise a problem that will be unfamiliar to most of your readers, you will first have to argue that the problem exists and it is in their interest that something should be done about it.
What is my solution?	**State your proposed solution.** You need to have a clear, definite statement of exactly what you are proposing. Say exactly what you want others to do. You might want to place this statement near the beginning of your argument, or later, after you have considered and rejected other possible solutions. **VAGUE:** Our city should encourage all citizens to conserve water. **SPECIFIC:** Our city should provide incentives to conserve water, including offering rain barrels for the minimal cost of $10, replacing at no cost old toilets with water-efficient toilets, and providing rebates up to $500 to those who replace grass with plants that require little water.
Will my solution work?	**Convince your readers that your solution will work.** When your readers agree that a problem exists and a solution should be found, your next task is to convince them that your solution is the best one to resolve the problem. Many college campuses suffer from transportation and parking problems. If your campus is one of them, then your readers likely will agree that the problems exist. The

question is what to do about them. One possible solution is to add a light-rail line to campus from your city's planned light-rail system. If you argue for adding a light-rail line, you must project how many people will ride it and how many car trips will be reduced.

Why is my solution better than others?

Show why your solution is better than other possible solutions. An obvious solution to a lack of parking is to build a parking garage. But parking garages also cost money, and they might even encourage more people to drive, further aggravating the traffic problem. Another solution is to provide more buses, which would not require building a light-rail line and likely would be cheaper. You must argue why rail would be preferable.

Will people be willing to implement my solution?

Demonstrate that your solution is feasible. Your solution not only has to work; it must have a realistic chance of being implemented. Can we afford it? Will it take too long to do? Will people accept it? What else might not get done? A light-rail link might be ideal for getting students to and from campus, but it would cost a great deal of money to construct. The rail proposal is feasible only if you have a concrete proposal for how it would be funded.

How can I convince my readers?

Arguments for light rail include reducing traffic, reducing air pollution, and encouraging the develoment of neighborhoods near rail routes.

Focus on the audience. All effective writing attends to the audience, but in no form of writing is the audience more important than in arguments for change. Readers have to be convinced that "we really have a problem, and we need to do something about it." It's not enough just to get readers to agree that the problem exists. They have to believe that the problem is worth solving.

Keys to proposal arguments

Convince readers that you can be trusted

To gain the trust of your readers, you first must convince them that you are well informed. You also must convince them that you are fair and sincere and that your heart is in the right place. Readers think favorably of good writers. Poor writers lose readers on all counts, even with the same ideas as a good writer.

Convince your readers that you have their best interests in mind

At the outset many readers may not have much interest in the problem you identify. If you are proposing adding bike lanes to streets in your city, you likely will need the support of people who will never use them. You could argue that if more people rode bicycles, there would be more parking places for those who drive and less air pollution for everyone.

Convince your readers with evidence

You may need a great deal of evidence for a problem that is unfamiliar to your readers. Statistics are often helpful in establishing that a problem affects many people. Likewise, you will need evidence that your solution will work and that it can be accomplished.

Emphasize what you have in common with your readers and be honest about differences

You may not share the assumptions and beliefs of your audience. Think about what may separate you from your audience and what you have in common. When you can establish common ground with your readers because you live in the same community, have similar goals, or share experiences, then you can be frank about any differences you might have. Readers appreciate honesty.

Show exactly how your proposal will have good consequences and possibly reduce bad consequences

Predicting the future is never easy. Think about how your proposal can make good things happen or reduce bad things. Has a solution similar to the one that you are proposing been tried elsewhere? Can you connect to other good consequences? For example, saving water also saves the energy required to run a water treatment plant and to pump it to a home or business.

End with strength

Remember that you want your readers to take action. If you have a powerful example, use it in the conclusion. Inspire your readers to want something better than the status quo. Leave them with a strong impression.

An effective proposal argument

Readers have to be motivated to take action to solve a problem.

The Declaration of Independence

Thomas Jefferson

The American Revolution had already begun with the battles of Lexington, Concord, and Bunker Hill, and George Washington had been named to head the colonial army by June 7, 1776, when the Continental Congress moved to draft a Declaration of Independence. Thomas Jefferson was given eighteen days to complete the task with the help of Benjamin Franklin and John Adams.

IN CONGRESS, JULY 4, 1776.

The unanimous Declaration of the thirteen united States of America.

When, in the Course of human events, it becomes necessary for one people to dissolve the political bands which have connected them with another, and to assume among the powers of the earth, the separate and equal station to which the laws of nature and of nature's God entitle them, a decent respect to the opinions of mankind requires that they should declare the causes which impel them to the separation.

> Jefferson maintains that the drastic solution of declaring independence is justified if the problem is of great magnitude.

We hold these truths to be self-evident: That all men are created equal; that they are endowed by their Creator with certain unalienable rights; that among these are life, liberty and the pursuit of happiness. That, to secure these rights, governments are instituted among men, deriving their just powers from the consent of the governed; that, whenever any form of government becomes destructive of these ends, it is the right of the people to alter or to abolish it, and to institute new Government, laying its foundation on such principles, and organizing its powers in such form, as to them shall seem most likely to effect their safety and happiness. Prudence,

> The rationale for the proposal is a definition argument. According to Jefferson, the purpose of a government is to ensure the rights of the governed. When a government fails to achieve its defined purpose—to ensure the rights of the people—the people have the right to abolish it. The British used similar arguments to justify the revolution against King James II in 1688.

indeed, will dictate that governments long established should not be changed for light and transient causes; and accordingly all experience hath shown, that mankind are more disposed to suffer, while evils are sufferable, than to right themselves by abolishing the forms to which they are accustomed. But when a long train of abuses and usurpations, pursuing invariably the same object evinces a design to reduce them under absolute despotism, it is their right, it is their duty, to throw off such government and to provide new guards for their future security. Such has been the patient sufferance of these colonies, and such is now the necessity which constrains them to alter their former systems of government. The history of the present king of Great Britain is a history of repeated injuries and usurpations, all having in direct object the establishment of an absolute tyranny over these States. To prove this, let facts be submitted to a candid world.

He has refused his assent to laws, the most wholesome and necessary for the public good.

He has forbidden his governors to pass laws of immediate and pressing importance, unless suspended in their operation till his Assent should be obtained, and, when so suspended, he has utterly neglected to attend to them.

He has refused to pass other laws for the accommodation of large districts of people, unless those people would relinquish the right of representation in the legislature–a right inestimable to them and formidable to tyrants only.

He has called together legislative bodies at places unusual, uncomfortable, and distant from the depository of their public Records, for the sole purpose of fatiguing them into compliance with his measures.

He has dissolved representative houses repeatedly, for opposing with manly firmness his invasions on the rights of the people.

The burden for Jefferson is to convince others of the severity of the problem—that life is intolerable under the King. He goes on to detail a long list of complaints. His goal is to prove the need for change rather than to outline how the solution will work.

He has refused for a long time, after such dissolutions, to cause others to be elected; whereby the legislative powers, incapable of annihilation, have returned to the people at large for their exercise; the State remaining in the mean time exposed to all the dangers of invasion from without, and convulsions within.

He has endeavored to prevent the population of these states; for that purpose obstructing the laws for naturalization of foreigners; refusing to pass others to encourage their migrations hither, and raising the conditions of new appropriations of lands.

He has obstructed the administration of justice by refusing his assent to laws for establishing judiciary powers.

He has made judges dependent on his will alone, for the tenure of their offices, and the amount and payment of their salaries.

He has erected a multitude of new offices, and sent hither swarms of officers to harass our people, and eat out their substance.

He has kept among us, in times of peace, standing armies without the consent of our legislatures.

He has affected to render the military independent of and superior to the civil power.

He has combined with others to subject us to a jurisdiction foreign to our constitution, and unacknowledged by our laws; giving his assent to their acts of pretended legislation:

For quartering large bodies of armed troops among us;

For protecting them, by a mock trial, from punishment for any murders which they should commit on the inhabitants of these States;

For cutting off our trade with all parts of the world;

For imposing taxes on us without our consent;

For depriving us in many cases, of the benefits of trial by jury;

The legalistic list of charges is made more vivid by the use of metaphors such as "swarms of officers," which likens the British to a plague of insects.

For transporting us beyond seas to be tried for pretended offences;

For abolishing the free system of English laws in a neighboring province, establishing therein an arbitrary government, and enlarging its boundaries so as to render it at once an example and fit instrument for introducing the same absolute rule into these colonies;

For taking away our charters, abolishing our most valuable laws, and altering fundamentally the forms of our governments;

For suspending our own legislatures, and declaring themselves invested with power to legislate for us in all cases whatsoever.

He has abdicated government here, by declaring us out of his protection and waging war against us.

He has plundered our seas, ravaged our coasts, burnt our towns, and destroyed the lives of our people.

He is at this time transporting large armies of foreign mercenaries to complete the works of death, desolation and tyranny, already begun with circumstances of cruelty and perfidy scarcely paralleled in the most barbarous ages, and totally unworthy the head of a civilized nation.

He has constrained our fellow citizens taken captive on the high seas to bear arms against their country, to become the executioners of their friends and brethren, or to fall themselves by their hands.

He has excited domestic insurrections amongst us, and has endeavored to bring on the inhabitants of our frontiers, the merciless Indian savages, whose known rule of warfare is an undistinguished destruction of all ages, sexes and conditions.

In every stage of these oppressions we have petitioned for redress in the most humble terms; our repeated petitions have been answered only by repeated injury. A prince,

The strongest charges against the king are placed at the end of the list.

whose character is thus marked by every act which may define a tyrant, is unfit to be the ruler of a free people.

Nor have we been wanting in attentions to our British brethren. We have warned them from time to time of attempts by their legislature to extend an unwarrantable jurisdiction over us. We have reminded them of the circumstances of our emigration and settlement here. We have appealed to their native justice and magnanimity, and we have conjured them by the ties of our common kindred to disavow these usurpations, which would inevitably interrupt our connections and correspondence. They too have been deaf to the voice of justice and of consanguinity. We must, therefore, acquiesce in the necessity, which denounces our separation, and hold them, as we hold the rest of mankind, enemies in war, in peace, friends.

We, therefore, the representatives of the United States of America, in general congress, assembled, appealing to the Supreme Judge of the world for the rectitude of our intentions, do, in the name, and by authority of the good people of these colonies, solemnly publish and declare, that these united colonies are, and of right ought to be free and independent states; that they are absolved from all allegiance to the British crown, and that all political connection between them and the state of Great Britain, is and ought to be totally dissolved; and that as free and independent states, they have full power to levy war, conclude peace, contract alliances, establish commerce, and to do all other acts and things which independent states may of right do. And for the support of this declaration, with a firm reliance on the protection of Divine Providence, we mutually pledge to each other our lives, our fortunes and our sacred honor.

> To build credibility Jefferson makes a case that the colonists' frustration with the British government is justified. He argues that the colonists have tried the peaceful approach only to be rebuffed.

> The proposal is that the colonies no longer have any political connection to Great Britain and possess all the rights of an independent country.

Explore Current Issues

Should the government help the Lower Ninth Ward rebuild after Katrina?

By 2007, around 56% of the population of New Orleans had returned to the city. However, only 7% of the residents of the Lower Ninth Ward came back. Residents of this devastated area have seen little rebuilding since storm waters from Hurricane Katrina overflowed the levees and flooded the city in 2005. The rebuilding that has occurred in the Lower Ninth Ward is due mainly to various religious and nonprofit organizations who have pledged to rebuild the community one house at a time. The leadership of many of these groups feels that the federal government has failed not only the city as a whole, but the Lower Ninth Ward in particular.

However, how responsible is the federal government for rebuilding New Orleans? Some, such as former Speaker of the House Dennis Hastert, feel that the government should not be involved in rebuilding the homes of people who knowingly live in a flood-prone area. Others feel that areas such as the Lower Ninth Ward should not be rebuilt, but instead demolished to make way for an entirely new New Orleans.

Those who believe that the federal government should be responsible for the rebuilding efforts argue that New Orleans is both culturally unique and economically essential to the United States. Senator Mary Landrieu has even suggested that the billions of dollars in revenue that the U.S. receives from offshore petroleum leases in Louisiana could be used for wetlands and flood protection projects. In May of 2008, the argument for federal rebuilding efforts was given more fuel when the Army Corps of engineers was found liable for the failure of the MR-GO (Mississippi River-Gulf Outlet), which routed storm surges towards New Orleans and resulted in the fateful levee breaches.

Write about it

1. If you were a spokesperson for FEMA (Federal Emergency Management Agency), what reasons would you give to residents of the Lower Ninth Ward that your agency should not be responsible for rebuilding houses in the area?

2. If you were a spokesperson for a nonprofit organization building houses in the Lower Ninth Ward, what reasons would you give to a local corporation to sponsor your work?

3. If you were a developer who wanted to remove most of the old structures in the Lower Ninth Ward and build entirely new, mixed-income multiple- and single-family dwellings, what reasons would you give the residents of that area to support this change?

How to read proposal arguments

Make notes as you read, either in the margins or on paper or a computer file. Circle any words or references that you don't know and look them up.

What is it?	• What kind of a text is it? An editorial? an essay? an advertisement? a grant proposal? a Web site? a business proposal? What are your expectations for this kind of text? • What media are used? (Web sites, for example, often combine images, words, and sounds.)
Where did it come from?	• Who wrote this material? • Where did it first appear? In a book, newspaper, magazine, online, in a company, or in an organization?
What is the problem?	• Where is the evidence for the problem? Does this evidence establish that the problem exists? • How important is the problem? • Whom does the problem affect? (These people are called the stakeholders.) • What else has been written about the problem?
What is the solution?	• What exactly is the solution that the writer proposes? • Where is the evidence for the proposed solution? Does this evidence convince you that the proposal will solve the problem? • What kinds of sources are cited? Are they from books, newspapers, periodicals, or the Web? Are they completely documented?
How feasible is the proposed solution?	• Does the writer make a case that this is practical, and will people support the solution? • If the solution costs money, where does the money come from?
How is it composed?	• How is the piece of writing organized? • How does the writer represent herself or himself? • How would you characterize the style? • How effective is the design? Is it easy to read? • If there are any photographs, charts, or other graphics, what information do they contribute?

Building the Interstate Highway System

(SPEECH)

Richard Nixon

In July 1954, President Eisenhower was scheduled to deliver a speech to the annual conference of United States Governors held at Lake George, New York, but was called away by a death in the family. Then-Vice President Richard Nixon filled in for the president and, speaking from Eisenhower's notes, unveiled a startling plan: the federal government proposed to dedicate $50 billion—an enormous sum in 1954—to create a system of interstate highways connecting the country from coast to coast, and from border to border. The proposal was electrifying news, and led directly to the creation of the Interstate Highway System we use today.

Return to these questions after you have finished reading.

Analyzing and Connecting

1. What evidence does the vice president present that the state of America's highways is indeed a problem? What are the specific problems this plan is intended to solve?

2. Traffic in many locations today is more congested than it was when Nixon delivered his speech in 1954. Some politicians today argue for building more roads. How are arguments for more roads today similar to and different from Nixon's arguments?

3. Nixon's speech was covered in the media for the general public, whose approval was needed in order for the proposal to pass through Congress into law. But the immediate audience for the speech consisted of forty-eight state governors. What gestures do you see in this speech that show the vice president and president wanted to appeal to them specifically, and understood their unique concerns?

4. Vice President Nixon delivered this speech on President Eisenhower's behalf, using Eisenhower's notes. Therefore, the occasion required Nixon both to present the president's ideas as worthy and to present himself as a credible substitute. How does he try to accomplish these goals? Is he effective? Why or why not?

Finding Ideas for Writing

How many of the problems outlined by Nixon were actually solved by the Interstate Highway System? Write a brief "progress" report in which you assess what problems have been solved and what other problems have arisen because of the Interstate Highway System.

BUILDING THE INTERSTATE HIGHWAY SYSTEM

A Cabinet committee has just been established by the President to explore and to help formulate a comprehensive transportation policy for the Nation, taking into account the vital interests of carriers, shippers, the States and communities, the public at large. But more specifically, our highway net is inadequate locally, and obsolete as a national system.

To start to meet this problem at this session of the Congress, we have increased by approximately 500 million dollars the Federal monies available to the States for road development. This seems like a very substantial sum. But the experts say that 5 billion dollars a year for ten years, in addition to all current, normal expenditures, will pay off in economic growth; and when we have spent 50 billion dollars in the next ten years, we shall only have made a good start on the highways the country will need for a population of 200 million people.

A 50 billion dollar highway program in ten years is a goal toward which we can—and we should—look.

Now, let us look at the highway net of the United States as it is. What is wrong with it? It is obsolete because in large part it just happened. It was governed in the beginning by terrain, existing Indian trails, cattle trails, arbitrary section lines. It was designed largely for local movement at low speeds of one or two horsepower. It has been adjusted, it is true, at intervals to meet metropolitan traffic gluts, transcontinental movement, and increased horsepower. But it has never been completely overhauled or planned to satisfy the needs ten years ahead.

At this point in his notes, the President had a personal anecdote illustrating the problem. Thirty-five years ago this month, the Secretary of War initiated a transcontinental truck convoy to prove that the gas engine had displaced the mule, even on our relatively primitive roads. A Second

Lieutenant named Dwight Eisenhower went along as an observer. All-weather roads in the United States at that time totaled 300,000 miles. The autos and trucks numbered 7.6 million. That truck convoy left Washington July the 7th. It arrived in San Francisco on September the 5th, sixty days and 6000 breakdowns later.

Today, all-weather mileage is approximately 1.8 million as compared with 300,000 miles. But autos and trucks number more than 56 million, as compared with 7.6 million.

It is obvious, then, that the increase in mileage has lagged behind the increase in vehicles. The road system, moreover, is fundamentally the same, either haphazard or completely arbitrary in its origin, designed for local movement, in an age of transcontinental travel.

Now, what are the penalties of this obsolete net which we have today? Our first most apparent [is] an annual death toll comparable to the casualties of a bloody war, beyond calculation in dollar terms. It approaches 40,000 killed and exceeds 1.3 million injured annually.

And second, the annual wastage of billions of hours in detours, traffic jams, and so on, measurable by any traffic engineer and amounting to billions of dollars in productive time.

Third, all the civil suits that clog up our courts. It has been estimated that more than half have their origins on highways, roads and streets.

Nullification of efficiency in the production of goods by inefficiency in the transport of goods is another result of this obsolete net that we have today.

And finally, the appalling inadequacies to meet the demands of catastrophe or defense, should an atomic war come.

These penalties warrant the expenditures of billions to correct them.

Now, let us look at the highway net as it should be. The President believes that the requirements are these: a grand plan for a properly

articulated system that solves the problems of speedy, safe, transcontinental travel; intercity communication; access highways; and farm-to-market movement; metropolitan area congestion; bottlenecks; and parking.

Second, a financing proposal based on self-liquidation of each project, wherever that is possible, through tolls or the assured increase in gas tax revenue, and on Federal help where the national interest demands it.

And third, and I would emphasize this, particularly at this Conference, because I know how deeply the President believes in this principle: a cooperative alliance between the Federal government and the states so that local government and the most efficient sort of government in the administration of funds, will be the manager of its own area.

And the fourth, very probably, a program initiated by the Federal government, with State cooperation, for the planning and construction of a modern State highway system, with the Federal government functions, for example, being to advance funds or guarantee the obligations of localities or States which undertake to construct new, or modernize existing highways.

And then I would like to read to you the last sentence from the President's notes, exactly as it appears in them, because it is an exhortation to the members of this Conference: "I hope that you will study the matter, and recommend to me the cooperative action you think the Federal government and the 48 States should take to meet these requirements, so that I can submit positive proposals to the next session of the Congress."

And I know that in making this request to the Governors Conference, that the President believes it is essential that we have cooperation in this field. He believes that only with cooperation, and with the maximum of State and local initiative and control can we make a program which will deal with the problem and deal with it effectively.

Why Bother?

(ESSAY)

Michael Pollan

Michael Pollan is an author and professor of journalism at the University of California, Berkeley. His most recent book is *In Defense of Food: An Eater's Manifesto* (2008). His previous book, *The Omnivore's Dilemma: A Natural History of Four Meals*, was named one of the ten best books of 2006 by the *New York Times* and the *Washington Post*. This article appeared in a special "Green" issue of the *New York Times Magazine* in April 2008.

Return to these questions after you have finished reading.

Analyzing and Connecting

1. The success of Pollan's argument depends on his being able to grab his audience's attention, make them care about the problem at hand, and make them responsible for the solution. How does he try to achieve these goals? Do you think he is successful? Why or why not?

2. Pollan begins the article by describing his reaction to Al Gore's "puny" solution to the seemingly insurmountable problem of global warming—changing our light bulbs. How do Pollan's solutions compare? Do they seem in proportion to the problem, or are they more in proportion to what is possible? What, according to Pollan, is more important?

3. What kind of tone does Pollan set up with the title, "Why Bother?" Does he carry this tone throughout the essay? Is the tone appropriate for the argument? Why or why not? How does his tone affect his credibility with his audience?

4. Pollan again revisits Gore's request that we change our light bulbs, explaining that "Gore probably can't imagine us doing anything much more challenging, like, say, growing some portion of our own food." What is the causal relationship that Pollan sets up to explain our helplessness? How does this causal relationship support his overall argument?

Finding Ideas for Writing

Pollan mourns the downfall of the word *virtue*, asking "how did it come to pass that virtue—a quality that for most of history has generally been deemed, well, a virtue—became a mark of liberal softheadedness?" What other words have similarly lost favor, being relegated now to derogatory or ironic usage? Choose one of these words and write a short opinion piece detailing its fall from grace.

Why Bother?

Why bother? That really is the big question facing us as individuals hoping to do something about climate change, and it's not an easy one to answer. I don't know about you, but for me the most upsetting moment in *An Inconvenient Truth* came long after Al Gore scared the hell out of me, constructing an utterly convincing case that the very survival of life on earth as we know it is threatened by climate change. No, the really dark moment came during the closing credits, when we are asked to . . . change our light bulbs. That's when it got really depressing. The immense disproportion between the magnitude of the problem Gore had described and the puniness of what he was asking us to do about it was enough to sink your heart.

But the drop-in-the-bucket issue is not the only problem lurking behind the "why bother" question. Let's say I do bother, big time. I turn my life upside-down, start biking to work, plant a big garden, turn down the thermostat so low I need the Jimmy Carter signature cardigan, forsake the clothes dryer for a laundry line across the yard, trade in the station wagon for a hybrid, get off the beef, go completely local. I could theoretically do all that, but what would be the point when I know full well that halfway around the world there lives my evil twin, some carbon-footprint *doppelgänger* in Shanghai or Chongqing who has just bought his first car (Chinese car ownership is where ours was back in 1918), is eager to swallow every bite of meat I forswear and who's positively itching to replace every last pound of CO_2 I'm struggling no longer to emit. So what exactly would I have to show for all my trouble?

A sense of personal virtue, you might suggest, somewhat sheepishly. But what good is that when virtue itself is quickly becoming a term of derision? And not just on the editorial pages of the *Wall Street Journal* or on the lips of the vice president, who famously dismissed energy conservation as a "sign of personal virtue." No, even in the pages of the *New York Times* and the *New Yorker*, it seems the epithet "virtuous," when applied to an act of personal environmental responsibility, may be used only ironically. Tell me: How did it come to pass that virtue—a quality that for most of history has generally been deemed, well, a virtue—became a mark of liberal softheadedness? How peculiar, that doing the right thing by the environment—buying the hybrid, eating like a locavore—should now set you up for the Ed Begley Jr. treatment.

And even if in the face of this derision I decide I am going to bother, there arises the whole vexed question of getting it right. Is eating local or walking to work really going to reduce my carbon footprint? According to one analysis, if walking to work increases your appetite and you consume more meat or milk as a result, walking might actually emit more carbon than driving. A handful of studies have recently suggested that in certain cases under certain conditions, produce from places as far away as New Zealand might account for less carbon than comparable domestic products. True, at least one of these studies was co-written by a representative of agribusiness interests in (surprise!) New Zealand, but even so, they make you wonder. If determining the carbon footprint of food is really this complicated, and I've got to consider not only "food miles" but also whether the food came by ship or truck and how lushly the grass grows in New Zealand, then maybe on second thought I'll just buy the imported chops at Costco, at least until the experts get their footprints sorted out.

There are so many stories we can tell ourselves to justify doing nothing, but perhaps the most insidious is that, whatever we do manage to do, it will be too little too late. Climate change is upon us, and it has arrived well ahead of schedule. Scientists' projections that seemed dire a decade ago turn out to have been unduly optimistic: the warming and the melting is occurring much faster than the models predicted. Now truly terrifying feedback loops threaten to boost the rate of change exponentially, as the shift from white ice to blue water in the Arctic absorbs more sunlight and warming soils everywhere become more biologically active, causing them to release their vast stores of carbon into the air. Have you looked into the eyes of a climate scientist recently? They look really scared.

So do you still want to talk about planting gardens?

I do.

Whatever we can do as individuals to change the way we live at this suddenly very late date does seem utterly inadequate to the challenge. It's hard to argue with Michael Specter, in a recent *New Yorker* piece on carbon footprints, when he says: "Personal choices, no matter how virtuous [N.B.!], cannot do enough. It will also take laws and money." So it will. Yet it is no less accurate or hardheaded to say that laws and money cannot do enough, either; that it will also take profound changes in the way we live. Why? Because the climate-change crisis is at its very bottom a crisis of lifestyle—of character, even. The Big Problem is nothing more or less than the sum total of countless little everyday choices, most of them made by us (consumer spending represents 70 percent of our economy), and most of the rest of them made in the name of our needs and desires and preferences.

For us to wait for legislation or technology to solve the problem of how we're living our lives suggests we're not really serious about changing—something our politicians cannot fail to notice. They will not move until we do. Indeed, to look to leaders and experts, to laws and money and grand schemes, to save us from

our predicament represents precisely the sort of thinking—passive, delegated, dependent for solutions on specialists—that helped get us into this mess in the first place. It's hard to believe that the same sort of thinking could now get us out of it.

Thirty years ago, Wendell Berry, the Kentucky farmer and writer, put forward a blunt analysis of precisely this mentality. He argued that the environmental crisis of the 1970s—an era innocent of climate change; what we would give to have back that environmental crisis!—was at its heart a crisis of character and would have to be addressed first at that level: at home, as it were. He was impatient with people who wrote checks to environmental organizations while thoughtlessly squandering fossil fuel in their everyday lives—the 1970s equivalent of people buying carbon offsets to atone for their Tahoes and Durangos. Nothing was likely to change until we healed the "split between what we think and what we do." For Berry, the "why bother" question came down to a moral imperative: "Once our personal connection to what is wrong becomes clear, then we have to choose: we can go on as before, recognizing our dishonesty and living with it the best we can, or we can begin the effort to change the way we think and live."

For Berry, the deep problem standing behind all the other problems of industrial civilization is "specialization," which he regards as the "disease of the modern character." Our society assigns us a tiny number of roles: we're producers (of one thing) at work, consumers of a great many other things the rest of the time, and then once a year or so we vote as citizens. Virtually all of our needs and desires we delegate to specialists of one kind or another—our meals to agribusiness, health to the doctor, education to the teacher, entertainment to the media, care for the environment to the environmentalist, political action to the politician.

As Adam Smith and many others have pointed out, this division of labor has given us many of the blessings of civilization. Specialization is what allows me to sit at a computer thinking about climate change. Yet this same division of labor obscures the lines of connection—and responsibility—linking our everyday acts to their real-world consequences, making it easy for me to overlook the coal-fired power plant that is lighting my screen, or the mountaintop in Kentucky that had to be destroyed to provide the coal to that plant, or the streams running crimson with heavy metals as a result.

Of course, what made this sort of specialization possible in the first place was cheap energy. Cheap fossil fuel allows us to pay distant others to process our food for us, to entertain us and to (try to) solve our problems, with the result that there is very little we know how to accomplish for ourselves. Think for a moment of all the things you suddenly need to do for yourself when the power goes out—up to and including entertaining yourself. Think, too, about how a power failure causes your neighbors—your community—to suddenly loom so much larger in your life. Cheap energy allowed us to leapfrog community by making it possible to sell our specialty over great distances as well as summon into our lives the specialties of countless distant others.

Here's the point: Cheap energy, which gives us climate change, fosters precisely the mentality that makes dealing with climate change in our own lives seem impossibly difficult. Specialists ourselves, we can no longer imagine anyone but an expert, or anything but a new technology or law, solving our problems. Al Gore asks us to change the light bulbs because he probably can't imagine us doing anything much more challenging, like, say, growing some portion of our own food. We can't imagine it, either, which is probably why we prefer to cross our fingers and talk about the promise of ethanol and nuclear power—new liquids and electrons to power the same old cars and houses and lives.

The "cheap-energy mind," as Wendell Berry called it, is the mind that asks, "Why bother?" because it is helpless to imagine—much less attempt—a different sort of life, one less divided, less reliant. Since the cheap-energy mind translates everything into money, its proxy, it prefers to put its faith in market-based solutions—carbon taxes and pollution-trading schemes. If we could just get the incentives right, it believes, the economy will properly value everything that matters and nudge our self-interest down the proper channels. The best we can hope for is a greener version of the old invisible hand. Visible hands it has no use for.

But while some such grand scheme may well be necessary, it's doubtful that it will be sufficient or that it will be politically sustainable before we've demonstrated to ourselves that change is possible. Merely to give, to spend, even to vote, is not to do, and there is so much that needs to be done—without further delay. In the judgment of James Hansen, the NASA climate scientist who began sounding the alarm on global warming 20 years ago, we have only 10 years left to start cutting—not just slowing—the amount of carbon we're emitting or face a "different planet." Hansen said this more than two years ago, however; two years have gone by, and nothing of consequence has been done. So: eight years left to go and a great deal left to do.

Which brings us back to the "why bother" question and how we might better answer it. The reasons not to bother are many and compelling, at least to the cheap-energy mind. But let me offer a few admittedly tentative reasons that we might put on the other side of the scale:

If you do bother, you will set an example for other people. If enough other people bother, each one influencing yet another in a chain reaction of behavioral

change, markets for all manner of green products and alternative technologies will prosper and expand. (Just look at the market for hybrid cars.) Consciousness will be raised, perhaps even changed: new moral imperatives and new taboos might take root in the culture. Driving an S.U.V. or eating a 24-ounce steak or illuminating your McMansion like an airport runway at night might come to be regarded as outrages to human conscience. Not having things might become cooler than having them. And those who did change the way they live would acquire the moral standing to demand changes in behavior from others—from other people, other corporations, even other countries.

All of this could, theoretically, happen. What I'm describing (imagining would probably be more accurate) is a process of viral social change, and change of this kind, which is nonlinear, is never something anyone can plan or predict or count on. Who knows, maybe the virus will reach all the way to Chongqing and infect my Chinese evil twin. Or not. Maybe going green will prove a passing fad and will lose steam after a few years, just as it did in the 1980s, when Ronald Reagan took down Jimmy Carter's solar panels from the roof of the White House.

Going personally green is a bet, nothing more or less, though it's one we probably all should make, even if the odds of it paying off aren't great. Sometimes you have to act as if acting will make a difference, even when you can't prove that it will. That, after all, was precisely what happened in Communist Czechoslovakia and Poland, when a handful of individuals like Vaclav Havel and Adam Michnik resolved that they would simply conduct their lives "as if" they lived in a free society. That improbable bet created a tiny space of liberty that, in time, expanded to take in, and then help take down, the whole of the Eastern bloc.

So what would be a comparable bet that the individual might make in the case of the environmental crisis? Havel himself has suggested that people begin to "conduct themselves as if they were to live on this earth forever and be answerable for its condition one day." Fair enough, but let me propose a slightly less abstract and daunting wager. The idea is to find one thing to do in your life that doesn't involve spending or voting, that may or may not virally rock the world but is real and particular (as well as symbolic) and that, come what may, will offer its own rewards. Maybe you decide to give up meat, an act that would reduce your carbon footprint by as much as a quarter. Or you could try this: determine to observe the Sabbath. For one day a week, abstain completely from economic activity: no shopping, no driving, no electronics.

But the act I want to talk about is growing some—even just a little—of your own food. Rip out your lawn, if you have one, and if you don't—if you live in a high-rise, or have a yard shrouded in shade—look into getting a plot in a community garden. Measured against the Problem We Face, planting a garden sounds pretty benign, I know, but in fact it's one of the most powerful things an individual can do—to reduce your carbon footprint, sure, but more important, to reduce your sense of dependence and dividedness: to change the cheap-energy mind.

A great many things happen when you plant a vegetable garden, some of them directly related to climate change, others indirect but related nevertheless. Growing food, we forget, comprises the original solar technology: calories produced by means of photosynthesis. Years ago the cheap-energy mind discovered that more food could be produced with less effort by replacing sunlight with fossil-fuel fertilizers and pesticides, with a result that the typical calorie of food energy in your diet now requires about 10 calories of fossil-fuel energy to produce. It's estimated that the way we feed ourselves (or rather, allow ourselves to be fed) accounts for about a fifth of the greenhouse gas for which each of us is responsible.

Yet the sun still shines down on your yard, and photosynthesis still works so abundantly that in a thoughtfully organized vegetable garden (one planted from seed, nourished by compost from the kitchen and involving not too many drives to the garden center), you can grow the proverbial free lunch—CO_2-free and dollar-free. This is the most-local food you can possibly eat (not to mention the freshest, tastiest and most nutritious), with a carbon footprint so faint that even the New Zealand lamb council dares not challenge it. And while we're counting carbon, consider too your compost pile, which shrinks the heap of garbage your household needs trucked away even as it feeds your vegetables and sequesters carbon in your soil. What else? Well, you will probably notice that you're getting a pretty good workout there in your garden, burning calories without having to get into the car to drive to the gym. (It is one of the absurdities of the modern division of labor that, having replaced physical labor with fossil fuel, we now have to burn even more fossil fuel to keep our unemployed bodies in shape.) Also, by engaging both body and mind, time spent in the garden is time (and energy) subtracted from electronic forms of entertainment.

You begin to see that growing even a little of your own food is, as Wendell Berry pointed out 30 years ago, one of those solutions that, instead of begetting a new set of problems—the way "solutions" like ethanol or nuclear power inevitably do—actually beget other solutions, and not only of the kind that save carbon. Still more valuable are the habits of mind that growing a little of your

own food can yield. You quickly learn that you need not be dependent on specialists to provide for yourself—that your body is still good for something and may actually be enlisted in its own support. If the experts are right, if both oil and time are running out, these are skills and habits of mind we're all very soon going to need. We may also need the food. Could gardens provide it? Well, during World War II, victory gardens supplied as much as 40 percent of the produce Americans ate.

But there are sweeter reasons to plant that garden, to bother. At least in this one corner of your yard and life, you will have begun to heal the split between what you think and what you do, to commingle your identities as consumer and producer and citizen. Chances are, your garden will re-engage you with your neighbors, for you will have produce to give away and the need to borrow their tools. You will have reduced the power of the cheap-energy mind by personally overcoming its most debilitating weakness: its helplessness and the fact that it can't do much of anything that doesn't involve division or subtraction. The garden's

season-long transit from seed to ripe fruit—*will you get a load of that zucchini?!*—suggests that the operations of addition and multiplication still obtain, that the abundance of nature is not exhausted. The single greatest lesson the garden teaches is that our relationship to the planet need not be zero-sum, and that as long as the sun still shines and people still can plan and plant, think and do, we can, if we bother to try, find ways to provide for ourselves without diminishing the world.

How to write a proposal argument

These steps for the process of writing an argument for change may not progress as neatly as this chart might suggest. Writing is not an assembly-line process.

As you write and revise, imagine that you are in a conversation with an audience that contains people who both agree and disagree with you. Think about what you would say to both and speak to these diverse readers.

1 IDENTIFY THE PROBLEM

- Read your assignment carefully and note exactly what you are being asked to do.

- Identify the problem, what causes it, and whom it affects.

- Do background research on what has been written about the problem and what solutions have been attempted.

- Describe what has been done or not done to address the problem.

- Make a claim advocating a specific change or course of action. Put the claim in this form: We should (or should not) do _____.

2 PROPOSE YOUR SOLUTION

- State your solution as specifically as you can.

- Consider other solutions and describe why your solution is better.

- Examine if the solution will have enough money and support to be implemented.

- Analyze your potential readers. How interested will your readers be in this problem? How would your solution benefit them directly and indirectly?

3 WRITE A DRAFT

- Define the problem. Give the background your readers will need.

- Discuss other possible solutions.

- Present your solution. Explain exactly how it will work, how it will be accomplished, and if anything like it has been tried elsewhere.

- Argue that your proposal will work. Address any possible arguments that your solution will not work.

- Describe the positive consequences of your solution and the negative consequences that can be avoided.

- Conclude with a call for action. Be specific about exactly what readers need to do.

- Write a title that will interest readers.

- Include any necessary images, tables, or graphics.

4 REVISE, REVISE, REVISE

- Recheck that your proposal fulfills the assignment.

- Make sure that your proposal claim is clear and focused.

- Add detail or further explanation about the problem.

- Add detail or further explanation about how your solution addresses the problem.

- Make sure you have considered other solutions and explain why yours is better.

- Examine your organization and think of possible better ways to organize.

- Review the visual presentation of your report for readability and maximum impact.

- Proofread carefully.

5 SUBMITTED VERSION

- Make sure your finished writing meets all formatting requirements.

1: Identify the problem

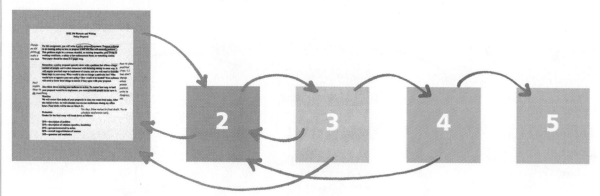

Analyze the assignment

- Read your assignment slowly and carefully. Look for the key words *propose* or *problem* and *solution*. These key words tell you that you are writing a proposal.

- Highlight any information about the length specified, date due, formatting, and other requirements. You can attend to this information later. At this point you want to zero in on the subject and your proposal claim.

Identify the problem

- What exactly is the problem?
- Who is most affected by the problem?
- What causes the problem?
- Has anyone tried to do anything about it? If so, why haven't they succeeded?
- What is likely to happen in the future if the problem isn't solved?

Do background research in online and print library sources, Web sources, government documents, experts in the field, and possibly field research such as a survey

- What has been written about the problem?
- What other solutions have been proposed?
- Where have other solutions been effective?
- Where have other solutions failed?

Make a proposal claim

- Proposal claims advocate a specific change or course of action. Put the claim in this form: We should (or should not) do _____.

Write Now

Make an idea map

When you have a number of ideas and facts about a topic, write them on sticky notes. Then post the sticky notes and move them around, so you can begin to see how they might fit together. When you find an organization that suits your subject, make a working outline from your sticky notes.

PROBLEM:
Citizens of the United States born in another country cannot run for president

EXCEPTION:
Foreign-born citizens whose parents are American citizens

REQUIRED:
2/3s majority of Congress and 2/3s of state legislatures must approve

SOLUTION:
Amend the U.S. Constitution to allow foreign-born American citizens to run for and serve as the president of the United States

HOW WOULD IT WORK?
Grass-roots campaign

WHO WOULD SUPPORT?
Probably Asian Americans, Mexican Americans, and other recent immigrant groups

WHO WOULD OPPOSE?
1) politicians afraid of angering voters
2) Americans who are afraid of foreigners

HOW LONG WOULD IT TAKE?
Probably years because of the approval process

PRO ARGUMENTS
1) Fairness
2) America's image of itself as a land of opportunity

COUNTERARGUMENT
Point out that foreign born doesn't mean untrustworthy

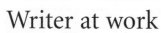

Writer at work

Kim Lee was asked to write a proposal argument for her Rhetoric and Writing course. Upon receiving the assignment, she made the following notes and observations.

RHE 306 Rhetoric and Writing
Policy Proposal

Change an old policy or make a new one.

For this assignment, you will write a policy proposal argument. Propose a change to an existing policy or law, or propose a new law, that will correct a problem. This problem might be a revenue shortfall, an existing inequality, poor living or working conditions, a safety or law-enforcement threat, or something similar. Your paper should be about 5–7 pages long.

Remember, a policy proposal typically deals with a problem that affects a large number of people, and is often concerned with bettering society in some way. It will require practical steps to implement of course, and you will need to describe these steps in your essay. What would it take to change a particular law? Who would have to approve your new policy? How would it be funded? Your audience will need to know these things to decide if they agree with your proposal.

have to show practical steps. U.S. laws don't change unless people protest, write to Congress, etc.

Must inspire them to do something.

Also think about moving your audience to action. No matter how easy or hard your proposal would be to implement, you must persuade people to act upon it.

Timeline
We will review first drafts of your proposals in class one week from today. After this initial review, we will schedule one-on-one conferences during my office hours. Final drafts will be due on March 31.

Ten days from review to final draft. Try to schedule conference early.

Evaluation
Grades for the final essay will break down as follows:

20%—description of problem
25%—description of solution (specifics, feasibility)
25%—persuasiveness/call to action
20%—overall support/citation of sources
10%—grammar and mechanics

Read the assignment closely

Kim Lee began by highlighting key words in the assignment and noting specifics about the length and due date.

Choose a topic

Kim listed possible topics and then considered the strengths and weaknesses of each. She chose one that could be developed adequately and could motivate her audience.

Plan research strategies

Kim made a list of possible sources of information to begin her research.

POSSIBLE TOPICS

— Create a standardized form of testing for steroid use in all American sports (professional, educational, recreational).

> Might be too broad. Also, the science involved might be hard to explain in 5-7 pages

— Move the U.S. capital to Nashville, Tennessee.

> Too regional?

— Amend the Constitution to allow foreign-born American Citizens (or naturalized citizens) to serve as president of the United States.

An issue of fair treatment.
Good for motivating audience.

— Revitalize Youngstown, Ohio, by building a tourist trade around its previous Mafioso reputation as "Little Chicago." Could give lots of specific steps (funding, building plans, tourist info).

— Reformulate the means by which the Corporation for Public Broadcasting receives federal funds. Would be very dry, though T.V. shows like Sesame Street could be used to provoke interest/make people want to act.

To Do:

— Search Internet for current discussion on this topic. What kinds of sites are discussing the "natural-born" clause? AmendforArnold.com, Orrin Hatch.

— Search periodicals for discussions of this topic.

— Search academic and law journals for more sophisticated discussions.

— Any books???

— What groups (political, ideological) are discussing this right now?

2: Propose your solution

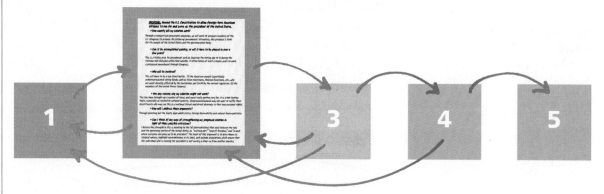

State your solution as specifically as you can

- What exactly do you want to achieve?
- How exactly will your solution work?
- Can it be accomplished quickly, or will it have to be phased in over a few years?
- Has anything like it been tried elsewhere?
- Who will be involved?
- Is it possible that your solution might not work?
- How will you address those arguments?
- Can you think of any ways of strengthening your proposed solution in light of those possible criticisms?

Consider other solutions

- What other solutions have been or might be proposed for this problem, including doing nothing?
- What are the advantages and disadvantages of those solutions?
- Why is your solution better?

Examine the feasibility of your solution

- How easy is your solution to implement?
- Will the people who will be most affected be willing to go along with it? (For example, lots of things can be accomplished if enough people volunteer, but groups often have difficulty getting enough volunteers to work without pay.)
- If it costs money, how do you propose paying for it?
- Who is most likely to reject your proposal because it is not practical enough?
- How can you convince your readers that your proposal can be achieved?

Analyze your potential readers

- Whom are you writing for?
- How interested will your readers be in this problem?
- How much does this problem affect them?
- How would your solution benefit them directly and indirectly?

Staying on Track

Acknowledging other points of view

Write for readers who may disagree with you

Proposal arguments that ignore other points of view and other possible solutions tend to convince only those who agree with you before you start writing. Your goal is to convince those who haven't thought about the problem and those who might disagree at the outset but can be persuaded. Think about why readers might disagree.

- Are they misinformed about the problem? If so, you will need to provide accurate information.
- Do they have different assumptions about the problem? If so, can you show them that your assumptions are better?
- Do they share your goals but think your solution is not the right one? If so, you will need to explain why your solution is better.

You might have to do some research to find out the views of others. If you are writing about a local problem, you may need to talk to people.

Deal fairly with other solutions and other points of view

OFF TRACK

Free tuition for all state high school graduates who attend state colleges is an idea too ridiculous to consider.
(No reason is given for rejecting an alternative solution, and those who propose it are insulted.)

ON TRACK

Free tuition for all state high school graduates is a desirable solution to get more students to attend college, but it is not likely to be implemented because of the cost. A solution targeted to low-income students similar to the HOPE scholarship program in Georgia, which is funded by state lottery money, could be implemented in our state.
(The author offers a reason for rejecting an alternative solution and proposes a solution that has some common ground with the alternative.)

Writer at work

Kim Lee began laying out her proposal by first stating her solution as specifically as possible. She used the following list of questions to guide her proposal argument.

PROPOSAL: Amend the U.S. Constitution to allow foreign-born American citizens to run for and serve as the president of the United States.

- **How exactly will my solution work?**

Through a nonpartisan grassroots campaign, we will work to pressure members of the U.S. Congress to propose the following amendment. Ultimately, this proposal is both for the people of the United States and the governmental body.

- **Can it be accomplished quickly, or will it have to be phased in over a few years?**

This is a tricky area. An amendment such as lowering the voting age to 18 during the Vietnam War did pass within four months. It often takes at least a couple years to work a proposed amendment through Congress.

- **Who will be involved?**

This will have to be a two-front battle. (1) the American people, specifically underrepresented voting blocks such as Asian Americans, Mexican Americans, etc., who are most directly affected by the limitations put forth by the current regulation. (2) the members of the United States Congress.

- **Are any reasons why my solution might not work?**

This has been brought up a number of times and never really gotten very far. It is a hot-button topic, especially as related to national security. Congressmen/women may not want to ruffle their constituents who may see this as a national threat and direct decrease in their own personal rights.

- **How will I address those arguments?**

Through pointing out the faulty logic which states foreign born=shifty and natural-born=patriotic.

- **Can I think of any ways of strengthening my proposed solution in light of those possible criticisms?**

I believe the strength in this is pointing to the (a) contradictions that exist between the rule and the governing notion of the United States as "melting pot," "land of freedom," and "a land where everyone can grow up to be president." The heart of this argument is to drive home its illogical nature, highlight contradictions in its logic, and include stipulations which ensure that the individual who is running for president is not merely a drop-in from another country.

OTHER SOLUTIONS
- **Solutions that have been discussed recently seem to differ in the length of required residence.**

Not necessarily disadvantages, but have been ineffective in achieving the goal. It comes from the people and not in support of one candidate, but an idea.

FEASIBILITY
- **How easy is my solution to implement?**

It all depends on the people's ability to move Congress to action.

- **Will the people who will be most affected be willing to go along with it?**

I believe the answer is yes.

- **How will we pay for it?**

Again, grass roots political fundraising. A major source may be ethic/immigrant groups, etc.

- **Who is most likely to reject my proposal because it is not practical enough?**

Most likely (a) politicians who see support of the change as a threat to their positions (due to voter dissent) and (b) citizens who live in a state of fear.

- **How can I convince my readers that my proposal can be achieved?**

It must be proposed as being about the people and their ability to enact change. It is about empowerment.

POTENTIAL READERS
- **Whom am I writing for?**

American people (specifically the immigrant population).

- **How interested will my readers be in this problem?**

It is currently a hot topic and hopefully making it more personally relevant will peak interest (not just about Governor Schwarzenegger).

- **How much does this problem affect them?**

It withholds a basic right for them and their children.

- **How would my solution benefit them directly and indirectly?**

Directly, it allows for naturalized citizens to run for president (or vice president). Indirectly, it fosters a sense of pride in one's ethnic identity and helps (through visibility and legislative legitimacy) to create an image of diversity and success.

3: Write a draft

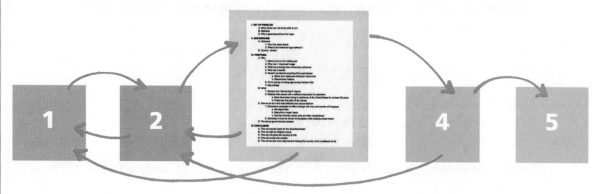

Define the problem

- Set out the issue or problem. If the problem is local, you might begin by telling about your experience or the experience of someone you know. You might need to argue for the seriousness of the problem, and you might have to give some background on how it came about.

Present your solution

- Describe other solutions that have been attempted and others that are possible. Explain why other solutions either don't solve the problem or are unrealistic.

- Make clear the goals of your solution. Many solutions cannot solve problems completely.

- Describe in detail the steps in implementing your solution and how they will solve the problem you have identified. You can impress your readers by the care with which you have thought through this problem.

- Explain the positive consequences that will follow from your proposal. What good things will happen and what bad things will be avoided if your proposal is implemented?

Argue that your solution can be done

- Your proposal for solving the problem is a truly good idea only if it can be put into practice. If people have to change the ways they are doing things now, explain why they would want to change. If your proposal costs money, you need to identify exactly where the money would come from.

Conclude with a call for action

- Make a call for action. You should put your readers in a position such that if they agree with you, they will take action. You might restate and emphasize what exactly they need to do.

Writer at work

Here is the outline that Kim Lee used to write the first draft of her proposal essay.

I. SET UP PROBLEM
   A. Story about son not being able to run
   B. Statistics
   C. Why it goes beyond just the hype

II. BACKGROUND
   A. Historical
      1. How this came about
      2. What is the historical logic behind it
   B. Current - Arnold

III. PROPOSAL
   A. Why
      1. Nation built on the melting pot
      2. Why now > improved image
      3. What have foreign-born Americans achieved
      4. Who has it barred
      5. Haven't we learned anything from past biases
         a. Gitmo and Japanese American internment
         b. Natural-born traitors
      6. Tie to raising of voting age during Vietnam War
      7. Not a threat
   B. What
      1. Remove the "natural-born" clause
      2. Replace that clause with a different stipulation for president
         a. Must have been living in residence of the United States for at least 25 years
         b. Preserves the spirit of the clause
   C. How to do so in the most efficient and secure fashion
      1. Grassroots campaign to effect change with men and women of Congress
         a. We elect them
         b. Make this a major issue
         c. Use the minority voices who are often marginalized
      2. Ultimately it must be driven to Congress while keeping voices heard
   D. The actual governmental process

IV. CONCLUSION
   A. This will provide hope for the disenfranchised
   B. This will right an illogical wrong
   C. This will not place the country at risk
   D. This will create role models
   E. This will be one more step toward making this country what it professes to be

4: Revise, revise, revise

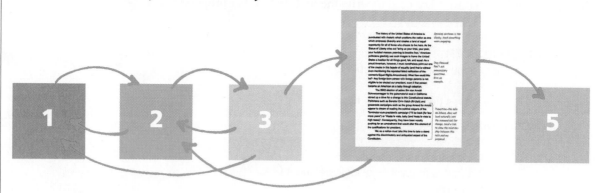

Take a break from your writing and come back to it with "fresh eyes." When you return, imagine you are someone who has never seen your proposal before. Read the proposal out loud. When you are done, ask yourself: Do I understand the problem? Does it really seem like a problem that must be dealt with? Is the solution clear? Does it seem like it is worth the trouble? Do I think it will really work? How much will it cost me, in money, effort, or inconvenience? The biggest trap you can fall into is starting off with the little stuff first. Leave the small stuff for last.

Does your paper or project meet the assignment?	• Look again at your assignment. Does your paper or project do what the assignment asks?
	• Look again at the assignment for specific guidelines, including length, format, and amount of research. Does your work meet these guidelines?
Is the proposal claim clear and focused?	• Does the proposal claim address the problem?
	• Does the proposal claim issue a clear call to action?
Do you identify the problem adequately?	• Do you need more evidence that the problem exists and is a serious concern?
	• Will your readers find credible any sources you include? Can you think of other sources that might be more persuasive?
Is it clear how your solution will address the problem?	• Can you find more evidence that your solution will resolve the problem?
	• Do you address potential objections to your solution?
	• Do you provide evidence that your solution is feasible? For example, if your solution requires money, where will the money come from?

Do you consider alternative solutions?	• Do you explain why your solution is better than the alternatives?
Is your organization effective?	• Is the order of your main points clear to your reader? • Are there any places where you find abrupt shifts or gaps? • Are there sections or paragraphs that could be rearranged to make your draft more effective?
Is your introduction effective?	• Can you get off to a faster start, perhaps with a striking example? • Can you think of a better way to engage your readers to be interested in the problem you identify? • Does your introduction give your readers a sense of why the problem is important?
Is your conclusion effective?	• Does your conclusion have a call for action? • Do you make it clear exactly what you want your readers to do?
Do you represent yourself effectively?	• To the extent you can, forget for a moment that you wrote what you are reading. What impression do you have of you, the writer? • Does "the writer" create an appropriate tone? • Has "the writer" done his or her homework?
Is the writing project visually effective?	• Is the font attractive and readable? • Is the overall layout attractive and readable? • If headings are used, do they make clear what comes under each of them? • Is each photograph, chart, graph, map, or table clearly labeled? Does each visual have a caption?
Save the editing for last.	When you have finished revising, edit and proofread carefully.

A peer review guide is on page 27.

Writer at work

During peer review of her paper with fellow classmates, and in her meeting with her instructor, Kim Lee made notes on her rough draft. She used these comments to guide her revision of the essay.

The history of the United States of America is punctuated with rhetoric which positions the nation as one that embraces diversity and creates a land of equal opportunity for all of those who choose to live here. As the Statue of Liberty cries out "bring us your tired, your poor, your huddled masses yearning to breathe free," American politicians gleefully use such images to frame the United States a bastion for all things good, fair, and equal. As a proud American, however, I must nonetheless point out one of the cracks in this façade of equality ~~(and that is without even mentioning the repeated failed ratification of the women's Equal Rights Amendment). What flaw could this be?~~ Any foreign-born person with foreign parents is not eligible to be elected our president, even if that person became an American as a baby through adoption.

> *Opening sentence is too clunky. Need something more engaging.*

> *Stay focused. Don't ask unnecessary questions. Give an example.*

The 2003 election of action film star Arnold Schwarzenegger to the gubernatorial seat in California stirred up a drive for a change to this Constitutional statute. Politicians such as Senator Orrin Hatch (R-Utah) and grassroots campaigns such as the group Amend for Arnold appear to dream of reading the political slogans of the Terminator-cum-president's campaign: "I'll be back (for four more years") or "Hasta la vista, baby (and hasta la vista to high taxes)." Consequently, they have been vocally pushing for an amendment that would alter this element of the qualifications for president.

We as a nation must take this time to take a stand against this discriminatory and antiquated aspect of the Constitution.

> *Transition—the info on Schwrz. does not lead naturally into the renewed call for change. Need a link to show the relationship between this info and my proposal.*

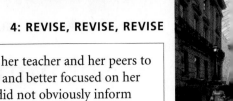

Look for ways to focus	Kim Lee responded to suggestions from her teacher and her peers to make her opening paragraph less wordy and better focused on her main point. She removed material that did not obviously inform readers about the problem she was interested in.
Check transitions	She also worked on strengthening transitions between paragraphs.
Read your paper aloud	Finally, Kim Lee read her essay aloud to check for misspelled words, awkward phrasing, and other mechanical problems.

Staying on Track

Reviewing your draft

Give yourself plenty of time for reviewing your draft. For detailed information on how to participate in a peer review, how to review it yourself, and how to respond to comments from your classmates, your instructor, or a campus writing consultant, see pages 24–28.

Some good questions to ask yourself when reviewing an argument for change

- Do you connect the problem to your readers? Even if the problem doesn't affect them directly, at the very least you should appeal to their sense of fairness.
- Can you explain more specifically how your solution will work?
- If resources including people and money are required for your solution, can you elaborate where these resources will come from?
- Do you include other possible solutions and discuss the advantages and disadvantages of each? Can you add to this discussion?
- Does your conclusion connect with the attitudes and values of your readers in addition to making clear what you want them to do? Can you add an additional point? Can you sharpen your call to action?

5: Submitted version

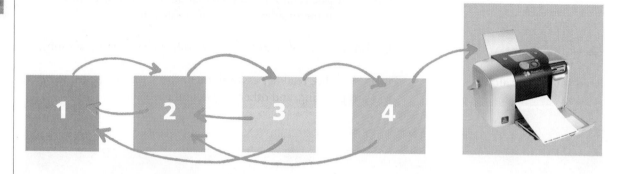

Kim Lee
Professor Patel
RHE 306
31 March 2008

Let's Make It a Real Melting Pot with Presidential Hopes for All

The image the United States likes to advertise is a country that embraces diversity and creates a land of equal opportunity for all. As the Statue of Liberty cries out "give me your tired, your poor, your huddled masses yearning to breathe free," American politicians gleefully evoke such images to frame the United States a bastion for all things good, fair, and equal. As a proud American, however, I must nonetheless highlight one of the cracks in this façade of equality. Imagine an infertile couple decides to adopt an orphaned child from China. They follow all of the legal processes deemed necessary by both countries. They fly abroad and bring home their (once parentless) six-month-old baby boy. They raise and nurture him, and while teaching him to embrace his ethnicity, they also teach him to love Captain Crunch, baseball, and *The Three Stooges*. He grows and eventually attends an ethnically diverse

American public school. One day in the fifth grade his teacher tells the class that anyone can grow up to be president. To clarify her point, she turns to the boy, knowing his background, and states, "No, you could not be president, Stu, but you could still be a senator. That's something to aspire to!" How do these parents explain this rule to this American-raised child? This scenario will become increasingly common. Senator Larry Craig of Idaho states that Americans adopt over 25,000 foreign-born children annually (Epstein A5). As the Constitution currently reads, only "natural-born" citizens may run for the offices of president and vice president. Neither these children nor the thousands of hardworking Americans who chose to make America their official homeland may aspire to the highest political position in the land. While the huddled masses may enter, it appears they must retain a second-class citizen ranking.

The "natural-born" stipulation regarding the presidency stems from the self-same meeting of minds which brought the American people the Electoral College. During the Constitutional Convention of 1787, the Congress formulated the regulatory measures associated with the office of the president. A letter sent from John Jay to George Washington during this period read as follows:

> "Permit me to hint," Jay wrote, "whether it would not be wise and seasonable to provide a strong check to the admission of foreigners into the administration of our national government; and to declare expressly that the Command in Chief of the American army shall not be given to, nor devolve on, any but a natural-born citizen." (Mathews A1)

Shortly thereafter, Article II, Section I, Clause V of the Constitution declared that "No Person except a natural born Citizen, or a Citizen of the United States at the time of the Adoption of this Constitution, shall be eligible to the Office of President." Jill A. Pryor

states in *The Yale Law Journal* that "some writers have suggested that Jay was

responding to rumors that foreign princes might be asked to assume the presidency"

(881). Many cite disastrous examples of foreign rule in the eighteenth century are the

impetus for the "natural born" clause. For example, in 1772—only fifteen years prior to

the adoption of the statute—Poland had been divided up by Prussia, Russia, and

Austria, (Kasindorf). Perhaps an element of self-preservation and *not* ethnocentrism

led to the questionable stipulation. Nonetheless, in the twenty-first century this clause

reeks of xenophobia.

The 2003 election of action film star Arnold Schwarzenegger as governor of

California stirred up movement to change this Constitutional statute. Politicians such as

Senators Orrin Hatch (R-Utah) and Ted Kennedy (D-Massachusetts and Arnold's uncle

by marriage) have created a buzz for ratifying a would-be twenty-eighth amendment. In

addition, grassroots campaigns like "Amend for Arnold" are trying to rally popular

support as they dream of the Terminator-cum-president's political slogans ("I'll be back

. . . for four more years" or "Hasta la vista, baby, and hasta la vista to high taxes").

Schwarzenegger has become the face—and the bulked-up body—of the viable

naturalized president.

We as a nation should follow the lead set by those enamored of the action star,

but distance the fight from this one extremely wealthy actor. We must instead take a

stand against the discriminatory practice applied to all foreign-born American citizens

by this obsolete provision of the Constitution. Congress has made minor attempts to

update this biased clause. The Fourteenth Amendment clarified the difference

Lee 4

between "natural-born" and "native born" citizens by spelling out the citizenship status of children born to American parents *outside* of the United States (Ginsberg 929). (Such a clause qualifies individuals such as Senator John McCain—born in Panama—for presidency.) This change is not enough. I propose that the United States abolish the "natural born" clause and replace it with a stipulation that allows naturalized citizens to run for president. This amendment would state that a candidate must have been naturalized and lived in residence in the United States for a period of at least twenty-five years. The present time is ideal for this change. This amendment could simultaneously honor the spirit of the Constitution, protect and ensure the interests of the United States, promote an international image of inclusiveness, and grant heretofore withheld rights to thousands of legal and loyal United States citizens.

In our push for change, we must make clear the importance of this amendment. It would not provide special rights for would-be terrorists. To the contrary, it would fulfill the longtime promises of the nation. The United States claims to allow all people to blend into the great stew of citizenship. It has already suffered embarrassment and international cries of ethnic bias as a result of political moves such as Japanese American internment and the Guantanamo Bay detention center. This amendment can help mend the national image as every American takes one more step toward equality. Naturalized citizens have been contributing to the United States for centuries. Many nameless Mexican, Irish, and Asian Americans sweated and toiled to build the American railroads. The public has welcomed naturalized Americans such as Bob Hope, Albert Pujols, and Peter Jennings into their hearts and living rooms. Individuals such as German-born Henry Kissinger and Czechoslovakian-born Madeleine Albright have held high posts in the American government and served as respected aides to its presidents. The amendment must make clear that it is not about one man's celebrity. Approximately 700 foreign-born Americans have won the Medal of Honor and over 60,000 proudly serve in the United States military today (Siskind 5). The "natural-born" clause must be removed to provide each of these people—over half a million naturalized in 2003 alone—with equal footing to those who were born into citizenship rather than working for it (U.S. Census Bureau).

Since the passing of the Bill of Rights, only seventeen amendments have been ratified. This process takes time and overwhelming congressional and statewide support. To alter the Constitution, a proposed amendment must pass with a two-thirds "super-majority" in both the House of Representatives and the Senate. In addition, the proposal must find favor in two-thirds (thirty-eight) of state legislatures. In short, this task will not be easy. In order for this change to occur, a grassroots campaign must work to dispel misinformation regarding naturalized citizens and force the hands of senators and representatives wishing to retain their congressional seats. We must take this proposal to ethnicity-specific political groups from both sides of the aisle, business organizations, and community activist groups. We must convince representatives that this issue matters. Only through raising voices and casting votes can the people enact change. Only then can every American child see the possibility for limitless achievement and equality. Only then can everyone find the same sense of pride in the possibility for true American diversity in the highest office in the land.

Works Cited

Epstein, Edward. "Doubt About a Foreign-Born President." *San Francisco Chronicle* 6 Oct. 2004: A5. *LexisNexis Academic*. Web. 6 Mar. 2008.

Facts for Features. US Dept. of Commerce, 27 June 2005. Web. 17 Mar. 2008.

Ginsberg, Gordon. "Citizenship: Expatriation: Distinction Between Naturalized and Natural Born Citizens." *Michigan Law Review* 50 (1952): 926-29. *JSTOR*. Web. 6 Mar. 2008.

Mathews, Joe. "Maybe Anyone Can Be President." *Los Angeles Times* 2 Feb. 2005: A1. *LexisNexis Academic*. Web. 6 Mar. 2008.

Kasindorf, Martin. "Should the Constitution Be Amended for Arnold?" *USA Today* 2 Dec. 2004. *LexisNexis Academic*. Web. 8 Mar. 2008.

Pryor, Jill A. "The Natural Born Citizen Clause and Presidential Eligibility: An Approach for Resolving Two Hundred Years of Uncertainty." *The Yale Law Journal* 97.5 (1988): 881-99. Print.

Siskind, Lawrence J. "Why Shouldn't Arnold Run?" *The Recorder* 10 Dec. 2004: 5. *LexisNexis Academic*. Web. 10 Mar. 2008.

United States. Dept. of Commerce. Census Bureau. "The Fourth of July 2005."

Projects

If you want to persuade your readers to do something, you must convince them that a problem exists and that something needs to be done about it. You'll likely make the best argument for change if the problem matters to you. Most groups and organizations are faced with problems. You'll be able to argue with conviction, and you might even bring about change.

The following projects will give you experience in the kinds of proposals frequent in the workplace and in public life.

Proposal essay

Write a proposal of 1000–1250 words (about five to seven double-spaced pages) that would solve a problem that you identify.

Choose a problem with which you have personal experience, but you should also think about how many other people this problem affects. Your proposal should take them into account as part of your audience.

Find out who would be in a position to enact your proposal. How can you make your solution seem like a good idea to these people?

Propose your solution as specifically as you can. What exactly do you want to achieve? How exactly will your solution work? Has anything like it been tried elsewhere? Who will be involved?

Consider other solutions that have been or might be proposed for this problem, including doing nothing. What are the advantages and disadvantages of those solutions? Why is your solution better?

Examine how easy your solution is to implement. Will the people most affected be willing to go along with it? Lots of things can be accomplished if enough people volunteer, but groups often have difficulty getting enough volunteers to work without pay. If it costs money, how do you propose paying for it?

Reconstructing a proposal

You may not have a lot of experience writing proposals. Nevertheless, proposals have had a profound impact on your life. Almost every program, law, policy, or business that affects you had to be proposed before it became a reality.

↓

Think of some things in your life that were proposed by people: the building where you attended high school, for example. At some point, that building was proposed as a way of solving a certain problem—perhaps your town had one old, overflowing high school, and your building was proposed to solve the overcrowding. Its location was probably chosen carefully, to avoid causing more problems with traffic, and to ensure that it was easy for students to reach.

↓

Choose something you are familiar with that went through a proposal process. Try to reconstruct the four components of the original proposal. What problem do you think people were trying to solve? How did concerns about fairness and feasibility shape the program, building, or policy?

↓

Outline your re-created proposal in a page or two.

↓

Ask yourself if this policy, program, or business truly solved the problem it was intended to solve. Clearly, the proposal itself was successful, for the school was built, the law was passed, or the business was started. But how successful was the proposed solution in reality?

Teamwork: counterproposals

Find a proposal argument that you and three or four classmates are interested in. This might be a proposal to widen a road in your town, to pass a law making English the official language of your state government, or something similar.

↓

As a group discuss the four components of the proposal as outlined in this chapter: What is the problem being addressed? What is the solution? Is it workable and fair? Is it feasible?

↓

Then have each person in the group construct a one- or two-page counterproposal. Your counterproposals should address the same problem as the original proposal, but should offer different solutions. Your analysis of the workability, fairness, and feasibility of the original proposal will help you shape your counterproposals. Is there a way to solve the problem that is cheaper? less disruptive? more fair? less risky?

↓

Present your counterproposals to the rest of your group, and discuss which is the most appealing. You may find that a combination of elements of the different proposals ends up being the best.

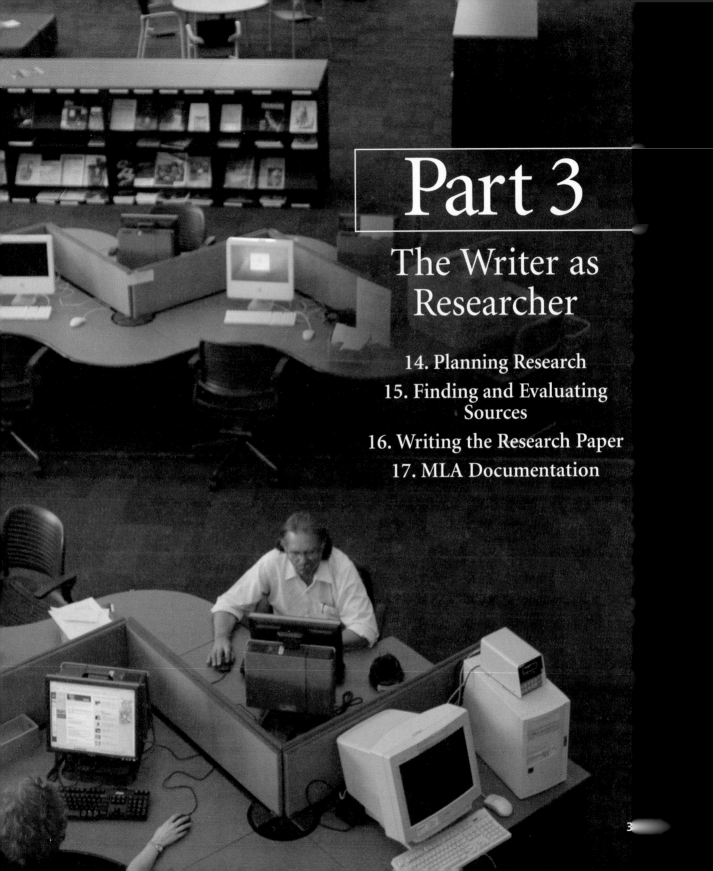

Part 3

The Writer as Researcher

14 Planning Research

Understand the different kinds of possible research and plan your strategy in advance.

Analyze the research task

If you have an assignment that requires research, look closely at what you are being asked to do. The assignment may ask you to review, compare, survey, analyze, evaluate, or prove that something is true or untrue. You may be writing for experts, for students like yourself, or for the general public. The purpose of your research and your potential audience will help guide your strategies for research.

The key is understanding what is expected of you. You are being asked to

1. Determine your goals.
2. Find a subject.
3. Ask a question about the subject.
4. Find out what has been said about this subject.
5. Make a contribution to the discussion about this subject.

Determine your goals

Often your assignment will tell you how to get started. Look for key words:

- An *analysis* or *examination* requires you to look at an issue in detail, explaining how it has evolved, who or what it affects, and what is at stake.
- A *survey* requires you to gather opinions about a particular issue, either by a questionnaire or by interviews.
- An *evaluation* requires you to make critical judgments.
- An *argument* requires you to assemble evidence in support of a claim you make.

Ask your instructor for guidance if you remain unsure what is expected.

Find a subject that interests you

When you ask meaningful questions, your research will be enjoyable. Your courses may give you some ideas about questions to ask. Personal experience is often a good source of questions related to your research topic: What was the cause of something that happened to you? Was your experience typical or atypical? How can you solve a problem you have? What do experts think about the issues that concern you? Working with a topic that has already aroused your curiosity makes it more likely that your findings will interest others.

A good way to begin is by browsing a subject directory, either in your library or on the Web. Subject directories can show you many different aspects of a single topic.

[Reproduced with permission of Yahoo! Inc. Copyright © 2008 by Yahoo! Inc. YAHOO! and the YAHOO! logo are trademarks of Yahoo! Inc.]

Ask a question

Often you'll be surprised by the amount of information your initial browsing uncovers. Your next task will be to identify in that mass of information a question for your research project. This researchable question will be the focus of the remainder of your research and ultimately of your research project or paper. Browsing on the topic of solid waste recycling might lead you to a researchable question such as

- Do cities save or lose money on recycling programs?
- Why can't all plastics be recycled?
- Are Americans being persuaded to recycle more paper, aluminum, and plastic?

Focus your research question

Think about how to make your research question specific enough so that you can treat it thoroughly in a paper. Reading about your subject will help you to focus your research question.

- Why did the number of tons of recycled plastic and glass in our city peak in 2005 and decline slightly ever since?
- Should our state mandate the use of degradable plastics that decay along with kitchen and yard waste in compost heaps?
- Besides paper bags that deplete forests, what are the alternatives to plastic bags that contaminate soil in landfills and sabotage the recycling system by jamming the machinery that sorts bottles and cans?

Determine what kinds of research you need to do

Once you have formulated a research question, begin thinking about what kind of research you will need to do to address the question.

Secondary research

Most researchers rely partly or exclusively on the work of others as sources of information. Research based on the work of others is called **secondary research**. In the past this information was contained almost exclusively in collections of print materials housed in libraries, but today enormous amounts of information are available through library databases and the World Wide Web.

Primary research

Much of the research done in college creates new information through **primary research**: experiments, data-gathering surveys and interviews, detailed observations, and the examination of historical documents. Although some undergraduates do not do primary research, sometimes you may be researching a question that requires you to gather firsthand information. For example, if you are researching a campus issue such as the impact of a new library fee on students' budgets, you may need to conduct interviews, make observations, or take a survey.

Determine what you need

Is the scope of your issue . . .	Then research might include . . .
Local? (Inadequate bike lanes, local noise ordinances, school policies)	• interviews and observations • local newspapers • other local media: television, radio
Regional? (County taxes, toll road construction, watershed protection)	• some of the sources above • state government offices • regional organizations, clubs, or associations—e.g., the Newark Better Business Bureau, Brazos Valley Mothers Against Drunk Driving
National? (Federal agricultural subsidies, immigration, major league sports)	• some of the sources above • federal government offices • national organizations, clubs, or associations—e.g., the American Automobile Association • national network news on television and radio • national newspapers or magazines—e.g., the *New York Times* or *Rolling Stone*
International? (Trade imbalances, military conflicts, global climate change)	• some of the sources above • federal government offices • international agencies such as UNICEF • international news outlets such as Reuters • foreign newspapers or magazines like *Le Monde* and *der Spiegel*

You can also find sources you need by thinking about people affected by your issue and noting where it is being discussed.

Who is interested in this issue?	Where would they read, write, talk, or hear about it?	In what different media might the information appear?
scientists teachers voters minors senior citizens policy makers stock brokers	scientific journals political journals scholarly journals newspapers books Web forums government documents	online television radio print film/DVD

Set a Schedule

Use your assignment, your personal schedule, and your knowledge of the sources you'll need to schedule your research. Allow yourself some large blocks of uninterrupted time, especially during the browsing stage.

Project: Research paper for a government course, analyzing a recent financial fraud

Days until first draft is due: 17

Days 1–3:
PRELIMINARY research, one hour each evening

Days 4–6:
IN-DEPTH library research—Schedule appointment with reference librarian for periodicals search tutorial

Days 7–9:
Go over collected material, think about research question/hypothesis

Days 10–12:
Begin drafting

Days 13–14:
Revise rough draft for clarity, organization, and ideas

Days 15–16:
Follow-up research or verify questionable sources as needed

Day 17:
Fine-tune draft

Project: Paper utilizing field research for an introduction to social research course

Weeks until project due: 7

Week 1:
Research and brainstorm topics; discuss short list of possible topics/methods with professor; make final decision

Week 2:
Research survey/interview methods; design appropriate method

Week 3:
Conduct field research

Week 4:
Analyze data and do follow-up if necessary

Week 5:
Draft paper—go back to library if necessary

Week 6:
Take draft to writing center; revise

Week 7:
Proofread, fine tune, and make sure all charts and images print correctly

Draft a working thesis

Once you have done some preliminary research into your question, you need to craft a working thesis. Perhaps you have found a lot of interesting material on the home economics movement of the 1950s and 1960s. You have discovered that food companies—particularly makers of packaged foods—were deeply involved in shaping and funding the movement. As you research the question of why food companies fostered the home economics movement, a working thesis begins to emerge.

Write your topic, research question, and working thesis on a note card or sheet of paper. Keep your working thesis handy. You may need to revise it several times until the wording is precise. As you research, ask yourself, does this information tend to support my thesis? Information that does not support your thesis is still important! It may lead you to adjust your thesis, or even abandon it altogether. You may need to find another source or reason that shows your thesis is still valid.

TOPIC:
The Home Economics Movement of the 1950s and 1960s.

RESEARCH QUESTION:
Why did the major American food corporations fund the Home Economics movement of the 50s and 60s?

WORKING THESIS:
Major American food corporations invested in the development and spread of Home Economics in order to create a ready market for their products by teaching women to rely on prepared foods instead of cooking "from scratch." They used Home Economics programs to change the way Americans thought about food and cooking.

Write Now

Determine what information you need

Select one of the possible topics below or identify a topic that will work for your assignment. Write a brief list or paragraph describing the types of research that might be used to investigate the question. What kinds of information would you need? Where would you look for it?

1. How much does an average American couple spend to adopt a child from overseas?
2. What determines the price of gasoline that you pay at the pump?
3. How effective was drafting soldiers in the North and South during the Civil War?
4. Why does the U.S. Postal Service spend part of its budget to encourage stamp collecting?

15 Finding and Evaluating Sources

Know how to find and identify the best information available.

Find information in databases

You can learn how to use databases in your library with the help of a reference librarian. Your library may also have online and printed tutorials on using databases. Once you know how to access the databases you need, you can work from computers in other locations.

Most databases are by subscription only and must be accessed through your library's Web site, but a few like Google Scholar are free to everyone.

Academic Search Premier and Academic Search Complete	Provides full text articles for thousands of scholarly publications, including social sciences, humanities, education, computer sciences, engineering, language and linguistics, literature, medical sciences, and ethnic studies journals.
ArticleFirst	Indexes journals in business, the humanities, medicine, science, and social sciences.
EBSCOhost Research Databases	Gateway to a large collection of EBSCO databases, including Academic Search Premier and MasterFILE Premier.
Expanded Academic ASAP	Indexes periodicals from the arts, humanities, sciences, social sciences, and general news, with full-text articles and images.
Factiva	Provides news and business information from over 10,000 sources including the *Wall Street Journal.*
FirstSearch	Offers millions of full-text articles from many databases.
Google Scholar	Searches scholarly literature according to criteria of relevance.
InfoTrac OneFile	Contains millions of full-text articles on a wide range of academic and general interest topics.
JSTOR	Provides scanned copies of scholarly journals.
LexisNexis Academic	Provides full text of a wide range of newspapers, magazines, government and legal documents, and company profiles from around the world.
OmniFile Full Text	Provides full-text articles, indexes, and abstracts for most subjects.

Construct effective searches

To use databases effectively, make a list of keywords in advance.

Select a database

Your next decision is to choose a database to begin your research. Newspapers might include stories on local deer populations and changes in hunting policy. Popular journals such as *Field and Stream* might have articles on national trends in deer hunting, and might also summarize scholarly research on the subject. Scholarly journals, perhaps in the field of wildlife biology, would contain articles about formal research into the effects of deer hunting on population density, average size and weight of animals, range, and other specific factors.

To find newspaper stories, begin with LexisNexis Academic. To find popular and scholarly journal articles, go Academic Search Premier, Academic Search Complete, EBSCOhost, Expanded Academic ASAP, FirstSearch, or InfoTrac OneFile.

Evaluate database sources

Databases collect print sources and put them in digital formats. Evaluate database sources the same way you evaluate print sources.

1. **Source:** Is the source a scholarly or popular journal?
2. **Author:** What are the author's qualifications?
3. **Timeliness:** How current is the source?
4. **Evidence:** Where does the evidence come from?
5. **Biases:** Can you detect particular biases?
6. **Advertising:** Is advertising prominent?

Evaluate for relevance

Even reliable sources may not pertain to your topic. Consider the relevance of each source for your subject.

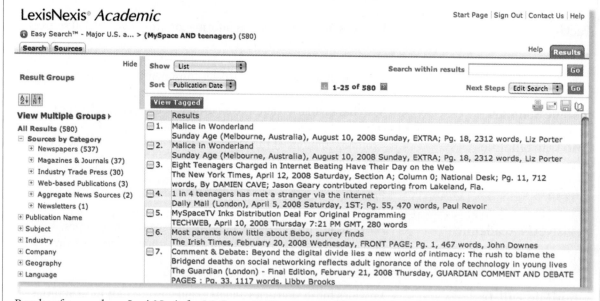

Results of a search on LexisNexis for MySpace AND teenagers. If your topic is the danger of predators taking advantage of younger teenagers on MySpace, probably articles 1, 4, 6, and 7 would be the first ones to examine.

Locate elements of a citation

To cite a source from a database, you will need the

- Author if listed
- Title of article
- Name of periodical
- Volume and issue number (for journals)
- Date of publication (and edition for newspapers)

- Section (for newspapers) and page numbers
- Name of database
- Medium of publication (*Web*)
- Date of access (the day you found the article in the database)

A sample article from the Academic Search Premier search for "steroids" and "high school." The confusing part of citing this example is distinguishing between the database and the vendor. The vendor's name often appears at the top of the screen, making the vendor's name look like the name of the database. In this case, EBSCO is the vendor—the company that sells your library access to Academic Search Premier and many other databases. Often you have to look carefully to find the name of the database.

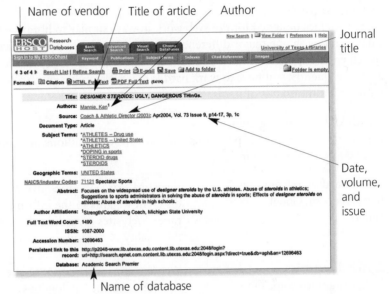

Name of vendor / Title of article / Author

Journal title

Date, volume, and issue

Name of database

A citation for an article that you find on a database looks like this in MLA style:

Mannie, Ken. "Designer Steroids: Ugly, Dangerous Things." *Scholastic Coach and Athletic Director* 73.9 (2004): 14–17. *Academic Search Premier*. Web. 26 July 2008.

Working Together

Compare databases

In a group of three or four students

Identify keywords for your research topic, and use the same keywords for searches on three or more databases. If the search yields too many items, use AND to connect the terms or add another keyword plus AND. Copy the results from each search and paste this into a file. Which database turned up more items? Which turned up more scholarly articles? Which turned up more articles in popular journals? Which will be most helpful for your research topic?

Find information on the Web

Because anyone can publish on the Web, there is no overall quality control and there is no system of organization as you would find in a library. Nevertheless, the Web offers you some resources for current topics that would be difficult to find in a library. The keys to success are knowing where you are most likely to find current and accurate information about the particular question you are researching, and knowing how to access that information.

Search engines

Search engines designed for the Web work in ways similar to library databases and your library's online catalog, but with one major difference. Databases typically do some screening of the items they list, but search engines potentially take you to every Web site that isn't password protected—millions of pages in all. Consequently, you have to work harder to limit searches on the Web; otherwise you can be deluged with tens of thousands of items.

Kinds of search engines

A search engine is a set of programs that sort through millions of items at incredible speed. There are four basic kinds of search engines.

1. Keyword search engines (e.g., Ask.com, Google, MSN, Yahoo!)	Keyword search engines give different results because they assign different weights to the information they find. Google, for example, ranks Web sites according to how many other sites link to them and the quality of the linking sites.
2. Web directories (e.g., Britannica.com, Yahoo! Directory)	Web directories classify Web sites into categories and are the closest equivalent to the cataloging system used by libraries. On most directories professional editors decide how to index a particular Web site. Web directories also allow keyword searches.
3. Metasearch agents (e.g., Dogpile, HotBot, Metacrawler)	Metasearch agents allow you to use several search engines simultaneously. While the concept is sound, metasearch agents are limited by the number of hits they can return and their inability to handle advanced searches.
4. Specialized search engines (e.g., Froogle [shopping], Google Scholar [academic], Monster.com [jobs], Baidu [regional for China], WebMD [medicine])	Specialized search engines have been developed in recent years for specific subjects.

Google™ Advanced Search   Advanced Search Tips | About Google

Find results	with **all** of the words	murder rate major cities	10 results	Google Search
	with the **exact phrase**			
	with **at least one** of the words			
	without the words			

Language	Return pages written in	any language
File Format	Only return results of the file format	any format
Date	Return web pages updated in the	anytime
Occurrences	Return results where my terms occur	anywhere in the page
Domain	Only return results from the site or domain	.gov
		e.g. google.com, .org More info

An advanced search on Google for government sites only (.gov).

Advanced searches

Search engines often produce too many hits and are therefore not always useful. If you look only at the first few items, you may miss what is most valuable. The alternative is to refine your search. Most search engines offer you the option of an advanced search, which gives you the opportunity to limit numbers.

The advanced searches on Google and Yahoo! give you the options of using a string of words to search for sites that contain (1) all the words, (2) the exact phrase, (3) any of the words, or (4) that exclude certain words. They also allow you to specify the language of the site, the date range, the file format, and the domain. For example, government statistics on crime are considered the most reliable, so if you want to find statistics on murder rates, you can specify the domain as .gov in an advanced search.

Discussion forums, groups, and blogs

The Internet allows you to access other people's opinions on thousands of topics. The Groups section of Google (groups.google.com) has an archive of several hundred million messages that can be searched. Much of the conversation on these sites is undocumented and highly opinionated, but you can still gather important information about people's attitudes and get tips about other sources, which you can verify later.

Web logs, better known as blogs, also are sources of public opinion. Several tools have been developed to search blogs: Bloglines, Google Blog Search, Technorati, and IceRocket. Blogs are not screened and are not considered authoritative sources, but blogs can sometimes lead you to quality sources.

Evaluate Web sources

All electronic search tools share a common problem: They often give you too many sources. Web search engines not only pull up thousands of hits, but these hits may vary dramatically in quality. No one regulates or checks information put on the Web, and it's no surprise that much information on the Web is highly opinionated or false.

Misleading Web sites

Some Web sites are put up as jokes. Other Web sites are deliberately misleading. Many prominent Web sites draw imitators who want to cash in on the commercial visibility. The Web site for the Campaign for Tobacco-Free Kids (www.tobaccofreekids.org), for example, has an imitator (www.smokefreekids.com) that sells software for antismoking education. The .com URL is often a tip-off that a site has a profit motive.

Biased Web sites

Always approach Web sites with an eye toward evaluating content. For example, the Web site Thinktwice.com, sponsored by the Global Vaccine Institute, opposes the vaccination of children. On the site you can find claims that the polio vaccine administered to millions in the United States causes cancer because it was contaminated with Simian Virus 40. Always look for other sources for verification. The U.S. Centers for Disease Control publishes fact sheets on the latest information about diseases and their prevention, including one on polio vaccine and Simian Virus 40.

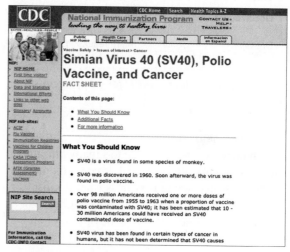

Fact sheet on Simian Virus 40, Polio Vaccine, and Cancer from the Centers for Disease Control (http://www.cdc.gov/nip/vacsafe/concerns/cancer/sv40-polio-cancer-facts.htm).

Locate elements of a citation

To cite a Web site you will need

- Author if listed
- Title of the work (in italics unless part of a larger work)
- Title of the overall Web site (in italics if distinct from the work)
- Version of the site (if relevant)
- Publisher or sponsor of the site (if no publisher is given, use *N.p.*)
- Date of publication (if no date is given, use *n.d.*)
- Medium of publication (Web)
- Date of access

Ogintz, Eileen. "Hiking Italy's Amalfi Coast." *CNN.com.* Cable News Network, 1 July 2008. Web. 3 July 2008.

A citation for a Web page looks like this in MLA style.

Criteria for evaluating Web sources

The criteria for evaluating print sources can be applied to Web sources if the special circumstances of the Web are acknowledged. For example, when you find a Web page by using a search engine, often you go deep into a complex site without having any sense of the context for that page. To evaluate the credibility of the site, you would need to examine the home page, not just the specific page you saw first.

Source	Look for the site's ownership in the Web address. If a Web site doesn't indicate ownership, then you have to make judgments about who put it up and why. The suffix can offer clues: .gov is used by government bodies, and .edu by educational institutions, generally colleges and universities. These sites are generally more reliable than .com sites.
Author	Often Web sites give no information about their authors other than an e-mail address, if that. In such cases it is difficult or impossible to determine the author's qualifications. Look up the author on Google. If qualifications are listed, is the author an expert in the field?
Timeliness	Many Web pages do not list when they were last updated; thus you cannot determine their currency.
Evidence	The accuracy of any evidence found on the Web is often hard to verify. The most reliable information on the Web stands up to the tests of print evaluation, with clear indication of the sponsoring organization and the sources of any factual information.
Biases	Many Web sites announce their viewpoint on controversial issues, but others conceal their attitude with a reasonable tone and seemingly factual evidence such as statistics. Citations and bibliographies do not ensure that a site is reliable. Look carefully at the links and sources cited.
Advertising	Many Web sites are infomercials aimed at getting you to buy a product or service. While they might contain useful information, they are no more trustworthy than other forms of advertising.

Wikipedia

Wikipedia is not considered a reliable source of information for a research paper by many instructors and the scholarly community in general. The problem with Wikipedia is not so much that erroneous information exists on Wikipedia but that the content changes frequently. There is no guarantee that what you find on Wikipedia today will still be there tomorrow. Many Wikipedia entries, however, do list reliable sources that you can consult and cite in a research paper.

Find visual sources online

You can find images published on the Web using Google and other search engines that allow you to specify searches for images. For example, if you are writing a research paper on invasive plant species, you might want to include an image of kudzu, an invasive vine common in the American South. In Google, choose Images and type *kudzu* in the search box. You'll find a selection of images of plant, including several from the National Park Service.

Three major search engines are designed specifically to find images.

- Google Image Search (images.google.com). The most comprehensive image search tool.

- Picsearch (www.picsearch.com). Provides thumbnails of images linked to the source on the Web.

- Yahoo Search (images.search.yahoo.com). Has tools to limit results on the Advanced Search similar to Google.

Other useful visual sites for visual resources include

- *Statistical Abstract of the United States* (www.census.gov/compendia/statab/). Contains statistical data represented in charts and graphs.

- Directory of map sites (www.lib.utexas.edu/maps/map_sites/ map_sites.html).

Kudzu

Pueraria montana var. lobata (Willd.) Maesen & S. Almeida
Pea family (Fabaceae)

NATIVE RANGE: Asia

DESCRIPTION: Kudzu ia a climbing, semi-woody, perennial vine in the pea family. Deciduous leaves are alternate and compound, with three broad leaflets up to 4 inches across. Leaflets may be entire or deeply 2-3 lobed with hairy margins. Individual flowers, about 1/2 inch long, are purple, highly fragrant and borne in long hanging clusters. Flowering occurs in late summer and is soon followed by production of brown, hairy, flattened, seed pods, each of which contains three to ten hard seeds.

Kudzu was planted widely in the South to reduce soil erosion but has itself become a major pest, smothering native trees and plants.

Follow copyright requirements

Just because images are easy to download from the Web does not mean that you are free to use every image you find. Look for the image creator's copyright notice and suggested credit line. This notice will tell you if you can reproduce the image. You should acknowledge the source of any image you use.

In many cases you will find a copyright notice that reads something like this, "Any use or re-transmission of text or images in this Web site without written consent of the copyright owner constitutes copyright infringement and is prohibited." You must write to the creator to ask permission to use an image from a site that is not in the public domain, even if you cannot find a copyright notice.

Write Now

Evaluate Web sites

Hoaxbusters (http://hoaxbusters.ciac.org/) provides an index of Internet hoaxes sorted into categories. Read several of the hoaxes, and select one to explore further. To evaluate your site use the criteria for evaluating Web sources on the opposite page. On which criteria does it fail to be reliable?

Next do a Google search for Ritalin, a commonly prescribed drug for attention deficit disorder (ADD) and attention deficit hyperactivity disorder (ADHD). You will find that the drug is quite controversial. Look at five different Web sites. Which sites do you find most reliable and the least reliable?

Find books

Nearly all college libraries now shelve books according to the Library of Congress Classification System, which uses a combination of letters and numbers to give you the book's unique location in the library. The Library of Congress call number begins with a letter or letters that represent the broad subject area into which the book is classified.

The Library of Congress system groups books by subject, and you can often find other items relevant to your search shelved close to the particular one you are looking for. You can search the extensive Library of Congress online catalog (catalog.loc.gov) to find out how your subject might be indexed, or you can go straight to your own library's catalog and conduct a subject search. The call number will enable you to find the item in the stacks. You will need to consult the locations guide for your library to find the book on the shelves.

When you find a book in your library catalog, take time to notice the subject headings under which it is indexed. For example, if you locate Jeff Hawkins's *On Intelligence*, you will probably find it cross-listed under several subject categories, including

```
Brain

Intellect

Artificial intelligence

Neural networks (Computer science)
```

Browsing within these categories, or using some of their keywords in a new search, may lead you to more useful sources.

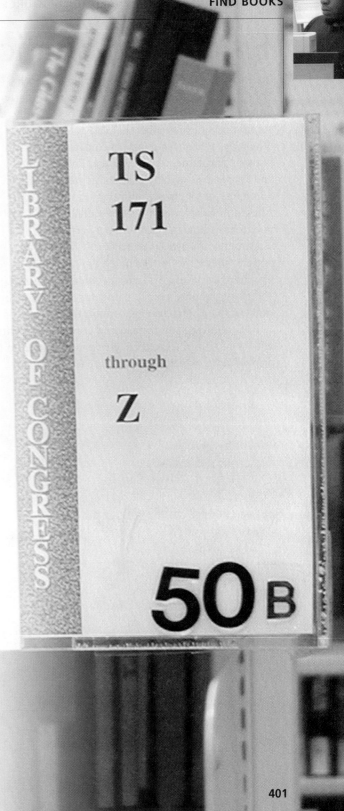

Find journal articles

Like books, scholarly journals provide in-depth examinations of subjects. The articles in scholarly journals are written by experts, and they usually contain lists of references that can guide you to other research on a subject. In contrast, articles in popular magazines like *Newsweek*, *Rolling Stone*, and *People* are typically written by journalists. Some instructors frown on using popular magazines, but these journals can be valuable for researching current opinion on a particular topic.

Searching for articles in scholarly journals and popular magazines works much the same way as searching for books. Indexes for scholarly journals and magazines are available on your library's Web site. Databases increasingly contain the full text of articles, allowing you to read and copy the contents onto your computer. Others give you a citation to a print journal, which you then have to find on a shelf in your library.

Your library has a list of databases and indexes by subject. Find this subject index either on your library's Web site or in the reference section of your library. Follow these steps to find articles:

1. Select an index appropriate to your subject. (For researching multiple sclerosis, you might start with Health Reference Center, MEDLINE, and PsycINFO.)

2. Search the index using relevant subject heading(s). (You could start with multiple sclerosis and then combine MS with other terms to narrow your search.)

3. Print or copy the complete citation to the article(s).

4. Print or copy the full text if it is available.

5. If the full text is not available, check the periodicals holdings to see if your library has the print journal.

Your library will probably have printed handouts or information on the Web that tell you which specialized index to use for a particular subject. Ask a librarian who works at the reference or information desk to help you.

Evaluate print sources

Whether you use print or online sources, a successful search will turn up many more items than you can expect to use in your final product. You have to make a series of decisions about what is important and relevant. Return to your research question and working thesis (see Chapter 14) to determine which items are relevant.

How reliable are your sources? Books are expensive to print and distribute, so book publishers generally protect their investment by providing some level of editorial oversight. Print sources in libraries have an additional layer of oversight because someone has decided that a book or journal is worth purchasing and cataloging. Web sites, in contrast, can be put up and changed quickly, so information can be—and often is—posted thoughtlessly.

But print sources contain their share of biased, inaccurate, and misleading information. Over the years librarians have developed a set of criteria for evaluating print sources.

Source	Who published the book or article? Scholarly books and articles in scholarly journals are reviewed by experts in the field before they are published. They are generally more reliable than popular magazines and books, which tend to emphasize what is entertaining at the expense of comprehensiveness.
Author	Who wrote the book or article? What are the author's qualifications?
Timeliness	How current is the source? If you are researching a fast-developing subject such as vaccines for Asian bird flu, then currency is very important. Currency might not be as important for a historical subject, but even historical figures and events are often reinterpreted.
Evidence	Where does the evidence come from: facts, interviews, observations, surveys, or experiments? Is the evidence adequate to support the author's claims?
Biases	Can you detect particular biases of the author? How do the author's biases affect the interpretation offered?
Advertising	Is advertising a prominent part of the journal or newspaper? How might the ads affect what gets printed?

Write Now

Evaluate information

Think of three or four different types of writing you have read recently: a novel, textbook, blog, letter, flyer, comic book, or online review. Evaluate each source according to the criteria above. Which item is the most reliable? For what purpose? Which is the least reliable?

16 Writing the Research Paper

Thorough reasearch gives you a wealth of ideas and information to communicate.

Plan your organization

Review your goals and thesis

Before you begin writing your paper, review the assignment and your goals (see Chapter 14). Your review of the assignment will remind you of your purpose, your potential readers, your stance on your subject, and the length and scope you should aim for.

By now you should have formulated a working thesis, which will be the focus of your paper. You should also have located, read, evaluated, and taken notes on enough source material to write your paper. At this stage in the writing process, your working thesis may be rough and may change as you write your draft, but having a working thesis will help keep your paper focused.

Determine your contribution

A convincing and compelling research paper does not make claims based solely on the word of the writer. It draws on the expertise and reputations of others as well. Thus it is critical to show your readers which elements of your paper represent your original thinking.

Determine exactly what you are adding to the larger conversation about your subject.

- Who do you agree with?
- Who do you disagree with?
- What can you add to points you agree with?
- What original analysis or theorizing do you have to offer?
- What original findings from field research do you have to offer?

Determine your main points and group your findings

Look back over your notes and determine how to group the ideas you researched. Decide what your major points will be, and how those points support your thesis. Group your research findings so that they match up with your major points.

Now it is time to create a working outline. Always include your thesis at the top of your outline as a guiding light. Some writers create formal outlines with roman numerals and the like; others compose the headings for the paragraphs of their paper and use them to guide their draft; still others may start writing and then determine how they will organize their draft when they have a few paragraphs written. Experiment and decide which method works best for you.

405

Avoid plagiarism

You know that copying someone else's paper word for word or taking an article off the Internet and turning it in as yours is plagiarism. That's plain stealing, and people who take that risk should know that the punishment can be severe. But plagiarism also means using the ideas, melodies, or images of someone else without acknowledging them, and it is important to understand exactly what defines plagiarism.

What you don't have to document

Fortunately, common sense governs issues of academic plagiarism. The standards of documentation are not so strict that the source of every fact you cite must be acknowledged. Suppose you are writing about the causes of maritime disasters and you want to know how many people drowned when the *Titanic* sank on the early morning of April 15, 1912. You check the *Britannica Online* Web site and find that the death toll was around 1,500. Since this fact is available in many other reference works, you would not need to cite *Britannica Online* as the source.

But let's say you want to challenge the version of the sinking offered in the 1998 movie *Titanic*, which repeats the usual explanation that the *Titanic* side-swiped an iceberg, ripping a long gash along the hull that caused the ship to go down. Suppose that, in your reading, you discover that a September 1985 exploration of the wreck by an unmanned submersible did not find the long gash previously thought to have sunk the ship. The evidence instead suggested that the force of the collision with the iceberg broke the seams in the hull, allowing water to flood the ship's watertight compartments. You would need to cite the source of your information for this alternative version of the *Titanic*'s demise.

What you do have to document

For facts that are not easily found in general reference works, statements of opinion, and arguable claims, you should cite the source. You should also cite the sources of statistics, research findings, examples, graphs, charts, and illustrations. For example, if you state that the percentage of obese children aged 6 to 11 in the United States rose from 4% in 1974 to 15% in 2000, you need to cite the source.

As a reader you should be skeptical about statistics and research findings when the source is not mentioned. When a writer does not cite the sources of statistics and research findings, there is no way of knowing how reliable the sources are or whether the writer is making them up.

From the writer's perspective careful citing of sources lends credibility. If you take your statistics from a generally trusted source, your readers are more likely to trust whatever conclusions or arguments you are presenting. When in doubt, always document the source.

Be careful when taking notes and copying material online

The best way to avoid unintentional plagiarism is to take care to distinguish source words from your own words.

- Don't mix words from the source with your own words. If you copy anything from a source when taking notes, place those words in quotation marks and note the page number(s) where those words appear.

- Write down all the information you need for each source.

- If you copy words from an online source, take special care to note the source. You could easily copy online material and later not be able to find where it came from.

- Photocopy printed sources and print out online sources. Having printed copies of sources allows you to double-check later that you haven't used words from the source by mistake and that any words you quote are accurate.

Quote sources without plagiarizing

Effective research writing builds on the work of others. You can summarize or paraphrase the work of others, but often it is best to let the authors speak in your text by quoting their exact words. Indicate the words of others by placing them inside quotation marks.

Most people who get into plagiarism trouble lift words from a source and use them without quotation marks. Where the line is drawn is easiest to illustrate with an example. In the following passage, Steven Johnson takes sharp issue with the metaphor of surfing applied to the Web:

> The concept of "surfing" does a terrible injustice to what it means to navigate around the Web. . . . What makes the idea of cybersurf so infuriating is the implicit connection drawn to television. Web surfing, after all, is a derivation of channel surfing—the term thrust upon the world by the rise of remote controls and cable panoply in the mid-eighties. . . . Applied to the boob tube, of course, the term was not altogether inappropriate. Surfing at least implied that channel-hopping was more dynamic, more involved, than the old routine of passive consumption. Just as a real-world surfer's enjoyment depended on the waves delivered up by the ocean, the channel surfer was at the mercy of the programmers and network executives. The analogy took off because it worked well in the one-to-many system of cable TV, where your navigational options were limited to the available channels.
>
> But when the term crossed over to the bustling new world of the Web, it lost a great deal of precision. . . . Web surfing and channel surfing are genuinely different pursuits; to imagine them as equivalents is to ignore the defining characteristics of each medium. Or at least that's what happens in theory. In practice, the Web takes on the greater burden. The television imagery casts the online surfer in the random, anesthetic shadow of TV programming, roaming from site to site like a CD player set on shuffle play. But what makes the online world so revolutionary is the fact that there are connections between each stop on a Web itinerant's journey. The links that join those various destinations are links of association, not randomness. A channel surfer hops back and forth between different channels because she's bored. A Web surfer clicks on a link because she's interested.
>
> Steven Johnson. *Interface Culture: How New Technology Transforms the Way We Create and Communicate*. New York: Harper, 1997. 107–09. Print.

If you were writing a paper or putting up a Web site that concerned Web surfing, you might want to mention the distinction that Johnson makes between channel surfing and surfing on the Web. You could then expand on the distinction.

Use quotation marks for direct quotations

If you quote directly, you must place quotation marks around all words you take from the original:

> One observer marks this contrast: "A channel surfer hops back and forth between different channels because she's bored. A Web surfer clicks on a link because she's interested" (Johnson 109).

Notice that the quotation is introduced and not just dropped in. This example follows Modern Language Association (MLA) style, where the citation–(Johnson 109)–goes outside the quotation marks but before the final period. In MLA style, source references are made according to the author's last name, which refers you to the full citation in the list of works cited at the end. Following the author's name is the page number where the quotation can be located. (Notice also that there is no comma after the name.)

Attribute every quotation

If the author's name appears in the sentence, cite only the page number, in parentheses:

> According to Steven Johnson, "A channel surfer hops back and forth between different channels because she's bored. A Web surfer clicks on a link because she's interested" (109).

Quoting words that are quoted in your source

If you want to quote material that is already quoted in your source, use single quotes for that material:

> Steven Johnson uses the metaphor of a Gothic cathedral to describe a computer interface: " 'The principle of the Gothic architecture,' Coleridge once said, 'is infinity made imaginable.' The same could be said for the modern interface" (42).

Summarize and paraphrase sources without plagiarizing

Summarizing

When you summarize, you state the major ideas of an entire source or part of a source in a paragraph or perhaps even a sentence. The key is to put the summary in your own words. If you use words from the source, you have to put those words within quotation marks.

> **PLAGIARIZED**
>
> Steven Johnson argues in *Interface Culture* that the concept of "surfing" is misapplied to the Internet because channel surfers hop back and forth between different channels because they're bored, but Web surfers click on links because they're interested.

[Most of the words are lifted directly from the original; see page 407.]

> **ACCEPTABLE SUMMARY**
>
> Steven Johnson argues in *Interface Culture* that the concept of "surfing" is misapplied to the Internet because users of the Web consciously choose to link to other sites while television viewers mindlessly flip through the channels until something catches their attention.

Paraphrasing

When you paraphrase, you represent the idea of the source in your own words at about the same length as the original. You still need to include the reference to the source of the idea. The following example illustrates what is not an acceptable paraphrase.

> **PLAGIARIZED**
>
> Steven Johnson argues that the concept of "surfing" does a terrible injustice to what it means to navigate around the Web. What makes the idea of Web surfing infuriating is the association with television. Web surfing and channel surfing are truly different activities; to imagine them as the same is to ignore their defining characteristics. A channel surfer skips around because she's bored while a Web surfer clicks on a link because she's interested (107-09).

Even though the source is listed, this paraphrase is unacceptable. Too many of the words in the original are used directly here, including much or all of entire sentences.

When a string of words is lifted from a source and inserted without quotation marks, the passage is plagiarized. Changing a few words in a sentence is not a paraphrase. Compare these two sentences:

SOURCE

Web surfing and channel surfing are genuinely different pursuits; to imagine them as equivalents is to ignore the defining characteristics of each medium.

UNACCEPTABLE PARAPHRASE

Web surfing and channel surfing are truly different activities; to imagine them as the same is to ignore their defining characteristics.

The paraphrase takes the structure of the original sentence and substitutes a few words. It is much too similar to the original.

A true paraphrase represents an entire rewriting of the idea from the source

ACCEPTABLE PARAPHRASE

Steven Johnson argues that "surfing" is a misleading term for describing how people navigate on the Web. He allows that "surfing" is appropriate for clicking across television channels because the viewer has to interact with what the networks and cable companies provide, just as the surfer has to interact with what the ocean provides. Web surfing, according to Johnson, operates at much greater depth and with much more consciousness of purpose. Web surfers actively follow links to make connections (107-09).

Even though there are a few words from the original in this paraphrase, such as *navigate* and *connections*, these sentences are original in structure and wording while accurately conveying the meaning of the source.

Frame each paraphrase

Each paraphrase should begin by introducing the author and conclude with a page reference to the material that is paraphrased.

Incorporate quotations

Quotations are a frequent problem area in research papers. Review every quotation to ensure that each is used effectively and correctly.

- Limit the use of long quotations. If you have more than one blocked quotation on a page, look closely to see if one or more can be paraphrased or summarized.

- Check that each quotation supports your major points rather than making major points for you. If the ideas rather than the original wording are what's important, paraphrase the quotation and cite the source.

- Check that each quotation is introduced and attributed. Each quotation should be introduced and the author or title named. Check for verbs that signal a quotation: Smith *claims*, Jones *argues*, Brown *states*.

- Check that you cite the source for each quotation. You are required to cite the sources of all direct quotations, paraphrases, and summaries.

- Check the accuracy of each quotation. It's easy to leave out words or mistype a quotation. Compare what is in your paper to the original source. If you need to add words to make the quotation grammatical, make sure the added words are in brackets.

- Read your paper aloud to a classmate or a friend. Each quotation should flow smoothly when you read your paper aloud. Put a check beside rough spots as you read aloud so you can revise later.

When to quote directly and when to paraphrase
Use direct quotations when the original wording is important.

DIRECT QUOTATION

Smith notes that

> Although the public grew to accept film as a teaching tool, it was not always aware of all it was being taught. That was because a second type of film was also being produced during these years, the "attitude-building" film, whose primary purpose was to motivate, not instruct. Carefully chosen visuals were combined with dramatic story lines, music, editing, and sharply drawn characters to create powerful instruments of mass manipulation. (21)

Prose quotations longer than four lines (MLA) or forty words (APA) should be indented one inch in MLA style or one-half inch in APA style. Shorter quotations should be enclosed within quotation marks.

PARAPHRASE

Smith points out that a second kind of mental hygiene film, the attitude-building film, was introduced during the 1940s. It attempted to motivate viewers, whereas earlier films explicitly tried to teach something. The attitude-building films were intended to manipulate their audiences to feel a certain way (21).

PARAPHRASE COMBINED WITH QUOTATION

In his analysis of the rise of fascism in twentieth-century Europe, George Mosse notes that the fascist movement was built on pre-existing ideas like individualism and sacrifice. It "scavenged" other ideologies and made use of them. "Fascism was a new political movement but not a movement which invented anything new," Mosse explains (xvii).

In the second example, the original wording provides stronger description of the attitude-building films. The direct quotation is a better choice.

Often, you can paraphrase the main idea of a lengthy passage and quote only the most striking phrase or sentence.

Verbs that introduce quotations and paraphrases

acknowledge	claim	emphasize	offer
add	comment	explain	point out
admit	compare	express	refute
advise	complain	find	reject
agree	concede	grant	remark
allow	conclude	illustrate	reply
analyze	contend	imply	report
answer	criticize	insist	respond
argue	declare	interpret	show
ask	describe	maintain	state
assert	disagree	note	suggest
believe	discuss	object	think
charge	dispute	observe	write

Staying on Track

Quotations don't speak for themselves

OFF TRACK

Don't rely on long quotations to do the work of writing for you.

These quotations are picked up out of context and dropped into the paper. Readers have no clue about why they are relevant to the writer's text.

Richard Lanham writes:

> Economics . . . studies the allocation of scarce resources. Normally we would think that the phrase "information economy," which we hear everywhere nowadays, makes some sense. It is no longer physical stuff that is in short supply, we are told, but information about it. So, we live in an "information economy." but information is not in short supply in the new information economy. We're drowning in it. What we lack is the human attention needed to make sense of it all. (xi)

Lanham goes on to say:

> "Rhetoric" has not always been a synonym for humbug. For most of Western history, it has meant the body of doctrine that teaches people how to speak and write and, thus, act effectively in public life. Usually defined as "the art of persuasion," it might as well have been called "the economics of attention." It tells us how to allocate our central scarce resource, to invite people to attend to what we would like them to attend to. (xii-xiii)

ON TRACK

When sources are used effectively, they are woven into the fabric of a research project but still maintain their identity.

Most of the source is paraphrased, allowing the discussion to be integrated into the writer's text. The writer centers on how two key concepts, the "information economy" and "rhetoric," are reinterpreted by Richard Lanham. Only those words critical to representing Lanham's position are quoted directly.

In *The Economics of Attention*, Richard Lanham begins by pointing out that the "information economy" stands traditional economics on its head because there is no shortage of information today. Instead Lanham argues that attention is what is in short supply and that the discipline of rhetoric can help us to understand how attention is allocated. Rhetoric historically has meant the art and study of speaking and writing well, especially for participating in public life. Lanham maintains that what rhetoric has really been about is what he calls "the economics of attention" (xii). The central goal of rhetoric, according to Lanham, is "to invite people to attend to what we would like them to attend to" (xii-xiii).

Incorporate visuals

Here are a few guidelines to keep in mind for incorporating visual sources into your research paper.

- Use visuals for examples and supporting evidence, not for decoration. For example, if the subject of your research is Internet crime in San Francisco, including a picture of the Golden Gate Bridge is irrelevant and will detract from your paper.

- Refer to images and other graphics in the body of your research paper. Explain the significance of any images or graphics in the body of your paper.

- Respect the copyright of visual sources. You may need to request permission to use a visual from the Web.

- Get complete citation information. You are required to cite visual sources in your list of works cited just as you are for other sources.

- Describe the content of the image or graphic in the caption.

Façade of the Last Judgment, Orvieto, Italy, c. 1310–1330. Medieval churches frequently depicted Christ as a judge, damning sinners to hell.

Write Now

Summarize, paraphrase, and quote directly

Read this quotation and then
- Write a summary of it;
- Write a paraphrase of it;
- Incorporate a direct quotation from it into a sentence.

There is no strife, no prejudice, no national conflict in outer space as yet. Its hazards are hostile to us all. Its conquest deserves the best of all mankind, and its opportunity for peaceful cooperation may never come again. But why, some say, the moon? Why choose this as our goal? And they may well ask why climb the highest mountain? Why, 35 years ago, fly the Atlantic? Why does Rice play Texas?

We choose to go to the moon. We choose to go to the moon in this decade and do the other things, not because they are easy, but because they are hard, because that goal will serve to organize and measure the best of our energies and skills, because that challenge is one that we are willing to accept, one we are unwilling to postpone, and one which we intend to win, and the others, too. (President John F. Kennedy, September 12, 1962).

Review your research project

Read your project aloud and put checks in the margin in places where you think it sounds rough or might need more development. When you finish, try to imagine yourself as a reader who doesn't know much about your subject or has a different viewpoint. What could you add to benefit that reader?

Reviewing another student's research project

Read through a paper twice. The first time you read through a paper, concentrate on comprehension and overall impressions. On your second reading show the writer where you got confused or highlight parts that were especially good by adding comments in the margins.

Questions for reviewing a research project

- Does the title describe the subject of the paper? Does it create interest in the subject?

- Are the introductory paragraphs effective and relevant to the paper that follows?

- Is the thesis clearly stated in the beginning paragraphs of the paper?

- Does the writer offer support for the thesis from a variety of valid and reliable sources?

- Does the paper go into enough detail to support the thesis, and are the details relevant to the thesis?

- Do the arguments presented in the paper flow logically? Is the paper well organized?

- Is the tone of the paper consistent throughout? Is the word choice varied and appropriate throughout?

- Did you have to read some parts more than once to fully understand them?

- Are quotations properly introduced and integrated into the text?

- Are all facts and quotations that are not common knowledge documented?

- Is the documentation in the correct form?

- Is the paper free of errors of grammar and punctuation?

Revise your research project

From your review and possibly reviews of other students, make a list of changes you might make. Start with the large concerns—reorganizing paragraphs, cutting unnecessary parts, and adding new sections. When you have finished revising, edit and proofread carefully.

415

17 MLA Documentation

MLA is the preferred style in the humanities and fine arts.

Works Cited

"Donna." Personal interview. 30 Mar. 2008.

Drum, Kevin. "You Own You." *Washington Monthly.* Washington Monthly, Dec. 2005. Web. 9 Apr. 2008.

"Equifax Annual Profit at $246.5 Million." Atlanta Business Chronicle. *Atlanta Business Chronicle,* 2 Feb. 2006. Web. 9 Apr. 2008.

Kuehner-Hebert, Katie. "Colorado Banks Would Fund ID Theft Task Force." *American Banker* 21 Mar. 2006: 1-4. *Business Source Premier.* Web. 7 April 2008.

Monahan, Mary T. 2007 Identity Fraud Survey Report. Javelin Strategy and Research, Feb. 2007. Web. 12 Apr. 2008.

Moyer, Liz. "Credit Agencies in the Clover." *Forbes.com.* Forbes, June 2005. Web. 10 Apr. 2008.

Solove, Daniel J. *The Digital Person: Technology and Privacy in the Information Age.* New York: NYU P, 2004. Print.

CHAPTER CONTENTS

If you have questions that the examples in this chapter do not address, consult the *MLA Handbook for Writers of Research Papers*, 7th ed. (2009), and the *MLA Style Manual and Guide to Scholarly Publishing*, 3rd ed. (2008).

Elements of MLA documentation

In MLA style, quotations, summaries, and paraphrases from outside sources are indicated by in-text citations in parentheses. When readers find a parenthetical reference in the body of a paper, they can turn to the list of works cited at the end of the paper to find complete publication information for the cited source.

Walker 3

... But how important is face-to-face interaction to maintaining good, "social" behavior in a group?

Describing humans as "innate mind readers," one observer argues that "our skill at imagining other people's mental states ranks up there with our knack for language and our opposable thumbs" (Johnson 196). The frequency of "flame wars" on Internet message boards and list serves, however, indicates that our innate skill at reading minds isn't always accurate. Some crucial information must be lacking in these forums that causes people to misread others' mental states.

The writer quotes a passage from page 196 of Johnson's book.

Walker 5

Works Cited

Darlin, Damon. "'Wall-E': An Homage to Mr. Jobs." *New York Times*. New York Times, 29 June 2008. Web. 7 July 2008.

Johnson, Steven. *Emergence: The Connected Lives of Ants, Brains, Cities, and Software.* New York: Scribner, 2001. Print.

"Listen to the Brain Drain." *Irish Times* 24 June 2008, final ed.: 17. *LexisNexis Academic.* Web. 8 July 2008.

The reader can find the source by looking up Johnson's name in the list of works cited. The information there can be used to locate the book, to check whether the writer accurately represents Johnson, and to see how the point quoted fits into Johnson's larger argument.

Entries in the works-cited list

The list of works cited is organized alphabetically by authors or, if no author is listed, the first word in the title other than *a*, *an*, or *the*. MLA style uses four basic forms for entries in the list of works cited: books, periodicals (scholarly journals, newspapers, magazines), online sources, and database sources.

1. WORKS-CITED ENTRIES FOR BOOKS

Entries for books have three main elements:

1. Author's name.

2. *Title of book*.

3. Publication information.

Sterling, Bruce. *Shaping Things*. Cambridge: MIT P, 2005. Print.

1. Author's name.
- List the author's name with the last name first, followed by a period.

2. Title of book.
- Find the exact title on the title page, not the cover.
- Separate the title and subtitle with a colon.
- Italicize the title and put a period at the end.

3. Publication information.
- The place (usually the city) of publication,
- The name of the publisher,
- The date of publication,
- The medium of publication (Print).

Use a colon between the place of publication and the publisher's name (using accepted abbreviations), followed by a comma and then the publication date.

2. WORKS-CITED ENTRIES FOR PERIODICALS

Entries for periodicals have three main elements:

1. Author's name.

2. "Title of article."

3. Publication information.

Danielewicz, Jane. "Personal Genres, Public Voices." *College Composition and Communication* 59.3 (2008): 420-50. Print.

1. Author's name.
- List the author's name with the last name first, followed by a period.

2. "Title of article."
- Place the title of the article inside quotation marks.
- Insert a period before the closing quotation mark.

3. Publication information.
- Italicize the title of the journal.
- For scholarly journals follow the title immediately with the volume and issue number.
- List the date of publication, in parentheses, followed by a colon.
- List the inclusive page numbers, separated by a hyphen, followed by a period.
- Give the medium of publication.

3. WORKS-CITED ENTRIES FOR WEB SOURCES

Publications on the Web vary widely. For works other than newspapers, magazines, and other journals published on the Web, include the following components if you can locate them. Include a URL only if your readers probably cannot find the source without it.

1. Author's name.

2. "Title of work."

3. *Title of overall Web site.*

4. Version or edition used.

5. Publisher or sponsor of the site,

6. Date of publication.

7. Medium of publication *(Web).*

8. Date of access.

Dalenberg, Alex. "University of Arizona Looks Beyond Mars Mission." *CNN.com.* Cable News Network, 2 July 2008. Web. 24 July 2008.

4. WORKS-CITED ENTRIES FOR DATABASE SOURCES

Basic entries for database sources have five main elements.

1. Author's name.

2. Print publication information.

3. *Name of database.*

4. Medium of publication *(Web).*

5. Date of access.

Hede, Jesper. "Jews and Muslims in Dante's Vision." *European Review* 16.1 (2008): 101-14. *Academic Search Premier.* Web. 14 Sept. 2008.

1. **Author's name**
- List the author's or editor's name if you can find it; otherwise begin with the title of the work.

2. **"Title of work."**
- Place the title of work inside quotation marks if it is part of a larger Web site.

3. **Title of overall Web site.**
- Italicize the name of the overall site if it is different from 2.

4. **Version or edition used.**
- Some Web sites are updated, so list the version if you find it (e.g., 2006 edition).

5. **Publisher or sponsor of the site,**
- Follow the publisher's or sponsor's name with a comma. If not available, use *N.p.*

6. **Date of publication.**
- Use day, month, and year if available; otherwise use *n.d.*

7. **Medium of publication (*Web*).**

8. **Date of access.**
- List the day, month, and year you accessed the source.

1. **Author's name**
- List the author's or editor's name with the last name first, followed by a period.

2. **Print publication information.**
- Give the print publication information in standard format, in this case for a periodical.

3. **Name of database.**
- Italicize the name of the database, followed by a period.

4. **Medium of publication.**
- For all database sources, the medium of publication is Web.

5. **Date of access.**
- List the date you accessed the source (day, month, and year).

In-text citations in MLA style

1. Author named in your text

Put the author's name in a signal phrase in your sentence.

> Sociologist Daniel Bell called this emerging U.S. economy the "postindustrial society" (3).

2. Author not named in your text

> In 1997, the Gallup poll reported that 55% of adults in the United States think secondhand smoke is "very harmful," compared to only 36% in 1994 (Saad 4).

3. Work by one author

The author's last name comes first, followed by the page number. There is no comma.

> (Bell 3)

4. Work by two or three authors

The authors' last names follow the order of the title page. If there are two authors, join the names with *and*. If there are three, use commas between the first two names and a comma with *and* before the last name.

> (Francisco, Vaughn, and Lynn 7)

5. Work by four or more authors

You may use the phrase *et al.* (meaning "and others") for all names but the first, or you may write out all the names. Make sure you use the same method for both the in-text citations and the works-cited list.

> (Abrams et al. 1653)

6. Work by no named author

Use a shortened version of the title that includes at least the first important word. Your reader will use the shortened title to find the full title in the works-cited list.

> A review in *The New Yorker* of Ryan Adams's new album focuses on the artist's age ("Pure" 25).

Notice that "Pure" is in quotation marks because it refers to the title of an article. If it were a book, the short title would be in italics.

7. Work by a group or organization	Treat the group or organization as the author. Try to identify the group author in the text and place only the page number in the parentheses.

> According to the *Irish Free State Handbook*, published by the Ministry for Industry and Finance, the population of Ireland in 1929 was approximately 4,192,000 (23).

8. Quotations longer than four lines	NOTE: When using indented ("block") quotations of longer than four lines, the period appears *before* the parentheses enclosing the page number.

> In her article "Art for Everybody," Susan Orlean attempts to explain the popularity of painter Thomas Kinkade:
>> People like to own things they think are valuable. . . .The high price of limited editions is part of their appeal: it implies that they are choice and exclusive, and that only a certain class of people will be able to afford them—a limited edition of people with taste and discernment. (128)
>
> This same statement could possibly also explain the popularity of phenomena like PBS's *Antiques Roadshow*.

If the source is longer than one page, provide the page number for each quotation, paraphrase, and summary.

9. Web sources including Web pages, blogs, podcasts, wikis, videos, and other multimedia sources	MLA prefers that you mention the author in the text instead of putting the author's name in parentheses.

> Andrew Keen ironically used his own blog to claim that "blogs are boring to write (yawn), boring to read (yawn) and boring to discuss (yawn)."

If you cannot identify the author, mention the title in your text.

10. Work in an anthology	Cite the name of the author of the work within an anthology, not the name of the editor of the collection. Alphabetize the entry in the list of works cited by the author, not the editor. For example, Melissa Jane Hardie published the chapter "Beard" in *Rhetorical Bodies*, a book edited by Jack Selzer and Sharon Crowley.

> In "Beard," Melissa Jane Hardie explores the role assumed by Elizabeth Taylor as the celebrity companion of gay actors including Rock Hudson and Montgomery Clift (278-79).

Note that Hardie, not Selzer and Crowley, is named in parenthetical citations.

> (Hardie 278-79)

11. Two or more works by the same author	Use the author's last name and then a shortened version of the title of each source.
	The majority of books written about coauthorship focus on partners of the same sex (Laird, *Women* 351).
	Note that *Women* is italicized because it is the name of a book.
12. Different authors with the same last name	If your list of works cited contains items by two or more different authors with the same last name, include the initial of the first name in the parenthetical reference. Note that a period follows the initial.
	Web surfing requires more mental involvement than channel surfing (S. Johnson 107).
13. Two or more sources within the same sentence	Place each citation directly after the statement it supports.
	Many sweeping pronouncements were made in the 1990s that the Internet is the best opportunity to improve education since the printing press (Ellsworth xxii) or even in the history of the world (Dyrli and Kinnaman 79).
14. Two or more sources within the same citation	If two sources support a single point, separate them with a semicolon.
	(McKibbin 39; Gore 92)
15. Work quoted in another source	When you do not have access to the original source of the material you wish to use, put the abbreviation *qtd. in* (quoted in) before the information about the indirect source.
	National governments have become increasingly what Ulrich Beck, in a 1999 interview, calls "zombie institutions"—institutions which are "dead and still alive" (qtd. in Bauman 6).
16. Literary works	To supply a reference to literary works, you sometimes need more than a page number from a specific edition. Readers should be able to locate a quotation in any edition of the book. Give the page number from the edition that you are using, then a semicolon and other identifying information.
	"Marriage is a house" is one of the most memorable lines in *Don Quixote* (546; pt. 2, bk. 3, ch. 19).

Books in MLA-style works cited

COLLAPSE

HOW SOCIETIES CHOOSE

TO FAIL OR SUCCEED

■ ■ ■ ■ ■ ■ ■ ■ ■ ■ ■

JARED DIAMOND

VIKING

TITLE PAGE

Title of book

Subtitle of book

Author's name

Publisher's imprint

VIKING
Published by the Penguin Group
Penguin Group (USA) Inc. 375 Hudson Street
New York, New York 10014, U.S.A.
Penguin Group (Canada), 10 Alcorn Avenue, Toronto, Ontario, Canada M4V 3B2
(a division of Pearson Penguin Canada Inc.)
Penguin Books Ltd, 80 Strand, London WC2R 0RL, England
Penguin Ireland, 25 St. Stephen's Green, Dublin 2, Ireland
(a division of Penguin Books Ltd)
Penguin Books Australia Ltd, 250 Camberwell Road, Camberwell, Victoria 3124, Australia
(a division of Pearson Australia Group Pty Ltd)
Penguin Books India Pvt Ltd, 11 Community Centre, Pancheel Park,
New Delhi–110 017, India
Penguin Group (NZ), Cnr Airborne and Rosendale Roads, Albany,
Aukland 1310, New Zealand
(a division of Pearson New Zealand Ltd)
Penguin Books (South Africa) (Pty) Ltd, 24 Sturdee Avenue,
Rosebank, Johannesburg 2196, South Africa

Penguin Books Ltd, Registered Offices: 80 Strand, London WC2R 0RL, England

First published in 2005 by Viking Penguin, a member of Penguin Group (USA) Inc.

20 19 18

Copyright © Jared Diamond, 2005
All rights reserved

Maps by Jeffrey L. Ward

COPYRIGHT PAGE

Place of publication
(When more than one city is listed
for the publisher, use the first city.)

Copyright date
(usually indicates date of original
publication)

Diamond, Jared. *Collapse: How Societies Choose to Fail or Succeed.*
New York: Viking, 2005. Print.

1. Author's or editor's name
- The author's last name comes first, followed by a comma and the first name.
- For edited books, put the abbreviation *ed.* after the name, preceded by a comma:

Kavanaugh, Peter, ed.

2. Book title
- Use the exact title, as it appears on the title page (not the cover).
- Italicize the title.
- All nouns, verbs, pronouns, adjectives, and subordinating conjunctions, and the first word of the title are capitalized. Do not capitalize articles, prepositions, or coordinating conjunctions unless they are the first word of the title.

3. Publication information

Place of publication
- If more than one city is given, use the first.
- For cities outside the United States add an abbreviation of the country or province if the city is not well known.

Publisher
- Omit words such as Press, Publisher, and Inc.
- For university presses, use UP:

New York UP

- Shorten the name. For example, shorten W.W. Norton & Co. to Norton.

Date of publication
- Give the year as it appears on the copyright page.
- If no year is given, but can be approximated, put a *c.* ("circa") and the approximate date in brackets: [c. 1999].
- Otherwise, put *n.d.* ("no date"):

Boston: Harvard UP, n.d.

Medium of publication
- Print.

Sample works-cited entries for books

ONE AUTHOR

17. Book by one author

The author's last name comes first, followed by a comma, the first name, and a period.

Doctorow, E. L. *The March*. New York: Random, 2005. Print.

18. Two or more books by the same author

In the entry for the first book, include the author's name. In the second entry, substitute three hyphens and a period for the author's name. List the titles of books by the same author in alphabetical order.

Grimsley, Jim. *Boulevard*. Chapel Hill: Algonquin, 2002.
---. *Dream Boy*. New York: Simon, 1995. Print.

MULTIPLE AUTHORS

19. Book by two or three authors

The second and subsequent authors' names appear first name first. A comma separates the authors' names. If all are editors, use eds. after the names.

Cruz, Arnaldo, and Martin Manalansan, eds. *Queer Globalizations: Citizenship and the Afterlife of Colonialism*. New York: New York UP, 2002. Print.

20. Book by four or more authors

You may use the phrase *et al.* (meaning "and others") for all authors but the first, or you may write out all the names. You need to use the same method in the in-text citation as you do in the works-cited list.

Britton, Jane et al. *The Broadview Anthology of Expository Prose*. New York: Broadview, 2001. Print.

ANONYMOUS AND GROUP AUTHORS

21. Book by an unknown author

Begin the entry with the title.

The Baseball Encyclopedia. 10th ed. New York: MacMillan; 1996. Print.

22. Book by a group or organization

Treat the group as the author of the work.

United Nations. *The Charter of the United Nations: A Commentary*. New York: Oxford UP, 2000. Print.

23. Religious texts

The New Oxford Annotated Bible. Ed. Bruce M. Metzger and Roland E. Murphy. New York: Oxford UP, 1991. Print.

EDITIONS, REPRINTS, AND ILLUSTRATED BOOKS

24. Book with an editor

List an edited book under the editor's name if your focus is on the editor. Otherwise, cite an edited book under the author's name.

Lewis, Gifford, ed. *The Big House of Inver*. By Edith Somerville and Martin Ross. Dublin: Farmar, 2000. Print.

25. Reprinted works

For works of fiction that have been printed in many different editions or reprints, give the original publication date after the title.

Wilde, Oscar. *The Picture of Dorian Gray*. 1890. New York: Norton, 2001. Print.

26. Illustrated book or graphic narrative

After the title of the book, give the illustrator's name, preceded by the abbreviation *Illus*. If the emphasis is on the illustrator's work, place the illustrator's name first, followed by the abbreviation *illus.*, and list the author after the title, preceded by the word *By*.

Strunk, William, Jr., and E. B. White. *The Elements of Style Illustrated*. Illus. Maira Kalman. New York: Penguin, 2005. Print.

PARTS OF BOOKS

27. Introduction, Foreword, Preface, or Afterword

Give the author and then the name of the specific part being cited. If the author for the whole work is different, put that author's name after the word *By*. Place inclusive page numbers at the end.

Benstock, Sheri. Introduction. *The House of Mirth*. By Edith Wharton. Boston: Bedford-St. Martin's, 2002. 3-24. Print.

28. Single chapter written by same author as the book

Ardis, Ann. "Mapping the Middlebrow in Edwardian England." *Modernism and Cultural Conflict: 1880-1922*. Cambridge: Cambridge UP, 2002. 114-42. Print.

29. Selection from an anthology or edited collection

Sedaris, David. "Full House." *The Best American Nonrequired Reading 2004*. Ed. Dave Eggers. Boston: Houghton, 2004. 350-58. Print.

Periodicals in MLA-style works cited

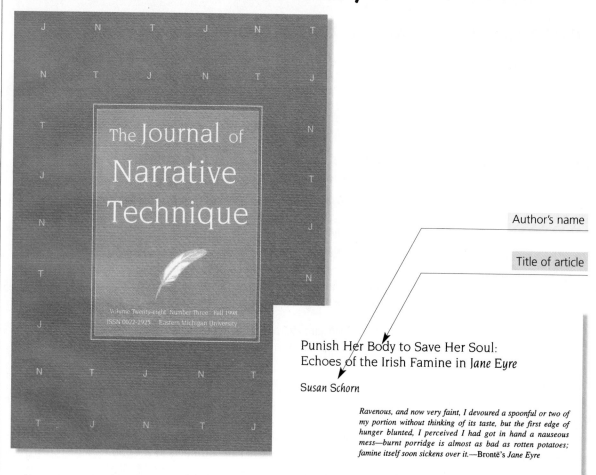

Author's name

Title of article

Punish Her Body to Save Her Soul:
Echoes of the Irish Famine in *Jane Eyre*

Susan Schorn

> *Ravenous, and now very faint, I devoured a spoonful or two of my portion without thinking of its taste, but the first edge of hunger blunted, I perceived I had got in hand a nauseous mess—burnt porridge is almost as bad as rotten potatoes; famine itself soon sickens over it.*—Brontë's *Jane Eyre*

In 1846, the second year of the Irish Potato Famine, Charles Trevelyan, Assistant Secretary in charge of the relief of Ireland, stated "The great evil with which we are to contend is not the physical evil of famine, but the moral evil of the selfish, perverse and turbulent character of the people" (Clarity). That same year, Charlotte Brontë penned the following speech for the character of Mr. Brocklehurst in her novel *Jane Eyre*: "Oh, madam, when you put bread and cheese, instead of burnt porridge, into these children's mouths, you may indeed feed their vile bodies, but you little think how you starve their immortal souls!" The similarity between the sentiment and policy of these two men, one fictional, one very real indeed, is no coincidence. Both express ideas that were then common currency with regard to "the Irish Problem." The connections between starvation, moral improvement, discipline, and nationality were familiar ones in Victorian England, and Brontë's use of this public, political sentiment in her novel—and of numerous other images borrowed from accounts of the

Name of journal, volume number, issue number, date of publication, page numbers

The Journal of Narrative Technique 28.3 (Fall 1998): 350–365. Copyright © 1998 by *The Journal of Narrative Technique*.

Schorn, Susan. "'Punish Her Body to Save Her Soul': Echoes of the Irish

Famine in *Jane Eyre*." *The Journal of Narrative Technique* 28.3 (1998):

350-65. Print.

1. Author's or editor's name
- The author's last name comes first, followed by a comma and the first name.

2. Title of article
- Use the exact title, which appears at the top of the article.
- Put the title in quotation marks. If a book title is part of the article's title, italicize the book title. If a title requiring quotation marks is part of the article's title, use single quotation marks around it.
- All nouns, verbs, pronouns, adjectives, and subordinating conjunctions, and the first word of the title are capitalized. Do not capitalize articles, prepositions, or coordinating conjunctions unless they are the first word of the title.

3. Publication information

Name of journal
- Italicize the title of the journal.
- Abbreviate the title of the journal if it commonly appears that way.

Volume, issue, and page numbers
- For scholarly journals give the volume number and issue number. Place a period between the volume and issue numbers: "28.3" indicates volume 28, issue 3.
- Some scholarly journals use issue numbers only.
- Give the page numbers for the entire article, not just the part you used.

Date of publication
- For magazines and journals identified by the month or season of publication, use the month (or season) and year in place of the volume.
- For weekly or biweekly magazines, give both the day and month of publication, as listed on the issue. Note that the day precedes the month and no comma is used.

Medium of publication
- Print.

Sample works-cited entries for periodicals

JOURNAL ARTICLES

30. Article by one author

> Mallory, Anne. "Burke, Boredom, and the Theater of Counterrevolution." *PMLA* 118.2 (2003): 224-38. Print.

31. Article by two or three authors

> Higgins, Lorraine D., and Lisa D. Brush. "Personal Experience Narrative and Public Debate: Writing the Wrongs of Welfare." *College Composition and Communication* 57.4 (2006): 694-729. Print.

32. Article by four or more authors

You may use the phrase *et al.* (meaning "and others") for all authors but the first, or you may write out all the names.

> Breece, Katherine E. et al. "Patterns of mtDNA Diversity in Northwestern North America." *Human Biology* 76.1 (2004): 33-54. Print.

PAGINATION IN JOURNALS

33. Article in a scholarly journal

After the title of the article, give the journal name in italics, the volume and issue number, the year of publication in parentheses, a colon, the inclusive page numbers, and the medium of publication.

> Duncan, Mike. "Whatever Happened to the Paragraph?" *College English* 69.5 (2007): 470-95. Print.

34. Article in a scholarly journal paginated by issue that uses only issue numbers

Some scholarly journals use issue numbers only. List the issue number after the name of the journal.

> McCall, Sophie. "Double Vision Reading." *Canadian Literature* 194 (2007): 95-97. Print.

MAGAZINES

35. Monthly or seasonal magazines

Use the month (or season) and year in place of the volume. Abbreviate the names of all months except May, June, and July.

> Barlow, John Perry. "Africa Rising: Everything You Know about Africa Is Wrong." *Wired* Jan. 1998: 142-58. Print.

36. Weekly or biweekly magazines

Give both the day and month of publication, as listed on the issue.

> Toobin, Jeffrey. "Crackdown." *New Yorker* 5 Nov. 2001: 56-61. Print.

NEWSPAPERS

37. Newspaper article by one author

The author's last name comes first, followed by a comma and the first name.

> Marriott, Michel. "Arts and Crafts for the Digital Age." *New York Times* 8 June 2006, late ed.: C13. Print.

38. Article by two or three authors

The second and subsequent authors' names are printed in regular order, first name first:

> Davis, Howard, June Allstead, and Jane Mavis. "Rice's Testimony to 9/11 Commission Leaves Unanswered Questions." *Dallas Morning News* 9 Apr. 2004, final ed.: C5. Print.

39. Newspaper article by an unknown author

Begin the entry with the title.

> "The Dotted Line." *Washington Post* 8 June 2006: final ed.: E2. Print.

REVIEWS, EDITORIALS, LETTERS TO THE EDITOR

40. Review

If there is no title, just name the work reviewed.

> Mendelsohn, Daniel. "The Two Oscar Wildes." Rev. of *The Imporatnce of Being Earnest,* dir. Oliver Parker. *The New York Review of Books* 10 Oct. 2002: 23-24. Print.

41. Editorial

> "Stop Stonewalling on Reform." Editorial. *Business Week* 17 June 2002: 108. Print.

42. Letter to the editor

> Patai, Daphne. Letter. *Harper's Magazine* Dec. 2001: 4. Print.

Web sources in MLA-style works cited

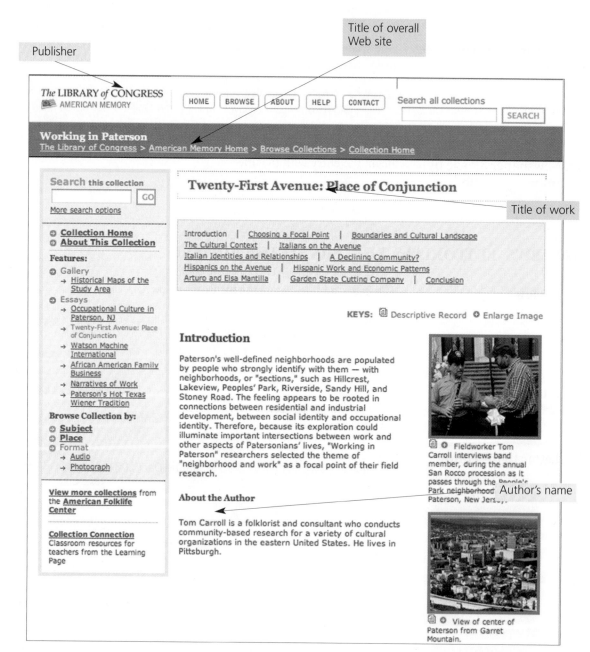

Publisher

Title of overall
Web site

Title of work

Author's name

Carrol, Tom. "Twenty-First Avenue: Place of Conjunction." *Working in Patterson*. Lib. of Cong., n.d. Web. 14 Mar. 2009.

1. Author's name
- Authorship is often difficult to determine for Web sources. If you know the author or creator, follow the rules for books and periodicals.
- If you cannot identify the author or creator, begin with the title.

2. Title of work and title of overall Web site
- Place the title of the work inside quotation marks if it is part of a larger Web site.
- Untitled works may be identified by a label (e.g., *Home page, Introduction*). List the label in the title slot without quotations marks or italics.
- Italicize the name of the overall site if it is different from the work.
- The name of the overall Web site will usually be found on its index or home page. If you can not find a link back to the home page, look at the URL for clues. You can work backward through the URL by deleting sections (separated by slashes) until you come to the home page.
- Some Web sites are updated; list the version if you find it (e.g., *Vers, 1.2*).

3. Publication information
- List the publisher's or sponsor's name followed by a comma. If it isn't available, use *N.p.*
- List the date of publication by day, month, and year if available. If you cannot find a date, use *n.d.*
- Give the medium of publication *(Web)*.
- List the date you accessed the site by day, month, and year.

When do you list a URL?

MLA style no longer requires including URLs of Web sources. URLs are of limited value because they change frequently and they can be specific to an individual search. Include the URL as supplementary information only when your readers probably cannot locate the source without the URL.

Sample works-cited entries for Web sources

ONLINE PUBLICATIONS

43. Publication by a known author

If you know the author or creator, follow the rules for periodicals and books.

> Boerner, Steve. "Leopold Mozart." *The Mozart Project: Biography.*
> The Mozart Project, 21 Mar. 1998. Web. 30 Oct. 2008.

44. Publication by an anonymous author

If a work has no author's or editor's name listed, begin the entry with the title.

> "State of the Birds." *Audubon*. National Audubon Society, 2008.
> Web. 19 Aug. 2008.

45. Publication on the Web with print publication data

Include the print publication information. Then give name of the Web site or database in italics, the medium of publication (*Web*), and the date of access (day, month, and year).

> Kirsch, Irwin S., et al. *Adult Literacy in America*. Darby: Diane, 1993.
> *Google Scholar*. Web. 30 Oct. 2008.

46. Government publication on the Web

Government publications are issued in many formats. If you cannot locate the author of the document, given the name of the government and agency that published it.

> United States. Dept of Health and Human Services. *Salmonellosis*
> *Outbreak in Certain Types of Tomatoes.* 5 July 2008. *U.S. Food*
> *and Drug Administration Site*. Web. 30 July 2008.

ONLINE PERIODICALS

47. Article in a scholarly journal

Some scholarly journals are published on the Web only. List articles by author, title, name of journal in italics, volume and issue number, and year of publication. If the journal does not have page numbers, use *n. pag.* in place of page numbers. Then list the medium of publication (*Web*) and the date of access (day, month, and year).

> Fleckenstein, Kristie. "Who's Writing? Aristotelian Ethos and the
> Author Position in Digital Poetics." *Kairos* 11.3 (2007): n. pag.
> Web. 6 Apr. 2008.

48. Article in a newspaper

The first date is the date of publication, the second is the date of access.

> Brown, Patricia Leigh. "Australia in Sonoma." *New York Times*. New York Times, 5 July 2008. Web. 3 Aug. 2008.

49. Article in a popular magazine

Follow the publisher's name with a comma. If no publisher is available, use *n.p.*

> Brown, Patricia Leigh. "The Wild Horse Is Us." *Newsweek*. Newsweek, 1 July 2008. Web. 3 July 2008.

ONLINE BOOKS AND SCHOLARLY PROJECTS

50. Online book

If the book was printed and then scanned, give the print publication information. Then give the name of the database or Web site in italics, the medium of publication (*Web*), and the date of access (day, month, and year).

> Prebish, Charles S. and Kenneth K. Tanaka. *The Faces of Buddhism in America*. Berkeley: U of California P, 2003. *eScholarship Editions*. Web. 22 May 2008.

51. Document within a scholarly project

Give the print information, then the title of the scholarly project or database, the medium of publication (*Web*), and the date of access (day, month, and year).

> "New York Quiet." *Franklin Repository* 5 Aug. 1863, 1. *Valley of the Shadow*. Web. 23 Feb. 2008.

LIBRARY DATABASE

52. Work from a library database

Begin with the print publication information, but omit the medium of original publication (*Print*). Give the name of the database in italics, the medium of publication (*Web*), and the day, month, and year you accessed the source.

> Mortensen, Daniel E. "The Loci of Cicero." *Rhetorica* 26.1 (2008): 31-56. *Academic Search Complete*. Web. 21 Sept. 2008.

Other sources in MLA-style works cited

53. E-mail

Give the name of the writer, the subject line, a description of the message, the date, and the medium of delivery.

> Ballmer, Steve. "A New Era of Business Productivity and Innovation." Message to Microsoft Executive E-mail. 30 Nov. 2006. E-mail.

54. Blog

If there is no sponsor or publisher for the blog, use *N.p.*

> Arrington, Michael. "Think Before You Voicemail." *TechCrunch*. N.p., 5 July 2008. Web. 10 Sept. 2008.

55. Personal home page

List *Home page* without quotation marks in place of the title. If no date is listed. use *n.d.*

> Graff, Harvey J. Home page. Dept. of English, Ohio State U, n.d. Web. 15 Nov. 2008.

56. Sound recording

List the composer, performer, composer, or group first, depending on which you wish to emphasize. Place a comma between the publisher and the date. Indicate the medium after the date.

> McCoury, Del, perf. "1952 Vincent Black Lightning." By Richard Thompson. *Del and the Boys*. Ceili, 2001. CD.

57. Film

Begin with the title in italics. List the director, the distributor, the date, and the medium. Other data, such as the names of the screenwriters and performers, is optional.

> *Wanted*. Dir. Timur Bekmambetov. Perf. James McAvoy, Angelina Jolie and Morgan Freeman. Universal, 2008. Film.

58. Video or DVD

Follow the same format for films.

> *No Country for Old Men*. Dir. Ethan Coen and Joel Coen. Perf. Tommy Lee Jones, Javier Bardem and Josh Brolin. Paramount, 2007. DVD.

59. Television or radio program

Provide the title of the episode or segment, followed by the title of the program and series (if any). After the titles, list any performers, narrators, directors, or others who might be pertinent. Then give the name of the network, call numbers and city for any local station, the broadcast date, and the medium of reception (*television or radio*).

> "Kaisha." *The Sopranos*. Perf. James Gandolfini, Lorraine Bracco, and Edie Falco. HBO. 4 June 2006. Television.

Visual sources in MLA-style works cited

60. Cartoon	Trudeau, Garry. "Doonesbury." Comic Strip. *Washington Post* 21 Apr. 2008. C15. Print.
61. Advertisement	Nike. Advertisement. ABC. 8 Oct. 2008. Television.
62. Map, graph, or chart	Treat a map, graph, or chart as an anonymous book, but add the appropriate descriptive label. List *Map* after the name of the map. *Greenland*. Map. Vancouver: International Travel Maps, 2004. Print.
63. Painting, sculpture, or photograph	Give the artist's name first if available, the title of the work in italics, the medium of composition, the name of the institution that houses the work and the city, or the name of the collection. In the text, mentioning the work and the artist is preferable to a parenthetical citation. Manet, Edouard. *Olympia*. 1863. Oil on canvas. Musée d'Orsay, Paris.

VISUAL SOURCES ON THE WEB

64. Video on the Web	Video on the Web often lacks a creator and a date. Begin the entry with a title if you cannot find a creator. Use *n.d.* if you cannot find a date. Wesch, Michael. *A Vision of Students Today. YouTube*. YouTube, 2007. Web. 28 May 2008.
65. Work of art on the Web	Gardner, Alexander. *The Home of a Rebel Sharpshooter, Gettysburg*. 1863. Prints and Photographs Div., Lib of Cong. *Selected Civil War Photographs*. Web. 5 Dec. 2008.
66. Map on the Web	"Lansing, Michigan." Map. *Google Maps*. Google, 3 Nov. 2008. Web. 3 Nov. 2008.

Sample MLA paper

Abukar 1

George Abukar
Professor Hernandez
English 1102
5 May 2008

It's Time to Shut Down the Identity Theft Racket

For many college students, a credit rating is something
you'll start to worry about after you graduate and get a job.
A friend of mine, whom I'll call "Donna," has never had a
credit card in her life, and protecting her credit rating was the
last thing on her mind her junior year. That is, until she
started getting disturbing calls from debt collectors accusing
her of not paying her credit card bill.

The first few times she got these calls, Donna explained to
the callers that she didn't have a credit card and didn't know
what account they were talking about. Then one debt collector
threatened to tell Donna's boss about her bad debts and take
her to court. Donna got scared.

It took several days of phone calls to her parents, her bank,
the police, and a credit-reporting agency before Donna found
out what was going on. During spring break of her sophomore
year, Donna had lost her wallet at a beach in South Carolina.
She got a new driver's license from the Department of Motor
Vehicles when she returned home, but she didn't report the
lost wallet to the police because it didn't have any money or
credit cards in it.

But whoever found Donna's wallet used her driver's license
information to apply for a credit card, and got one, with
Donna's name on it. He or she used the card to rack up several
thousand dollars in bills, mostly for clothes and stereo
equipment. When this criminal didn't pay the bill, the
creditors came looking for Donna instead.

It's bad enough that someone stole Donna's identity. What
was worse, to her, was that none of the people who should have
helped stop the crime did. The credit card company that issued
the card did not bother to check the applicant's identity. The

---

Include your last name and page number as page header, beginning with the first page, 1/2" from the top.

Center the title. Do not underline the title, put it inside quotation marks, or type it in all capital letters.

Indent each paragraph five spaces (1/2" on the ruler in your word processing program).

Specify 1" margins all around. Double-space everything.

MLA style does not require a title page. Check with your instructor to find out whether you need one.

Abukar 2

credit reporting agencies did nothing to help her get the bad information off her files. In fact, even after she has filled out forms for all three national credit reporting agencies, asking to have the information about the unpaid credit card bills removed from her file, the bad debts are still showing up. Donna worries that she will never have a clean credit record, and that she'll have trouble buying a house or car after she graduates. "All this information about me has been falsified," Donna said in an interview, "and I don't even get to set the record straight." Only the credit reporting agencies have the ability to do that, and since they do not stand to make any money from helping Donna, they are in no hurry to do it.

As long as credit-reporting agencies are protected from the effects of identity theft, they will not take steps to protect consumers. Therefore, I propose that the United States Congress pass federal legislation making credit-reporting agencies liable for damages when their actions or negligence lead to loss from identity theft.

> Akubar states his thesis in this paragraph after he has described the problem using the example of Donna.

This legislation is necessary because identity theft is out of control. In 2007 there were 8.4 million adult victims of identity theft in the United States for a total loss of $49.3 billion (Monahan). The great majority of victims learn of identity theft when they become victims; very few are alerted by proactive businesses. Clearly, identity theft is a huge and expensive problem. What is being done to prevent it?

Mostly, consumers are being told to protect themselves. The United States Federal Trade Commission has an entire Web site devoted to telling consumers how to minimize their risk of identity theft. Some of their advice is obvious, like "Keep your purse or wallet in a safe place at work." Some tips are more obscure: "Treat your mail and trash carefully." Some assume that people have a lot more time, patience, and knowledge than they really do:

> Quotations of more than four lines should be indented 1" or ten spaces.

> Ask about information security procedures in your workplace or at businesses, doctor's offices or other institutions that collect your personally identifying information. Find out who has access to your

Abukar 3

personal information and verify that it is handled securely. Ask about the disposal procedures for those records as well. Find out if your information will be shared with anyone else. If so, ask how your information can be kept confidential. *(Identity Theft: Minimizing).*

> Do not include a page number for items without pagination, such as Web sites.

Not many people are prepared to spend twenty minutes grilling the checkout person at Old Navy when she asks for their phone number. But even if someone takes all these steps and avoids even a simple mistake like Donna made by losing her wallet, is that enough.

Daniel J. Solove, in his book *The Digital Person: Technology and Privacy in the Information Age,* argues that it is not. "The underlying cause of identity theft," he says, "is an architecture that makes us vulnerable to such crimes and unable to adequately repair the damage" (115). He notes that

> Introduce blocked quotations rather than just dropping them into the text.

> We are increasingly living with digital dossiers about our lives, and these dossiers are not controlled by us but by various entities, such as private-sector companies and the government. These dossiers play a profound role in our existence in modern society. The identity thief taps into these dossiers and uses them, manipulates them, and pollutes them. The identity thief's ability to so easily access and use our personal data stems from an architecture that does not provide adequate security to our personal information and that does not afford us with a sufficient degree of participation in its collection, dissemination, and use. (115)

> Do not place blocked quotations within quotation marks.

Solove's proposal for reducing identity theft is to change the structure, or "architecture," of the systems we use to collect and store personal information. He recommends giving individuals more control over their personal information and requiring the companies that use that information to inform

For other examples of papers using MLA documentation, see pages 140–147, 326–331, and 376–381.

Abukar 8

Works Cited

"Donna." Personal interview. 30 Mar. 2008.

Drum, Kevin. "You Own You." *Washington Monthly*. Washington
Monthly, Dec. 2005. Web. 9 Apr. 2008.

"Equifax Annual Profit at $246.5 Million." *Atlanta Business
Chronicle*. Atlanta Business Chronicle, 2 Feb. 2006. Web.
9 Apr. 2008.

Kuehner-Hebert, Katie. "Colorado Banks Would Fund ID Theft
Task Force." *American Banker* 21 Mar. 2006: 1-4. *Business
Source Premier*. Web. 7 April 2008.

Monahan, Mary T. *2007 Identity Fraud Survey Report*. Javelin
Strategy and Research, Feb. 2007. Web. 12 Apr. 2008.

Moyer, Liz. "Credit Agencies in the Clover." *Forbes.com*. Forbes,
June 2005. Web. 10 Apr. 2008.

Solove, Daniel J. *The Digital Person: Technology and Privacy in the
Information Age*. New York: NY UP, 2004. Print.

United States. Dept. of Commerce. Federal Trade
Commission. *Identity Theft Survey Report*. McLean:
Synovate, 2004. Print.

---. ---. *Identity Theft: Minimizing Your Risk*. US Dept. of
Commerce, 2005. Web. 15 Apr. 2008.

Center "Works Cited" on a new page.

Double-space all entries. Indent all but the first line in each entry one-half inch.

Alphabetize entries by the last names of the authors or by the first important word in the title if no author is listed.

Italicize the titles of books and periodicals.

If an author has more than one entry, list the entries in alphabetical order by title. Use three hyphens in place of the author's name for the second and subsequent entries.

Go through your text and make sure all the sources you have used are in the list of works cited.

Photo Credits

p. 8: Oona Curley; **p. 40:** Oona Curley; **p. 60:** Time & Life Pictures/Getty Images; **p. 62:** Xen/Alamy; **p. 67:** Frank Capri/Hulton/Getty Images; **p. 92:** NASA; **p. 119:** Getty Images; **p. 161:** AP Images; **p. 163:** Ted Soqui/Corbis; **p. 172 (top):** Hoffmann/Getty Images; **p. 172 (bottom left):** Gaslight Ad Archives; **p. 172 (bottom right):** Volkswagen AG; **p. 173 (top left):** Photofest; **p. 173 (bottom):** © 2006 Volkswagen of America, Inc.; **p. 202:** Helene Rogers/Alamy; **p. 252:** Reuters/Corbis; **p. 295:** Unicef; **p. 298:** National Archives; **p. 305:** Vario images GmbH & Co.KG/Alamy; **p. 347:** Wally McNamee/Corbis; **p. 386:** Oona Curley.

Unless otherwise credited, all photos © Lester Faigley Photos.

Text Credits

danah boyd, "Web 2.0 Forum: Knowledge Access as a Public Good," *Britannica Blog,* June 2007. Reprinted with permission from the *Britannica Blog,* copyright © 2007 by Encyclopaedia Britannica, Inc.

Tim Collins, "Straight from the Heart" from *The Guardian,* July 13, 2005. Copyright © Tim Collins 2005. Reprinted by permission.

Lee Connell, "My Dropout Boyfriend Kept Dropping In," *New York Times,* June 1, 2008. Copyright © 2008 The New York Times. All rights reserved. Used by permission and protected by the Copyright Laws of the United States. The printing, copying, redistribution, or retransmission of the material without express written permission is prohibited.

Stephanie Coontz, "The Future of Marriage," *Cato Unbound,* January 14, 2008. Copyright © 2008 by Cato Institute. Reproduced with permission of Cato Institute via Copyright Clearance Center.

Stentor Danielson "Pesticides, Parasite May Cause Frog Deformities," *National Geographic News,* July 9, 2002. Reprinted by permission of the National Geographic Society.

EBSCO. Screen images from EBSCO Database are used by permission of EBSCO Publishing.

Sue Kunitomi Embrey, "Some Lines for a Younger Brother." Originally published in *Gidra,* Vol. II, No. 5, May 1970. Copyright © 1970 by Sue Kunitomi Embrey. Reprinted by permission.

Lori Gottlieb, "How Do I Love Thee?" *Atlantic Monthly,* March 2006. Reprinted by permission of the author.

Ted Koppel, "Take My Privacy Please!" *New York Times,* June 13, 2005. Copyright © 2005 by The New York Times Co. Reprinted with permission.

LexisNexis Copyright 2009, LexisNexis, a division of Reed Elsevier Inc. All Rights Reserved. LexisNexis and the Knowledge Burst logo are registered trademarks of Reed Elsevier Properties Inc. and are used with the permission of LexisNexis.

David T.Z. Mindich, "The Collapse of the Media: The Young and the Restless," *The Wilson Quarterly,* Spring 2005. Reprinted by permission of the author.

Lefteris Pavlides, "The Aesthetics of Wind Power," *Providence Journal,* March 7, 2005. Reprinted by permission of the author.

Michael Pollan, "Why Bother?" Reprinted by permission of International Creative Management, Inc. Copyright © 2008 by Michael Pollan. First appeared in *New York Times Magazine.*

Emily Raine, "Why Should I Be Nice to You? Coffee Shops and the Politics of Good Service" from *Bad Subjects,* Issue 74, December 2005. Reprinted by permission of the author.

Stephanie Rosenbloom, "The Nitpicking Nation," *The New York Times,* May 7, 2006. Copyright © 2006 The New York Times. All rights reserved. Used by permission and protected by the Copyright Laws of the United States. The printing, copying, redistribution, or retransmission of the material without express written permission is prohibited.

Chip Walter, "Affairs of the Lips: Why We Kiss," *Scientific American Mind,* February/March 2008. Reprinted with permission. Copyright © 2008 by Scientific American, Inc. All rights reserved.

Samuel Wilson, "*The Emperor's Giraffe*" The Emperor's Giraffe. Copyright © 1999 by Westview Press. Reprinted by permission of Westview Press, a member of Perseus Books Group.

Mark Winne, "When Handouts Keep Coming, the Food Line Never Ends," *Washington Post,* November 18, 2007, Reprinted by permission of the author.

YAHOO! Ince. Reproduced with permission of Yahoo! Inc. Copyright © 2008 by Yahoo! Inc. YAHOO! and the YAHOO! logo are trademarks of Yahoo! Inc.

Index

See student writers at work

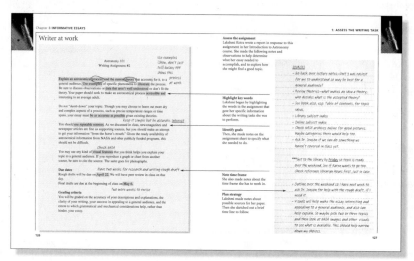

Understand the assignment

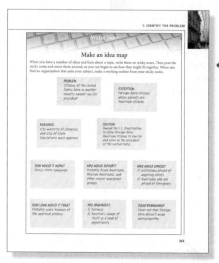

Discover ideas

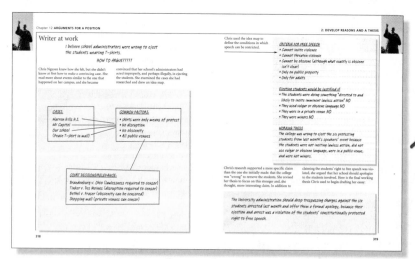

Explore the topic